MW01204010

OCP Developer PL/SQL Program Units Exam Guide

Steve O'Hearn

McGraw-Hill/Osborne

New York   Chicago   San Francisco
Lisbon   London   Madrid   Mexico City
Milan   New Delhi   San Juan
Seoul   Singapore   Sydney   Toronto

McGraw-Hill/Osborne
2600 Tenth Street
Berkeley, California 94710
U.S.A.

To arrange bulk purchase discounts for sales promotions, premiums, or fund-raisers,
please contact **McGraw-Hill**/Osborne at the above address. For information on
translations or book distributors outside the U.S.A., please see the International
Contact Information page immediately following the index of this book.

OCP Developer PL/SQL Program Units Exam Guide

1234567890 DOC DOC 0198765432

Book p/n 0-07-219337-9 and CD p/n 0-07-219338-7
parts of
ISBN 0-07-219336-0

Publisher	**Acquisitions Coordinator**
Brandon A. Nordin	Athena Honore
Vice President & Associate Publisher	**Technical Editor**
Scott Rogers	Pam Gamer
Acquisitions Editor	**Composition & Indexing**
Jeremy Judson	MacAllister Publishing
	Services, LLC
Project Manager	
Jenn Tust	**Cover Design**
	Damore Johann

This book was composed with QuarkXPress™.

To my mother Joan, who instills in me
the confidence to accomplish anything

About the Author

Steve O'Hearn has been an Oracle Certified Application Developer since 1999. He graduated from George Washington University in 1983 with a Bachelor's in Business Administration with a concentration in Information Processing. He has designed, developed, and administered a wide variety of Oracle databases for 17 years for clients such as the U.S. Army, U.S. Navy, the FAA, the World Bank, NASA, and more. His first published work appeared in 1996. He created the original web site for the Mid-Atlantic Association of Oracle Professionals (MAOP) and served as its vice president from 1998 to 2000. He is a principal of Information Systems Consortium, Inc., where he currently serves as Chief Technology Officer. He works as Director of Consulting by day, and authors curriculum and teaches Oracle and Java classes on nights and weekends for ISC's db-Training division. He is a member of MENSA and the National Press Club. For the past few years, he's been spending his time contributing to the building of ISC, but many years ago, rock and roll paid his college tuition, and he's been known to play guitar on occasion with many talented musicians when he's not in front of a PC. Steve loves getting e-mail at home at soh@corbinian.com.

Acknowledgments

Without the support of Jeremy Judson, the faithful persistence of Athena Honore, and the team at Oracle Press, this book would not exist. Thank you very much to both of you—you're terrific to work with.

Thanks to Molly Applegate and her team for their hard work and excellent contributions in the production of the book: Jeanne Henning, Michael Brumitt, Jennifer Earhart, Nonie Ratcliff, and Jeff Yesh.

A special thank you to the technical editing of Pam Gamer, whose sharp eye and excellent insight contributed significantly to the book in many key areas—thank you very much, Pam!

Thanks to Marlene Theriault for introducing me to the great people at Oracle Press; to Graham Seibert for encouraging me in my writing; to Michael Ault for his inspirational example; to Bert Spencer at European Oracle User Group (EOUG) for opportunities to present and network. Thanks to Steve Vandivier, with whom I served as vice president of the MAOP for two years.

A huge thanks to Dan Hinkle and his wife Brenda, my brilliant business associates for several years. As former president of the MAOP, Dan encouraged me in many pursuits and opened up several doors for me, and as CEO of our company, he has fearlessly led us into many great and successful adventures.

A very special thanks to Martin Kuhn at the National Press Club for some key suggestions and tremendous encouragement and to former NPC President Doug Harbrecht at *Business Week* magazine for making some key introductions for me. A great deal of thanks also to Roy Patterson and Jim Bauchspies whose management and leadership many, many years ago helped to start my Oracle career.

Finally, thanks to my father for teaching me the value of hard work and to my mother who has always listened, encouraged, and inspired me, and to whom this book is dedicated.

Contents

PART I

Language Syntax

1 Overview of PL/SQL 3
An Introduction to the PL/SQL Language 4
PL/SQL Syntax Fundamentals 7
Statements 8
Identifiers 8
Comments 8
Literals 9
Declaration Section 10
Variables 10
Datatypes 11
Constants 14
Other Declared Elements 14
Processing Section 15
Expressions 15
Assignment Statements 21
Conditional Statements 22
Loops 25
Cursors 28
Implicit Cursors 28
Explicit Cursors 30
Cursor Attributes 32
Loops Revisited: The Cursor FOR Loop 33

Advanced Datatype Declaration............................ 34
%TYPE 34
%ROWTYPE 35
Exception-Handling Section............................... 37
System-Defined Exceptions 38
User-Defined Exceptions 39
Working with Blocks 40
Nested Blocks 41
Scope: Declared Elements............................ 42
Exception Scope and Exception Propagation 44
An Introduction to Program Units........................... 47
Anonymous Blocks 47
Named Program Units............................... 47
Chapter Summary..................................... 49
Two-Minute Drill 51
Chapter Questions 53
Answers to Chapter Questions 57

2 Procedures **61**
Uses of Procedures.................................... 62
What Can You Do with Procedures? 63
Where Can You Store Procedures?...................... 64
Creating, Altering, and Dropping Procedures 66
Creating Procedures 66
Altering Procedures................................. 70
Dropping Procedures................................ 72
Invoking Procedures................................... 73
Executing a Procedure from a PL/SQL Block 73
Executing a Procedure from the SQL*Plus Command Line........ 74
Parameters 76
Parameter Declaration Syntax 76
Parameter Datatypes 77
Default Values..................................... 77
Parameter Types.................................... 78
Positional Notation versus Named Notation 83
Data Dictionary Resources for Procedures 85
USER_OBJECTS................................... 86
USER_OBJECT_SIZE 88
USER_SOURCE................................... 88
USER_ERRORS 89
SHOW ERRORS 91
Chapter Summary..................................... 93
Two-Minute Drill 95

Chapter Questions   96
Answers to Chapter Questions 100

3 Functions 103
Uses of Functions. 104
   Functions versus Procedures 105
Creating, Altering, and Dropping Functions 106
   Creating Functions. 106
   Altering Functions 107
   Dropping Functions. 108
Invoking Functions 109
   Functions Called from PL/SQL Expressions 110
   Functions Called from SQL Statements 112
   Client-Side Functions. 113
Parameters 115
   Passing Parameters by Reference 117
RETURN. 119
Chapter Summary. 123
Two-Minute Drill 123
Chapter Questions 124
Answers to Chapter Questions 129

4 Packages 133
Uses of Packages 134
Creating, Altering, and Dropping Packages. 137
   Creating a Package Specification 137
   Creating a Package Body 139
   Public versus Private Constructs. 140
   Global Constructs 141
   Altering a Package. 143
   Dropping a Package. 147
   Changes to a Package Specification that Require a Change
     to the Body 149
Invoking Packaged Constructs 151
   Referencing Packaged Constructs. 151
   Using Packaged Constructs 151
Data Dictionary Resources for Packages. 156
Chapter Summary. 158
Two-Minute Drill 159
Chapter Questions 160
Answers to Chapter Questions 164

5 Triggers **167**
   Uses of Triggers 168
   Creating, Altering, and Dropping Triggers 170
      Creating Triggers 171
      The :old and :new Qualifiers 175
      Conditional Predicates..................................... 177
      Firing Rules 178
      Restrictions 179
      Altering Triggers.. 181
      Dropping Triggers 181
   Enabling and Disabling Triggers 183
      Disabling and Enabling a Named Trigger 183
      Enabling and Disabling a Named Table's Triggers. 184
   INSTEAD OF Triggers 185
   Non-DML Triggers 188
      DDL Triggers 189
   Data Dictionary Resources for Triggers 190
      USER_TRIGGERS... 191
   Chapter Summary... 194
   Two-Minute Drill 195
   Chapter Questions 197
   Answers to Chapter Questions 200

6 Working with Program Units. **203**
   Client-Side versus Server-Side Program Units 204
      Invoking Server-Side Program Units......................... 205
      Invoking Client-Side Program Units 206
      The Trade-of—Where to Put Them? 207
   Local Subprograms... 209
      Forward Declarations 209
   Overloading... 214
      Creating Overloaded Modules............................... 215
      Namespaces for Program Units 217
   Initializing Variables with a One-Time-Only Procedure 219
   Functions and Purity Levels 221
      WNDS and RNDS.. 224
      WNPS and RNPS.. 224
      TRUST... 225
      Purity Levels for the Package Initialization Section. 225
      DEFAULT... 226
      The Benefits of PRAGMA.................................... 226
   Persistent States 228
      Persistent Variables and Constants 228

Persistent Tables, Records, and Types 231
Persistent Cursors 232
Chapter Summary 237
Two-Minute Drill 238
Chapter Questions 239
Answers to Chapter Questions 243

7 Working with Oracle's PL/SQL Packages **245**
DBMS_OUTPUT 247
SET SERVEROUTPUT ON 247
ENABLE and DISABLE 248
PUT_LINE, PUT, and NEW_LINE 248
GET_LINE and GET_LINES 249
DBMS_JOB 251
JOB_QUEUE_PROCESSES and JOB_QUEUE_INTERVAL 251
The SUBMIT Procedure 252
The REMOVE Procedure 253
The RUN Procedure 253
The CHANGE, NEXT_DATE, WHAT, INTERVAL,
and INSTANCE Procedures 254
Other Procedures: USER_EXPORT, BROKEN, and ISUBMIT 254
Monitoring Batch Jobs with USER_JOBS 255
DBMS_DDL 257
The ALTER_COMPILE Procedure 257
The ANALYZE_OBJECT Procedure 258
Monitoring the Results of ALTER_COMPILE
and ANALYZE_OBJECT 259
DBMS_PIPE 260
The PACK_MESSAGE Procedure 260
The SEND_MESSAGE Function 260
The RECEIVE_MESSAGE Function 261
The NEXT_ITEM_TYPE Function 262
The UNPACK_MESSAGE Procedure 262
Other Procedures 262
DBMS_SQL 263
The OPEN_CURSOR Function and the
CLOSE_CURSOR Procedure 268
The PARSE Procedure 268
The DEFINE_COLUMN Procedure 269
The EXECUTE Function 270
The FETCH_ROWS Function 270
The COLUMN_VALUE Procedure 271
The BIND_VARIABLE Procedure 271

Native Dynamic SQL. 272
Compilation Errors. 273
Chapter Summary. 274
Two-Minute Drill 275
Chapter Questions 276
Answers to Chapter Questions 278

PART II
Development Tools

8 Using Oracle PL/SQL Tools **283**
SQL*Plus 284
The SQL*Plus Buffer Editor 287
Using Text Editors 289
Executing Text Files 291
PL/SQL Blocks and the Buffer 291
Procedure Builder 292
Object Navigator. 294
Creating a Program Unit with Procedure Builder 298
Executing a Program Unit 305
Moving Program Units. 306
Working with Libraries 307
Creating Database Triggers. 308
Chapter Summary. 310
Two-Minute Drill 311
Chapter Questions 312
Answers to Chapter Questions 315

9 Debugging PL/SQL **317**
Debugging Concepts 318
Debugging Techniques 318
Code Formatting: An Example 320
Debugging Tools 321
Debugging with SQL*Plus 323
Debugging Compilation Errors with SQL*Plus. 323
SHOW ERROR 328
Debugging Execution Errors in SQL*Plus. 329
Debugging with Procedure Builder. 330
Starting Debugger: Setting Breakpoints 331
Chapter Summary. 340
Two-Minute Drill 340
Chapter Questions 341
Answers to Chapter Questions 344

PART III
Privileges and Interdependence

10 Managing Privileges 349
   System Privileges 350
   Roles 351
   System and Object Privilege Requirements for Program Units 353
      System Privileges for Program Units 353
      Object Privileges for Program Units 356
   Owner and Invoker Rights 358
      Owner Rights 358
      Invoker Rights 360
   Granting and Revoking Privileges 362
   Data Dictionary Resources 364
      SESSION_PRIVS 364
      SESSION_ROLES 365
      USER_SYS_PRIVS 365
      USER_ROLE_PRIVS 365
      DBA_SYS_PRIVS 366
      USER_TAB_PRIVS, USER_TAB_PRIVS_MADE, and
        USER_TAB_PRIVS_RECD 366
   Chapter Summary 368
   Two-Minute Drill 370
   Chapter Questions 371
   Answers to Chapter Questions 373

11 Managing Interdependencies 377
   Tracking Dependencies 378
      USER_DEPENDENCIES 378
      DEPTREE and IDEPTREE 382
   Dependency Issues Within a Single Database 386
   Dependency Issues Across Multiple Databases 388
      The Timestamp Mode 390
      The Signature Mode 390
   Avoiding Recompilation Errors 392
   Chapter Summary 394
   Two-Minute Drill 396
   Chapter Questions 396
   Answers to Chapter Questions 399

PART IV
Practice Exams

12 Practice Exams 403
    Practice Exam #1 404
    Answers to Practice Exam #1 425
    Practice Exam #2 436
    Answers to Practice Exam #2 452
    Practice Exam #3 462
    Answers to Practice Exam #3 478

Introduction

The car was careening out of control at a dangerously high speed on the mountainside road. Suddenly I could hear the screeching of tires as everyone in the car lurched to the right, and the vehicle's tires skidded dangerously on the edge of a cliff. I could see the 500-foot precipitous drop to certain death in the ravine below. Suddenly the driver (who must have been an Oracle Certified Developer) grabbed the wheel and confidently steered the vehicle back to safety. Then it came to me—I realized I had to turn off the television and get the introduction to this book written, fer cryin' out loud.

Okay, so maybe this book won't be a major motion picture any time soon, but it certainly has the potential to change your life and take you into some great adventures. If you're reading this at all, you probably understand the powerful importance of database systems in the world today. We live in an information age; every industry, every government organization, and every nonprofit operation anywhere in the world must have control over its information. The leading tool for collecting, controlling, analyzing, and distributing information today is unquestionably the Oracle database. Furthermore, Procedural Language/Structured Query Language (PL/SQL) is Oracle's proprietary language that enables you to manage your data in the most efficient manner. Although it's true that other languages, such as Java, provide ways to interact with database systems, the architecture of PL/SQL is inherently faster than any other language in a statement-level benchmark analysis. Because Oracle has embedded PL/SQL inside the database, as well as in various development tools that run throughout the network, statements you create in PL/SQL will process faster than statements in any other language, which have to go through drivers and gateways to reach the database. Even books about Java and database applications include chapters about how to call PL/SQL program units in the database from Java programs for the fastest and most efficient form of database processing.

I have been creating Oracle applications since the mid-1980s. I've worked with nonprofits, international agencies, corporations in the Fortune 500, and many organizations within the U.S. government. The requirements of all of these clients have had the same common themes. They all need their database applications to be as efficient as possible and their data to be as readily available as possible with the lowest possible maintenance costs and the best security available to protect sensitive data. The Oracle database has the capability to achieve all of this, but only in the hands of properly trained and experienced professionals. So how can you ensure that you and your team are knowledgeable enough and capable enough to provide the best services possible in the course of your application development efforts? Furthermore, how can you best communicate your level of expertise to those who would hire your services?

The answer is easy: Oracle certification. By incorporating experienced professionals on your team who are certified, you can vastly improve the odds of success in your efforts. By getting certification for yourself, you can reinforce your own knowledge, fill in the gaps of knowledge that you might not realize you have, and authoritatively announce to the world that you are, indeed, an Oracle professional who has been independently assessed and certified as an expert who is knowledgeable in his or her field. There is no more universally acceptable method of achieving such a high level of credibility in the Oracle industry.

Why You Should Become Certified

There was a time when an Oracle professional didn't need certification to stay competitive in the marketplace. Those days are over. Although information technology professionals such as network engineers and Microsoft administrators have required certification for years, the concept of controlled certification testing for application developers is a relatively new phenomenon in the Oracle industry. However, an increasing number of employers are asking for certified developers.

The Oracle business offers great promise for those who enter it. Frankly, I can't think of another industry in the world today that offers the same benefits and opportunities that the information technology field gives. Oracle, as the leading database product by far, is at the heart of the information age. To get Oracle certification is to secure a tremendous future for yourself.

Here are some of the specific benefits you will experience with Oracle certification:

■ *Raise your income and increase your marketability.* Certification definitely catches the attention of existing and potential employers. Although IT professionals have enjoyed little competition for jobs in the recent past, this situation cannot last forever—in fact, we are already starting to see the number of people in the IT work force increasing, and although the future of the industry still looks better than virtually any other industry in the world today, if you want to stand out among your peers, certification is your best approach.

■ *Solidify your knowledge.* Have you ever felt completely confident as an Oracle developer? Are you sure that you have a solid foundation of knowledge in all of the skills that Oracle Corporation intends for you to have as an Oracle professional? Have you ever wondered if there was some critical technique, some significant function that you don't know about, but that if you did, would save you hours of unnecessary work? Have you ever felt reluctant to speak out confidently, take a bold stand in a meeting, or assume a technical lead role because of uncertainty about your own knowledge and technical abilities? If any of this sounds familiar, then certification is for you. The confidence that comes from being declared to be Oracle Certified by Oracle Corporation is the confidence that paves the way to your career success.

■ *Declare your skills to the world.* You know what you can do. But how does the rest of the world know what you can do? When you interview for a job, how often does the interviewer really understand enough to ask you the important technical questions? After all, if your potential employer fully understood Oracle to begin with, perhaps they wouldn't require your skills after all. The truth is that most interviewers don't understand the difference between a PL/SQL cursor and a developer who's just really mad and uses a lot of foul language. However, nontechnical people do understand certification. When you can present yourself as Oracle Certified to a potential or existing employer, you are benefiting from the endorsement of Oracle Corporation itself, which carries a great deal of weight with your coworkers, management, and for that matter, friends and family. I know, that last part may sound corny, but trust me, I can tell you from personal experience that you'll be surprised how impressed your family and friends will be by your certification. The reason is simple: nontechnical people cannot appreciate the true depths of your technical knowledge, but everyone understands what it means to be certified.

■ *Enjoy extra benefits from Oracle Corporation.* Once you are Oracle Certified, you will be welcomed into an elite circle. The Oracle Corporation will send you a certificate, an identification card, and instructions on how to use the Oracle Certified logo, which you will be authorized to add to your resume and other personal marketing material, such as a web site. Just for fun, certified professionals are granted special access to Oracle Corporation events that noncertified participants cannot attend. For example, at the last Oracle Open World conference, there was a special section of the conference hall reserved for just OCP members that had better food (especially the gigantic extra-rich brownies, yum!), comfortable chairs and leather sofas not available elsewhere, and more importantly, an opportunity to engage in question-and-answer sessions with technical presenters in a much nicer, smaller, and relaxed environment that made the entire conference rather special. Also, at the time of this writing, Oracle Corporation is in the process of building an "OCP members only" web site, but it remains to be seen what this will include.

About Oracle Certification

Oracle has several different types of certification, which are divided into *tiers*, as shown in the following table.

Tier	Certification	Description
Oracle Certified Associate (OCA)	Oracle9*i*	Relatively new. A starting point, but not the required starting point. Ideal for junior team members.
Oracle Certified Professional (OCP)	Oracle Database Administrator: Oracle9*i*	For DBAs.
	Oracle Database Administrator: Oracle8*i*	
	Oracle8*i* Database Operator	For network engineers or system administrators who use Oracle, but not necessarily as their primary responsibility.
	Oracle Internet Application Developer, also known as Oracle Internet Application Developer, Forms Release 6/6*i*	For Oracle application developers.
	Oracle Java Developer	For serious Java database developers.
Oracle Certified Master (OCM)	Oracle9*i*	For those who already have OCP, but want to advance to the newest and most prestigious level.

As you can see in the previous table, each tier consists of one or more certifications. Each certification consists of one or more exams that you must take in order to earn the certification. Each exam must be successfully passed; the average scores for all exams within a single certification are not considered.

The OCA and OCM tiers are relatively new additions. As you can see from the table, most of the certifications are under the Oracle Certified Professional tier. This is why you will probably hear most people refer to Oracle certification as OCP.

Each certification requires that you successfully pass one or more exams. For the Oracle Internet Application Developer Certification, you must pass four exams, as listed in the following table.

Recommended Order	Exam #	Exam Title
1	1Z0-001	Introduction to Oracle: SQL and PL/SQL
2	1Z0-101	Develop PL/SQL Program Units
3	1Z0-131	Build Internet Applications I
4	1Z0-132	Build Internet Applications II

This book will prepare you to take the second exam in this series, Exam 1Z0-101, Develop PL/SQL Program Units, for the Oracle Internet Application Developer certification.

About the Exam

The exam is a multiple choice, proctored exam, which you must pass for certification. It has 57 questions. In order to pass, you must answer 39 questions correctly, which is 68 percent of the exam. The exam, as is the case with all of the Oracle Certification exams, is graded on a pass/fail basis. In other words, your actual grade is meaningless to your certification; the only result that matters is whether you passed or failed.

The estimated time to take the exam is two hours, which is longer than many of the other Oracle certification exams and for good reason—it's a more taxing exam. You will be presented with several code samples and asked several questions that will, in a single question, often challenge several knowledge areas at once. However, the two-hour period is more than sufficient time. I was able to completely read each question carefully, answer them all, and review each answer with time to spare.

How to Register For and Take the Exam

To take an Oracle certification exam, you must do the following:

■ *Contact Prometric.* Prometric is the testing company that administers the exam on behalf of Oracle Corporation. Their phone number is (800) 891-EXAM, which is (800) 891-3926, and their web site is at www.2test.com. Personally, I hate to say this, but as much of a fan of the Internet as I am, I found the telephone support much more helpful. At the time I registered, I found the web site to be rather time-consuming, but I was able to register on the phone within a few minutes. You will need to locate a testing center near you, but that shouldn't be difficult; just provide your zip code and Prometric can quickly tell you the address of the nearest testing center to you. Testing centers are located in urban areas throughout the United States as well as some rural areas. I found 2 within a 10-minute walk of my office in Tyson's Corner, Virginia. When you register for a test, you will reserve a seat at the testing center for a specific date and time. It's recommended that you call and register at least a few days in advance of the exam itself. Prometric should give you some sort of registration number when you call; make a note of this number and plan to bring it to the exam testing center.

■ *Get a good night's sleep.* That's just common sense. Eat something beforehand, but don't drink a gallon of water. You want to show up to the exam alert and prepared to sit still for two hours.

■ *Show up for the exam at least 15 minutes early, with your registration information.* If you don't show up at least 15 minutes early, the testing proctor can elect to not seat you, if he or she determines it would be disruptive to other test takers. Prometric will provide a registration number that you will need at the testing center to identify yourself—be sure to take it with you. You will be required to show two forms of identification and at least one of those must be a government-issued photo identification, such as a driver's license. You will need to arrive a few minutes early so you can sign in, and you will not be allowed to take certain things with you into the testing center, such as a laptop computer, palm pilot, cell phone, or Blackberry. At the testing center I attended, I was given a locker for temporary use to place my cell phone and pager that I had with me. The exam is proctored, meaning that a person will monitor you to make sure you aren't passing answers back and forth with other test takers. You cannot take anything in to the exam with you, but notepaper will be provided if you want to write notes during the exam. However, you are required to turn in those notes upon completion of the exam; you cannot take any notes away from the exam.

■ *Take the exam.* You will be sitting at a computer workstation, answering multiple-choice questions. You will be able to mark any questions that you aren't sure about or that you want to skip, and at any time, you can display a summary of all the questions, which will show which questions remain unanswered and which questions you have marked for review. You can jump to any question at any time, you can change your answers at any time, and once you are satisfied that you are done, you can submit the entire exam for grading at any time—but, of course, once you grade it, you are done and cannot change anything so you obviously don't want to do this until you are done. You will get credit for each question answered correctly and no credit for incorrect answers. Therefore, you're better off to at least guess at questions you're not sure about. You won't get anything deducted for a wrong answer and you just might get it correct.

Your exam will be graded immediately and the results will be sent to the sign-in desk, where you can pick up a printed summary of your exam results. Results are also sent immediately to the Oracle Certification management for compilation and credit toward your certification.

■ *When you have completed the exam, return to the sign-in desk.* Here you can pick up a printed copy of your exam results. You will need to keep these for your records. Even if you fail the exam, you want to get these results. Although the specific questions and answers won't be listed on the printout, the general test categories will be, along with a count of how many questions addressed different topics and how many questions you answered correctly by topic. This is valuable information to know how to prepare for any retest you may require, not to mention a great reinforcement to yourself for the topics that you do understand. Also, don't forget to pick up your cell phone or anything else you may have placed in a locker.

■ *If you need to retake an exam, you must wait at least 30 calendar days.*

■ *Once you have successfully passed all of the exams required for certification, you are immediately considered certified.* You will be automatically sent a package through the mail containing your welcome letter, a pin, an identification card, your certificate, and additional information.

How to Read This Book

This book is designed specifically to prepare you for the exam. It intentionally uses repetition to teach you about the material you'll need for the exam. Each chapter will summarize the topics addressed in the chapter and explain each key concept in detail. Each chapter repeats key concepts in chapter summaries, two-minute drills, and chapter questions to reinforce your knowledge so that by the time you complete the practice exams at the end of the book, you'll be ready to pass your Oracle Certification exam.

Who Should Read This Book

This book is obviously perfect for anyone who is thinking about taking the Oracle Certified Internet Application Developer exams. However, it is also ideal for anyone who wants to round out his or her knowledge of PL/SQL and make sure he or she has a full understanding of what it means to create and manage PL/SQL program units.

We assume that you have a working knowledge of the Structured Query Language (SQL). The book makes references to Data Definition Language (DDL) and Data Manipulation Language (DML), and it is assumed that you understand the difference. DDL consists of those SQL statements that create database objects, such as CREATE, ALTER, and DROP. DML consists of those SQL statements that work with existing objects—SELECT, INSERT, UPDATE, and DELETE.

It is suggested that you already know something about PL/SQL syntax, but in case you don't, Chapter 1 provides an excellent summary of the basic language syntax of PL/SQL.

The book refers to *database objects*, but please note that this is not a reference to the relatively new concept of objects in the database. The kind of database objects that this book references are those database objects found in the Oracle data dictionary view USER_OBJECTS. These include tables, indexes, synonyms, sequences, and, of course, PL/SQL program units.

Let's Get Started!

Welcome to a great experience—one that will move you ahead in your career, build your confidence, and enhance your reputation in the professional community. So what are you waiting for? Turn to Chapter 1!

PART
I

Language Syntax

CHAPTER
1

Overview of PL/SQL

o understand Procedural Language/Structured Query Language (PL/SQL) program units, you must first understand the basic language syntax of PL/SQL. That is the subject of this chapter. These topics are tested in the first exam of the Oracle Internet Application Developer's certification, but these same topics are the backdrop and foundation of the entire exam on program units. Many issues of working with program units, such as privileges, permissions, interdependencies, and parameter syntax, are built upon the fundamentals that are reviewed in this chapter. So, although these topics are not explicitly tested in the exam, a complete understanding of them is required to perform successfully on the exam. Even if you already know this material, it is advised that you skim it before moving to the next chapter.

In this chapter, you will review and understand the following topics:

■ An introduction to the PL/SQL language

■ PL/SQL syntax fundamentals

■ Declaration section

■ Processing section

■ Cursors

■ Advanced datatype declaration

■ Exception handling

■ Working with blocks

■ An introduction to program units

An Introduction to the PL/SQL Language

PL/SQL is a proprietary computer programming language that is owned by the Oracle Corporation. It combines the power of SQL with the best and most commonly used features of some popular third-generation languages, such as C, FORTRAN, COBOL, Ada, Pascal, and PL/1. PL/SQL's features include variable declaration, assignment statements, conditional logic, loops, subprogram and parameter passing, and error handling, all integrated with the full power of the SQL language. Using PL/SQL, application developers can create programs that process database records individually with far more control that a stand-alone SQL script will enable, such as fully controllable conditional logic and looping.

SQL's Data Manipulation Language (DML) commands, including SELECT, INSERT, UPDATE, and DELETE, can be used in PL/SQL statements. Some SQL statements, such as SELECT, require some minor accommodations (such as the INTO clause). Most of Oracle's SQL functions can be used from within PL/SQL expressions inside of PL/SQL programs.

PL/SQL programs can be structured as program units, such as procedures and functions. Program units can be placed on either the server side or the client side. On the server side, program units can be stored in the database and be called to execute from other PL/SQL applications as well as from simple SQL*Plus command-line statements. On the client side, Oracle Corporation has built support for PL/SQL program units into various Oracle development tools, such as Form Builder and Report Builder, to extend the capability of those tools and provide capabilities for detailed data manipulation. By having the flexibility to store program units on either the client or the server, the developer is empowered to choose either implementation for each program unit in order to tune the application for optimal performance; in other words, by being able to move the program unit around, the developer can choose to put program units that frequently interact with the database on the server side and move those program units that perform more direct interaction with the user on the client side. The choice is up to the developer, and the result is an optimally tuned application.

Procedures and functions can be combined into larger program units called *packages.* There are several advantages to using packages; they offer some security and performance improvement advantages, not to mention the simple benefit of organizing a set of program units in one place. When several applications are stored in the same database, it's a lot easier to see which program units support which applications when they are collected in a package than if they are thrown into a schema's alphabetical listing of objects. Even if only one application is stored in a schema, some of the program units might be intended for one work purpose, perhaps accounting, and another set of program units might be meant for something else, such as application maintenance and user account tracking. By storing the relevant program units in separate packages, it's easier for developers to understand and maintain the application.

Oracle Corporation provides some prewritten PL/SQL packages to extend the capability of the PL/SQL language, and Oracle also provides support for special features and techniques, such as scheduling batch jobs, working with operating system files, or working with Oracle database snapshots. PL/SQL program units can be stored inside the database in the form of database triggers, which are associated with events and are "fired" in response to various activities, such as SQL UPDATEs and DELETEs, whether the triggering SQL transaction originated from another PL/SQL program or not. In addition, PL/SQL program units can be created for use from within SQL statements or be used to "wrap" Java programs for storage in the database.

There are two major categories of PL/SQL programs: *anonymous* and *named.* Generally, *program units* refer to named PL/SQL programs. An example of an anonymous PL/SQL program, generally known as a *block,* is shown here:

```
DECLARE
   v_counter NUMBER(3);
   v_user    ALL_USERS.USERNAME%TYPE;
   v_today   DATE;
BEGIN
   -- First, get the current date and time,
   -- and the schema of the user running
   -- this program.  Print the results on the screen.
   SELECT    SYSDATE, USER
   INTO      v_today, v_user
   FROM      DUAL;

   DBMS_OUTPUT.PUT_LINE(
      'Today : ' ||
      TO_CHAR(v_today, 'FMDay, Month DD, YYYY'));
   DBMS_OUTPUT.PUT_LINE('Schema: ' || v_user);
   -- Next, set up a loop
   v_counter := 0;
   LOOP
      v_counter := v_counter + 1;
      EXIT WHEN v_counter > 10;
      DBMS_OUTPUT.PUT_LINE('Line: ' || v_counter);
   END LOOP;
EXCEPTION
   WHEN OTHERS THEN
      INSERT INTO ERRORS
         VALUES (SEQ_ERROR_ID.NEXTVAL, 'Something went wrong.');
      COMMIT;
END;
/
```

A PL/SQL block consists of the following sections:

- **Declaration section** Includes the declaration of variables, constants, cursors, and user-defined exceptions for use in the processing section. This section is only required if there is anything to declare. If the processing section doesn't require any user-declared elements, the declaration section is not required.

- **Processing section** This is the main body of the block and is the only required section of the block. It includes assignment statements, conditional logic, loops, and more.

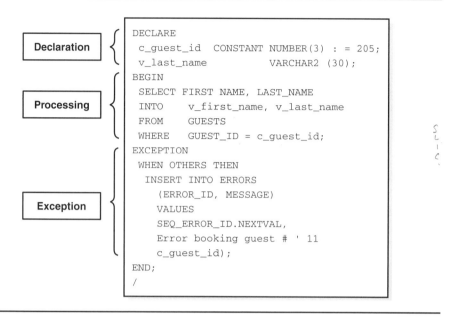

```
         ⎧ DECLARE
Declaration ⎨   c_guest_id  CONSTANT NUMBER(3)  : = 205;
         ⎩   v_last_name              VARCHAR2 (30);
         ⎧ BEGIN
           SELECT FIRST NAME, LAST_NAME
Processing ⎨ INTO     v_first_name, v_last_name
           FROM     GUESTS
         ⎩ WHERE    GUEST_ID = c_guest_id;
         ⎧ EXCEPTION
           WHEN OTHERS THEN
             INSERT INTO ERRORS
               (ERROR_ID, MESSAGE)
Exception ⎨    VALUES
               SEQ_ERROR_ID.NEXTVAL,
               Error booking guest # ' 11
         ⎩     c_guest_id);
           END;
           /
```

FIGURE 1-1.   *The structure of a PL/SQL block*

- **Exception-handling section**   This is an optional section that will handle any exceptions that may be raised in the processing section. Exceptions may or may not be raised in the processing section during execution, but regardless of whether they are raised or not, this section is optional.

Figure 1-1 shows an example of a PL/SQL block and identifies the various sections.

PL/SQL Syntax Fundamentals
In this section, you will cover

- Statements
- Identifiers
- Comments, single-line and multiline
- Literals

Statements

PL/SQL programs are built as a combination of statements, and statements consist of a combination of identifiers, expressions, operators, and PL/SQL reserved words. Semicolons terminate these statements. Furthermore, white space between the elements within expressions is ignored. In other words, statements can continue across many lines until a semicolon is encountered, which terminates the statement and opens the way for the next statement. The job of understanding PL/SQL consists of understanding the rules of the language elements and understanding how to put the elements together into functional programs.

Identifiers

Identifiers are used in PL/SQL to define the names of various elements. Identifiers are words that you make up. They must start with a character, can be up to 30 characters in length, and cannot include spaces, but can include dollar signs ($), pound signs (#), and underscores (_). Identifiers are used to name variables, constants, explicit cursors, user-named exceptions, and program units such as procedures, functions, database triggers, and packages.

   PL/SQL is a case-insensitive language, meaning that the language elements are not case sensitive. However, data is case sensitive; in other words, string literals and the values of variables and constants that are defined with character-based datatypes are case sensitive.

Comments

Comments can be included in PL/SQL code by preceding the comments with special characters. These special characters tell the PL/SQL parser to ignore the line, or lines, that follow.

   Single-line comments are preceded by two dashes in succession. A single-line comment can be placed on a line by itself or at the end of a line of valid PL/SQL code.

   A multiline comment starts with the characters, /*, and is terminated with the characters, */. A multiline comment can span as many lines as you wish. It can begin on a line of existing PL/SQL code and at its termination can be followed by PL/SQL on the same line as the termination characters.

   The following code listing shows two examples of single-line comments and one of a multiline comment:

```
DECLARE
   v_schema VARCHAR2(30);   -- This is a single line comment
BEGIN
   -- This is a single line comment
   SELECT USER
```

```
  INTO    v_schema
  FROM    DUAL;
  /*  This is a multi line comment.  It can continue
      on as many consecutive lines as you wish,
      as long as you end it with the proper
      characters. */  DBMS_OUTPUT.PUT_LINE(v_schema);
      DBMS_OUTPUT.PUT_LINE('All done.');
END;
/
```

Literals

The rules for literals in PL/SQL are the same as the rules used in SQL. Character literals, also known as string literals, are delimited with single quotes. Numeric literals have no quotes, commas, dollar signs, or any other special characters, but they should include any necessary decimal points. Date literals are delimited with single quotes. The date value itself must be in the appropriate format for the database and the format mask that may apply. The default format for dates is 'DD-MON-YY', as in '01-JAN-03' for January 3, 2003. Most Oracle installations also accept the alternative format of 'DD-MON-YYYY' as a default, as in '01-JAN-2003'. A date literal can be expressed in a format that varies from the default, provided the appropriate format mask, according to the rules of SQL, accompanies them.

When using string literals, sometimes it's necessary to define a value that includes the single quote symbol, which is the string delimiter itself. This requires special attention. To include a single quote within the string without delimiting the end of the string, you must include two single quote characters in succession within the string literal. In other words, to specify my last name as a string literal, I have to use the following syntax:

```
'O''Hearn'
```

This will be seen within PL/SQL as the following literal value:

```
O'Hearn
```

One important datatype that PL/SQL uses is the BOOLEAN datatype. This datatype doesn't exist in the database and isn't formally recognized in SQL, but is used in PL/SQL. The BOOLEAN datatype is quite simple; the options for values are either TRUE or FALSE. (NULL, of course, is an option as well.) BOOLEAN literal values are expressed with the reserved words TRUE and FALSE without any quotes.

Finally, the reserved word NULL is considered a valid value of any variable of any datatype. The definition of NULL is properly understood as "the absence of information." In other words, it is not a blank, nor is it a zero; a blank and a zero are defined values. NULL indicates that the PL/SQL program just doesn't know what the value is.

Literal values can be used throughout PL/SQL, as we shall see in the following sections.

Declaration Section

The declaration section is where you set up variables, constants, and other elements for use in the processing section. The declaration section is only required if the processing section requires any of these elements. The declaration section can be used to declare variables, constants, cursors, and user-defined exceptions. Each is described in the following sections.

Variables

Variables are declared with the following format:

```
VARIABLE_NAME DATATYPE;
```

For example, the following code declares a variable called v_last_name and declares it with the variable character datatype at a maximum length of 30 characters:

```
v_last_name VARCHAR2(30);
```

Variable names must start with a letter and can be up to 30 characters with no spaces. Names can include the following special characters:

```
#$_
```

A variable's datatype must be declared. The list of available datatypes follows this section.

As an option, a variable can be initialized at declaration with the assignment statement, as in the following examples:

```
v_last_name VARCHAR2(30) := 'Hoddlestein';
v_found     BOOLEAN      := TRUE;
v_order     NUMBER(5,2)  := 150.57;
```

Without initialization, a variable's value at the beginning of the processing section will be NULL.

Datatypes

To declare variables, constants, and, as we shall see later, parameters, you must be familiar with PL/SQL's datatypes. They are explained here:

■ **CHAR(*n*)**   Accepts alphanumeric data up to *n* characters in length. The *n* indicator is required. The CHAR(n) right pads the data with blanks to ensure that a total of *n* characters will be stored no matter what; for example, if you store the string "Joe" in a variable whose datatype is CHAR(5), then "Joe   " is stored—two extra blanks are automatically added to force the string to be five characters long. The maximum length is 32,767 characters. CHAR is short for CHARACTER, which is also accepted, that is, CHARACTER(*n*). In practice, CHAR is not used nearly as much as the alternative, which is VARCHAR2, described later in this list. The length specifier, *n*, is not required. It defaults to 1.

■ **VARCHAR2(*n*)**   Accepts alphanumeric data up to *n* characters in length. As with CHAR(*n*), the *n* indicator is required, but contrary to CHAR(*n*), VARCHAR2(*n*) will not pad values, but will instead store only as much data as required by the entered value. For example, for a variable declared as VARCHAR2(30), if the provided value is Smith, then only 5 characters are stored, even though up to 30 characters are allowed. The longest VARCHAR2 length allowed is 32,767 characters.

■ **DATE**   Accepts date descriptions in the same date format required by the database. The default format is 'DD-MON-YY', where DD is the numeric day of the month, MON is the first three letters, capitalized, of the month, and YY is the last two digits of the year. For example, September 28, 1989 is represented as '28-SEP-89'.

■ **NUMBER(n,m)**   Accepts numeric data only. The value for *n* is the size specification, and the value of *m* is the precision. Both are optional, but *m* cannot be used without the presence of *n*. Up to *n* significant digits are accepted. For example, the declaration NUMBER(3) will accept numbers no higher than the number 999. The value for *m* is used to specify the portion of *n* that is defined to the right of the decimal point. In other words, NUMBER(*n,m*) will accept up to *n* significant digits of which *m* are to the right of the decimal point. For example, the declaration NUMBER(3,1) will accept numbers no higher than 99.9. See Figure 1-2 for some examples of variables declared with NUMBER.

The variable v_number_1 is declared with NUMBER and no size or precision. If both *n* and *m* are left out, then the 40 most significant digits are

```
± Oracle SQL*Plus                                        _ □ ×
File  Edit  Search  Options  Help
SQL> SET SERVEROUTPUT ON
SQL> DECLARE
  2      v_number_1 NUMBER;
  3      v_number_2 NUMBER(42);
  4      v_number_3 NUMBER(40);
  5  BEGIN
  6      v_number_1 := 123456789012345678901234567890123456789112345;
  7      v_number_2 := 123456789012345678901234567890123456789112;
  8      v_number_3 := 123456789012345678901234567890123456789891;
  9      DBMS_OUTPUT.PUT_LINE('v_number_1 = ' || v_number_1);
 10      DBMS_OUTPUT.PUT_LINE('v_number_2 = ' || v_number_2);
 11      DBMS_OUTPUT.PUT_LINE('v_number_3 = ' || v_number_3);
 12  END;
 13  /
v_number_1 = 123456789012345678901234567890123456789000000
v_number_2 = 123456789012345678901234567890123456789100
v_number_3 = 123456789012345678901234567890123456789891

PL/SQL procedure successfully completed.

SQL>
```

FIGURE 1-2. *Three examples of variables declared with NUMBER*

stored. The resulting variable can receive numbers that are larger than 40 significant digits, but will only record the first 40 most significant digits, rounded off. The next variable, v_number_2, demonstrates that the maximum allowable value for *n* is documented at 38, but a declared value of 42 works in PL/SQL 8.1.5, and a variable declared as NUMBER(42) accepts up to 40 actual significant digits. Finally, Figure 1-2 shows v_number_3 as an example of a declaration of NUMBER(40), which stores precisely 40 significant digits.

■ **BOOLEAN**   Stores values corresponding to the keywords TRUE or FALSE and, of course, can also be NULL. For example, an acceptable declaration is as follows:

```
v_found BOOLEAN := TRUE;
```

■ **LONG**   Accepts very large blocks of alphanumeric data, up to 32,760 bytes.

- **RAW** Accepts binary data, such as multimedia files, and accepts lengths of up to 32,767 characters. PL/SQL will not interpret the contents of a RAW variable.

- **LONG RAW** Accepts very large blocks of binary data, up to 32,760 bytes. Note that this is actually less than the ultimate length accepted by RAW.

- **MLSLABEL** A secure operating system label, used in Trusted Oracle.

- **ROWID** A value that is defined by the Oracle system to uniquely identify the physical storage address of a row in the Oracle database. The value is obtained from the pseudocolumn that is automatically added to every Oracle table by the Oracle system.

There are several datatypes for working with large objects (LOBs):

- **BLOB** A Binary Large Object that accepts up to 4 gigabytes of binary data.

- **CLOB** A Character Large Object that accepts up to 4 gigabytes of alphanumeric data.

- **NCLOB** The multibyte character set alternative to CLOB.

- **BFILE** A pointer to a binary operating system file.

There are several numeric datatypes that store whole number integers:

- **BINARY_INTEGER and PLS_INTEGER** Both enable the storage of integers ranging from $(-2^{31} + 1)$ to $(2^{31} - 1)$. The difference between the two is that PLS_INTEGER will raise an exception if an overflow occurs, whereas BINARY_INTEGER may not do the same when the result is assigned to a NUMBER datatype.

- **INT, also INTEGER** The same as NUMBER, but it does not accept decimal values. In other words, INT does not accept a precision component, only a size component. For example, INTEGER(5) is accepted.

- **SMALLINT** The same as NUMBER(38).

- **POSITIVE** The same as BINARY_INTEGER, but with a more limited range, from (1) to (2^{31}).

- **NATURAL** The same as BINARY_INTEGER, but with a more limited range, from (0) to (2^{31}).

There are several numeric datatypes that store real numbers:

- **NUMERIC, DEC, and DECIMAL**   The same as NUMBER, except that they declare fixed-point numbers.

- **REAL, FLOAT, and DOUBLE_PRECISION**   The same as NUMBER, but these declare floating-point numbers.

- **TABLE**   This is a complex datatype, also known as a composite datatype. A PL/SQL table is similar to an array structure that most third-generation programming languages support.

- **RECORD**   This is another composite datatype. A variable declared with a RECORD datatype is a single variable that represents a combination of scalar datatypes (all of the other datatypes mentioned above, except for TABLE) as well as other RECORD variables. A RECORD variable, for example, might be declared that is called PHONE_NUMBER but represents a combination of VARCHAR2 variables AREA_CODE, PHONE, and EXTENSION.

Constants

A PL/SQL constant is a declared element with a value that is assigned when it's declared in the declaration section. Its value cannot be changed by any code that references it, such as that found in the processing or exception-handling section.

The syntax to declare a constant is similar to that used for a variable. The only differences are the use of the reserved word CONSTANT, and the fact that the assignment statement that initializes the value is required, not optional, for a constant. Here's an example:

```
c_tax_rate CONSTANT NUMBER(4,3) := 0.045;
```

The previous sample declares a constant called c_tax_rate. Constants, as with variables, require that a datatype be used in the declaration. The same datatypes that can be used to declare a variable are also available for use with constants.

Once the initialized value is set, it cannot be changed. In other words, in the course of the PL/SQL block's execution, the processing section cannot assign a new value to the constant; neither can the exception-handling section change the constant's value.

Other Declared Elements

You can declare more than just variables and constants in the declaration section. You can also declare explicit cursors and user-defined exceptions. These will be discussed at a later point in this chapter.

Processing Section

The processing section contains the executable statements that form the main body of your PL/SQL block. A PL/SQL block must have a processing section; it is the only required section in the block.

The processing section includes the following elements:

- Expressions
- Assignment statements
- Conditional statements
- Loops
- Cursor control statements

Expressions

Expressions are not stand-alone statements, but are instead small units of code that are included in other stand-alone statements. Uses of expressions include assignment statements and conditional statements.

There are two general types of expressions: arithmetic expressions and comparison expressions. Arithmetic expressions combine variables, constants, and literal values with arithmetic operators or SQL functions to produce a single result. For example, consider the following expression:

```
v_wholesale_price + v_admin_expense
```

This expression takes two variables and adds them together, producing a single answer. This expression, as with all expressions, is not a complete stand-alone PL/SQL statement, but could be used within an assignment statement or elsewhere to build a complete statement. The arithmetic operators that PL/SQL uses are the same that SQL uses (see Table 1-1).

Expressions are subject to the rule of operator precedence. The rule of operator precedence dictates which operator is given priority over another operator within an expression.

For example, consider the following expression:

```
3 + 4 * 5
```

The rules of operator precedence dictate that the multiplication operator is evaluated first, which produces an interim result as follows:

```
3 + 20
```

Operator	Description	Operator Precedence
()	Parentheses	1
*	Multiplication	2
/	Division	
+	Addition	3
—	Subtraction	

TABLE 1-1. *Arithmetic Operators*

Finally, this remaining expression is evaluated, and the result is computed to be 23. In other words

```
3 + 4 * 5 = 23
```

However, parentheses can be used to override the rules of operator precedence, as follows:

```
(3 + 4) * 5 = 35
```

By overriding the rule of operator precedence, we have altered the expression.

Nested parentheses are allowed, and the innermost set of parentheses will be evaluated before the others. In situations where multiple operators are within the same expression and are at the same level of operator precedence, the leftmost operators are evaluated first. The PL/SQL rules of operator precedence are the same rules that SQL uses.

SQL Functions

Almost all of the SQL functions can be used in PL/SQL expressions. For example, this expression is considered valid in PL/SQL:

```
SUBSTR(v_lastname,1,1)
```

This expression uses the SQL function SUBSTR, or substring, and in this example, produces the first single character from within the variable v_lastname.

The only SQL function that is not allowed in PL/SQL expressions is the DECODE function. The SQL DECODE function is essentially a conditional logic function, and PL/SQL has the more comprehensive alternative of the IF-THEN-END

Decode is NOT allowed in PL/SQL

IF statement, which we will address later. As a result of the presence of IF statements in PL/SQL, the DECODE function is not required, nor is it allowed. (Note that although DECODE cannot be used in PL/SQL expressions, it can be used in cursors, which are addressed later.)

Presence of Null +100 = Null → Arithmetic Exp
Null + Values = Values → character Exp

NULL

The presence of NULL requires special attention. Consider the following expression:

```
v_salary + v_commission
```

If the value of v_salary is 100, and the value of v_commission is NULL, then the evaluated result is NULL. After all, what is the result of 100 plus "I don't know."? The answer is, obviously, "I don't know." This is an important point. The presence of a NULL value in an arithmetic expression will produce a NULL result.

On the other hand, the presence of a NULL value in a character expression will not necessarily produce a NULL result. Here's an example:

```
v_first_name   := "James"
v_middle_name := NULL;
v_last_name    := "Waters"
v_full_name := v_first_name || ' ' || v_middle_name || ' ' || v_last_name
```

The value for v_full_name will be "James Waters". The NULL value for v_middle_name will simply be ignored in a character expression.

For those situations where the possible presence of a NULL value is unacceptable, you can use the SQL function NVL, which will replace any occurrences of NULL values with some specified value of your choosing. For example, in the case of the PL/SQL expression we looked at earlier, we can use NVL to ensure that a NULL value will not NULL out the entire result:

```
NVL(v_salary,0) + NVL(v_commission,0)
```

This expression now will always produce some sort of answer. If the commission value is NULL, then the NVL function will replace the presence of NULL with the zero value we provided as the second parameter. On the other hand, if the v_commission variable holds a non-NULL value, then the value will be left alone, and the equation will simply use the assigned value for v_commission.

Comparison Operators and BOOLEAN Expressions

BOOLEAN expressions use comparison operators to obtain a TRUE or FALSE result. BOOLEAN expressions are used in IF statements and elsewhere, and are equivalent to the SQL WHERE clause.

An example of a BOOLEAN expression is shown here:

```
v_last_name = 'Smith'
```

This expression will compare the value contained in the v_last_name variable with the literal value of 'Smith'. If the two values are identical, the expression will evaluate to TRUE. Otherwise, the expression evaluates to FALSE.

Comparison operators can be used to compare two arithmetic expressions. Here's an example:

```
(3+4)*5 >= (v_answer / v_rate);
```

In this example, the two expressions on either side of the comparison operator will be evaluated, and the results will be compared to determine if the expression on the left side is greater than or equal to the expression on the right side. If yes, then a value TRUE for the entire expression is the result. Otherwise, a FALSE results. The two sides of the comparison operator must represent the same general datatypes, meaning they must both be DATEs, character strings, or numeric datatypes.

Furthermore, PL/SQL honors the same rules that SQL uses for the comparison for datatypes:

- **DATE** Earlier dates are *lesser* dates, and later dates are *greater* dates.

- **VARCHAR2** A is less than Z. Adam is less than Albert. Uppercase Z is less than lowercase a. The number 2 is greater than 10. If this seems strange, remember that when numbers are stored as character strings, PL/SQL won't recognize them as numbers and will treat them as the equivalent of dictionary entries.

- **Numeric datatypes, such as NUMBER and INTEGER** The number 1 is less than the number 2. The number 10 is less than the number 100.

Comparison operators are all collectively at the same level of operator precedence as each other and are considered inferior to the arithmetic operators. In other words, arithmetic operators are evaluated before comparison operators in any given expression, excluding, of course, the effect of any parentheses, which can be used to override default precedence rules.

Operator	Description
=	Equals
>=	Greater than or equal to
>	Greater than
<=	Less than or equal to
<	Less than
!=	Not equal
<>	Not equal
^=	Not equal
IN	Compares one value on the left with a set of values on the right. The set is enclosed in parentheses, with each value separated by commas, as in ('Smith', 'Jones', 'Grant', 'Waters') or (1999, 2000, 2001).
LIKE	Activates wildcard characters. The two wildcard characters are as follows: _ An underscore represents one single unknown character. % A percent sign represents an unknown number of unknown characters, from zero to infinity. Here's an example: IF ('_c%') LIKE v_lastname THEN The '_c%', combined with the LIKE keyword, is interpreted to refer to any string with a second character that is a lowercase c and that's followed by any characters, from zero to an infinite number. Possible matches might include "McLean", "Acktinson", and "Ochs". If the reserved word LIKE is replaced with a standard comparison operator, such as the equals sign ("="), then the wildcard characters are no longer recognized as wildcards, but as literal values. In other words, without LIKE in the previous example, we'd be looking for someone whose last name really is "_c%", and I'm not sure what planet that person would be on, but chances are this isn't what we meant.

TABLE 1-2. *Comparison Operators*

Logical Operators

Finally, multiple BOOLEAN expressions can be combined with logical operators. Here's an example:

```
IF ((3+4)*5     = v_answer) AND
   (v_last_name = 'Smith') THEN
```

In this example, the logical operator AND combines the two BOOLEAN expressions, which are evaluated first, to create an overall TRUE or FALSE for the entire IF condition.

The logical operators are shown in Table 1-3.

The rules of operator precedence dictate that expressions combined with AND are resolved before expressions combined with OR. Also, logical operators are evaluated after arithmetic and comparison operators.

For example, consider the following code sample:

```
DECLARE
   v_last_name   VARCHAR2(30) := 'Waters';
   v_department  VARCHAR2(10) := 'President';
   v_order_total NUMBER(5,2)  := 49.99;
BEGIN
   IF (v_department = 'President') OR
      (v_department = 'Marketing') AND
      (v_order_total > 79.84)       THEN
     DBMS_OUTPUT.PUT_LINE('Found it');
   ELSE
     DBMS_OUTPUT.PUT_LINE('Did not find it.');
   END IF;
END;
/
```

Operator	Description	Operator Precedence
AND	Requires both sides of the logical operator expression to be TRUE. Otherwise, it returns a FALSE.	1
OR	Requires only one of the sides of the logical operator expression to be TRUE. If both sides are FALSE, the result is FALSE.	2

TABLE 1-3. *Logical Operators*

The result: Contrary to what you might think, it's 'Found it'. The reason is operator precedence of logical operators. Consider each expression:

- (v_department = 'President') evaluates to TRUE.
- (v_department = 'Marketing') evaluates to FALSE.
- (v_order_total > 79.84) evaluates to FALSE.

As a result, we have

```
TRUE OR FALSE AND FALSE
```

Operator precedence says that the AND comparison should be evaluated first. A comparison of FALSE AND FALSE produces a result of FALSE, resulting in

```
TRUE OR FALSE
```

And this, at long last, evaluates to TRUE.

If this is not what is desired, then once again parentheses can be used to override the behavior of operator precedence. For example, this is the same code sample, but with a careful placement of parentheses to alter the logic:

```
DECLARE
   v_last_name    VARCHAR2(30) := 'Waters';
   v_department   VARCHAR2(10) := 'President';
   v_order_total NUMBER(5,2)   := 49.99;
BEGIN
   IF ((v_department  = 'President')  OR
      (v_department   = 'Marketing')) AND
       (v_order_total > 79.84)          THEN
     DBMS_OUTPUT.PUT_LINE('Found it');
   ELSE
     DBMS_OUTPUT.PUT_LINE('Did not find it.');
   END IF;
END;
/
```

Now the result is 'Did not find it.' The default behavior of operator precedence has been overridden with parentheses.

Assignment Statements

Assignment statements are built with the assignment symbol, :=, and are used to change the value of the element on the left side of the assignment symbol to be the same as the value resulting from the expression on the right side. The left side of the assignment statement is one variable. The right side of the assignment can be anything from one variable or constant, a literal value, or an expression with an evaluated result that is a single value.

The datatype on the right side of the assignment statement must match the datatype of the variable on the left. However, Oracle does perform automatic datatype conversions in many situations when it is appropriate. But proper design dictates that you as the developer should ensure, through the use of conversion functions and whatever else is appropriate, that the expression on the right produces a datatype that matches the datatype of the variable on the left.

For example, consider the following assignment statement:

```
v_lastname := 'Smith';
```

This assignment statement changes the value of the variable v_lastname to be equal to the character string Smith.

Here is an example of an assignment statement that uses an expression on the right side:

```
v_order_total := v_order_subtotal + v_tax + v_shipping;
```

Upon the execution of this statement, the value of v_order_total will be equal to the result of the expression on the right, which is the addition of the three variables v_order_subtotal, v_tax, and v_shipping.

Conditional Statements

Conditional statements enable you to control the flow of execution through your code by testing for conditions and branching the process flow in different ways depending on the outcome. In PL/SQL, as in most languages, conditional statements are **If** statements.

Consider the following code sample:

```
DECLARE
   v_day_of_week VARCHAR2(30);
BEGIN
   v_day_of_week := TO_CHAR(SYSDATE,'DY');
   IF (v_day_of_week IN ('SAT','SUN')) THEN
     DBMS_OUTPUT.PUT_LINE('The office is closed today');
   ELSE
     DBMS_OUTPUT.PUT_LINE('The office is open today.');
   END IF;
END;
/
```

In this example, either one of two different sentences will be printed, depending on the value of the variable v_day_of_week. If the value is either SAT or SUN, then the sentence, The office is closed today, will print. Otherwise, the sentence, The office is open today, will print.

The syntax of a simple PL/SQL IF statement is as follows:

- The reserved word IF.

- Some expression that evaluates to a BOOLEAN value, in other words, either TRUE or FALSE. This expression can use literals, variables, constants, SQL functions, PL/SQL program units, arithmetic and logical operators, and, of course, comparison operators.

- The reserved word THEN.

- One or more PL/SQL statements, which are only executed when the IF expression evaluates to TRUE.

- The reserved words END IF and the semicolon, which mark the conclusion of this IF block.

The IF statement is considered a single statement, so the semicolon only appears at the end, which is at the end of END IF. However, the IF statement nests other complete statements within itself. You can place any number of valid PL/SQL statements after the THEN keyword, including assignment statements, SQL statements, and even other IF statements.

The previous code sample shows the IF statement in its simplest form. You may optionally extend the logic of this IF statement by including one or more occurrences of the reserved word ELSIF followed by another BOOLEAN expression and then a set of PL/SQL executable statements. Finally, you can optionally include the reserved word ELSE followed by a set of PL/SQL executable statements.

The following code sample demonstrates all of these options:

```
DECLARE
  CURSOR cur_employees IS
    SELECT    E.EMPLOYEE_ID,
              E.POSITION,
              EC.SALARY
    FROM      EMPLOYEES E,
              EMP_COMPENSATION EC
    WHERE     E.EMPLOYEE_ID = EC.EMPLOYEE_ID
      AND     EC.START_DATE =
                (SELECT MAX(EC2.START_DATE)
                 FROM   EMP_COMPENSATION EC2
                 WHERE  EC2.EMPLOYEE_ID = E.EMPLOYEE_ID)
```

```
      ORDER BY POSITION;
  rec_employees cur_employees%ROWTYPE;
  v_salary_increase NUMBER(4,2);
BEGIN
  OPEN cur_employees;
  LOOP
    FETCH cur_employees INTO rec_employees;
    EXIT WHEN cur_employees%NOTFOUND;
    IF    (rec_employees.POSITION = 'Executive')
    THEN
      v_salary_increase := 0;
    ELSIF (rec_employees.POSITION = 'Manager')
    THEN
      v_salary_increase := .02;
    ELSIF (rec_employees.POSITION = 'Engineer')
    THEN
      v_salary_increase := .04;
    ELSE -- for all other positions, do this
      v_salary_increase := .06;
    END IF;
    INSERT INTO EMP_COMPENSATION
      (EMP_COMPENSATION_ID,
       EMPLOYEE_ID,
       SALARY,
       START_DATE)
    VALUES
      (SEQ_EMP_COMPENSATION_ID.NEXTVAL,
       rec_employees.EMPLOYEE_ID,
       rec_employees.SALARY * v_salary_increase,
       SYSDATE);
  END LOOP;
  COMMIT;
END;
/
```

This code sample uses an IF statement that employs two ELSIF clauses and one single ELSE clause. In this example, if the value for rec_employees.POSITION is determined to be equal to the literal string Executive, then the first set of processing statements will be executed through to completion; in other words, the value for v_salary_increase will be set to zero, and the section that starts with the ELSIF that tests for the literal string Manager will be skipped, as will the rest of the IF block. Execution will pick up after the END IF keywords.

On the other hand, if the value for rec_employees.POSITION is Manager, then the second set of statements will be executed, and processing will jump past the Engineer section and pick up with the first executable statement after END IF.

Finally, if none of the specified values for rec_employees.POSITION are found—in other words, if it's not Executive, Manager, or Engineer—then the ELSE clause will capture control and set the value of v_salary_increase to .06.

In any IF statement, if an ELSIF clause is included, it must include a BOOLEAN expression, and the THEN keyword. The ELSIF clause is not required, but you may include as many as you wish.

If the ELSE clause is included, it cannot have a BOOLEAN expression, nor does it use a THEN keyword. There can only be one ELSE clause, although it is not required. The ELSE clause, if used, must be last, after any and all ELSIF clauses.

Remember that the first IF expression that tests for TRUE is where control will stop and process, and the rest of the ELSIF expressions that follow, whether they might be TRUE or not, will not even be evaluated. The first one that is TRUE is the first one that is processed.

The expressions in IF statements can use comparison and logical operators, variables, constants, SQL functions, and all of the other features available for use with expressions.

Loops

Loops are structures that "nest" other PL/SQL statements inside. All statements in a loop will execute all the way through the loop, after which control will return to the top of the loop and repeat the entire set of statements again. Any variables with values that are changed as the loop executes will retain those changed values. In other words, the results of the first loop's execution is retained and built upon as the loop repeats.

Consider the following code sample:

```
DECLARE
  v_loop_counter NUMBER(3) := 1;
BEGIN
  LOOP
    DBMS_OUTPUT.PUT_LINE('Loop ' || v_loop_counter);
    v_loop_counter := v_loop_counter + 1;
    EXIT WHEN v_loop_counter >= 10;
  END LOOP;
END;
/
```

This loop will print the word Loop nine times, each of which will be followed with a number corresponding to the value of v_loop_counter. The keywords EXIT WHEN determine when the loop will terminate, and control will leave the loop and be passed to the first executable statement after the END LOOP statement. The syntax is

- The reserved word LOOP
- Any number of valid PL/SQL statements
- The reserved words END LOOP, followed by a semicolon

The LOOP . . . END LOOP statement is one single statement. Just as the IF . . . END IF statement nests statements within itself, so does the LOOP . . . END LOOP statement. In fact, you can nest LOOP statements within other LOOP statements.

Also notice that the LOOP statement requires an EXIT to avoid behaving as an infinite loop. Without an EXIT statement of some kind, the loop will never terminate. It's the developer's responsibility to define the conditions upon which the loop will be eventually exited and include the EXIT statement.

The EXIT statement can be on a line by itself, as in the following code snippet:

```
IF (v_condition = TRUE)
THEN
   EXIT;
END IF;
```

The EXIT statement can also be used with a WHEN clause to define a BOOLEAN expression of some sort, as in the following:

```
EXIT WHEN v_condition = TRUE;
```

Either is acceptable, but the LOOP . . . END LOOP requires some sort of EXIT somewhere. You can even provide multiple EXIT statements if you wish. The first one encountered in the execution of the block is the one that will force control to leave the loop.

The LOOP statement has a few variations, such as the WHILE LOOP, the Numeric FOR LOOP, and the Cursor FOR LOOP. These are described in the next few sections.

WHILE LOOP

The WHILE LOOP statement uses a conditional expression to test whether or not control should enter the loop. Furthermore, this expression is checked again at the top of every pass through the loop.

The following is an example of a WHILE LOOP:

```
DECLARE
   v_loop_limit NUMBER(3) := 0;
BEGIN
```

```
  WHILE (v_loop_limit < 10)
  LOOP
    v_loop_limit := v_loop_limit + 1;
    DBMS_OUTPUT.PUT_LINE('In the loop: ' || v_loop_limit);
  END LOOP;
  DBMS_OUTPUT.PUT_LINE('Out of the loop.');
END;
/
```

The primary difference between the simple loop and the WHILE LOOP is that the WHILE LOOP could theoretically not execute the first time through the loop, although the simple loop will always enter the loop at least once. The expression that the WHILE LOOP tests can be the same sort of expression that an IF statement uses, with comparison and logical operators.

Numeric FOR LOOP

The Numeric FOR LOOP uses a predefined numeric range to determine how many passes through the loop will be performed. The following code sample will repeat 10 times:

```
BEGIN
  FOR v_loop_limit IN 1..10
  LOOP
    DBMS_OUTPUT.PUT_LINE('In the FOR loop: ' || v_loop_limit);
  END LOOP;
END;
/
```

Notice that the variable v_loop_limit is not declared here. This is not a mistake. The Numeric FOR LOOP automatically declares and initializes the counter variable and automatically increments it by a value of one (1) each pass through the loop.

The downside is that the v_loop_limit variable will not be available upon the completion of the loop. The scope of this variable is the inner portion of the Numeric FOR LOOP. Once the loop concludes, you cannot reference the v_loop_limit variable again for any reason.

Note that the EXIT statement is not required here in order to define a logical exit point for the loop, but the PL/SQL syntax parser will accept it. If an EXIT is used, and if it executes before FOR loop completes, the Numeric FOR LOOP will exit according to what the EXIT statement requires and not complete the predefined cycle.

Cursor FOR LOOP

To understand Cursor FOR LOOPs, you must first understand cursors, which are discussed in the next section. At the end of the next section, Cursor FOR LOOPs are addressed.

Cursors

Contrary to popular belief, cursors are *not* Oracle programmers whose code won't work. (Well, maybe that's true some of the time.)

The PL/SQL explicit cursor element is the single most important feature of the PL/SQL language and is the entire reason for using the language. It empowers the developer to obtain record-level control over database queries, stepping any query through its returned data one row at a time and pausing for as long as required between rows to perform other processing—even to the point of interacting with the database objects and choosing to terminate the query at any moment, if the need arises.

There are two types of cursors in PL/SQL: implicit cursors and explicit cursors. First, let's look at what an implicit cursor is; then we'll discuss explicit cursors, which is the more powerful form.

Implicit Cursors

Implicit cursors are not declared. They are DML statements, such as the SELECT statement, that are used in the processing section of a PL/SQL block.

For example, consider the following code sample:

```
DECLARE
   v_port_name VARCHAR2(80);
BEGIN
   SELECT    PORT_NAME
   INTO      v_port_name
   FROM      PORTS
   WHERE     PORT_ID = 101;
   DBMS_OUTPUT.PUT_LINE(v_port_name);
END;
```

The SELECT statement is an example of an implicit cursor. Notice the presence of the reserved word INTO. Implicit cursors built on the SELECT statement must use the INTO reserved word to define the list of variables that will capture the data from the columns of the SELECT statement. For each column selected, there must be a corresponding variable to receive the data.

Here's an example:

```
DECLARE
   v_ship_name   VARCHAR2(80);
   v_capacity    NUMBER(10);
   v_length      NUMBER(10);
BEGIN
   SELECT SHIP_NAME, CAPACITY, LENGTH
   INTO   v_ship_name, v_capacity, v_length
```

```
    FROM    SHIPS
    WHERE   SHIP_ID = 2;
    DBMS_OUTPUT.PUT_LINE('Ship information:');
    DBMS_OUTPUT.PUT_LINE('Name    : ' || v_ship_name);
    DBMS_OUTPUT.PUT_LINE('Capacity: ' || v_capacity);
    DBMS_OUTPUT.PUT_LINE('Length  : ' || v_length);
END;
```

The previous example shows an implicit cursor that obtains three values and SELECTs all three columns INTO the three variables. The first column's data is stored in the first variable, the second column's data is stored in the second variable, and the third column's data is stored in the third variable.

Implicit cursors are, in essence, SQL statements that are embedded in PL/SQL blocks. Embedded SQL statements can be any valid SQL statement that would work in the SQL*Plus interface. This includes SELECT, INSERT, UPDATE, and DELETE statements. Any SQL function can be used, including DECODE, which is not allowed in PL/SQL expressions but is accepted in embedded SQL.

Implicit cursors, by definition, can only work with individual variables. The implication of this is that the SELECT statement defined in an implicit cursor must return one and only one record. Otherwise, PL/SQL will encounter an error condition, known as an *exception*, which is covered later.

The important point here is that SELECT statements written as implicit cursors must define a query that results in the returning of one single record—no more, no less—or else an exception is raised, and processing in the block will halt. This isn't necessarily an undesirable situation, as is discussed in the exception-handling section, but is something that you must consider when building your code.

The intention behind this language feature is simple: A SELECT statement written as an implicit cursor performs its query on the database in total and stores the entirety of its results into the variables you define in the INTO clause. Variables can only handle one value at a time. Therefore, the SELECT statement better not return something other than one value per variable. If you think this could happen— that is, if you think the SELECT statement could theoretically return more than one row—and if this condition is acceptable, then don't use an implicit cursor; declare an explicit cursor instead. On the other hand, if the presence of more than one row is a bad sign, then use an implicit cursor, and the database will force an exception to be raised when this bad sign occurs.

For example, if your SELECT statement is querying for records based on a primary key, then it better return one row or else the primary key constraint isn't performing its UNIQUE constraint correctly in the database. Perhaps someone has disabled the constraint and bad data has entered the database. This would be bad, and an implicit cursor that queries on a primary key but that returns multiple rows is definitely a problem you want to be notified about. So, use an implicit cursor and you'll get the exception raised if and when the database becomes problematic.

On the other hand, there are many situations where it's OK to return some number of records from the database other than one single record. For these situations, explicit cursors are the choice.

Explicit Cursors

Explicit cursors are declared in the declaration section and are used in the processing section. They are called explicit cursors largely because you have to name them when you declare them; thus, they are "explicitly" referenced.

When you work with explicit cursors, you need to work with four statements, with the following keywords:

- **CURSOR** The keyword CURSOR is used to declare an explicit cursor in the declaration section. To declare a CURSOR, you use the keyword CURSOR, followed by a name you make up, and then the keyword IS, followed by a complete valid SELECT statement. SELECT statements used in a cursor can include anything that would execute in the database on its own. In other words, you can use joins, functions, subqueries, and so on.

- **OPEN** The keyword OPEN is used in the processing section to parse the SELECT statement that is declared in the CURSOR statement and prepare it for execution.

- **FETCH . . . INTO** These reserved words are used to obtain one and only one of the rows that the explicit cursor's SELECT statement returns. The FETCH statement can be invoked multiple times to return each of the SELECT statement's rows, one by one. However, the FETCH statement does not necessarily have to be used until all of the rows are returned. It can be used as often as is desired and stop short of returning all of the rows. The sequence in which the rows are returned is defined by the SELECT statement's ORDER BY clause. The FETCH syntax requires a reference to the name of the cursor as declared in the CURSOR declaration, followed by the reserved word INTO as well as by a list of variables with numbers that must match the number of columns selected in the declared CURSOR and with datatypes that must match as well.

- **CLOSE** This keyword is used to terminate the use of the explicit cursor. The PL/SQL parser will not issue a compilation error if the CLOSE statement is left out. But use of the CLOSE keyword is not only considered good design because it frees up memory allocation for other uses, it also empowers your PL/SQL block to re-open the cursor and begin all over again, should that be required by your code. However, if you leave out the CLOSE keyword, the Oracle processes will eventually figure it out and free up memory automatically.

Consider the following code listing:

```
DECLARE
  v_today  DATE;
  -- declare the explicit cursor
  CURSOR cur_cruises IS
    SELECT C.CAPTAIN_ID,
           E.LAST_NAME || ', ' || E.FIRST_NAME FULL_NAME
    FROM   CRUISES C,
           EMPLOYEES E
    WHERE  C.CAPTAIN_ID = E.EMPLOYEE_ID
      AND  START_DATE >= v_today
      AND  END_DATE   <= v_today;
  v_captain_id NUMBER(3);
  v_full_name  VARCHAR2(40);
BEGIN
  -- use an implicit cursor
  SELECT     TRUNC(SYSDATE)
  INTO       v_today
  FROM       DUAL;
  DBMS_OUTPUT.PUT_LINE(
    'Captains currently at sea include:');
  OPEN cur_cruises;  -- open the explicit cursor
  LOOP
    -- fetch the explicit cursor
    FETCH cur_cruises INTO v_captain_id, v_full_name;
    EXIT WHEN cur_cruises%NOTFOUND;
    DBMS_OUTPUT.PUT_LINE('Captain ID: ' || v_captain_id);
    DBMS_OUTPUT.PUT_LINE('Name      : ' || v_full_name);
  END LOOP;
  CLOSE cur_cruises;  -- close the explicit cursor
END;
```

The previous code listing is an example of both an explicit cursor, declared with the name cur_cruises, and an implicit cursor, which immediately follows the BEGIN statement that starts the processing section. The explicit cursor cur_cruises is a named SELECT statement. Explicit cursors can be defined with any valid SELECT statement that would execute on its own. For example, if you can execute the SELECT statement in a SQL*Plus window, you can use that SELECT statement to build an explicit cursor.

However, explicit cursors can also include variables that have already been defined from within PL/SQL. In the previous example, notice that the variable v_today is declared prior to the declaration of the cur_cruises explicit cursor. This means that the cur_cruises can include the variable in its own definition, even though the value for the v_today variable is not yet defined. In order for the PL/SQL parser to function correctly, the variable must be declared before the cursor. But it does not need to be initialized at declaration. Instead, the moment the OPEN statement is issued on the cursor is when the variable's definition will be identified and the cursor's definition will be based on the value of the variable at the time of the OPEN statement.

Cursor Attributes

Cursors have four values defined by the system that you can optionally choose to reference in your code. These are the four attributes:

- **NOTFOUND**   A BOOLEAN value that is TRUE if the most recent FETCH statement issued for the associated cursor did not return a row.

- **FOUND**   A BOOLEAN value that is TRUE if the most recent FETCH statement for the associated cursor returned a record.

- **ISOPEN**   A BOOLEAN value that is TRUE if the associated cursor is currently open.

- **ROWCOUNT**   A numeric value that indicates the total number of rows affected so far by the associated cursor.

The syntax for using cursor attributes is to indicate the cursor's name, followed by a percent sign (%) and the attribute. For example, a typical combination of statements is shown here:

```
FETCH cur_employees INTO rec_employees;
IF (cur_employees%NOTFOUND) THEN
   ...
```

The cursor cur_employees, once fetched, either found a row or it didn't. The story is in the value of cur_employees%NOTFOUND, which is TRUE if no row was found.

This works for explicit cursors, where you have a declared name of a cursor. For implicit cursors, there is no name, so instead we use the generic name SQL, which refers to the most recently executed implicit cursor in the code.

Here is an example of an implicit cursor attribute:

```
DECLARE
   UPDATE EMPLOYEES
      SET SALARY = SALARY * 1.05;
      DBMS_OUTPUT.PUT_LINE('Number of raises: ' ||
                          SQL%ROWCOUNT);
END;
/
```

The text will print out the number of rows affected by the UPDATE statement, which is an implicit cursor.

Loops Revisited: The Cursor FOR Loop

Now that we know what cursors are, we can revisit the Cursor FOR LOOP. The Cursor FOR LOOP is similar to the Numeric FOR LOOP, but uses a PL/SQL cursor instead. The cursor is considered an anonymous explicit cursor. It's anonymous because we don't know its name, but it is explicit because it will fetch automatically through the set of records that the query returns.

The following code demonstrates a simple Cursor FOR LOOP:

```
BEGIN
  FOR rec_employees IN (SELECT EMPLOYEE_ID FROM EMPLOYEES)
  LOOP
    DBMS_OUTPUT.PUT_LINE('In the FOR loop: ' || rec_employees.EMPLOYEE_ID);
  END LOOP;
END;
/ \
```

Notice that the FOR LOOP counter variable is rec_employees, which in the Cursor FOR LOOP is a %ROWTYPE variable. The presence of the SELECT statement after the IN keyword is what makes this a Cursor FOR LOOP.

The Cursor FOR LOOP automatically does the following:

- Declares the %ROWTYPE variable rec_employees. (The %ROWTYPE is discussed in the next section.)

- Declares an anonymous cursor for the SELECT statement and opens the cursor upon the first pass through the loop.

- Performs a fetch from the anonymous cursor for each pass through the loop and repeats the loop until the condition of SQL%NOTFOUND exists with the anonymous cursor.

- Upon exiting the loop, a CLOSE statement is issued on the cursor.

Just as with the Numeric FOR LOOP, the Cursor FOR LOOP does not require an EXIT statement, but it is accepted.

The Cursor FOR LOOP automatically declares a lot of elements that could be declared individually. However, when you declare a cursor explicitly, you have much more control. Just as with the Numeric FOR LOOP, the Cursor FOR LOOP's loop counter variable, which is rec_employees in the previous example, is local to the loop, so it cannot be referenced by any code outside the loop.

Advanced Datatype Declaration

As you know, PL/SQL code is generally used to interact with the database, and the database already has tables and columns with declared datatypes. Furthermore, most PL/SQL variables are used to hold data obtained from the database through SELECT statements and related commands. As a result, most of the variables you will declare should have the same datatype as the columns in the tables of the database that you will be working with.

For example, if you are obtaining data from a table called CRUISES, and you are intending to SELECT data from that table, including the START_DATE, then you'll probably want to have a variable that is already declared with the same datatype as START_DATE to hold the data that you'll be fetching from the database.

The PL/SQL language features some special capabilities for declaring variables based on the datatypes of existing table columns from the database. The %TYPE declaration is used to declare a single variable based on a database object, and the %ROWTYPE can be used to declare multiple variables within a single declarative statement.

%TYPE

The %TYPE declaration lets you declare a variable at design time with a datatype that isn't decided until execution time, and the datatype is automatically extracted from the Oracle database data dictionary from the column of a table that you specify.

For example, if you want to declare a variable with the purpose of receiving data from the CRUISES table's CRUISE_NAME column, you want your variable to have the same datatype as that particular column as it is declared in the database. You could look it up and manually match them up, but the %TYPE declaration will do that for you. Better still, if the column's datatype is modified in the future, your %TYPE declared variable will ensure that future executions of your PL/SQL code will use the correct datatype. However, this does run the risk that a significant datatype change, such as a change from a VARCHAR2 to a NUMBER, may cause other problems in the processing section, but the risk is considered worth the benefit that the %TYPE declaration provides. In other words, %TYPE is considered good design.

The format for the %TYPE declaration is as follows:

```
variable_name TABLE.COLUMN%TYPE;
```

Following the example of a variable that will receive data from the CRUISES table's CRUISE_NAME column, the code would look like this:

```
v_cruise_name CRUISES.CRUISE_NAME%TYPE;
```

The declaration for the v_cruise_name variable will be resolved at execution time by the PL/SQL block, which will inspect the data dictionary and locate the datatype for the CRUISE table's CRUISE_NAME column, and that will be the datatype for the v_cruise_name variable.

There is no requirement that you, as the developer, must associate the %TYPE declaration with the table and column that you later will fetch data from for the declared variable. PL/SQL will not bother to follow up and ensure that you have in fact tied these two elements together, the table's column and the variable, in your processing section. Technically, any table and column can be used, regardless of what you intend to do with the variable, but naturally the table and column selection is probably going to be relevant to your use of the variable in the processing section.

%ROWTYPE

The %ROWTYPE declaration builds on the concept of the %TYPE declaration. A single declaration with %ROWTYPE can actually result in more than one variable.

The %ROWTYPE declaration ties the variable declaration to the declaration of a CURSOR in a PL/SQL block. The resulting declaration will produce, in a single statement, one variable for each of the columns selected in the CURSOR declaration. The %ROWTYPE declaration can therefore conceivably declare many variables in a single statement.

The resulting variables have a slightly unusual naming convention. Their names will be a combination of the %ROWTYPE variable name, followed by a period, followed by the name of the column as defined in the CURSOR that is referenced by the %ROWTYPE declaration.

Consider the following code sample:

```
DECLARE
  CURSOR cur_employees IS
    SELECT EMPLOYEE_ID,
           LAST_NAME || ', ' || FIRST_NAME FULL_NAME,
           POSITION
    FROM    EMPLOYEES
    ORDER BY LAST_NAME;
  rec_employees cur_employees%ROWTYPE;
BEGIN
  OPEN cur_employees;
  LOOP
    FETCH cur_employees INTO rec_employees;
    EXIT WHEN cur_employees%NOTFOUND;
    DBMS_OUTPUT.PUT_LINE(rec_employees.EMPLOYEE_ID);
    DBMS_OUTPUT.PUT_LINE(rec_employees.FULL_NAME);
```

```
    DBMS_OUTPUT.PUT_LINE(rec_employees.POSITION);
  END LOOP;
  CLOSE cur_employees;
END;
```

The variable rec_employees is declared as a %ROWTYPE variable and is based on the cursor cur_employees. This means that the resulting variables will be as follows:

■ **rec_employees.EMPLOYEE_ID**   The datatype is inherited from the EMPLOYEES table's EMPLOYEE_ID datatype.

■ **rec_employees.FULL_NAME**   This represents the column alias name of the concatenated result of the LAST_NAME and the FIRST_NAME columns, along with the string literal ' , '. The datatype of rec_employees.FULL_NAME is the datatype of the expression, which is determined by combining the datatypes of the elements within the expression. For example, if LAST_NAME is VARCHAR2(30) and FIRST_NAME is VARCHAR2(20), then FULL_NAME will be VARCHAR2(52), including the ' , ' string literal. Since these columns are combined using SQL functions in the original SELECT statement, then a column alias must be used for the rec_employees %ROWTYPE variable to be named.

■ **rec_employees.POSITION**   The datatype is inherited from the EMPLOYEES table's POSITION datatype.

Also, note how the %ROWTYPE variable works in a FETCH statement. Although the use of standard variables requires a FETCH statement that specifies each column in the explicit cursor, and each variable that is receiving the fetched data, the use of a %ROWTYPE variable greatly simplifies the FETCH statement:

```
FETCH cur_employees INTO rec_employees;
```

This format automatically fetches all of the columns defined in the cursor into all of the appropriate variables in the %ROWTYPE variable.

Once the FETCH statement has executed, the %ROWTYPE variables can be used. Here's an example:

```
    DBMS_OUTPUT.PUT_LINE(rec_employees.EMPLOYEE_ID);
```

In short, %ROWTYPE variables are the ideal choice for creating variables to be used with an explicit cursor.

Exception-Handling Section

PL/SQL programs are primarily designed to interact with the database. The database is a large and potentially complex environment and its condition at any given moment is beyond the control of the PL/SQL parser. In other words, while the PL/SQL parser can analyze the syntax of your PL/SQL program when you compile it, there is no guarantee that the database with which it interacts will even be up and running later when the PL/SQL program executes or that the database objects that are named within your PL/SQL program still exist, let alone reflect the structure that your program requires.

This poses a problem. Although you can compile your PL/SQL program today and produce an accurately written program unit, you have no assurance that the database elements that your code interacts with, such as the relationship of data in one table to another, are going to remain unchanged in the future when your PL/SQL program is executed.

In order to handle these unpredictable situations, PL/SQL provides a mechanism known as exceptions. Exceptions are not errors, but instead are show-stopping problems based on circumstances beyond the control of the PL/SQL parser that result in your code being unable to continue.

When an exception occurs in the course of your PL/SQL program unit's execution, the exception is said to be raised. After the exception is raised, execution within the particular PL/SQL block terminates. Any open cursors are automatically closed, and any loops are exited. Execution control leaves the processing section of the block.

Furthermore, when execution exits the block due to a raised exception, control will pass into the exception-handling section of the block, if such a section has been included with the block. The exception-handling section is an optional section in which you can declare *exception handlers*. An exception handler is a section of PL/SQL code that is included with the PL/SQL block, and that will only execute if and when the associated exception is raised within the processing section.

If your PL/SQL program is executed and an exception is raised, and if you've included an exception-handling section, and if that exception-handling section includes an exception handler that is appropriate for the particular raised exception, then the code you've provided for your exception will be executed, and the PL/SQL block will terminate with a message indicating that the PL/SQL program was successfully completed.

On the other hand, if the same situation arises, but you have not provided an exception handler appropriate for the exception, then the PL/SQL program will still terminate, but with an error message indicating that an unhandled exception was raised in your PL/SQL program.

Note that the exception-handling section is not required. Exceptions may be raised whether you have provided an exception-handling section or not.

There are two general categories of exceptions: system-defined exceptions and user-defined exceptions.

System-Defined Exceptions

System-defined exceptions are exceptions that you, as a developer, do not declare, but that are raised automatically by the system. There are several predefined exceptions:

- **CURSOR_ALREADY_OPEN** This is raised when your code attempts to issue an OPEN statement on a cursor that is already opened.

- **DUP_VAL_ON_INDEX** You've attempted to INSERT or UPDATE a database table that includes a UNIQUE constraint on at least one column, and the UNIQUE constraint has been violated in the INSERT or UPDATE issued from your code.

- **INVALID_CURSOR** This results from an attempt to fetch or close a cursor that hasn't been opened.

- **INVALID_NUMBER** An automatic datatype conversion was attempted on a literal that is being passed to some mechanism in PL/SQL (such as a parameter) that's expecting a numeric value, and Oracle attempted the conversion but failed.

- **LOGIN_DENIED** An attempt to log in to the database from your program was rejected by the database, probably due to an invalid user ID or password.

- **NO_DATA_FOUND** Generally, this exception indicates that you've attempted a SELECT . . . INTO command on a table that returned no rows, either as a result of the logic in the WHERE clause, or because the table truly has no rows. This exception can also result from an attempt to read past the end of file marker using the UTL_FILE package or from an attempt to refer to a row in a PL/SQL table that hasn't been initialized.

- **NOT_LOGGED_ON** Your program has attempted some sort of database access, such as a SELECT statement, at a time that it is not logged on to the database.

- **PROGRAM_ERROR** This exception generally is serious and is accompanied with a Contact Oracle Support message.

- **STORAGE_ERROR** Generally, this indicates a memory problem.

- **TIMEOUT_ON_RESOURCE** While attempting to access some resource in the database, a timeout was experienced.

- **TOO_MANY_ROWS** This results from a SELECT . . . INTO statement that returns more than one row, as determined by the WHERE clause.

- **TRANSACTION_BACKED_OUT** A remote transaction is rolled back for some reason beyond the control of your program.

- **VALUE_ERROR** This results from a variety of problems, generally related to attempts to convert values from one variable to another, such as truncation, constraint violations, or something related.

- **ZERO_DIVIDE** Your code attempted to divide by zero. This can result from equations that divide by some variable with a value you can't necessarily predict, such as a parameter or some value fetched from a database object, and that turns out to be zero in some particular execution of your code.

Some of the more commonly encountered system-defined exceptions are NO_DATA_FOUND and TOO_MANY_ROWS, both of which result from the use of the SELECT . . . INTO statement, which must always return a single row from the database in order to populate the single value variable (or variables) defined in the INTO clause. However, an easy way to avoid receiving the NO_DATA_FOUND or the TOO_MANY_ROWS system-defined exceptions is to simply use explicit cursors all of the time. Explicit cursors cannot experience either of these exceptions.

User-Defined Exceptions

User-defined exceptions are exceptions that you, the developer, declare in the declaration section and then explicitly raise with the RAISE statement somewhere in the processing section.

Consider the following code sample:

```
DECLARE
  CURSOR cur_work_schedule IS
    SELECT WORK_SCHEDULE_ID, START_DATE, END_DATE
    FROM   WORK_SCHEDULE;
  rec_work_schedule cur_work_schedule%ROWTYPE;
  ex_dates_incorrect EXCEPTION;
BEGIN
  OPEN cur_work_schedule;
  LOOP
    FETCH cur_work_schedule INTO rec_work_schedule;
    EXIT WHEN cur_work_schedule%NOTFOUND;
    IF rec_work_schedule.START_DATE >
       rec_work_schedule.END_DATE
    THEN
      RAISE ex_dates_incorrect;
```

```
      END IF;
    END LOOP;
    CLOSE cur_work_schedule;
EXCEPTION
  WHEN ex_dates_incorrect THEN
     INSERT INTO ERRORS
       (ERROR_ID, MESSAGE)
     VALUES
       (SEQ_ERROR_ID.NEXTVAL,
        rec_work_schedule.WORK_SCHEDULE_ID ||
        'START_DATE follows END_DATE');
END;
```

The user-defined exception ex_dates_incorrect is raised in the processing section explicitly with the RAISE command. In this example, the exception is only raised when the START_DATE value is determined to be greater than the END_DATE. When this condition is found to be true with a particular record, the processing section will immediately terminate, and control will pass to the exception-handling section, where the exception is handled with the WHEN ex_dates_incorrect exception handler. Information is then recorded in the ERRORS table, along with the primary key of the bad record, for future reference. The block will terminate with a PL/SQL procedure successfully completed message.

If there is no exception-handling section for the ex_dates_incorrect exception, then the generic WHEN OTHERS exception, if it exists, will execute, and the "successfully completed" message will display upon the completed execution of the PL/SQL code. Otherwise, the block will exit with an error message indicating that an unhandled exception was raised.

Working with Blocks

The statement that builds a PL/SQL block must include, as a minimum, a BEGIN and an END, as the following demonstrates:

```
BEGIN
    ... processing statements go here ...
END;
```

If the block includes a declaration section, then the DECLARE statement is required:

```
DECLARE
    ... declarations go here ...
BEGIN
    ... processing statements go here ...
END;
```

If the block includes an exception-handling section, then the EXCEPTION keyword is used:

```
BEGIN
    ... processing statements go here ...
EXCEPTION
    ... exception handling statements go here ...
END;
```

Finally, a block that includes all sections uses all four keywords:

```
DECLARE
    ... declarations go here ...
BEGIN
    ... processing statements go here ...
EXCEPTION
    ... exception handling statements go here ...
END;
```

Nested Blocks

Blocks can be nested within other blocks. Consider that the DECLARE . . . BEGIN . . . EXCEPTION . . . END statement is a single statement, and that the BEGIN . . . END that delineates the processing section can contain any other valid PL/SQL statement. It stands to reason therefore that one of those processing section statements can be another DECLARE . . . BEGIN . . . EXCEPTION . . . END statement. Furthermore, the nested block can contain another nested block and so on. Here's an example:

```
DECLARE
  v_highest_salary PAY_HISTORY.SALARY%TYPE;
BEGIN
  -- get the current highest salary
  SELECT MAX(SALARY)
  INTO   v_highest_salary
  FROM   PAY_HISTORY
  WHERE  END_DATE IS NULL;
  DECLARE
    c_highest_salary CONSTANT
                     PAY_HISTORY.SALARY%TYPE := v_highest_salary;
    CURSOR cur_pay_history IS
      SELECT PAY_HISTORY_ID, SALARY
      FROM   PAY_HISTORY
      WHERE  END_DATE IS NULL;
      rec_pay_history cur_pay_history%ROWTYPE;
  BEGIN
    OPEN cur_pay_history;
```

```
    LOOP
      FETCH cur_pay_history INTO rec_pay_history;
      EXIT WHEN cur_pay_history%NOTFOUND;
      IF (rec_pay_history.SALARY/c_highest_salary < .10)
      THEN
         -- Give a 6 percent pay raise to the lowest
         -- compensated employees
         UPDATE PAY_HISTORY
            SET SALARY = SALARY * 1.06
         WHERE  PAY_HISTORY_ID = rec_pay_history.PAY_HISTORY_ID;
      END IF;
    END LOOP;
    CLOSE cur_pay_history;
    COMMIT;
  END;
END;
/
```

The previous block is a block within a nested block. The outer block declares a variable and then uses that variable to fetch a value from the database. The nested block, also known as an inner block, uses the value that's been fetched from the database to declare a constant c_highest_salary, which is then used in the inner block.

Nested blocks can declare their own elements, including variables, constants, exceptions, and cursors. Nested blocks must subscribe to all of the rules required of any block. The DECLARE is optional, and the optional EXCEPTION reserved word can be used to handle any exceptions that are raised within the block.

However, once nested blocks are brought into an outer block, there are some issues of variable scope and exception scope that must be considered, which are discussed in the next few sections.

Scope: Declared Elements

A declared element, such as a variable, constant, user-defined exception, or cursor, is recognized within the block that declares it. The declared element is said to be "local" to its own block.

But when nested blocks are involved, the elements declared in one block may or may not be available for another block, depending on the scope of the variable.

For example, consider the following code sample:

```
DECLARE -- Outer block
  v_employee_id NUMBER(3) := 101;
  v_last_name   VARCHAR2(30) := 'Smith';
BEGIN
  DECLARE -- Inner block
```

```
   v_last_name VARCHAR2(30) := 'Jones';
   v_hire_date DATE;
 BEGIN
   DBMS_OUTPUT.PUT_LINE('Employee ID = ' || v_employee_id);
   DBMS_OUTPUT.PUT_LINE('Last Name (Inner) = ' || v_last_name);
 END; -- End of inner block
 DBMS_OUTPUT.PUT_LINE('Last Name (Outer)=' || v_last_name);
END; -- End of outer block
/
```

The output from this block will be as follows:

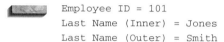

```
Employee ID = 101
Last Name (Inner) = Jones
Last Name (Outer) = Smith
```

Let's consider the different variables declared in this example.

The variable v_employee_id is declared only in the outer block. It's considered local to the outer block and global to the inner block. The variable can be referenced in either block. Any changes made to the variable in one block will be understood by the other one.

The variable v_last_name is declared in the outer block, and another is declared in the inner block. This results in two different variables. The v_last_name that is declared in the outer block behaves just like the v_employee_id variable, but there's a twist: The inner block, which would otherwise recognize the outer block's v_last_name variable, has its own variable of the same name, which overrides the attempt in this example to reference the variable of the same name in the outer block. The result: Any reference in the inner block to v_last_name is directed to the local block's variable of that name.

The variable v_hire_date is declared in the inner block. Therefore, it can be used in the inner block where v_hire_date is considered a local variable, but it cannot be referenced in this example in the outer block.

The general rule is that variables that are declared in a block are local to that block and global to any nested blocks. Local variables that have the same name as global variables take precedence in any variable references.

Block labels can be used to resolve conflicts between outer block and inner block elements. Here's an example:

```
<<outer_block>>
DECLARE
  v_lastname VARCHAR2(30) := 'Nader';
BEGIN
  <<inner_block>>
  DECLARE
```

```
      v_lastname VARCHAR2(30) := 'Keyes';
   BEGIN
      DBMS_OUTPUT.PUT_LINE(outer_block.v_lastname);
   END;
END;
```

In this example, each block is given a label. The DBMS_OUTPUT.PUT_LINE statement uses the label prefix to directly reference the outer block variable, bypassing the inner block variable, and resulting in the string "Nader" printing out on the screen.

Exception Scope and Exception Propagation

Remember that there are two kinds of exceptions: system-defined and user-defined. System-defined exceptions are raised automatically by the system. Their scope is not an issue. User-defined exceptions are exceptions that you define in the declaration section. When nested blocks are involved, the same rules of scope that apply to variables also apply to exceptions.

Consider the following code sample:

```
DECLARE
   ex_no_cabins EXCEPTION;
   v_cabins      BOOLEAN := FALSE;
   v_cruises     BOOLEAN := TRUE;
BEGIN
   DECLARE
      ex_no_cabins  EXCEPTION;
      ex_no_cruises EXCEPTION;
   BEGIN
      IF NOT (v_cabins)
      THEN
        RAISE ex_no_cabins;
      END IF;
      IF NOT (v_cruises)
      THEN
        RAISE ex_no_cruises;
      END IF;
   EXCEPTION
      WHEN ex_no_cruises THEN
        DBMS_OUTPUT.PUT_LINE('No cruises!');
   END;
EXCEPTION
   WHEN ex_no_cabins THEN
     DBMS_OUTPUT.PUT_LINE('No cabins!');
END;
/
```

Notice that there are three exceptions declared in this code sample:

- **ex_no_cabins, defined in the outer block** This exception is local to the outer block and global to the inner block.

- **ex_no_cabins, defined in the inner block** This exception is local to the inner block. It has the same name as the outer block's exception, but PL/SQL recognizes it as a different exception.

- **ex_no_cruises, defined in the inner block** This exception is local to the inner block and is unknown to the outer block, as are all inner-block-declared elements.

The previous code sample will produce the following output:

```
DECLARE
*
ORA-06510: PL/SQL: unhandled user-defined exception
ORA-06512: at line 12
```

The reason: The inner block will raise the exception ex_no_cabins. But this is the inner block's exception that is being raised.

At the moment that this exception is raised, control will automatically exit the inner block's processing section and be sent to the exception-handling section of the inner block. But there is no appropriate exception handler; there is neither a specific WHEN ex_no_cabins handler nor is there the generic WHEN OTHERS exception handler.

Note that had there been an appropriate exception handler in the inner block, then the inner block's exception handler would execute, and control would be passed to the next executable statement after the inner block within the outer block. However, there is no inner block exception handler. Therefore, control is passed to the outer block's exception handler, as PL/SQL looks for an exception-handling section.

In the outer block's exception-handling section, there is a WHEN ex_no_cabins handler, but this ex_no_cabins that is referenced is the outer block's ex_no_cabins, which is seen by PL/SQL as a different declared element from the inner block's ex_no_cabins exception. Therefore, PL/SQL does not recognize this exception handler as being relevant to the inner block's ex_no_cabins exception that was raised. As a result, the message that an unhandled exception was raised is the message displayed to the user.

Inner-block exception handlers can be used to handle exceptions that would otherwise terminate all processing. The inner block can handle the exception and move on if you set it up correctly.

Consider the following example:

```
DECLARE
  CURSOR cur_cruises IS
    SELECT    CRUISE_ID, CRUISE_NAME, START_DATE, END_DATE, STATUS
    FROM      CRUISES
    ORDER BY  START_DATE;
  rec_cruises cur_cruises%ROWTYPE;
BEGIN
  OPEN cur_cruises;
  LOOP
    FETCH cur_cruises INTO rec_cruises;
    EXIT WHEN cur_cruises%NOTFOUND;
    --
    IF  (TRUNC(rec_cruises.START_DATE) <= TRUNC(SYSDATE))
    AND (rec_cruises.STATUS            =  'Scheduled')
    THEN
       BEGIN -- the start of the nested block
         UPDATE CRUISES
           SET STATUS = 'Disembarked'
         WHERE CRUISE_ID = rec_cruises.CRUISE_ID;
       EXCEPTION
         WHEN OTHERS THEN
           INSERT INTO ERRORS
             (ERROR_ID, MESSAGE)
             VALUES
             (SEQ_ERROR_ID.NEXTVAL,
              'Procedure CRUISE_LIST:  UPDATE statement.');
       END; -- the end of the nested block
    END IF;
  END LOOP;
  CLOSE cur_cruises;
EXCEPTION
  WHEN OTHERS THEN
    INSERT INTO ERRORS
      (ERROR_ID, MESSAGE)
      VALUES
      (SEQ_ERROR_ID.NEXTVAL,
       'Procedure CRUISE_LIST experienced an error.');
    COMMIT;
END;
/
```

The previous code sample shows an outer block and an inner block. The inner block is nested inside a loop of the outer block. The inner block also is set up to handle any exception, using the WHEN OTHERS exception handler.

Notice the placement of this block: It is within a loop of the outer block. This loop is structured to fetch one row at a time from a declared cursor.

Normally, if an exception were to be raised at any time during these fetches, the outer block would terminate the loop and close the cursor, regardless of where it might be in the series of records it is returning from the database.

However, by placing a block around the code that might raise the exception, the exception could now be handled within the loop. Once the exception is handled in the inner block, the inner block completes and passes control to the next executable statement in the outer block, which is still within the loop, enabling the fetching of rows from the database to continue.

This design choice of using inner blocks is just one alternative available to you, as the developer. Whether you choose to use it or not is not an issue of good design or proper structure, but rather a business rule decision driven by whether or not an exception raised during the fetch could truly be a show-stopping problem or merely a flag that one record is bad, but not so bad that the processing of other records should be terminated. The choice is up to you.

An Introduction to Program Units

PL/SQL blocks are also known as program units. Program units can be unnamed—in other words, anonymous—or they can be named. This chapter, up to this point, has dealt with anonymous PL/SQL blocks. However, the rest of this book deals with named program units. This section discusses the difference between anonymous blocks and named program units.

Anonymous Blocks

Anonymous blocks are blocks that are not named. Any PL/SQL block without a name is considered an anonymous block. Anonymous blocks are often used in files that are submitted directly to the database. For example, the SQL*Plus command-line interface easily accepts anonymous PL/SQL blocks for execution. Also, anonymous blocks can be included within a larger PL/SQL block. The larger block may be anonymous or named.

Named Program Units

The alternative to anonymous blocks is named program units. Named program units include procedures, functions, packages, and database triggers. The 1Z0-101 Test 2 exam focuses on named program units.

The name given to a PL/SQL program unit must follow the standard rules that Oracle requires for naming any database object. Names must be 30 characters or less in length and can include any letter or number, as well as the underscore (_), pound sign (#), and dollar sign ($). Names cannot start with a number and must not include any spaces.

Named PL/SQL program units that are stored in the database are automatically logged and tracked by Oracle's Data Dictionary. The Data Dictionary will store everything from the actual source code to information about the named program unit (that is, metadata) that will be discussed later.

It's important to realize that although the PL/SQL language is case insensitive, the Oracle Data Dictionary stores everything about the PL/SQL program unit, such as the name, in uppercase letters. Note that the source code itself is not converted to uppercase letters; it is stored exactly as it is presented to the database. But the name of the program unit and other information about it are stored in uppercase letters. Therefore, although you could create a program unit with a name such as CreateShipment, as you might do in Java, it will end up being stored in the database as CREATESHIPMENT. As a result, the general practice is to use underscore characters to separate words, as in CREATE_SHIPMENT, so that the uppercase conversion will not produce a confusing name.

The categories of named program units include the following:

- Procedure
- Function
- Package
- Database trigger

Each of these is introduced in the following sections and is discussed in much more detail in the chapters that follow.

Procedure

A PL/SQL procedure is a named program unit that can be called on directly by its name. It can optionally receive values in the form of IN parameters and can even return values back to the calling source in the form of OUT parameters. Procedures can be stored on either the client or the server. They can be called by name from within other PL/SQL program units. Procedures that are stored in the database can be called from anywhere on the network where PL/SQL program units can execute.

Functions

A PL/SQL function is a named program unit that returns a single value. Functions can take parameters, but only for incoming values. The only value a function returns, and it must always return a single value, is sent back in the syntax of the function call itself. As a result, functions cannot be called in the same way that procedures are called and vice versa. Functions, for example, can be called from within a SQL statement, such as the column specification of a SELECT statement, whereas a procedure cannot.

The choice therefore of whether to create a PL/SQL program unit as a procedure or a function is not so much a choice based on what you, as the developer, want to accomplish within the program unit, but rather a decision based on how you want the program unit to be invoked, or called upon, and therefore how the data may or may not be returned to the calling source. This and all other issues of procedures and functions are addressed in detail in upcoming chapters.

Package

A PL/SQL package is a combination of procedures and/or functions. Packages may optionally include other declared elements, such as PL/SQL constants, or exceptions.

The reasons for combining procedures and functions are many and include the following:

- The logical association of a particular set of procedures and functions that support a particular application

- The performance benefits of loading multiple program units simultaneously rather than individually

- The security benefits uniquely associated with packages that enable the developer to selectively grant execute privileges on program units without necessarily publishing the actual source code

Database Trigger

A PL/SQL database trigger is a program unit that is not executed explicitly by the developer, but instead is associated with certain predetermined events that, if and when those events occur in the database, fire the program unit automatically. Database triggers are generally associated with DML functions on a given table. For example, you can create a database trigger that will always execute when anyone performs an UPDATE or DELETE on the CRUISES table.

The execution of the database trigger is unknown to the user, or process, that triggers its execution. Database triggers can invoke other PL/SQL program units, such as procedures and functions.

Chapter Summary

This chapter is an overview of the PL/SQL language. PL/SQL programs are structured in blocks. Each block can have a declaration section, a processing section, and an exception-handling section. The only required section is the processing section. The keywords DECLARE . . . BEGIN . . . EXCEPTION . . . END form a complete block.

In the declaration section, you can declare variables, constants, cursors, and exceptions. Variables and constants can be assigned the same datatypes used in SQL, plus BOOLEAN. Variables may be initialized when declared; constants must be initialized when declared. Variables and constants can make use of the dynamic datatype declaratives %TYPE and %ROWTYPE. %TYPE bases the definition of a variable on a named database table and column, while %ROWTYPE is associated with an explicit cursor and defines one variable for each column selected in that explicit cursor.

In the processing section, you can use assignment statements, conditional logic statements, and loops to work with the declared elements of your block. You can open a cursor, so that you can then fetch as many records as you wish from it, and close the cursor when you are done with it. Loops can be simple loops, which will only terminate if and when an EXIT statement inside the loop is invoked. Numeric FOR LOOPs will pass through a predetermined set of times, based on the way you declare the loop. The loop counter in the Numeric FOR LOOP is automatically declared in the opening Numeric FOR LOOP statement. Cursor FOR LOOPs use cursors to determine the number of passes through the loop and automatically declare a %ROWTYPE style variable to automatically receive data that is fetched from the database.

Exceptions may be raised in the processing section. Exceptions are show-stoppers; that is, they are conditions that prevent processing from continuing in any sort of logical fashion. When an exception is raised, the processing section of the block is terminated at the point of the exception, any loops are exited, cursors are closed, and all required cleanup is performed automatically.

The optional exception-handling section is where you can choose to handle exceptions, including system-defined exceptions that are raised automatically by the system, or it is where you can choose to handle user-defined exceptions, which you explicitly raise with the RAISE statement somewhere in the processing section. Exceptions may or may not be raised, regardless of whether or not there is a corresponding exception handler. If they are raised and not handled, then an unhandled exception message will be returned from the database when the PL/SQL block is executed. But if an exception is raised and handled, then a success message will be returned. Exception handlers name the exception they are handling, as in WHEN NO_DATA_FOUND, and a series of exception handlers can be included in an exception-handling section. But the generic WHEN OTHERS can handle any exception that isn't otherwise handled in an exception-handling section and should be included last, if it's included at all.

A block can be nested in another block. One of the principle advantages of nesting blocks is the capability to handle exceptions within an inner set of code, enabling the outer block's code to continue processing. Any declared elements, such as variables, that are declared in the outer block's declaration section are local to the outer block and global to the inner block. This means that they can be understood in both places, but may be overridden in the inner block since the inner block can declare its own variables, and those variables will be local to the inner block. Local variables take precedence over global variables, but block labels allow inner blocks to reference outer block elements in the event of a naming conflict. A PL/SQL block that starts with the reserved word DECLARE is an anonymous block. The rest of the book looks at named program units, such as procedures, functions, packages, and database triggers.

Two-Minute Drill

- Character literals are delineated in single quotes, such as 'Sandy', as are date literals, such as '15-JUN-2004'. Numeric literals have no quotes, such as 1126.

- Single-line comments are indicated with a pair of successive dashes: --. Multiline comments start with a slash-asterisk, as in /*, and continue until the first occurrence of the opposite, the asterisk-slash, as in */. The parser ignores comments.

- Variables may be declared for use in your processing section. Constants may also be declared with the reserved word CONSTANT. Both variables and constants must be given datatypes. The same datatypes used in SQL, such as NUMBER, NUMBER(n), NUMBER(n,m), VARCHAR2(n), and DATE, can be used, as can the new datatype BOOLEAN.

- To optionally initialize the value of a variable, use the assignment operator, :=. Constants must be initialized.

- Assignment statements in the processing section change the value of the specified variable on the left to be equal to whatever value will result from the evaluation of the expression on the right.

- SQL functions, such as LAST_DAY, SUBSTR, INSTR, ABS, and more can be used in PL/SQL blocks. However, DECODE cannot be used in PL/SQL expressions. Instead, use the PL/SQL conditional statement IF . . . THEN . . . END IF.

- The IF . . . THEN . . . END IF statement can include the optional ELSIF clause as many times as you wish and up to one single ELSE clause, which, if included, must be at the end.

- Expressions in IF statements must evaluate to either TRUE or FALSE. Expressions may use comparison operators such as equals (=), greater than (>), and others. Also, logical operators such as AND and OR can be used.

- The LOOP . . . END LOOP statement doesn't formally include an EXIT statement, but you should always include at least one EXIT statement, and be sure to define logic to invoke the EXIT statement at some eventual iteration of the loop.

- In the Numeric FOR . . . LOOP . . . END LOOP, the loop counter variable is first identified in the FOR loop and is automatically declared and incremented as the loop progresses. The lower limit and upper limit of the counter are specified in the FOR loop. The EXIT is not required either, since the FOR loop automatically exits when the upper limit is reached. An example would be FOR I IN 1..10 LOOP . . . END LOOP.

- An explicit cursor can be declared as any valid SELECT statement and can optionally include references to declared elements, such as variables, provided that the variable is declared in a statement that precedes the statement declaring the cursor. The value of the variable that will be used in the cursor is whatever the value is at the time the OPEN statement is issued on the cursor.

- In the Cursor FOR LOOP, the loop counter is actually a %ROWTYPE variable, and the lower and upper limits are replaced with a SELECT statement, which is an automatically declared anonymous explicit cursor. Furthermore, the loop automatically performs an OPEN, FETCH, and CLOSE. The loop will pass through once for each record automatically fetched from the database and will exit when no more records remain.

- A variable declared in a block is considered local to the block and global to any nested blocks. If the nested block makes any declarations, the declared elements are unknown to the outer block and will override references to any outer-block-declared elements of the same name, unless block labels are used.

- All cursors have four attributes that are system-defined variables describing the state of the cursor. The four attributes are %FOUND, %NOTFOUND, %ISOPEN, and %ROWCOUNT. An attribute for an explicit cursor is identified by appending the name of the explicit cursor at the beginning of the attribute, such as cur_employees%NOTFOUND, where cur_employees is the name of the cursor. Implicit cursors are anonymous, so the generic name SQL is used to refer to the most recently executed implicit cursor to get its attributes. An example would be SQL%ROWCOUNT.

- The exception-handling section is always at the end of the block and always starts with the reserved word EXCEPTION, followed by one or more exception handlers. Exception handlers start with the reserved word WHEN, followed by the name of the exception, the reserved word THEN, and then one or more lines of executable statements.

■ System-defined exceptions have predetermined names. The most commonly encountered system-defined exceptions are VALUE_ERROR and ZERO_DIVIDE, or in the case of implicit cursors, NO_DATA_FOUND and TOO_MANY_ROWS.

■ User-defined exceptions are declared in the declaration section and are then raised with the RAISE statement somewhere in the processing section. You define the names of these exceptions and should create exception handlers for your user-defined exceptions.

■ Exceptions that are raised, but not handled, will propagate out of the block and look for an outer block. If there is an outer block, then the outer block's exception handler will be investigated for an appropriate exception handler. If there isn't one, then the exception will propagate out again and continue until the exception either locates an exception handler or until there are no more outer blocks. The block's execution is terminated with an unhandled exception message when no exception handler is found.

Chapter Questions

I. **Which of the following keywords are required in any PL/SQL block? (Choose all that apply.)**

   A. DECLARE

   B. BEGIN

   C. EXCEPTION

   D. END

2. **What is wrong with the following code? (Choose all that apply.)**

```
DECLARE
  v_answer VARCHAR2(30);
BEGIN
  v_answer + v_result := v_one / v_two;
END;
```

   A. Three variables need to be declared.

   B. You cannot use two variables on the left side of an assignment statement.

   C. You cannot use the slash in an expression.

   D. Nothing is wrong with this code.

3. **Assuming the existence of an explicit cursor named ships and a declared %ROWTYPE variable named current_ship, which of the following FETCH statements are correct? (Choose all that apply.)**

   A. FETCH ships INTO current_ship%ROWTYPE;

   B. FETCH ships INTO current_ship.SHIP_ID;

   C. FETCH current_ship INTO ships;

   D. None of the above.

4. **What will happen when the following code is executed? (Choose all that apply.)**

```
DECLARE
  CURSOR cur_cruises IS
    SELECT CRUISE
    FROM  CRUISES;
  rec_cruises cur_cruises%ROWTYPE;
BEGIN
  OPEN cur_cruises;
  SELECT CRUISE
    INTO rec_cruises
    FROM CRUISES;
  CLOSE cur_cruises;
EXCEPTION
  WHEN OTHERS THEN
    INSERT INTO ERRORS
      (ERROR_ID, MESSAGE)
    VALUES
      (SEQ_ERROR_ID.NEXTVAL,'Something is wrong');
    COMMIT;
END;
```

   A. Nothing, the code will not parse correctly.

   B. The TOO_MANY_ROWS exception will be raised, which is not handled, and the PL/SQL code will terminate with an error message.

   C. It depends on how many rows are in the database.

   D. The message, 'Something is wrong', will definitely be inserted into the ERRORS table.

5. **Which of the following is not a cursor attribute? (Choose all that apply.)**

   A. %ISOPEN

   B. %ISNOTOPEN

   C. %FOUND

   D. %NOTFOUND

6. **What will happen when the following code is executed?**

```
BEGIN
  CREATE TABLE HOLIDAYS
    (HOLIDAY_ID NUMBER(3),
     HOLIDAY    VARCHAR2(30));
END;
```

   A. The HOLIDAYS table will be created.

   B. The TOO_MANY_ROWS exception will be raised, but since it's not handled, nothing will happen.

   C. A parsing error will occur.

   D. The table will be created, but won't be declared since it isn't created in the DECLARE section.

7. **Which of the following are valid names for program units? (Choose all that apply.)**

   A. PROCESS_ORDER

   B. SETUP-THE-DATABASE

   C. 100_SAMPLE_RECORDS

   D. GET_ORDER_#

8. **Consider the following code sample:**

```
DECLARE
  total_cabins  NUMBER(5) := 250;
  booked_cabins NUMBER(5);
  no_vacancies  EXCEPTION;
BEGIN
  booked_cabins := 250;
  DECLARE
    booked_cabins CONSTANT NUMBER(5) := 199;
  BEGIN
    IF (booked_cabins >= total_cabins)
    THEN
      RAISE no_vacancies;
    END IF;
  EXCEPTION
```

```
      WHEN no_vacancies THEN
        DBMS_OUTPUT.PUT_LINE('Inner block says: no vacancies');
    END;
    DBMS_OUTPUT.PUT_LINE('Complete');
EXCEPTION
    WHEN no_vacancies THEN
      DBMS_OUTPUT.PUT_LINE('Outer block says: no vacancies.');
END;
/
```

What will be the result when this code is executed?

A. Inner block says: no vacancies.

B. Outer block says: no vacancies.

C. Complete.

D. An unhandled exception message.

9. **You have created a PL/SQL block that declares variables using the %TYPE feature. When you created the block, the column upon which you based the %TYPE declaration had a datatype of NUMBER, but since you first created the block, it has been altered to have a datatype of VARCHAR2. Which of the following system-defined exceptions is most likely to occur in your block if you were you to execute the block now without modification?**

A. NO_DATA_FOUND

B. VALUE_ERROR

C. PROGRAM_ERROR

D. VALUE_CONFLICT

10. **How many passes through the loop will occur? (Choose all that apply.)**

```
DECLARE
  FOR rec_ships IN (SELECT SHIP_ID FROM SHIPS)
  LOOP
    IF (rec_ships.SHIP_ID = 1)
    THEN
      EXIT;
    END IF;
  END LOOP;
END;
/
```

A. Once for each record in the SHIPS table.

B. Only one. The EXIT will execute on the first record returned.

C. None, this code won't parse since you can't have an EXIT statement in a Cursor FOR LOOP.

D. None of the above.

Answers to Chapter Questions

1. B, D.   BEGIN and END

Explanation   Only BEGIN and END are required. DECLARE is only used in anonymous blocks that require elements to be declared. EXCEPTION is only used when exception handlers are specified.

2. A, B.   A: Three variables need to be declared. B: You cannot use two variables on the left side of an assignment statement.

Explanation   Any and all variables and constants that are used in a PL/SQL block must be declared. In this example, only the variable v_answer is declared. The others, v_result, v_one, and v_two, all need to be declared. The left side of the assignment statement is the target of the assignment, and therefore must be one single variable. The slash is the symbol for division and is completely acceptable.

3. D.   None of the above.

Explanation   The proper FETCH statement is `FETCH ships INTO current_ship;`

4. C.   It depends on how many rows are in the database.

Explanation   Note that the explicit cursor, which is opened and closed, is never fetched. Instead, an implicit cursor has been slipped in between the OPEN and CLOSE statements. If there are no rows in the CRUISES table, then the NO_DATA_FOUND exception will be automatically raised by the system. That exception is not handled, but the WHEN OTHERS exception handler will catch the exception, and the message, 'Something is wrong', will be stored in the ERRORS table. On the other hand, if there is one single row in the CRUISES table, then the SELECT . . . INTO will execute fine, placing the single row's column values into the rec_cruises variable, and no exception is raised. Finally, if the table has more than one row, then the TOO_MANY_ROWS exception will be raised, which is not handled, but once again the WHEN OTHERS exception handler will catch the exception, and the message, 'Something is wrong', will be stored in the ERRORS table.

5. B.   %ISNOTOPEN

Explanation   The four attributes are %ISOPEN, %FOUND, %NOTFOUND, and %ROWCOUNT. There is no such thing as %ISNOTOPEN.

6. C.   A parsing error will occur.

Explanation   The block is attempting to execute a DDL statement, and DDL statements aren't allowed in PL/SQL. Note, however, that there is a special package in PL/SQL that will support the execution of DDL statements by building them as text strings and sending them off to the database in another manner. But that is not what is being performed here.

7. A, D.   PROCESS_ORDER and GET_ORDER_#

Explanation   B is not allowed because of the use of hyphens. C is not allowed because names of program units cannot begin with numbers.

8. C.   Complete.

Explanation   A would have been correct had the IF statement evaluated to TRUE. Even though the user-defined exception is defined in the outer block, it is global to the inner block, and the inner block's exception handler will recognize the RAISE statement. If the RAISE statement would be executed, then the inner block's exception handler would have handled the exception, and the outer block's exception handler would never have been relevant, so B is not true. And since the user-defined exceptions are handled in both blocks, then D is not true. But C is true because the IF statement considers booked_cabins as the locally declared constant with a value of 199 and total_cabins as the globally declared variable with a value of 250. The comparison in the IF statement evaluates to FALSE, and the inner block completes, followed by the statement that prints the word Complete.

9. B.   VALUE_ERROR

Explanation   A occurs when you write an implicit cursor that attempts to SELECT . . . INTO a variable, but the SELECT returns no rows. C generally indicates some sort of major system bug. D is not a system-defined exception; I just made that up, but get used to that. Oracle loves to make up bogus names like this on the real OCP. The answer is B because VALUE_ERROR occurs when datatype conflicts exist, and if you've written code that was expecting a NUMBER datatype that is now a VARCHAR2 datatype, then datatype conflicts within your code are possible.

10. D.   None of the above.

Explanation   You really can't tell how many passes through the loop will occur. A is wrong. The IF statement will EXIT upon the first occurrence of a rec_ships.SHIP_ID of 1, but you cannot be sure of B since you really have no way of knowing when that will occur. And C is just completely wrong. Although there are some people in the business who say that the use of an EXIT in a Cursor FOR LOOP is ill-advised, it's accepted by the parser. D is the answer, since the number of rows returned will be all of the rows defined in the SELECT statement until the first occurrence of rec_ships.SHIP_ID is equal to 1, which could be any time, if ever; perhaps that value never occurs. D is the answer.

CHAPTER
2

Procedures

his chapter discusses the Procedural Language/Structured Query Language (PL/SQL) program unit known as a procedure. The PL/SQL procedure is the next level up from an anonymous block. Any serious professional application involving PL/SQL will make use of procedures to consolidate common code, to speed development and support cost-effective maintenance and enhancements, and to leverage the power of the database in a networked multiuser application supporting concurrent user sessions. This is done so that applications with distributed components, such as forms and database objects, can reference centralized PL/SQL code and share PL/SQL code blocks. Anonymous blocks cannot be used in this capacity; only named program units can do this, and procedures are the starting point of PL/SQL named program units.

In this chapter, you will review and understand the following topics:

- Uses of procedures
- Creating, altering, and dropping procedures
- Invoking procedures
- Parameters
- Data dictionary resources for procedures

Uses of Procedures

PL/SQL procedures are one of the PL/SQL program units. Procedures are used to store a PL/SQL block under an assigned name, so that the block can be called repeatedly, as needed, from any location on the network that has access to the Oracle database.

In addition, an anonymous PL/SQL block is parsed each time it is submitted for execution. But if that same anonymous block is assigned a name and created as a procedure, then Oracle will parse the procedure once, at the time it is created. Each subsequent call to that procedure will not require reparsing; it will simply execute, saving time over an anonymous block.

A PL/SQL procedure can be invoked from a single executable statement in another PL/SQL statement. These other PL/SQL statements could be in an anonymous PL/SQL block or in a named program unit, such as another procedure. A PL/SQL procedure can also be invoked from a single command-line executable statement in a SQL*Plus session.

A procedure may use parameters, at the option of the developer, to provide run-time information that can customize its behavior each time it's invoked as well as to pass information back out of the procedure to the calling source.

What Can You Do with Procedures?

The general textbook explanation for PL/SQL procedures is that they "do something," as opposed to functions, which "return a value." (Functions are discussed in the next chapter.) This description is true, but as is always the case in Oracle programming, there is more to the difference between procedures and functions than this simple explanation.

Procedures are excellent for defining a PL/SQL code block that you know you will need to call more than once, and whose work may produce results largely seen in the database or perhaps some module, like an Oracle Form, or a client-side form, as opposed to work whose result is some single answer; that would probably be more appropriate for a function.

For example, consider the following code sample:

```
PROCEDURE PROC_UPDATE_CRUISE_STATUS IS
  v_today DATE;
BEGIN
  SELECT TRUNC(SYSDATE)
  INTO   v_today
  FROM   DUAL;
  --
  UPDATE CRUISES
     SET STATUS = 'Disembarked'
   WHERE  TRUNC(START_DATE) < v_today
     AND  TRUNC(END_DATE)   > v_today
     AND  STATUS <> 'Cancelled';
  --
  UPDATE CRUISES
     SET STATUS = 'Completed'
   WHERE  TRUNC(END_DATE)   < v_today
     AND  STATUS <> 'Cancelled';
  --
  COMMIT;
EXCEPTION
  WHEN OTHERS THEN
    ROLLBACK;
    INSERT INTO ERRORS
     (ERROR_ID,
      MESSAGE)
      VALUES
     (SEQ_ERROR_ID.NEXTVAL,
      'PROC_UPDATE_CRUISE_STATUS:  Error updating CRUISE status');
  COMMIT;
END;
```

The procedure PROC_UPDATE_CRUISE_STATUS will review the existing table CRUISES and update the status of each cruise based on the current system date. The result of this procedure is that the CRUISES table will now reflect updated STATUS values for each record.

This is a PL/SQL code block that should probably execute on a regular basis, perhaps daily. In order to make it easily accessible for daily executions, it should be stored in the database as a procedure, where it can be called upon as needed to perform its work. This is a superior alternative to keeping the PL/SQL block in an operating system text file. Once in the database, any user, from anywhere on the network, can invoke the procedure as needed. Furthermore, the database functionality that supports security and controls privileges is available for the procedure. You may choose to selectively grant the privilege to execute this procedure to various schemas. And, whereas a simple anonymous PL/SQL block in a text file can only be executed by schemas with the appropriate privileges to the corresponding tables that are used in the block, you don't have this limitation with procedures. Once a user is granted execute privileges on a procedure, that user can execute the procedure, even if the procedure performs actions on tables that the user is not specifically granted access to. The result: You can use procedures to grant finer levels of access to tables and views in the database by merely granting execute privileges on the procedure, and not granting direct access to the tables, yet the user who executes the procedure will be able to execute the procedure successfully.

Procedures can also use parameters. Parameters are variables whose values are defined at execution by the process that calls upon the procedure. In other words, it's a way of "passing in" data from an outside source and thereby modifying the procedure's behavior each time the procedure is executed.

Where Can You Store Procedures?

Procedures can be stored in the database, alongside tables and other database objects. Once a procedure is stored in the database, it can be invoked from any process with database access. If a process, such as a SQL*Plus window, Java program, Oracle Form, or another PL/SQL procedure, has access to the database, it can execute the procedure, provided that the proper privileges have been granted on the procedure (more on this later) to the schema under which the process is running.

Procedures can also be stored within client-side processes, such as applications built with Oracle Form Builder or Oracle Report Builder. Procedures that are stored in such client-side processes can be used from within those tools as required; however, the procedure is only available to that application. In other words, if a procedure is stored in a Form, then some user elsewhere on the network who might be logged in to SQL*Plus cannot invoke that Form's procedure.

Procedures can be collected with other program units and stored together in a *package*. Also, procedures can be combined with packages and/or other program units in *libraries*.

For Review

1. Procedures can be stored in the database or on the client. They can be called from the SQL*Plus command line or from a single executable statement within another PL/SQL block, such as an anonymous block or a named program unit.

2. Parameters are a mechanism you can use to pass values to a procedure at execution time. They are treated as something like variables in the procedure code.

Exercises

1. **Which of the following is an advantage of a procedure? (Choose all that apply.)**

    A. The procedure is parsed once at the time it is created and does not need to be reparsed with each new execution, as is required with anonymous blocks.

    B. Procedures can be automatically granted to tables, even when the tables have been already granted.

    C. A user can be granted execute privileges on a procedure that uses tables that the user may not necessarily have access to, yet the user will be able to successfully execute the procedure, providing the developer with more selected and detailed control over table security.

    D. Procedures can take values at run time, and their behavior can be customized through these values.

2. **Where can you store a procedure? (Choose all that apply.)**

    A. Oracle Forms

    B. Oracle Reports

    C. In an Oracle database schema

    D. As part of an Oracle package

Answer Key
1. A, C, D. 2. A, B, C, D.

Creating, Altering, and Dropping Procedures

There are two main ways to create a procedure:

- Using the CREATE PROCEDURE command in a PL/SQL command script that executes in the SQL*Plus command-line interface

- Using GUI tools, such as Oracle's Procedure Builder

This section will explore the first method: working within the SQL*Plus command-line interface. Chapter 8 will explore the use of Oracle's Procedure Builder.

Creating Procedures

The following is a code sample that will create a stored procedure named PROC_RESET_ERROR_LOG:

```
CREATE PROCEDURE PROC_RESET_ERROR_LOG IS
BEGIN
  -- Clean out the ERRORS table
  DELETE FROM ERRORS;
  COMMIT;
END;
/
```

If this script is submitted to the SQL*Plus command-line interface, the result will be that a procedure called PROC_RESET_ERROR_LOG will be created and stored in the database, as shown in Figure 2-1.

The syntax for this command is as follows:

- The reserved words CREATE PROCEDURE.

- A name you make up, following the rules of object names described in Chapter 1 (up to 30 characters, no spaces).

- The reserved word IS or the reserved word AS— either is accepted.

- A valid PL/SQL block. The keywords BEGIN and END are required; EXCEPTION is optional. The keyword DECLARE, however, is never used. Instead of using DECLARE to begin the optional declarative section of the block, make any required declarations after the reserved word IS and before the reserved word BEGIN.

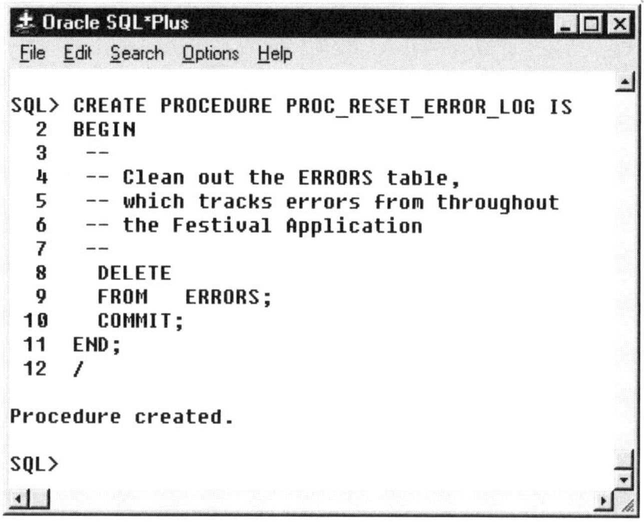

FIGURE 2-1. *SQL*Plus session: creating procedure PROC_RESET_ERROR_LOG*

Notice the slash (/) at the end of the file. In the SQL*Plus interface, a single slash at the end of the PL/SQL block on a line by itself as the first character is required to submit the PL/SQL block to the SQL*Plus interface for processing.

When you submit a CREATE PROCEDURE command to SQL*Plus, the following happens:

- The code is stored in the data dictionary.

- The code is parsed for syntax and determined to be either VALID or INVALID.

- If the code is VALID, you are provided with a "Procedure created" message, and the procedure is now given a status of VALID and is available for execution.

- If the code is INVALID, you are provided with some sort of error message, and the code, which is now stored in the data dictionary, is given a status of INVALID and is not available for execution.

Please note that whether the procedure is successfully parsed or not, it will be stored in the data dictionary.

```
Oracle SQL*Plus                                            _ □ X
File  Edit  Search  Options  Help
SQL> CREATE PROCEDURE PROC_RESET_ERROR_LOG IS
  2  BEGIN
  3  --
  4  -- Clean out the ERRORS table,
  5  -- which tracks errors from throughout
  6  -- the Festival Application
  7  --
  8    DELETE
  9    FROM   ERRORS;
 10    COMMIT;
 11  END;
 12  /
CREATE PROCEDURE PROC_RESET_ERROR_LOG IS
                      *
ERROR at line 1:
ORA-00955: name is already used by an existing object


SQL> |
```

FIGURE 2-2. *SQL*Plus session: attempting to create a procedure that already exists*

Also note that this process of storing the procedure does not actually execute the procedure itself. That is a separate command. The command we are considering is CREATE PROCEDURE. Your goal here is to create the procedure; executing it is a separate step.

Once the procedure is stored in the database, you cannot create another procedure of the same name. If you reexecute the same CREATE PROCEDURE block, you will get the results shown in Figure 2-2.

The attempt to reexecute the same code, once the procedure has been stored in the data dictionary, results in an error.

However, an option in the CREATE PROCEDURE command enables you to automatically overwrite any preexisting procedure of the same name. The OR REPLACE option enables you, as the developer, to create a procedure and, if it already exists, overwrite the code already stored in the data dictionary with the new code you are creating now. An example of the code is shown here:

```
CREATE OR REPLACE PROCEDURE PROC_RESET_ERROR_LOG IS
BEGIN
  -- Clean out the ERRORS table
```

```
  DELETE FROM ERRORS;
  COMMIT;
END;
/
```

This code will successfully store the procedure, as shown in Figure 2-3.

The OR REPLACE option in the CREATE PROCEDURE command guarantees that the procedure is created and stored, whether an existing procedure of the same name is already stored in the database or not.

Procedures can optionally include something called an END label, which is the name of the procedure repeated after the END statement. The following code listing displays an example of an END label:

```
CREATE OR REPLACE PROCEDURE PROC_RESET_ERROR_LOG IS
BEGIN
  -- Clean out the ERRORS table
  DELETE FROM ERRORS;
  COMMIT;
END PROC_RESET_ERROR_LOG;
/
```

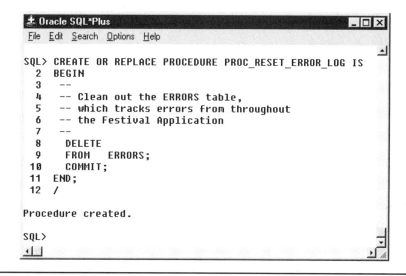

FIGURE 2-3. *SQL*Plus session: an example of CREATE OR REPLACE*

The advantage to an END label becomes more apparent once you begin combining many procedures into a package, when several procedures may be included, one after the other, in a lengthier code listing. In such a situation, it may be difficult to be sure where one procedure ends and another begins. The use of the END label can help prevent confusion.

Altering Procedures

Once a procedure has been created, you can use two methods to "alter" the procedure. If you are replacing the original source code with a new set of source code, use the OR REPLACE option discussed in the previous section. This is true for any code modification at all. If, however, you are recompiling the procedure without changing the code, then use the ALTER PROCEDURE command.

The ALTER PROCEDURE command is required when your stored procedure has not been changed in and of itself, but another database object referenced from within your procedure, such as a table, has been changed. This automatically causes your procedure to be flagged as INVALID.

For example, let's consider the example of the PROC_RESET_ERROR_LOG procedure we created in Figure 2-3. After the code in Figure 2-3 is executed, the status of the PROC_RESET_ERROR_LOG is VALID, as shown in Figure 2-4.

The PROC_RESET_ERROR_LOG procedure references a table called ERRORS. Let's change the ERRORS table, as follows:

```
ALTER TABLE ERRORS ADD ERROR_SOURCE VARCHAR2(30);
```

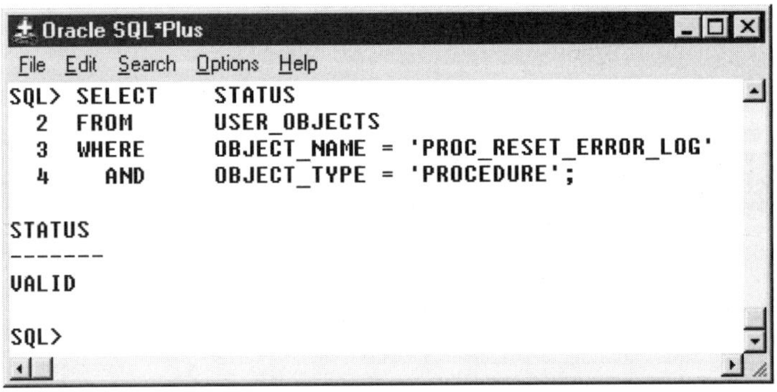

FIGURE 2-4. *Querying the STATUS of PROC_RESET_ERROR_LOG*

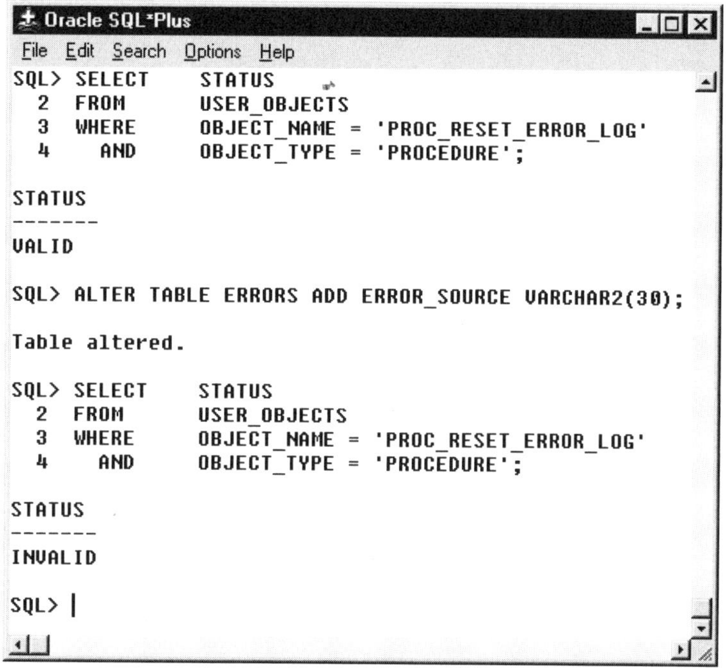

```
± Oracle SQL*Plus                                        _ □ ×
File  Edit  Search  Options  Help
SQL> SELECT      STATUS
  2  FROM        USER_OBJECTS
  3  WHERE       OBJECT_NAME = 'PROC_RESET_ERROR_LOG'
  4       AND    OBJECT_TYPE = 'PROCEDURE';

STATUS
-------
VALID

SQL> ALTER TABLE ERRORS ADD ERROR_SOURCE VARCHAR2(30);

Table altered.

SQL> SELECT      STATUS
  2  FROM        USER_OBJECTS
  3  WHERE       OBJECT_NAME = 'PROC_RESET_ERROR_LOG'
  4       AND    OBJECT_TYPE = 'PROCEDURE';

STATUS
-------
INVALID

SQL> |
```

FIGURE 2-5.   *Changing a table of PROC_RESET_ERROR_LOG changes its STATUS.*

The table is successfully changed. However, now that this table has been changed, Oracle automatically has flagged the procedure PROC_RESET_ERROR_LOG as INVALID (see Figure 2-5).

This change of STATUS is meant to force the developer to review the procedure and ensure that the table change doesn't materially change the syntax or logic of the procedure. In order to restore the STATUS of the procedure to VALID, the following command can be issued:

```
ALTER PROCEDURE PROC_RESET_ERROR_LOG COMPILE;
```

Assuming that the earlier change to the ERRORS table doesn't materially change the procedure, it should successfully recompile, and the STATUS of the procedure object should be restored to VALID.

Dropping Procedures

An example of a command that drops a procedure is shown in the following code listing:

```
DROP PROCEDURE PROC_RESET_ERROR_LOG;
```

Once this command is successfully executed, the database response "Procedure dropped" will be displayed.

For Review

1. The command CREATE OR REPLACE PROCEDURE is used to store a procedure in the database. After it has been stored, you can choose to issue an additional command to actually execute the procedure.

2. The source code of the procedure can be found in the USER_SOURCE view in the data dictionary, whether the procedure is VALID or not.

3. If the procedure is successfully stored and declared VALID, but something occurs in the database later, such as an ALTER on a table that the procedure uses, then the procedure will be flagged as INVALID and require recompilation. One way to restore the procedure to validity is to issue the ALTER PROCEDURE . . . COMPILE command, which will resubmit for parsing the same code that the database already stores. If everything reparses successfully, the procedure will be restored to a status of VALID, as indicated in the USER_OBJECTS data dictionary view.

Exercises

1. You have already stored a procedure in the database called RECONCILE_BOOKINGS, and it takes no parameters. You have made some changes to the source code, and you issue a command with the following opening line:

```
CREATE PROCEDURE RECONCILE_BOOKINGS IS ... END;
```

Assuming the body of the statement is correct, what will be the result of this command?

A. The procedure will be successfully stored and will be VALID.

B. The attempt will fail.

C. The procedure will be stored in the database, but will be INVALID.

D. The procedure will be stored and executed.

2. Which of the following statements will remove the
   RECONCILE_BOOKINGS procedure from the database?

   A. DELETE PROCEDURE RECONCILE_BOOKINGS;

   B. DROP RECONCILE_BOOKINGS;

   C. DROP PROCEDURE RECONCILE_BOOKINGS CASCADE;

   D. DROP PROCEDURE RECONCILE_BOOKINGS;

Answer Key
1. B. **2.** D.

Invoking Procedures

Once a procedure has been created and stored in the database, it can be invoked
from

- An executable statement of a PL/SQL block
- A command entered in the SQL*Plus command-line interface

Both are described in the following paragraphs.

Executing a Procedure from a PL/SQL Block

To invoke a procedure from another PL/SQL block, use a single statement that
names the procedure. For example, suppose you've created a procedure called
PROC_UPDATE_CRUISE_STATUS. The following PL/SQL block will execute the
procedure:

```
BEGIN
  PROC_UPDATE_CRUISE_STATUS;
END;
```

The previous anonymous block will execute the procedure
PROC_UPDATE_CRUISE_STATUS. Of course, multiple procedure calls can be
issued and can be mixed with other standard PL/SQL code, as follows:

```
DECLARE
  v_day_of_week VARCHAR2(3);
BEGIN
```

```
    PROC_RESET_ERROR_LOG;
    PROC_CHECK_CRUISE_LEGS;
    -- Determine if it's a weekday or not
    SELECT TO_CHAR(SYSDATE,'DY') DAY_OF_WEEK
    INTO   v_day_of_week
    FROM   DUAL;
    IF (v_day_of_week NOT IN ('SAT','SUN'))
    THEN
      PROC_UPDATE_CRUISE_STATUS;
    END IF;
END;
/
```

This anonymous PL/SQL block invokes three procedures, one of which is conditional upon the day of the week.

When a PL/SQL block calls a procedure, the calling block temporarily suspends execution at the point of the procedure call and waits while the called procedure executes. Once the called procedure completes execution, control passes back to the calling PL/SQL block, which then picks up with the next executable statement after the procedure call and continues execution. If another procedure is called, the calling block once again temporarily suspends execution until the called procedure is completed and then resumes execution.

The anonymous block shown in the previous code listing could be stored as a program unit itself. In other words, stored procedures can call other stored procedures.

Executing a Procedure from the SQL*Plus Command Line

You can execute a PL/SQL procedure from within the SQL*Plus command line without having to write another PL/SQL block to do it. The SQL command EXECUTE, or EXEC for short, must be used.

For example, if you have already stored a procedure called PROC_RUN_BATCH with no parameters, then the following statement, entered in the SQL*Plus window at the SQL prompt, will invoke the procedure:

```
EXECUTE PROC_RUN_BATCH;
```

The often-used shorter version is

```
EXEC PROC_RUN_BATCH;
```

If your procedure uses parameters, this will influence the manner in which you call the procedure. The subject of parameters is discussed in the next section.

For Review

1. To invoke a procedure from another PL/SQL program, use a statement that names the procedure on a line by itself. A procedure call is not part of an expression, but is a single statement unto itself.

2. To invoke a procedure from the SQL*Plus command-line interface, absent a PL/SQL block, use the SQL*Plus command EXECUTE, followed by the name of the procedure. The command EXEC is the short version of EXECUTE.

Exercises

1. **Assuming the referenced procedures exist, which of the following is a valid procedure call? (Choose all that apply.)**

   A. EXECUTE MODIFY_PRICES;

   B. ASSESS_DATES;

   C. GET_BOOK;

   D. EXEC SETUP_CRUISE;

2. **When one procedure calls another procedure, which of the following is true? (Choose all that apply.)**

   A. The calling block continues executing with the statements that follow the procedure call, while the called procedure starts up simultaneously.

   B. The called procedure executes and, upon completion, the calling block resumes where the called procedure was invoked and only then continues execution.

   C. The called procedure executes to completion, and this terminates all execution; the calling block cannot resume.

   D. The called procedure cannot be called from another procedure.

Answer Key
1. A, B, C, D. **2.** B.

Parameters

A parameter is a variable whose value can be defined at execution time and can be exchanged between the procedure and the calling PL/SQL block. Parameter values can be passed in to the procedure from the calling PL/SQL block and can optionally have their values passed back out of the procedure to the calling PL/SQL block upon the completion of the procedure's execution.

Parameter Declaration Syntax

Parameters are declared at the top of the procedure within a set of parentheses. Each parameter declaration includes the following:

- A name, defined by the developer, and adhering to the rules of object names (discussed earlier).

- The type of parameter, which will either be IN, OUT, or IN OUT. The default is IN.

- The datatype. Note that no specification or precision is allowed in parameter datatype declarations. To declare something as an alphanumeric string, you can use VARCHAR2, but you cannot use, for example, VARCHAR2(30).

- Optionally, a parameter may be provided with a default value. This can be done by using the reserved word DEFAULT, followed by a value or expression that is consistent with the declared datatype for the parameter. The DEFAULT value identifies the value the parameter will have if the calling PL/SQL block doesn't assign a value.

After each parameter declaration, you may place a comma and follow it with another parameter declaration.

The following is an example of a procedure header that uses parameters:

```
PROCEDURE PROC_SCHEDULE_CRUISE
    ( p_start_date   IN DATE      DEFAULT SYSDATE
    , p_total_days   IN NUMBER
    , p_ship_id      IN NUMBER
    , p_cruise_name  IN VARCHAR2 DEFAULT 'Island Getaway')
IS
 ... code follows ...
```

This procedure declares four parameters. Each parameter is an IN parameter. Each parameter is assigned a datatype. The parameter p_cruise_name is given a datatype of VARCHAR2; the length cannot be specified in a parameter datatype declaration.

Two of the parameters are assigned default values. The first, p_start_date, uses the Oracle pseudocolumn SYSDATE, and the second, p_cruise_name, is assigned the string, 'Island Getaway'.

Parameter Datatypes

Parameters must be given a datatype. Datatype options include any datatype that a PL/SQL-declared variable or constant will accept.

Parameter datatypes cannot include length, precision, or scale. For example, the use of the NUMBER datatype is allowed, but NUMBER(2) is not.

Parameter datatypes can also employ the %TYPE attribute. For example, the following is a possible alternative parameter datatype declaration for our example:

```
PROCEDURE PROC_SCHEDULE_CRUISE
    ( p_start_date  IN DATE      DEFAULT SYSDATE
    , p_total_days  IN NUMBER
    , p_ship_id     IN SHIPS.SHIP_ID%TYPE
    , p_cruise_name IN VARCHAR2 DEFAULT 'Island Getaway')
IS
```

The p_ship_id parameter can be declared with the datatype SHIPS.SHIP_ID%TYPE, which is resolved at run time.

Default Values

Default values are not required for parameters; they are optional. If a default value is included as part of the parameter declaration, then it is the last part of the parameter declaration. Default values can only be assigned to IN parameters.

After the parameter's declared datatype, one of two reserved expressions is allowed, followed by the actual default value. The two reserved expressions that are allowed are

■ The reserved word DEFAULT

■ The assignment operator, :=

For example, see the following code listing, which uses both forms:

```
PROCEDURE PROC_SCHEDULE_CRUISE
    ( p_start_date  IN DATE      := SYSDATE
    , p_total_days  IN NUMBER
    , p_ship_id     IN SHIPS.SHIP_ID%TYPE
    , p_cruise_name IN VARCHAR2 DEFAULT 'Island Getaway')
IS
```

This procedure header declares the p_start_date parameter as having a default value of SYSDATE, using the assignment operator, which is the same assignment operator that can be used when declaring PL/SQL constants or initial values for variables. The p_cruise_name parameter in the example uses the reserved word DEFAULT to accomplish the same thing.

When default values are provided for a parameter, the calling block doesn't have to provide a value for that parameter. There are two ways to avoid providing a value for a parameter that has a default value. If, for example, the fourth parameter in a list of four parameters is assigned a default value, then the calling block can provide values for the first three parameters only. The fourth parameter's default value will be used.

For example, to call the procedure PROC_SCHEDULE_CRUISE described earlier and to take advantage of the default value assigned to the p_cruise_name parameter, the following call can be used:

```
PROC_SCHEDULE_CRUISE('03-JAN-2003',3,1);
```

This will ensure that the fourth parameter's default value of Island Getaway will be used.

If a procedure's parameters are all provided with default values, then none of them need to be accounted for in the calling block. For example, if PROC_SCHEDULE_CRUISE has default values assigned for all of its parameters, then this call would be sufficient:

```
PROC_SCHEDULE_CRUISE;
```

The parameters will all operate with their default values.

Some procedures have parameter lists in which an early parameter has a default value, but you may wish to assign specific values to later parameters. The PROC_SCHEDULE_CRUISE procedure, for example, has a default value for its first parameter. The only way to use that first parameter's default value while still defining values for the others is to use the parameter-passing approach known as *named notation*. This is discussed later in this section.

Parameter Types

Parameters in procedures are described as being one of the three types:

- **IN parameters**   These are parameters whose values must be supplied by the calling block. Inside the procedure, IN parameters are read-only.

- **OUT parameters**   These are parameters whose values are defined within the procedure as it executes, and whose values are passed back out to the calling block. Inside the procedure, OUT parameter values are changeable.

- **IN OUT parameters** These are parameters that combine the features of IN parameters and OUT parameters into a single parameter. Inside the procedure, IN OUT parameters can be read and changed.

IN Parameters
The most commonly used parameter is the IN parameter. The value for an IN parameter is defined in the calling PL/SQL block and is included in the call to the procedure. Once the parameter value is passed in and the procedure begins execution, the value of the parameter cannot be changed. In other words, IN parameters are read-only.

Here is a sample procedure that employs four IN parameters:

```
PROCEDURE PROC_SCHEDULE_CRUISE
   ( p_start_date  IN DATE      DEFAULT SYSDATE
   , p_total_days  IN NUMBER
   , p_ship_id     IN NUMBER
   , p_cruise_name IN VARCHAR2 DEFAULT 'Island Getaway')
IS
   -- A procedure to schedule a cruise
   v_cruise_type_id CRUISE_TYPES.CRUISE_TYPE_ID%TYPE;
BEGIN
   -- Determine the type of cruise involved
   SELECT CRUISE_TYPE_ID
   INTO   v_cruise_type_id
   FROM   CRUISE_TYPES
   WHERE  LENGTH_DAYS = p_total_days;
   -- Schedule cruise
   INSERT INTO CRUISES
      ( CRUISE_ID
      , SHIP_ID
      , CRUISE_TYPE_ID
      , CRUISE_NAME
      , START_DATE
      , END_DATE)
   VALUES
      ( SEQ_CRUISE_ID.NEXTVAL
      , P_SHIP_ID
      , v_cruise_type_id
      , p_cruise_name
      , p_start_date
      , (p_start_date + p_total_days));
   COMMIT;
EXCEPTION
   WHEN OTHERS THEN
```

```
   ROLLBACK;
   PROC_RECORD_ERROR('PROC_SCHEDULE_CRUISE');
END;
```

The syntax for the four parameters that are declared at the top of the procedure is part of the procedure header:

```
PROCEDURE PROC_SCHEDULE_CRUISE
   ( p_start_date  IN DATE       DEFAULT SYSDATE
   , p_total_days  IN NUMBER
   , p_ship_id     IN NUMBER
   , p_cruise_name IN VARCHAR2 DEFAULT 'Island Getaway')
IS
```

Since the default parameter type is IN, we could have declared this procedure with the following header:

```
PROCEDURE PROC_SCHEDULE_CRUISE
   ( p_start_date  DATE       DEFAULT SYSDATE
   , p_total_days  NUMBER
   , p_ship_id     NUMBER
   , p_cruise_name VARCHAR2 DEFAULT 'Island Getaway')
IS
```

In other words, we could have omitted the keywords IN from each parameter declaration, because IN is the default.

When this procedure is executed, the values for each of these four IN parameters will need to be provided by the calling PL/SQL block. There are two ways to pass parameters to a program unit: positional notation and named notation. The following is a sample PL/SQL block that calls this procedure:

```
DECLARE
   v_ship_id NUMBER(4) := 1;
BEGIN
   PROC_SCHEDULE_CRUISES('04-JAN-2003', 3, v_ship_id, 'Alaskan Voyage');
END;
```

This procedure call passes parameter values by position. In other words, each of the four values is provided in the order that the procedures are declared in the procedure code itself.

OUT Parameters

OUT parameters cannot accept values from the calling PL/SQL block. On the contrary, a procedure defines the values of OUT parameters within its own code block, and the OUT parameter passes that value back out to the calling block.

OUT parameters cannot be assigned a DEFAULT value in their parameter declaration. The declaration of an OUT parameter is accomplished by using the same syntax of an IN parameter declaration, except with the OUT keyword, and no default value.

The following code sample demonstrates some OUT parameters:

```
PROCEDURE PROC_GET_EMPLOYEE_INFO
  (  p_employee_id IN  NUMBER
   , p_first_name  OUT VARCHAR2
   , p_last_name   OUT VARCHAR2)
IS
  -- This procedure uses an
  -- employee ID to get the employee's
  -- first and last name.
BEGIN
  SELECT    FIRST_NAME, LAST_NAME
  INTO      p_first_name, p_last_name
  FROM      EMPLOYEES
  WHERE     EMPLOYEE_ID = p_employee_id;
END;
```

The procedure PROC_GET_EMPLOYEE_INFO has three parameters. One is an IN parameter, whose value is defined by the calling block. The second and third parameters are both OUT parameters, and their values are defined within the PROC_GET_EMPLOYEE_INFO procedure and sent back to the calling block.

Since the OUT parameter's values are defined within the calling block, then the calling block must have some sort of proper way to receive these values. In other words, the calling block must be prepared with some sort of variable to receive the OUT parameter's values.

The following is a sample of a PL/SQL block that calls the PROC_GET_EMPLOYEE_INFO procedure:

```
DECLARE
  v_lastname VARCHAR2(30);
  v_firstname VARCHAR2(30);
BEGIN
  PROC_GET_EMPLOYEE_INFO(15,v_firstname, v_lastname);
  DBMS_OUTPUT.PUT_LINE('The employee"s name is: ' ||
    v_firstname || ' ' || v_lastname);
END;
/
```

The IN parameter can be provided a literal value by this calling block, but the two OUT parameters will be sending data back out. Therefore, this block uses two declared variables to receive that returning information.

When the PROC_GET_EMPLOYEE_INFO procedure is invoked, this calling block will temporarily suspend execution while waiting for the called PROC_GET_EMPLOYEE_INFO procedure to execute. When the called procedure has completed execution, the values for the OUT parameters p_first_name and p_last_name will be defined and assigned to the receiving variables v_firstname and v_lastname. The calling block will then resume with the next executable statement, which prints the employee's information to the system console.

IN OUT Parameters

A procedure can be declared with parameters that behave as both IN parameters and OUT parameters, meaning that the parameter can have its value passed in, and then have its value changed within the procedure and passed back out. This is done so that the calling block will receive the value of the parameter at the time the procedure completes execution. IN OUT parameters cannot be defined with a DEFAULT value as part of their declaration.

The following is an example of a procedure that declares an IN OUT parameter:

```
PROCEDURE PROC_SKIP_WEEKENDS
  (p_date IN OUT DATE)
IS
BEGIN
  WHILE (TO_CHAR(p_date,'DY') IN ('SAT','SUN'))
  LOOP
    p_date := p_date + 1;
  END LOOP;
END;
```

This procedure PROC_SKIP_WEEKENDS takes in a date and changes it as needed so that by the time the procedure is completed, the date will be a weekday. If the date as originally provided is a weekday, it will be left unchanged. But if the provided date is a weekend, then it will be changed to be the first weekday that follows.

This use of an IN OUT parameter requires a variable of some sort to be employed in the calling block in order to be able to receive the value upon completion of the procedure's execution. The following is an example of a block that might call this procedure:

```
DECLARE
  v_start_date DATE := '04-JAN-2003';
BEGIN
```

```
    PROC_SKIP_WEEKENDS(v_start_date);
    PROC_SCHEDULE_CRUISE(v_start_date, 3, 1);
END;
```

This code block guarantees that the value of v_start_date will be a weekday before it's sent on to the procedure PROC_SCHEDULE_CRUISE as the starting date of a particular cruise.

Positional Notation versus Named Notation

So far, all the calling blocks we've seen have passed parameter values by position. In other words, the first value provided in the calling block is assigned to the first parameter declared in the procedure and so on. For example, we have called the procedure PROC_SCHEDULE_CRUISE with the following header:

```
PROCEDURE PROC_SCHEDULE_CRUISE
   ( p_start_date  DATE      DEFAULT SYSDATE
   , p_total_days  NUMBER
   , p_ship_id     NUMBER
   , p_cruise_name VARCHAR2 DEFAULT 'Island Getaway')
IS
```

To call this procedure, we've used the following executable statement from a calling block:

```
PROC_SCHEDULE_CRUISE('03-JAN-2004', 3, 1);
```

The value for '03-JAN-2004' is assigned to the first parameter declared in the procedure PROC_SCHEDULE_CRUISE, which is p_start_date. The second value provided, which is the number 3, is automatically assigned to the second declared parameter in the procedure, which is called p_total_days.

But what about that default value for p_start_date? What if we want to take advantage of that? We can't just omit that first value when we use this pass by position approach to passing values to the parameters.

We must use a different notation known as *named notation*. When you call a procedure using named notation, you must know the names of the parameters for which you are going to provide values.

The following code sample calls the same procedure, but only provides values for the second and third parameters:

```
PROC_SCHEDULE_CRUISE(p_ship_id => 1, p_total_days => 3);
```

This notation requires that you name the parameter, followed by the parameter value assignment operator, =>, followed by the value.

Using this approach enables you to assign any value to any parameter in any order. Depending on how the default values for a procedure are defined, you may have no choice but to use this notation on occasion when you want to use all the default values, but still need to provide values for other parameters.

A procedure call can mix notation only if all positional notation references precede all named notation. For example:

```
PROC_SCHEDULE_CRUISE(1, p_total_days => 3);
```

Finally, regardless of which type of notation is used, Oracle will perform limited amounts of appropriate automatic datatype conversion when passing in values to parameters. For example, if a procedure is declared with a single parameter with a VARCHAR2 datatype, but a numeric literal is passed in, Oracle will perform the datatype conversion and accept the numeric literal as a VARCHAR2 value.

For Review

1. Procedures can be defined with parameters. Any parameter can be an IN, OUT, or an IN OUT parameter. IN parameters are defined by the calling block and are sent in to the called procedure. OUT parameters have their values defined in the called procedures, and those values are passed back out to the calling blocks. IN OUT parameters do both.

2. IN parameters can be defined with a DEFAULT value. IN parameters with default values do not have to be defined by the calling block as they normally would be.

3. OUT parameters and IN OUT parameters must be passed a variable from the calling block. Literals cannot be passed, because the calling block must be able to receive the value assigned from within the procedure.

4. Each parameter must be assigned a datatype when declared. However, it is not legal to define length or precision. In other words, you can declare a parameter as having a datatype of NUMBER or VARCHAR2, but not NUMBER(2), or VARCHAR2(30).

5. Parameters can be passed with positional notation or named notation.

Exercises

1. **Consider the following procedure header:**

```
PROCEDURE ACT_UPDATE
        (account_id IN OUT NUMBER)
    IS
```

Assuming all variables referenced are declared, which of the following procedure calls are acceptable for this procedure? (Choose all that apply.)

A. ACT_UPDATE(account_number);

B. ACT_UPDATE(101);

C. ACT_UPDATE;

D. ACT_UPDATE();

2. **What is true about an OUT parameter? (Choose all that apply.)**

    A. It must be assigned a value in the procedure.

    B. It cannot have a default value.

    C. The calling block can use a literal value to define its incoming value.

    D. It acts like a constant in the procedure.

Answer Key

1. A. 2. A, B.

Data Dictionary Resources for Procedures

Oracle's data dictionary provides a variety of statistics and information about procedures that are stored in the database. The following data dictionary views track information about procedures and other PL/SQL program units that are owned by a schema:

- **USER_DEPENDENCIES**   We'll discuss this view later in Chapter 11.

- **USER_OBJECTS**   This view contains a master list of all objects, including tables, views, sequences, synonyms, and, for our purposes, PL/SQL program units.

- **USER_OBJECT_SIZE**   This view contains information about the size of the objects listed in USER_OBJECTS.

- **USER_SOURCE**   This is where the actual source code of the PL/SQL program units is found.

- **USER_ERRORS**   This is where errors resulting from compilation are stored.

As is true throughout much of the data dictionary, each of the views that start with the prefix USER_ has corresponding views that start with the prefix ALL_ and DBA_. The meaning of each is as follows:

- **USER_**   These are views that show information about objects owned by the current schema, meaning the schema, or user name, in which you are logged in to at the time you query the data dictionary.

- **ALL_**   These are views to which the current schema is granted privileges to the objects in the particular data dictionary view, regardless of which schema owns it. For example, ALL_TABLES shows a list of tables that the current schema is privileged to work with, regardless of what schema owns the tables.

- **DBA_**   These are views that show information about all objects in the database.

For example, the view ALL_SOURCE will show the source code of procedures to which the current user, or schema, has been granted access, regardless of who owns the procedure.

All data dictionary views are owned by the SYS schema, and in order to see them, your schema must have been granted SELECT on each of them. Depending on your installation, you may or may not have access to these views, depending on how the DBA has chosen to set up the data dictionary, but you can always ask the DBA to grant SELECT privileges for these data dictionary views.

USER_OBJECTS

The USER_OBJECTS data dictionary view displays many objects that the schema, or user, owns, such as tables, views, sequences, indexes, and more. PL/SQL procedures are included in this view, and it is in this view that you can determine the status of a PL/SQL procedure. The USER_OBJECTS data dictionary view is shown here:

```
SQL> DESC USER_OBJECTS;
 Name                          Null?    Type
 ----------------------------- -------- ----------------
 OBJECT_NAME                            VARCHAR2(128)
 SUBOBJECT_NAME                         VARCHAR2(30)
 OBJECT_ID                              NUMBER
 DATA_OBJECT_ID                         NUMBER
 OBJECT_TYPE                            VARCHAR2(18)
 CREATED                                DATE
 LAST_DDL_TIME                          DATE
 TIMESTAMP                              VARCHAR2(19)
```

```
STATUS                          VARCHAR2(7)
TEMPORARY                       VARCHAR2(1)
GENERATED                       VARCHAR2(1)
SECONDARY                       VARCHAR2(1)
```

The columns are defined as follows:

- **OBJECT_NAME**   This is the name assigned to the object by the developer.

- **SUBOBJECT_NAME**   The name of the subobject and it does not apply to PL/SQL program units.

- **OBJECT_ID**   A system-generated number assigned to this object as an internally unique ID.

- **DATA_OBJECT_ID**   The object number of the segment in which the object's data is stored.

- **OBJECT_TYPE**   The type of Oracle database object. For PL/SQL procedures, this will always be PROCEDURE. Other values include FUNCTION, PACKAGE, PACKAGE BODY, TABLE, VIEW, and more.

- **CREATED**   The date when this object was first created. If a PL/SQL procedure has already been created, and a CREATE OR REPLACE causes the source code to be replaced, this date will still reflect the original creation date.

- **LAST_DDL_TIME**   The date when this object was last modified. Modifications include CREATE OR REPLACE commands as well as ALTER, GRANT, and REVOKE commands.

- **TIMESTAMP**   Same as CREATED, but stored as a VARCHAR2.

- **STATUS**   Either VALID or INVALID. Determines if the object is usable. If a PL/SQL program unit, such as a procedure, doesn't parse successfully, its STATUS is set to INVALID until it is properly parsed.

- **TEMPORARY**   A flag to indicate a temporary table object.

- **GENERATED**   Set automatically to N or Y to indicate if the name of the object was system-generated or not.

- **SECONDARY**   Set to N or Y to indicate if this is a secondary index. Not applicable to PL/SQL program units.

The following is an example of a query that will display all PL/SQL program units with a status of INVALID:

```
SELECT    OBJECT_TYPE, OBJECT_NAME
FROM      USER_OBJECTS
WHERE     OBJECT_TYPE IN ('PROCEDURE','FUNCTION','PACKAGE','PACKAGE BODY')
  AND     STATUS = 'INVALID';
```

USER_OBJECT_SIZE

The USER_OBJECT_SIZE view contains one row per object stored in the schema, and it provides information about the size of the object. For PL/SQL program units, there are several sizes to consider: the size of the original source code, the size of the parsed version of the code, and, most significantly, the size of the compiled code, which is the executable version and the size you'll be most concerned with if you choose to do advanced application tuning. For example, if you combine several procedures into a single PL/SQL package, you may choose not to combine them all into a single large package and prefer to combine them into several packages. (The reasons will be explored later when we discuss packages.)

The columns of USER_OBJECT_SIZE are defined here:

- **NAME**   The user-defined name of the object. For procedures, this will be the name of the procedure.

- **TYPE**   The type of Oracle object. This could be TABLE, VIEW, SEQUENCE, and so on. For PL/SQL program units, this will be PROCEDURE, FUNCTION, and so on.

- **SOURCE_SIZE**   The size of the source code in bytes.

- **PARSED_SIZE**   The size of the parsed version of the code before compilation in bytes.

- **CODE_SIZE**   The size of the compiled version of the code in bytes.

- **ERROR_SIZE**   The size of any error messages resulting from compilation errors in bytes.

USER_SOURCE

Once a procedure has been sent to the database, regardless of whether or not it's successfully parsed, its source code is stored in the data dictionary. The Oracle data dictionary view that displays the source code of your own procedures is USER_SOURCE. The USER_SOURCE table is as follows:

```
SQL> DESC USER_SOURCE;
 Name                            Null?    Type
 ----------------------  -------- ----------------
 NAME                    NOT NULL VARCHAR2(30)
 TYPE                             VARCHAR2(12)
 LINE                    NOT NULL NUMBER
 TEXT                             VARCHAR2(4000)
```

This data dictionary view contains one row per line of source code for each procedure. The columns of this data dictionary view are defined as follows:

- **NAME** The name of the stored procedure.

- **TYPE** This will equal the text string 'PROCEDURE' for stored procedures. Other options include 'FUNCTION', 'PACKAGE', and 'PACKAGE BODY'.

- **LINE** This is the line number of the source code for a particular named procedure.

- **TEXT** This is the actual line of source code.

For example, if we wanted to look at the stored procedure for the procedure PROC_RESET_ERROR_LOG, we could use the following query:

```
SELECT   TEXT
FROM     USER_SOURCE
WHERE    NAME = 'PROC_RESET_ERROR_LOG'
  AND    TYPE = 'PROCEDURE'
ORDER BY LINE;
```

When executed in SQL*Plus, this query will produce the display shown in Figure 2-6.

The USER_SOURCE view is where you will find source code for PL/SQL procedures, functions, and packages. Each line of code is a separate record in the view. By using a query such as the sample shown, you can display all rows of source code for a given procedure, function, or package.

USER_ERRORS

The USER_ERRORS view consists of the following columns:

- **NAME** The name of the program unit that produced the compilation error.

- **TYPE** The type of program unit. For example, the TYPE could be a PROCEDURE, FUNCTION, PACKAGE, or PACKAGE BODY.

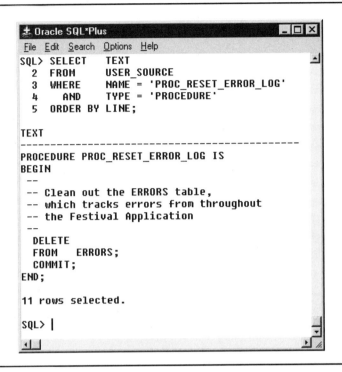

FIGURE 2-6. *SQL*Plus window: querying the USER_SOURCE view*

- **SEQUENCE** The sequence number of error messages. Each message for a given program unit's compilation attempt is assigned a sequence number, starting at 1, and incrementing by 1.

- **LINE** The line number in the original program unit where the problem occurred.

- **POSITION** The character position of the line identified in the LINE column of the program unit where the error occurred.

- **TEXT** The error message.

When you issue a command that attempts to store a program unit in the database, any compilation errors that might result are stored in the data dictionary and can be seen in this view. For example, let's say you were to submit the following procedure to the database for compilation:

```
CREATE OR REPLACE PROCEDURE PROC_SETUP_ORDER
IS
BEGIN
  INSERT INTO ORDERS (ORDER_ID, ORDER_DATE) (SEQ_ORDER_ID.NEXTVAL, SYSDATE);
  COMMIT;
END;
/
```

An attempt to execute this statement, which creates the stored procedure, will produce the following message:

```
Warning: Procedure created with compilation errors.
```

But the compilation errors themselves do not automatically display. You have to draw them out of the data dictionary. One way to do this is to inspect the data dictionary view where these messages can be found: USER_ERRORS. For example, the following query will work:

```
SELECT LINE, POSITION, TEXT
FROM    USER_ERRORS
WHERE   NAME = 'PROC_SETUP_ORDER'
  AND   TYPE = 'PROCEDURE'
ORDER BY SEQUENCE;
```

This query, when submitted to the database, will produce the output displayed in Figure 2-7.

Figure 2-7 demonstrates that the error messages from the compilation attempt are stored in the database and include specific information about the location and type of errors that occurred in the program unit.

The USER_ERRORS view shows error messages for any program units that were submitted to the database for storage, produced compilation errors, and have not yet been successfully compiled. However, once the program unit is successfully compiled and given a status of VALID, the compilation errors are removed from the USER_ERRORS view and are no longer available.

SHOW ERRORS

PL/SQL offers a shorthand method of reviewing the USER_ERRORS table when you're in the SQL*Plus interface. By issuing the command SHOW ERRORS, or the shorthand variation SHOW ERR, you can get a preformatted display from the USER_ERRORS data dictionary view of the error messages resulting from the most recent attempt to store a program unit.

```
Oracle SQL*Plus                                                                    _ □ ✕
File  Edit  Search  Options  Help
SQL> CREATE OR REPLACE PROCEDURE PROC_SETUP_ORDER
  2  IS
  3  BEGIN
  4    INSERT INTO ORDERS (ORDER_ID, ORDER_DATE) (SEQ_ORDER_ID.NEXTUAL, SYSDATE);
  5    COMMIT;
  6  END;
  7  /

Warning: Procedure created with compilation errors.

SQL> SET LINESIZE 100
SQL> COLUMN TEXT FORMAT A70
SQL> SELECT LINE, POSITION, TEXT
  2  FROM    USER_ERRORS
  3  WHERE   NAME = 'PROC_SETUP_ORDER'
  4    AND   TYPE = 'PROCEDURE'
  5  ORDER BY SEQUENCE;

    LINE  POSITION TEXT
--------- --------- ----------------------------------------------------------------------
       4        46 PLS-00103: Encountered the symbol "SEQ_ORDER_ID" when expecting one of
                   the following:

                      ( select
                   The symbol "select" was substituted for "SEQ_ORDER_ID" to continue.

       4        75 PLS-00103: Encountered the symbol ")" when expecting one of the follow
                   ing:

                      . ( , * @ % & - + / mod rem <an identifier>
                      <a double-quoted delimited-identifier> an exponent (**) as
                      from ||

SQL>
```

FIGURE 2-7. *Querying the USER_ERRORS data dictionary view*

However, keep in mind that the USER_ERRORS view retains this information as you work on other program units. Although the SHOW ERR command in SQL*Plus will demonstrate the compilation errors resulting from the most recent attempt to store a program unit, you can always review the USER_ERRORS view in the future for other program units you've been working on.

For Review

1. When any procedure is stored in the database, an entry is added to the data dictionary view USER_OBJECT.

2. The source code of a procedure can be found in the USER_SOURCE data dictionary view.

Exercises

1. **Which column in the USER_SOURCE view reflects the line number of a particular line of source code?**

   A. LINE_NUMBER

   B. LINE_NO

   C. NO

   D. LINE

2. **Which value in the TYPE column of USER_OBJECTS indicates the object is a procedure?**

   A. PROCEDURE

   B. PROGRAM_UNIT

   C. PROC

   D. PROCEDURE_OR_FUNCTION

Answer Key

1. D. **2.** A.

Chapter Summary

Procedures are a type of PL/SQL program unit that executes when called by name. Procedures can be called by another procedure or program unit, or by a call from the SQL*Plus command line using the EXECUTE, or EXEC, command. Procedures are generally used to provide a single code script for some job function that your application needs to perform more than once, either from various locations throughout the application or perhaps repeatedly over a period of time.

Procedures are PL/SQL blocks with an assigned name. Anything you can do in a block can be done in a procedure, including the declaration of elements such as variables, constants, cursors, and exceptions, as well as the full complement of capabilities in the processing section and the exception-handling section. However, you can do more in a procedure than you can do with a block.

Procedures can be defined with parameters. A parameter is like a variable whose value is exchanged between the calling block and the procedure. Parameters can be IN, OUT, or IN OUT parameters. IN parameters will take values at run time from the calling block, OUT parameter values are defined in the procedure and pass the value back out, and IN OUT parameters do both. IN parameters can be defined as having default values. If an IN parameter has a default value, then the calling block does not have to provide a value at run time; otherwise, it does.

OUT parameters cannot be passed literal values from the calling block. Instead, OUT parameter values are defined inside the procedure, and because the calling block must be prepared to receive the outgoing value from the procedure, OUT parameters must be provided with a variable in the calling block to receive the outgoing value. The same is true for IN OUT parameters, which will pass in whatever value the variable has at the time the procedure is called. At the conclusion of the called procedure's execution, the variable will be populated with the value being sent back out to the calling block.

Parameters must have their datatypes declared. However, you cannot specify the length or precision of a datatype in a parameter declaration. For example, you can define a parameter as having a datatype of VARCHAR2, but you cannot declare it with VARCHAR2(30).

A procedure is stored in the database with the CREATE PROCEDURE command or alternatively with the CREATE OR REPLACE PROCEDURE command. The first choice will not overwrite an existing procedure with the same name and set of parameters. (In Chapter 6, we'll explore how multiple copies of a procedure can be stored in the database as long as their parameter lists vary.) However, the OR REPLACE will overwrite the old code and replace it with new code. Once the procedure has been submitted to the database as part of the CREATE PROCEDURE command, the source code is stored in the data dictionary, and if it parses successfully, it is given a status of VALID. Otherwise, it is given a status of INVALID. Regardless, the source code is stored in the data dictionary.

Once a procedure is flagged as VALID, it can be used. However, if the procedure refers to any other database objects, such as a table, and that object is modified with the ALTER command for any reason, then even if there is no logical impact to the source code, the procedure is nevertheless automatically changed to a status of INVALID. To restore the VALID status, you must make any code changes if required and issue the ALTER PROCEDURE . . . COMPILE command. Assuming that the code can successfully reparse, the status will be restored to VALID.

Parameters can be passed to a procedure by positional notation, or by named notation. When passed by position, the parameters must be provided in the same order in which they are declared. When passed with named notation, then the parameter names must be specified, and the => operator can be used to indicate each parameter's value. Named notation allows you to provide the parameter values in random order, omitting any IN parameters that already have default values.

Two-Minute Drill

- Procedures are created with the CREATE OR REPLACE PROCEDURE procedure_name (parameter_list) IS command.

- The reserved word AS can be substituted for the reserved word IS.

- Procedures are PL/SQL blocks with assigned names. The reserved word DECLARE is never used; instead, declare variables after the reserved word IS and before BEGIN.

- After the final END of the procedure, you may optionally repeat the name of the procedure.

- If parameters are not included, then you may leave out the parentheses in the procedure call. But you must leave out the parentheses in the procedure declaration.

- To drop a procedure, use the DROP PROCEDURE procedure_name command.

- If a procedure has a status of INVALID, the existing code that is already stored in the data dictionary can be reparsed with the command ALTER PROCEDURE procedure_name COMPILE. Or, if you want to resubmit the code from outside the database, use the CREATE OR REPLACE PROCEDURE command.

- To execute a procedure from another PL/SQL program unit, repeat the procedure's name in a single statement by itself. Provide any parameter values as required by the specific procedure. For IN parameters, the calling block can provide literal values or variables containing assigned values. For OUT parameters, only a variable can be provided whose value at the time of the call will be ignored, but at the completion of the called procedure, the variable's value will be populated with whatever the called procedure defined for the OUT parameter. For IN OUT parameters, a variable must be provided, and its value at the time of the call is the value that will be passed in to the procedure, and any changes the procedure makes to the parameter will be sent back out to the calling block's variable at the completion of the called procedure's execution.

- To execute a procedure from a SQL*Plus login session, at the command line use the EXECUTE command (EXEC for short) followed by the procedure name.

- If a procedure is called using positional notation, each parameter's value must be provided in the order it is declared in the procedure. If named notation is used, then the parameter names, as they are declared in the procedure, must be used along with the => operator, followed by the value being provided.

Chapter Questions

1. **You want to create a procedure that will take a parameter named salary_amount whose value will be defined by the calling block. Assuming any database object references below are accurate, which of the following parameter declarations are acceptable? (Choose all that apply.)**

   A. salary_amount OUT EMPLOYEES.BONUS%TYPE

   B. salary_amount IN OUT NUMBER(2)

   C. salary_amount OUT VARCHAR2(30)

   D. salary_amount EMPLOYEES.SALARY%ROWTYPE

   E. None of the above

2. **You are working with a procedure that is declared with the following header:**

```
PROCEDURE PROC_HIRE_EMPLOYEE
   ( p_employee_id NUMBER
   , p_hire_date   DATE   DEFAULT LAST_DAY(SYSDATE)
   , p_lastname    VARCHAR2
   , p_firstname   VARCHAR2
   , p_results     OUT BOOLEAN)
IS
```

   Assuming that any of the following variables are properly declared, which of the following is an acceptable call to this procedure? (Choose all that apply.)

   A. PROC_HIRE_EMPLOYEE(p_lastname => 'Jones', p_firstname => 'Joe');

   B. PROC_HIRE_EMPLOYEE('Joe','Jones', TRUE);

   C. PROC_HIRE_EMPLOYEE(p_firstname => 'Joe', p_lastname => 'Jones', v_answer);

   D. PROC_HIRE_EMPLOYEE(101, '03-JAN-2003', 'Jones', 'Joe', v_result);

3. **A procedure called PROC_SHIPPING, with no declared parameters, is already stored in the database, but has a status of INVALID. What will happen when you execute the following statement in SQL*Plus? (Note: NULL is a valid PL/SQL statement.)**

```
CREATE PROCEDURE PROC_CHECK_SHIPPING
IS
BEGIN
  NULL;
END PROC_CHECK_SHIPPING;
```

   A. The procedure will overwrite the existing stored procedure, and the new status will be VALID.

   B. The attempt to create the procedure will fail due to a syntax error: The procedure name cannot be repeated after the END statement.

   C. The attempt to create the procedure will fail due to an error: You cannot create a procedure when another already exists with the same name.

   D. The procedure will overwrite the existing stored procedure, but the status will still be INVALID.

4. **You've created a stored procedure called ADD_EMPLOYEES that includes an INSERT statement for a table called EMPLOYEES. After you successfully store the procedure, you ALTER the EMPLOYEES table by dropping a column from the table. However, this new column isn't referenced in your procedure. What must you now do to guarantee that the procedure has a status of VALID? (Choose all that apply.)**

   A. ALTER PROCEDURE ADD_EMPLOYEES COMPILE;

   B. ALTER PROCEDURE ADD_EMPLOYEES RECOMPILE;

   C. ALTER PROCEDURE ADD_EMPLOYEES;

   D. Nothing

5. **You want to get rid of a procedure you no longer use called PROC_OBSOLETE. How do you do it?**

   A. DELETE PROCEDURE PROC_OBSOLETE;

   B. DROP PROCEDURE PROC_OBSOLETE;

   C. DROP PROCEDURE PROC_OBSOLETE CASCADE;

   D. DROP PROCEDURE PROC_OBSOLETE CASCADE CONSTRAINTS;

6. You have created a procedure and attempted to store it in the database using the **CREATE PROCEDURE** command. When you submitted it to the database, you received a syntax error. From the perspective of the schema that attempted the creation, which of the following data dictionary objects now contains the source code for this procedure? (Choose all that apply.)

   A. None of them

   B. USER_SOURCE

   C. ALL_SOURCE

   D. DBA_SOURCE

7. You submit the following code to the SQL*Plus interface:

```
CREATE OR REPLACE PROCEDURE PROC_HIRE_EMPLOYEE
  ( p_employee_id IN NUMBER DEFAULT SEQ_CUSTOMER_ID.NEXTVAL
  , p_hire_date   IN DATE   DEFAULT (SYSDATE+2)
  , p_lastname    IN VARCHAR2
  , p_result      OUT BOOLEAN)
IS
BEGIN
  IF (p_result IS NULL)
  THEN
    p_lastname := 'Smith';
  END IF;
END;
```

   Why will this procedure be given a status of INVALID? (Choose all that apply.)

   A. The IF statement cannot refer to p_result yet because its parameter declaration has no DEFAULT value.

   B. The assignment of 'Smith' to the p_lastname variable is not an option because p_lastname is an IN parameter.

   C. The p_employee_id parameter cannot use a SEQUENCE in its DEFAULT value expression.

   D. The p_hire_date parameter cannot be assigned a default value of SYSDATE+2.

8. You have created a procedure and stored it in the database under your own schema. Assuming you were to grant the required privileges, which of the following could invoke your procedure? (Choose all that apply.)

A. Another stored procedure in your own schema

B. Another stored procedure in a different schema, but in the same database

C. A procedure stored in an Oracle Form, located on a client machine on your network and logged in to a different schema in your database

D. An anonymous PL/SQL block, saved in a text file, and executed in a SQL*Plus session that's logged in as your own schema

9. **You are logged in to the SQL*Plus interface and want to invoke a procedure called PROC_UPDATE_STATUS that takes no parameters. From the SQL prompt, how can you execute this procedure? (Choose all that apply.)**

A. EXEC PROC_UPDATE_STATUS;

B. EXECUTE PROC_UPDATE_STATUS();

C. BEGIN
  PROC_UPDATE_STATUS;
  END;
  /

D. EXEC PROC_UPDATE_STATUS();

10. **Assume the following procedure is stored in the database:**

```
PROCEDURE PROCESS_ORDER
   (ORDER_ID      NUMBER,
    SALES_REP     VARCHAR2)
IS
BEGIN
  INSERT INTO ORDERS VALUES (ORDER_ID, SALES_REP);
END;
```

Assuming that the variable v_lastname has been properly declared, which of the following calls to this procedure will parse within a PL/SQL block and execute correctly without producing an error?

A. PROCESS_ORDER('101', 'Jones');

B. PROCESS_ORDER('101', v_lastname);

C. PROCESS_ORDER(101, SYSDATE);

D. PROCESS_ORDER(101, Jones);

Answers to Chapter Questions

1. E.   None of the above

Explanation   A is bad since it's only an OUT parameter. B is unacceptable because the NUMBER(2) datatype is invalid; no precision is allowed in parameter datatype declarations. C is unusable because it's only an OUT parameter and the VARCHAR2(30) defines length, which is unacceptable. D defaults as an IN parameter, which is acceptable, but the use of %ROWTYPE is invalid; the %TYPE attribute would have been preferable.

2. D.   PROC_HIRE_EMPLOYEE(101, '03-JAN-2003', 'Jones', 'Joe', v_result);

Explanation   A isn't good since there's no provision for the OUT parameter p_results. B isn't good for many reasons, but the first is that values are passed by positional notation instead of named notation, so the first value of Joe is sent to the parameter p_employee_id, but that parameter will only accept values of the datatype NUMBER. C would work except it combines passing parameters by positional notation and named notation, and this isn't acceptable if the named notation precedes the positional notation. D works, since values are passed by positional notation, and the final OUT parameter is provided a variable.

3. C.   The attempt to create the procedure will fail due to an error: You cannot create a procedure when another already exists with the same name.

Explanation   If the statement used the OR REPLACE option, it would have worked. But it certainly may repeat the name of the procedure after the END statement. In fact, that's considered good design.

4. A, D.   A: ALTER PROCEDURE ADD_EMPLOYEES COMPILE;
D: Nothing

Explanation   Regardless of what change was made to the table EMPLOYEES, and regardless of what specific action the procedure takes on that table, the fact is that if the table is used in any SQL statement from within the procedure, and if any ALTER is issued on the table, then the procedure should be recompiled. However, in reality, Oracle will automatically attempt to recompile the procedure on its next invocation, and since the procedure doesn't even reference the column, then the procedure will recompile fine at that time. The proper syntax for performing the recompilation is A, with the COMPILE keyword. There is no RECOMPILE keyword.

5. B.   DROP PROCEDURE PROC_OBSOLETE;

Explanation   No special keywords are required other than these. DELETE applies to tables whose records you wish to remove, but DROP is always used to eliminate a database object altogether.

6. B, C, D.   B: USER_SOURCE
C: ALL_SOURCE
D: DBA_SOURCE

Explanation   Any attempt of CREATE PROCEDURE will move source code into this set of data dictionary views, regardless of whether or not the attempt was successful.

7. B, C.   B: The assignment of 'Smith' to the p_lastname variable is not an option because p_lastname is an IN parameter. C: The p_employee_id parameter cannot use a SEQUENCE in its DEFAULT value expression.

Explanation   No IN parameters can be assigned values, and SEQUENCE generators are not allowed in DEFAULT value declarations for parameters. What A says is true, but not for the reason given; p_result should not be referenced because it is an OUT parameter, not an IN parameter, and it hasn't been assigned a value yet. As an OUT parameter, it cannot be assigned a DEFAULT value, but once the executable statements of the procedure begin, it can be assigned a value with a standard PL/SQL assignment statement. After that, it can be referenced in an IF statement. And D is allowable.

8. A, B, C, D.   A: Another stored procedure in your own schema. B: Another stored procedure in a different schema, but in the same database. C: A procedure stored in an Oracle Form, located on a client machine on your network and logged in to a different schema in your database. D: An anonymous PL/SQL block, saved in a text file, and executed in a SQL*Plus session that's logged in as your own schema

Explanation   A and D are true without any additional granting of privileges. B and C are true provided that you grant privileges to the appropriate schema first. (Note: the topic of granting privileges was introduced in this chapter, and will be explored in depth in Chapter 9.)

9. A, B, C, D.   A: EXEC PROC_UPDATE_STATUS;
B: EXECUTE PROC_UPDATE_STATUS();
C: BEGIN
   PROC_UPDATE_STATUS;
  END;
  /
D: EXEC PROC_UPDATE_STATUS();

Explanation C is a standard call from an anonymous PL/SQL block. A, B, and D are all acceptable SQL calls. When the procedure has no parameters, parentheses are not normally used, but are accepted.

    10. A, B, C.   A: PROCESS_ORDER('101', 'Jones');
                  B: PROCESS_ORDER('101', v_lastname);
                  C: PROCESS_ORDER(101, SYSDATE);

Explanation Thanks to Oracle's tendency to perform automatic datatype conversions, the character string '101' will be converted to a numeric value in A and B. And although it's a little silly for C to pass in the current system date as the value for the SALES_REP parameter, nevertheless it will work. But D will not work because Jones is not enclosed in single quotes.

CHAPTER
3

Functions

his chapter discusses functions, the second major type of Procedural Language/Structured Query Language (PL/SQL) program unit. A function is another way of storing a named PL/SQL block. Just like procedures, functions can be stored in the database or on a client as a part of an Oracle Form or attachable library of PL/SQL program units. A function, however, can be invoked within an expression, something that you cannot do with a procedure. Functions can be called from within SQL statements. They can be used to build assignment statements, IF ... THEN ... END IF statements, and more.

Oracle already provides several prewritten functions that we're used to using. For example, SUBSTR (sub-string), INSTR (in string), and ABS (absolute value) are all functions that have been prewritten and are built into the SQL language. However, by creating PL/SQL functions, we can, in essence, extend the capabilities of Oracle's SQL language.

In this chapter, you will review and understand the following topics:

- Uses of functions

- Functions versus procedures

- Creating, altering, and dropping functions

- Invoking functions

- Parameters

- RETURN

Uses of Functions

A function's main purpose is to return a single value of some sort, as opposed to a procedure, whose main purpose is to perform some particular business process. Like a procedure, a function is a PL/SQL block that's been assigned a name; but unlike a procedure, the function will always return one—and only one—value of some sort. This returned value is embodied in the function call in such a way that the function becomes, in essence, a variable.

When you create a function, you must consider how you intend to use the function. There are two major categories of functions you can create:

- Functions that are called from expressions in other PL/SQL program units. Any function can be used this way.

- Functions that are called from within SQL statements, whether the SQL statement is part of a PL/SQL program unit or not. Some functions you create in PL/SQL can be used in this way.

It's possible to create functions that can be invoked in both manners. However, if you intend to make a function that can be called from a valid SQL statement, there are some restrictions you have to consider. For example, a function that returns a BOOLEAN datatype, which is perfectly acceptable in PL/SQL, cannot be invoked from a SQL statement, where BOOLEAN datatypes are not recognized.

Functions versus Procedures

Functions can be used in places where procedures cannot be used. Whereas a procedure call is a statement unto itself, a call to a function is not; a function call is part of an expression. This means that functions can be used as a part, or all, of the right side of the assignment statement. Functions can be used as part, or perhaps all, of the Boolean expression in an IF statement. In short, wherever you might use a variable, you can use a function.

Functions always return a single value, embodied in the function call itself. In other words, contrary to the optional OUT parameter feature in procedures, which you may or may not use to return multiple values from a procedure, a function must always return one—and only one—value through the very call to the function itself. This value is not returned in the form of an OUT parameter, but instead it is returned in the body of the function itself, so that the function call behaves like a variable.

Technically, functions can use IN, OUT, and IN OUT parameters. In practice, functions are generally only given IN parameters, for reasons we will discuss in this chapter. However, it's important to know that OUT and IN OUT parameters will successfully compile.

For Review

1. Functions are called as part of an expression. A function returns a value in such a way that the function call in the expression behaves like a variable.

2. Functions can be called from within SQL statements, but only if the function is stored in the database and if the function returns a datatype that SQL recognizes. For example, the BOOLEAN datatype is recognized in PL/SQL, which will let you return a BOOLEAN datatype; but SQL cannot handle this.

Exercises

1. **You have a PL/SQL block that takes a value order_amount as a parameter, computes sales tax, and sends back the sales tax. You choose to store this program unit in the database. Which of the following is true?**

    A. It must be a function because it returns a value.

    B. It must be a procedure because it does something.

    C. It can be either a procedure or a function.

    D. It can be neither a procedure nor a function because it interacts with sales tax.

2. **You have created a function called scrub_invoice that returns a VARCHAR2 datatype. Which of the following is true? (Choose all that apply.)**

    A. You can invoke this function from the WHERE clause of a SELECT statement.

    B. You cannot store this function in the database.

    C. You can invoke this function from the Boolean expression of a WHILE . . . LOOP statement.

    D. You can store this function in an Oracle Form.

Answer Key
1. C. 2. A, C, D.

Creating, Altering, and Dropping Functions

The syntax to create, alter, and drop functions is similar to the syntax used for procedures, with a few additions. As with procedures, the command to create a function is not the same command required to execute the function.

Creating Functions

The syntax to create a function is similar to the syntax used to create a procedure, with one addition: the RETURN declaration. The following is a sample CREATE … FUNCTION statement.

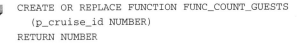

```
CREATE OR REPLACE FUNCTION FUNC_COUNT_GUESTS
  (p_cruise_id NUMBER)
RETURN NUMBER
```

```
IS
  v_count NUMBER(10)
BEGIN
  SELECT  COUNT(G.GUEST_ID)
  INTO    v_count
  FROM    GUESTS G,
          GUEST_BOOKINGS GB
  WHERE   G.GUEST_ID = GB.GUEST_BOOKING_ID
    AND   GB.CRUISE_ID = p_cruise_id;
  RETURN v_count;
END;
/
```

This function will take a single parameter, p_cruise_id. This parameter could include the parameter type declaration, such as IN, OUT, or IN OUT, but this example leaves it out, so this parameter is assumed to be the default IN parameter type, just as it would be assumed in a procedure. This function will use the p_cruise_id parameter to query the database and count the total number of guests for a single cruise. The result of the query is then returned to the calling block, using the RETURN statement at the end of the function.

If you think of the entire function as a variable, then think of the RETURN datatype as the function's datatype.

The function's processing section must include at least one RETURN statement that executes as the last logical statement of the function. The purpose of the RETURN statement is to return the actual value of the function. In other words, the function header declares the datatype of the value that will be returned, but the RETURN statement in the processing section does the actual return. Therefore, the datatype in the declaration and the datatype of the actual value returned must match in order for the function to be successfully parsed and, therefore, to be stored in the database as a VALID function.

Functions can RETURN any valid PL/SQL datatype, including NUMBER, VARCHAR2, and DATE, which are all recognized by SQL, as well as the datatypes that are recognized in PL/SQL but not in SQL, such as BOOLEAN. However, a word of warning: If the function returns a datatype that SQL does not recognize, then the function will only be able to be called from other PL/SQL expressions and not from SQL statements.

Altering Functions

As with a procedure, a function may reference database objects from within its code. As with a procedure, if those database objects are changed, then the function must be recompiled. To perform this recompilation, use the ALTER FUNCTION … COMPILE command.

If you do not perform the recompilation, then the function will be automatically recompiled at its next invocation. If the recompilation is successful, then the function will execute, and all that will be noticed is that the execution was a little longer than normal. However, if the function does not successfully recompile for any reason, then the attempt to execute the function will produce the following error message:

```
ORA-06575: Package or function [function_name] is in an invalid state
```

At this point, a developer will need to inspect the function's code. The command to recompile the function we created earlier is as follows:

```
ALTER FUNCTION FUNC_COUNT_GUESTS COMPILE;
```

The function's existing code, as stored in the data dictionary, is resubmitted for parsing, and assuming it parses successfully, it will be given a status of VALID.

Dropping Functions

To drop a function, use the DROP … FUNCTION statement. The following is a sample command that will drop our sample function:

```
DROP FUNCTION FUNC_COUNT_GUESTS;
```

No references to parameters is required, only the name of the function.

For Review

1. Function headers are the same as procedure headers, with the exception of the RETURN datatype declaration.

2. The RETURN statement should be the last executable statement in the function. The value returned should have a datatype that matches the declared datatype in the function header.

Exercises

1. **Once a function is stored in the database with the CREATE OR REPLACE FUNCTION statement, which of the following is true, assuming that the function returns a value with a datatype of NUMBER? (Choose all that apply.)**

   A. It is available for execution but only after it is compiled with the ALTER FUNCTION … COMPILE command.

   B. It can be invoked from SQL statements.

C. The same code cannot be stored as a procedure.

D. It can be invoked from PL/SQL expressions.

2. **You have created a function called compute_order and another called compute_tax. The compute_order function calls on the compute_tax function as part of its processing section. You attempt to drop the compute_tax function with the DROP FUNCTION command. Which of the following statements is true? (Choose all that apply.)**

A. You cannot drop the compute_tax function because it is called by compute_order, which you must drop first.

B. The compute_order function is left with a status of INVALID. You need to edit the code for compute_order to restore it to a status of VALID.

C. You can only drop the compute_tax function with the CASCADE option.

D. Any attempt to drop compute_tax will automatically drop compute_orders.

Answer Key
1. B, D. 2. B.

Invoking Functions

Functions are never called in a stand-alone statement as procedures are. Instead, a function call is always part of some other expression. Valid PL/SQL expressions can incorporate functions anywhere that a variable would be accepted. Valid SQL expressions may also invoke functions, but with a few limitations—only certain types of functions can be invoked from SQL.

The following is a sample of a block that might call our sample FUNC_COUNT_GUESTS function:

```
PROCEDURE PROC_ORDER_FOOD (p_cruise_number NUMBER)
IS
  v_guest_count NUMBER(10);
BEGIN
  -- Get the total number of guests
```

```
-- for the given cruise
v_guest_count := FUNC_COUNT_GUESTS(p_cruise_number);
-- Issue a purchase order
INSERT INTO PURCHASE_ORDERS
   (PURCHASE_ORDER_ID, SUPPLIER_ID, PRODUCT_ID, QUANTITY)
   VALUES
   (SEQ_PURCHASE_ORDER_ID.NEXTVAL, 524, 1, v_guest_count)
   COMMIT;
END;
```

In the calling block, which is a procedure, the call to the function FUNC_COUNT_GUESTS is made from the right side of an assignment statement. The function will be executed in full at that point and its RETURN value will be substituted into the place of the function in the assignment statement.

Functions Called from PL/SQL Expressions

Any PL/SQL function can be called from a PL/SQL expression of another program unit. Remember that expressions can be found in many places within PL/SQL:

- The right side of an assignment statement

- The Boolean expression of an IF ... THEN ... END IF statement

- The Boolean expression of a WHILE loop

- The calculation of a variable's default value

In short, anywhere you might use a PL/SQL variable, you can issue a function call.

Assume you have a function called leading_customer that returned a VARCHAR2 value of the customer's last name and that takes no parameters. The following code samples demonstrate various ways that the function leading_customer might be used. First, a call to the function that assigns the leading customer's last name as the default value for the variable v_last_name can be used:

```
DECLARE
   v_last_name VARCHAR2(30) DEFAULT leading_customer;
BEGIN
   DBMS_OUTPUT.PUT_LINE(v_last_name);
END;
/
```

This next sample demonstrates how the leading_customer function can be used in a PL/SQL assignment statement:

```
DECLARE
  v_official_statement VARCHAR2(1000);
BEGIN
  v_official_statement := 'The leading customer is ' ||
                          leading_customer;
END;
/
```

Finally, a function can be used in IF ... THEN ... END IF statements, as the following code sample demonstrates:

```
BEGIN
  IF (leading_customer = 'Iglesias')
  THEN
    DBMS_OUTPUT.PUT_LINE('Found the leading customer');
  END IF;
END;
/
```

As you can see, a function can be used anywhere within a PL/SQL block that a variable can be used. This is true of any function you can create in PL/SQL.

Functions can even be used as parameter values to other functions. For example,

```
BEGIN
  IF (leading_customer(get_largest_department) = 'Iglesias')
  THEN
    DBMS_OUTPUT.PUT_LINE('Found the leading customer');
  END IF;
END;
/
```

In this example, the function get_largest_department is executed and resolved, and its value is passed back out to the leading_customer function, which uses the value from get_largest_department as a parameter value. The assumption here, of course, is that the leading_customer function can take a parameter of the same datatype that the get_largest_department function returns.

As you can see, functions are powerful and flexible.

Functions Called from SQL Statements

Some functions that you create can be used from within SQL statements. If you want to create a function for use in SQL, you must recognize the following limitations on the function:

- It must be stored in the database. Note that functions can also be stored on the client, such as a function within an Oracle Form module or Report module, or a client-side PL/SQL library, but functions stored on the client are not available for use in SQL statements.

- It must not return datatypes that the database cannot understand, such as BOOLEAN, which is acceptable in PL/SQL, but not in SQL. No parameter definitions can include BOOLEAN datatypes or other non-SQL datatypes.

- Any parameters must be IN parameters.

Wherever you would use an Oracle predefined function, such as SUBSTR, LAST_DAY, or ROUND, you can use your own PL/SQL functions, provided your own PL/SQL functions respect these limitations. In other words, function calls are enabled in the SELECT statement (in the column list, or the WHERE, GROUP BY, HAVING, and ORDER BY clauses), in the UPDATE statement (in the SET and WHERE clauses), in the DELETE statement (the WHERE clause), and in the INSERT statement (VALUES list). These rules also apply to any and all subqueries.

Some examples of our leading_customer function called from within a SELECT statement are shown in the following code:

```
SELECT    leading_customer
FROM      DUAL;
```

or this alternative

```
SELECT    COUNT(SHIP_ID) NUMBER_OF_SHIPS,
          leading_customer
FROM      SHIPS;
```

or this

```
SELECT    GUEST_ID
FROM      GUESTS
WHERE     LASTNAME = leading_customer;
```

SELECT statements like this can be used within PL/SQL, or from anywhere in the database, assuming the function is stored in the database—in other words, if the function is stored on a client machine as part of a PL/SQL library or embedded in an

Oracle Form built with Form Builder, then it cannot be called in this fashion from within the database. It must be stored in the database.

When a column in a SELECT statement is sent to a function, the returned value will define the column's datatype. For example, consider the following code sample:

```
SELECT get_customer_name(101)
FROM    DUAL;
```

In this example, the stored database function get_customer_name is being invoked and is sent a single parameter value of 101. The parameter value is a numeric literal, but what is the datatype of the result? From this information alone, you cannot tell. If the function get_customer_name has a RETURN datatype of VARCHAR2, then that is the datatype of the column.

Furthermore, just like SQL predefined functions, the result of this function call could be passed to another function that expects a VARCHAR2 value. For example,

```
SELECT SUBSTR(get_customer_name(101), 1, 1)
FROM    DUAL;
```

The result of this is to identify the customer name based on the number 101, and then obtain the first letter from the customer name. The use of nested functions is enabled with any combination of your own functions and SQL predefined functions, in any order. When it comes to nested functions, as far as the database is concerned, all functions are alike, whether you created them or whether Oracle wrote them. The only concern is to make sure that the value you pass to any function's parameter has the correct datatype. You can provide a literal value, a variable, or a function. Just remember that if you think of a function as being a variable, then the function's RETURN datatype is its datatype.

Client-Side Functions

Functions that are stored in the database are available for use from anywhere in the database or on the network. Functions that are stored in the client, however, have some unusual issues.

For example, you can store a function in an Oracle Form. Functions that are stored in the Oracle Form can be referenced from other program units in the same client but only from within PL/SQL expressions. In other words, client-side functions cannot be referenced from SQL statements inside of PL/SQL program units, even if those program units are stored on the same Oracle Form on the same client. The only functions that can be referenced from within SQL statements are those functions that are stored in the database, even if the SQL statement (such as SELECT, INSERT, UPDATE, or DELETE) is stored in the same client-side program unit.

For Review

1. Any function can be called from any PL/SQL expression. Function calls can be substituted at any location within the expression where a variable would normally be used.

2. Many functions, but not all, can be called from any SQL expression. The RETURN datatype must be recognizable by SQL.

3. Functions that are stored in the database can be called upon by any PL/SQL or SQL expression. Functions that are stored in the client in a particular module, such as an Oracle Form or Report, can only be invoked as part of PL/SQL expressions in program units in that same exact client program.

Exercises

1. **You have created a function called get_customer_name and stored it as a function in an Oracle Form but not in the database. Next, you create a procedure that you store in the same Oracle Form, as follows:**

```
PROCEDURE PROC_INVOICE
IS
  v_customer_name VARCHAR2(30);
BEGIN
  SELECT get_customer_name
  INTO   v_customer_name
  FROM   DUAL;
  INSERT INTO INVOICE (INVOICE_ID, NAME) VALUES (1,
v_customer_name);
  COMMIT;
END;
```

What can be said of this procedure? (Choose all that apply.)

A. It will not compile.

B. It will compile, but it will not execute.

C. It will compile and execute, but it will contain logic errors.

D. It will compile and execute correctly.

2. **Consider the following code sample:**

```
DECLARE
  v_answer VARCHAR2(30);
BEGIN
  v_answer := invoice_amount(1, user_invoice_id);
END;
/
```

Assuming this code compiles and executes successfully, which of the following statements is correct? (Choose all that apply.)

A. invoice_amount is a procedure.

B. invoice_amount is a function.

C. user_invoice_id is a function.

D. user_invoice_id is a variable.

Answer Key

I. A. 2. B, C.

Parameters

Functions take parameters, just like procedures do, and just like procedures, a parameter for a function can be an IN, OUT, or an IN OUT parameter. The default parameter type is an IN parameter.

However, unlike a procedure, a function always returns a value through its unique RETURN statement, and this value replaces the original call to the function in the expression that calls the function. Given this, functions are not generally used to pass OUT or IN OUT parameters. Furthermore, the OUT and IN OUT parameter will not work with function calls that are made from SQL statements. For example, consider the following function:

```
FUNCTION FUNC_COMPUTE_TAX(p_order_amount IN OUT NUMBER)
RETURN NUMBER
IS
BEGIN
  p_order_amount := p_order_amount * 1.05;
  RETURN p_order_amount * .05;
END;
```

This function has an IN OUT parameter. The parameter comes IN as some dollar amount representing an order; it goes OUT with tax added. The function RETURNS the amount of the tax itself, as a NUMBER datatype.

This function cannot be invoked from a standard SQL statement. See Figure 3-1 for two attempts to invoke this function: one with a numeric literal as a parameter value and another with a database column.

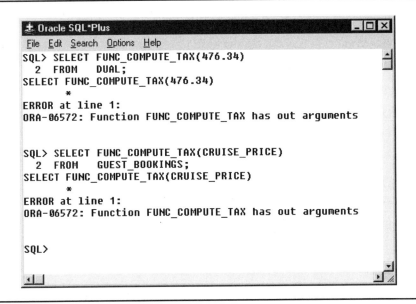

FIGURE 3-1. *Executing a function with an IN OUT parameter*

The figure represents two SQL calls that are made outside of a PL/SQL block and demonstrates that a stand-alone SQL statement cannot reference a function with an OUT or IN OUT parameter.

However, this function can be called from another PL/SQL block, from an expression in that block, provided that any parameter values that are sent to any of the function's OUT parameters are variables. This is, of course, the typical requirement of a procedure call with an OUT or IN OUT parameter.

Now consider the following procedure:

```
PROCEDURE PROC_PROCESS_ORDER IS
  v_order_amount NUMBER := 299.98;
  v_tax          NUMBER;
BEGIN
  v_tax := func_compute_tax(v_order_amount);
  DBMS_OUTPUT.PUT_LINE('The tax is: ' || v_tax);
  DBMS_OUTPUT.PUT_LINE('The new order amount is: ' || v_order_amount);
END;
```

This procedure will invoke the function and display both the results of the function's RETURN value and the modified value of v_order_amount that is changed via the IN OUT parameter.

This code works when used in this fashion—in other words, when the function is invoked from within a PL/SQL expression.

However, compare this code:

```
PROCEDURE PROC_PROCESS_ORDER IS
  v_order_amount NUMBER := 299.98;
  v_tax          NUMBER;
BEGIN
  SELECT func_compute_tax(v_order_amount)
  INTO   v_tax
  FROM   DUAL;
  DBMS_OUTPUT.PUT_LINE('The tax is: ' || v_tax);
  DBMS_OUTPUT.PUT_LINE('The new order amount is: ' || v_order_amount);
END;
```

This code will store correctly, but will produce an execution error:

```
SQL> exec proc_process_order;
BEGIN proc_process_order; END;

*
ERROR at line 1:
ORA-06572: Function FUNC_COMPUTE_TAX has out arguments
ORA-06512: at "FESTIVAL.PROC_PROCESS_ORDER", line 5
ORA-06512: at line 1
```

The function cannot be invoked from within a SQL statement. Even though the IN OUT parameter is provided a proper PL/SQL variable, it is still rejected at run time.

However, in practice, although the OUT or IN OUT parameter type will behave correctly in a function that is called from a PL/SQL expression, it's not generally considered good design. As a result, if a function has any parameters, they are generally all declared with the default IN parameter type.

Passing Parameters with Named Notation

Function calls from PL/SQL procedures can use the named notation that is enabled in procedures, but function calls from SQL statements cannot use this.

In other words, the function FUNC_COUNT_GUESTS can be called like this:

```
DECLARE
  v_total NUMBER(10);
BEGIN
  v_total := FUNC_COUNT_GUESTS(p_cruise_id => 101);
  DBMS_OUTPUT.PUT_LINE('The total is: ' || v_total);
END;
/
```

However, an attempt to call the same function with the same parameter-passing notation from SQL will produce an error message:

```
SELECT    FUNC_COUNT_GUESTS(p_cruise_id => 101)
FROM      DUAL;
                                          *
ERROR at line 1:
ORA-00907: missing right parenthesis
```

Function calls from SQL must use the positional notation for parameter values.

For Review

1. Functions can take parameters. Syntactically, a function can be defined with IN, OUT, and IN OUT parameters. Generally, however, if a function is defined with any parameters, the parameters are IN parameters.

2. Passing parameters by reference only works within function calls from PL/SQL expressions, not from SQL function calls.

Exercises

1. Assuming that any of the following variables are properly declared, which of the following PL/SQL statements includes a valid function call? (Choose all that apply.)

   A. get_shipping;

   B. v_answer := calculate_tax(order_amount, v_order_id => 240);

   C. SELECT best_customer INTO v_best FROM DUAL;

   D. get_shipping();

2. A function may defined with (Choose all that apply.):

   A. No parameters

   B. IN parameters

   C. OUT parameters

   D. IN OUT parameters

Answer Key
1. C. 2. A, B, C, D.

RETURN

The use of the RETURN statement is unique to functions. The RETURN statement is used to return some value. In fact, the primary reason for storing a PL/SQL block as a function is to return this value—this is the purpose of the function. For example, if a function is meant to compute the total payments received so far from guest reservations booked on a cruise, then the function will do whatever it needs to do to arrive at this final value and use the RETURN statement at the end to send the result back to the function call.

If you attempt to compile a function that has no RETURN statement, you will succeed, and the function will be stored in the data dictionary with a status of VALID. However, when you attempt to execute the function, you will receive a message like this:

```
ORA-06503: PL/SQL: Function returned without value
ORA-06512: at "[schema.function_name]", line 6
ORA-06512: at line 1
```

Therefore, it is the developer's responsibility to remember the RETURN statement. The compilation process won't remind you that it's required.

The function processes its statements until the RETURN statement is reached. Once the RETURN statement is processed, the execution of the function will stop. Any statements that follow will be ignored, and control is returned to the calling source. Therefore, it is considered good design to make the RETURN statement the last executable statement. However, the parser does not require this. Your function will compile without any RETURN statement or with a RETURN statement that precedes other valid PL/SQL statements.

Sometimes it makes sense to have multiple RETURN statements. Consider the following code:

```
FUNCTION FUNC_GET_CLASSIFICATION
   (p_duration NUMBER)
RETURN VARCHAR2
IS
BEGIN
  IF    (p_duration <= 4)
  THEN
    RETURN 'Weekend Getaway';
  ELSIF (p_duration >  4)
      AND (p_duration <= 7)
  THEN
    RETURN 'Weeklong Adventure';
  ELSE
```

```
    RETURN 'Romantic Voyage';
  END IF;
END;
/
```

In the preceding code sample, three different RETURN statements define the value that this function will send back. The IF statement determines which of the three RETURN statements will be executed. So although the function may include multiple RETURN statements, only one will actually execute—the first one that the function encounters. Also, this code guarantees that it is theoretically possible for one, and only one, of the RETURN statements to execute, depending on the IF statement's results.

The syntax of the RETURN statement is as follows:

```
RETURN [expression];
```

A RETURN statement can return a variable, constant, parameter, or any valid expression, including an expression that uses other functions. The only restriction is that the datatype of the returned value must match the datatype that is declared in the function header. However, note that Oracle will perform automatic datatype conversion where it makes sense. Consider the following code sample:

```
FUNCTION FUNC_A_NUMBER
RETURN NUMBER
IS
BEGIN
  RETURN '101';
END;
/
```

The declared datatype for the return is NUMBER, but the actual RETURN statement sends back a character string. However, the character string contains a string that is actually just a number and is a candidate for datatype conversion. This function will compile and execute successfully.

However, if the RETURN value is changed to, for example, 101A, then although the function will still compile successfully, an attempt to execute the function produces the following message:

```
ORA-06502: PL/SQL: numeric or value error: character to number conversion error
ORA-06512: at "FESTIVAL.FUNC_A_NUMBER", line 5
ORA-06512: at line 1
```

The attempt to execute the function yields the error in spite of the fact that it parsed correctly.

The fact that this example compiled correctly was due to Oracle's recognition at compilation time of the string as a candidate for automatic datatype conversion. However, although the string is a candidate, there's no guarantee that it can, in fact, be successfully converted every time. Consider this variation:

```
FUNCTION FUNC_A_NUMBER
   (p_some_string VARCHAR2)
RETURN NUMBER
IS
BEGIN
  RETURN p_some_string;
END;
/
```

This example will also parse correctly, even though the returned value is the formally declared parameter p_some_string with a datatype of VARCHAR2. At execution time, the following function call will successfully execute:

```
SELECT    FUNC_A_NUMBER('101')
FROM      DUAL;
```

But the following call to the same function

```
SELECT    FUNC_A_NUMBER('Washington Redskins')
FROM      DUAL;
```

will produce the PL/SQL: numeric or value error we saw earlier. The datatype conversion isn't attempted until execution.

On the other hand, if the PL/SQL compiler can recognize that there is no hope for automatic datatype conversion, it will not successfully parse the function. For example, consider the following CREATE FUNCTION statement:

```
CREATE OR REPLACE FUNCTION FUNC_A_NUMBER
   (p_some_string VARCHAR2)
RETURN DATE
IS
BEGIN
  RETURN 1;
END;
/
```

The compiler recognizes that no amount of automatic datatype conversion can translate a numeric value of 1 to any sort of valid DATE datatype. The function is flagged with a status of INVALID.

For Review

1. The RETURN statement is not required to compile a function but is required to execute it.

2. The syntax for a RETURN statement is RETURN [expression];.

3. Functions must declare the datatype of the RETURN value in the function header. The datatype of the RETURN value should match the datatype of the declared RETURN datatype. However, your function may compile with a RETURN statement that attempts to send back a construct (such as a variable, constant, or literal) whose datatype doesn't exactly match the declared RETURN datatype. If Oracle recognizes the possibility of an automatic datatype conversion, the RETURN will parse correctly. If there is no possibility of an automatic datatype conversion, it will not parse correctly.

Exercises

1. **How many RETURN statements can a function contain?**

   A. As many as you want.

   B. Only one.

   C. One for every RETURN declared in the function header.

   D. It depends on the number of parameters.

2. **How many RETURN statements will a function execute?**

   A. All of them.

   B. Only one.

   C. The one matching the declared datatype in the function header.

   D. It depends on the number of parameters.

Answer Key

1. A.   2. B.

Chapter Summary

Functions are another type of PL/SQL program unit. Functions can be stored in the database or on the client. Functions must be called as part of an expression. These can be SQL expressions, such as those found in SELECT statements, like a computed column, or a part of the WHERE clause. These can also be PL/SQL expressions, such as the right side of an assignment statement, or the Boolean expression of an IF statement or a WHILE loop.

The main purpose of a function is to return some sort of single value. All functions return one value through the RETURN statement. The RETURN statement must be included by the developer in the processing section of the function and will be the last statement that executes, because it will cause the function to terminate processing and will cause control to be sent back to the calling source. The RETURN statement's value is defined with a PL/SQL expression. This expression must evaluate to a single value. The RETURN value's datatype must be declared in the header of the function. Any valid PL/SQL datatype is acceptable. The declared RETURN datatype must match the actual expression used in the RETURN statement later. Although PL/SQL will perform automatic datatype conversion where appropriate, it's better to declare the proper datatype.

Functions are created with the CREATE FUNCTION statement, which includes the optional OR REPLACE clause. This statement is similar to the statement used to create procedures, with the exception that the CREATE FUNCTION statement requires that you declare the RETURN datatype. Functions can have IN, OUT, and IN OUT parameters, but in practice, functions are usually only declared with IN parameters.

Any function can be called from another PL/SQL expression. However, only certain functions can be called from SQL statements. If a function returns a datatype that SQL doesn't recognize, then the function cannot be called from a SQL statement, even though it's perfectly acceptable to create the function and call it from a PL/SQL statement. Functions that use OUT and/or IN OUT parameters cannot be called from SQL. Parameters can be passed by positional notation or by named notation, except for function calls from SQL statements, where named notation is not permitted.

You can use the same data dictionary resources for functions that you use for procedures. As you would expect, the value for the OBJECT_TYPE column in the USER_OBJECTS data dictionary view will be FUNCTION.

Two-Minute Drill

- ■ Functions always return a value. The datatype of the value that a function will return must be declared in the function header.

■ The RETURN statement will be the last executable statement in the function, regardless of where you place it in the code. The RETURN statement consists of the reserved word RETURN, followed by some valid PL/SQL expression, which must evaluate to a datatype that corresponds to the function's declared RETURN datatype.

■ Functions may take parameters. Functions can be defined with IN, OUT, and/or IN OUT parameters, but OUT and IN OUT parameters are not recommended.

■ Function parameters may be assigned default values, just like parameters in procedures.

■ Function calls from PL/SQL expressions simply name the function and include any appropriate parameters.

■ Function calls from embedded or stand-alone SQL statements have certain restrictions. They only work on functions that are stored in the database that have RETURN value datatypes and parameter datatypes that are consistent with acceptable datatypes in SQL. BOOLEAN datatypes are not enabled. Only IN parameters will work at execution time.

■ Just like a procedure, if a function's dependent objects, such as tables in cursors in the processing section, are changed in the database with the ALTER statement, then the function should be recompiled with the ALTER FUNCTION ... COMPILE command. However, failure to do this will cause the next invocation of the function to trigger a compile directive, and if the function compiles successfully, it will execute. On the other hand, if the function does not compile successfully, its status will remain INVALID, and it will be unavailable for execution until the code is modified.

■ Functions can be dropped with the DROP FUNCTION command.

Chapter Questions

1. **You have created a function called GET_TOTAL that takes no parameters. Assuming that any other variables are properly declared, which of the following PL/SQL statements includes a successful call to this function?**

   A. GET_TOTAL;

   B. v_total := GET_TOTAL();

   C. IF (GET_TOTAL = 101)

   D. v_total := GET_TOTAL;

2. Consider the following code sample:

```
CREATE OR REPLACE FUNCTION GET_TOTAL
   (cruise_id IN OUT NUMBER)
RETURN NUMBER
AS
   total   NUMBER(10);
BEGIN
   SELECT COUNT(*)
   INTO   total
   FROM   CRUISES
   WHERE  CRUISE_ID = cruise_id;
END;
/
```

What will happen when you submit this to the SQL*Plus client interface? (Choose all that apply.)

A. You will receive a parsing error because of the IN OUT parameter type, which is unacceptable in functions.

B. You will receive a parsing error because there is no RETURN statement at the end.

C. You will receive a parsing error because the parameter cruise_id cannot have the same name as the column CRUISE_ID in the CRUISES table.

D. You will receive the Function created message.

3. You have created a function called CUSTOMER_BALANCE, as follows:

```
CREATE OR REPLACE FUNCTION CUSTOMER_BALANCE
   (p_customer_id NUMBER)
RETURN NUMBER
IS
   order_amount NUMBER(10,2);
BEGIN
   SELECT SUM(ORDER_AMOUNT)
   INTO   order_amount
   FROM   ORDERS
   WHERE  CUSTOMER_ID = p_customer_id;
   RETURN order_amount;
END;
/
```

You store the function in the database, it compiles successfully, and you test its execution to demonstrate that it works as expected. Two weeks later, you issue the following command to the database:

```
ALTER TABLE ORDERS ADD ORDER_STATUS VARCHAR2(1);
```

Once this has been done, which of the following statements will now produce an error message?

A. ALTER FUNCTION CUSTOMER_BALANCE();

B. SELECT CUSTOMER_BALANCE FROM DUAL;

C. ALTER FUNCTION CUSTOMER_BALANCE COMPILE;

D. ALTER FUNCTION CUSTOMER BALANCE RECOMPILE;

4. You have stored a function in the database with the following header:

```
FUNCTION CALCULATE_DISCOUNT
RETURN BOOLEAN
IS
```

Assuming it has been successfully compiled and has a status of VALID, which of the following statements is true? (Choose all that apply.)

A. It can be called from a SQL statement.

B. It can be called from a PL/SQL expression.

C. You can execute it with the SQL*Plus EXEC command.

D. It takes no parameters.

5. You have stored a function in the database with the following header:

```
FUNCTION GET_BOOKINGS(guest_id IN NUMBER DEFAULT 0)
RETURN NUMBER
AS
```

Assuming that any referenced variables are properly declared, which of the following calls to this function will produce an error message? (Choose all that apply.)

A. SELECT GET_BOOKINGS(guest_id => 101) FROM DUAL;

B. SELECT GET_BOOKINGS(p_guest_id => 101) FROM DUAL;

C. v_answer := GET_BOOKINGS(101);

D. v_answer := GET_BOOKINGS;

6. **You are creating a new function with the following header and declaration section:**

    ```
    FUNCTION EMPLOYEE_HIRE_DATE
      (p_employee_id IN NUMBER)
    RETURN DATE
    IS
      v_date DATE;
    BEGIN
    ```

    Which of the following RETURN statements will be accepted by the compiler for this function? (Choose all that apply.)

    A. RETURN SYSDATE;

    B. RETURN 'No date was found';

    C. RETURN v_date;

    D. RETURN;

7. **You submit the following command to the SQL*Plus interface:**

    ```
    CREATE OR REPLACE FUNCTION GET_CEO_NAME
    RETURN VARCHAR2
    IS
    BEGIN
      RETURN 'Dale Houser';
    END;
    /
    ```

    Once you have submitted this to the database, which of the following is true?

    A. The function is stored in the data dictionary but not yet compiled.

    B. The function is stored and compiled but not yet executed.

    C. The function is stored, compiled, and executed.

    D. The function cannot be stored because of a syntax error.

8. **Consider the following call to a PL/SQL program unit:**

    ```
    FUNC_IDENTIFY_CRUISE(101);
    ```

    Assuming this statement compiles and executes accurately, which of the following can be said about this program unit? (Choose all that apply.)

   A. It takes only one parameter.

   B. It is not a function.

   C. It returns a value, although we can't be sure which one.

   D. The parameter represented by the value 101 is an IN parameter.

9. **You have two functions stored in the database: one called CABIN_STATUS with the following header:**

```
FUNCTION CABIN_STATUS (p_guest_name VARCHAR2 DEFAULT 'none')
RETURN VARCHAR2
IS
```

   and another called GUEST_NAME with the following header:

```
FUNCTION GUEST_NAME (p_guest_id NUMBER DEFAULT 0)
RETURN VARCHAR2
AS
```

   Assuming you have a third PL/SQL program unit, with a declared variable called v_answer VARCHAR2(80), which of the following PL/SQL statements are syntactically valid from your third program unit?

   A. v_answer := cabin_status || guest_name;

   B. v_answer := cabin_status(guest_name);

   C. v_answer := SUBSTR(cabin_status,1,1) || INSTR(guest_name,1);

   D. v_answer := guest_name(cabin_status);

10. **You have stored a function in an Oracle Form. From where can you invoke the function? (Choose all that apply.)**

   A. From a stored procedure in the database

   B. From a procedure stored in the same Oracle Form in which the function is stored

   C. From a procedure in a different Oracle Form in which the function is stored

   D. From an anonymous block in a text file that you execute from within the SQL*Plus interface

Answers to Chapter Questions

    1. B, C, D.   B: v_total := GET_TOTAL();
                        C: IF (GET_TOTAL = 101)
                        D: v_total := GET_TOTAL;

Explanation   A would work if GET_TOTAL were a procedure, but this doesn't work for functions. B is not usually used in PL/SQL, but it is actually accepted and will not produce an error.

    2. D. You will receive the Function created message.

Explanation   A is wrong because IN OUT parameters are declarable, although not usually useful, in functions. B is wrong because you can create a function without a RETURN statement, but you can't use it; the error will appear in execution. C is wrong because you are allowed to create variables whose names happen to match names of columns in the table; however, at execution, the SELECT statement will assume that both references to cruise_id are the column in the table, every row will return a TRUE as far as the SELECT statement is concerned, and the incoming parameter will be ignored. In other words, the SELECT statement will return each row from the CRUISES table where the value in the cruise_id column matches itself, and this will be true for every column. So although the function will compile, it will be logically erroneous, and besides, it doesn't RETURN anything, so it won't work anyway. However, it will be successfully stored in the database with a VALID status.

    3. A, D.   A: ALTER FUNCTION CUSTOMER_BALANCE();
                     D: ALTER FUNCTION CUSTOMER BALANCE RECOMPILE;

Explanation   Remember the question: which answers will produce an error? B will not produce an error message—even though the function has a status of INVALID after the change to the ORDERS table, it will still execute, but only after it is automatically recompiled by the system. Furthermore, the recompilation will be successful because the change to the ORDERS table will not produce an error in the function's recompilation. C will successfully recompile the function, but D is the correct answer to the question because the RECOMPILE directive doesn't exist, and A is bad syntax.

    4. B, D.   B: It can be called from a PL/SQL expression. D: It takes no parameters.

Explanation   A is not true because the function returns a datatype of BOOLEAN, which is not recognized in SQL. C is not true because the EXEC command is only used with procedures.

    5. A, B.   A: SELECT GET_BOOKINGS(guest_id => 101) FROM DUAL;
                 B: SELECT GET_BOOKINGS(p_guest_id => 101) FROM DUAL;

Explanation Both answers are unacceptable because passing parameters by named notation is not enabled from SQL statements. C is correct, and so is D, which will take advantage of the default value.

6. A, B, C.   A: RETURN SYSDATE;
               B: RETURN 'No date was found';
               C: RETURN v_date;

Explanation D is an incomplete statement. Note that upon execution, B will fail, but it will compile correctly since the parser recognizes that a string literal could, theoretically, contain a valid date, such as '01-JAN-2003'. Even though the string literal clearly does not contain a valid date in this example, the parser cannot recognize this fact; it is not until execution that the string literal is actually inspected for automatic datatype conversion.

7. B.   The function is stored and compiled but not yet executed.

Explanation There are no syntax errors with this function. The command is to CREATE OR REPLACE the function but not to execute it.

8. B, D.   B: It is not a function. D: The parameter represented by the value 101 is an IN parameter.

Explanation Gotcha! Trick question! Or maybe we didn't get you . . . this program unit must be a procedure. Functions, regardless of what prefix they are given, cannot be invoked as a single executable statement. So this must be a procedure. A is not necessarily true—this procedure could have more parameters defined for it, provided those parameters have default values, in which case the additional parameters just aren't required in this particular call to the program unit. C cannot be true because only functions really RETURN a value. Procedures can be compiled with a RETURN statement, and they will execute, but the RETURN statement in a procedure has no more effect than merely stopping execution of the procedure; it won't actually return anything. D must be true because the value 101 is a literal, and literals can only be provided for IN parameters. OUT and IN OUT parameters must have a mechanism to send back the data, such as a variable.

9. A, B, C, D.   A: v_answer := cabin_status || guest_name;
               B: v_answer := cabin_status(guest_name);
               C: v_answer := SUBSTR(cabin_status,1,1) ||
                  INSTR(guest_name,1);
               D: v_answer := guest_name(cabin_status);

Explanation A is okay because both cabin_status and guest_discount return VARCHAR2, and this is a simple string concatenation. B is okay because guest_discount has a default value for its parameter and returns a VARCHAR2, which is being passed to cabin_status as its parameter value. C is okay because the results of both functions are having standard SQL string functions applied to them. D is troublesome, but will be accepted by the compiler since the parser recognizes that the VARCHAR2 datatype returned by the function cabin_status might successfully convert in an automatic datatype conversion to the NUMBER datatype required by the guest_discount function.

10. B. From a procedure stored in the same Oracle Form in which the function is stored

Explanation A is not true because no database program unit can access a program unit stored in any client software. C is not true; no program unit in a Form can access any other program unit stored in another Form. (However, note that if the function were stored in a PL/SQL library that was shared between the Forms, then the answer would be yes.) D is false for the same reason that A is false.

CHAPTER
4

Packages

ost applications include several Procedural Language/Structured Query Language (PL/SQL) procedures and functions that are logically related together. These various procedures and functions could be left as stand-alone individual procedures and functions, stored in the database. However, they can also be collected in a package, where they can be more easily organized and where you will find certain performance improvements as well as access control and various other benefits. A PL/SQL package is a single program unit that contains one or more procedures and/or functions, as well as various other PL/SQL constructs such as cursors, variables, constants, and exceptions. Packages bring these various constructs together in a single program unit.

In this chapter, you will review and understand the following topics:

- Uses of packages

- Creating, altering, and dropping packages

- Invoking package constructs

- Data dictionary resources for packages

Uses of Packages

A package is a collection of PL/SQL program constructs, including variables, constants, cursors, user-defined exceptions, and PL/SQL procedures and functions, as well as PL/SQL-declared types. A package groups all of these constructs under one name. More than that, the package owns these constructs, and in so doing, affords them powers and performance benefits that would not otherwise exist if these constructs were not packaged together.

The benefits of a package include the following:

- *A package logically collects various program units and other declared constructs under one name*, to support one business process or application module and organize your work, keeping one application's set of constructs separate from another application that is stored in the same schema.

- *A package can improve application performance.* A package itself is never executed. Instead, other PL/SQL programs reference the constructs of the package individually, as required. If the constructs were stored separately, such as stand-alone procedures and/or functions, then each individual call to a program unit would cause the construct to be loaded, when called, into the System Global Area (SGA), which is the portion of RAM allocated for Oracle's database processes and user sessions. The process of loading a construct into the SGA is relatively time consuming but a necessary step.

However, when a construct of a stored package is invoked, the entire package is loaded into the SGA all at once. The result: Subsequent calls to package constructs are relatively faster. This process is automatic and completely dependent upon the use of packages.

- *A package enables the package developer to selectively publicize certain portions of the package while hiding others.* Packages consist of two parts: the package specification and the package body. Consider an example where a package contains one procedure and one function. The package specification for such a package would contain only the procedure header and the function header. This information includes the names of the procedure and function, their parameters, and the function's return datatype. That's it. This is all the information that a developer who wants to write calls to this procedure or function would need to know. The package body, on the other hand, includes the entire code for both the procedure and the function. It's possible for the package owner to grant privileges to the package by publishing only the package specification, while hiding the package body. The result: Other developers can make calls to the package without requiring the package owner to expose the code. Furthermore, it's possible for the developer to create procedures and/or functions that are only used by the packaged procedures and/or packaged functions, and that aren't included in the package specification at all. These private program units will not be available for use outside the package but can be used to streamline the package body code.

- *A package can create global constructs or persistent constructs.* The package specification can optionally include declarations for variables, constants, user-defined exceptions, cursors, and more. These constructs serve as global constructs within a user session. For example, a packaged variable that defines a tax rate can have its value set in one PL/SQL program, and a separate and subsequent PL/SQL program will be able to read that newly set value within the same user session. If a packaged cursor is opened in one program unit, it can be fetched in another.

- *Packages support code reuse.* By developing constructs that are documented in the package specifications and are contained as an autonomous program unit, a package can serve as a mechanism by which developers can share PL/SQL procedures, functions, and other constructs with other developers. In fact, Oracle Corporation has prewritten many sets of PL/SQL constructs in various built-in packages to support many purposes.

As you can see, there are many advantages to using packages. Although it's possible to create PL/SQL-based applications without packages, you miss many advantages if you do. Packages offer tremendous advantages to any PL/SQL-based application. It's not unusual for a single application development effort to include the creation of several custom-designed packages, as well as the incorporation of various packages prewritten by Oracle Corporation.

Packages can be stored in the database on the database server or on client-side machines in front-end tools, such as Oracle Forms or Oracle Reports. They can be included in client-side libraries as well. As with procedures and functions, if a package is stored in the database, it can be invoked from anywhere on the network. However, if the package is stored in the client, it can only be called from other PL/SQL code on that client.

For Review

1. Packages can contain variables, constants, exceptions, cursors, types, procedures, and functions.

2. The advantages to using packages include performance improvement, the selective publishing of code, the logical association of various PL/SQL constructs, and the ability to create global constructs.

Exercises

1. **Which of the following is an advantage of using PL/SQL packages? (Choose all that apply.)**

   A. They are easier to code.

   B. When one construct within the package is invoked, the entire package is loaded into the SGA.

   C. If a single construct is declared, then other global constructs are invoked automatically.

   D. It's possible to make a function header known to other developers without exposing the code contained within the function.

2. **Where can a package be stored? (Choose all that apply.)**

   A. In the database in a schema

   B. In a client-side Oracle Report

   C. As part of a PL/SQL library on the client

   D. As a part of an Oracle Form

Answer Key
1. B, D. 2. A, B, C, D.

Creating, Altering, and Dropping Packages

The statements used to create, alter, and drop packages are rather straightforward. However, this process is a little more involved than merely creating a procedure or function. The first point to understand is that a package consists of two parts: the package specification and the package body. The two parts are created separately. Any package must have a specification. A package may optionally include a package body but is not necessarily required to. The requirement for a package to have a body will be determined by what you declare in a package specification; you may simply declare a package specification and no body. However, most packages often include both the package specification and the package body.

You can declare a package specification without the package body and successfully store it in the database as a valid object. Furthermore, with only a package specification, it's possible to create other PL/SQL programs that call on the constructs of your package, even procedures or functions, whose code isn't written yet—the actual code can only be defined in the package body. However, the existence of the package specification enables other outside PL/SQL program units to reference the constructs of this package.

It's recommended that you create the package specification first, before the package body. The package specification, as we have seen, will successfully store, compile, and support the successful compilation of outside program units. A package body, on the other hand, cannot be compiled successfully without a corresponding package specification. However, the package body can be submitted and stored in the data dictionary without a package specification. The package body will simply be flagged with a status of INVALID in the USER_OBJECTS data dictionary view. After the package specification is successfully created, you need to either issue the ALTER PACKAGE . . . COMPILE statement, or simply reference a packaged construct and let the database automatically compile the package at that time.

Creating a Package Specification

The following is an example of a statement that creates a stored PL/SQL package specification:

```
CREATE OR REPLACE PACKAGE pack_booking AS
  c_tax_rate NUMBER(3,2) := 0.05;
  CURSOR cur_cruises IS
    SELECT CRUISE_ID, CRUISE_NAME
    FROM   CRUISES;
  rec_cruises cur_cruises%ROWTYPE;
  FUNCTION func_get_start_date
```

```
    (p_cruise_id IN CRUISES.CRUISE_ID%TYPE)
  RETURN DATE;
END pack_booking;
/
```

The syntax of the statement is the reserved word CREATE, followed by the optional OR REPLACE words, the reserved word PACKAGE, the name you choose for the package, and the reserved word AS. (The word IS is also accepted here.) Next is a series of declared constructs. Eventually, the closing END is included, followed by the package name, optionally repeated for clarity, and then the semicolon.

This package specification declares a constant c_tax_rate, a cursor cur_cruises, a record variable rec_cruises, and the function func_get_start_date. Notice that the function's actual code isn't included here, only the function header.

The package specification is the part of a package that declares the constructs of the package. These declared constructs may include any of the following:

- Variables and/or constants

- Compound datatypes, such as PL/SQL tables and TYPEs

- Cursors

- Exceptions

- Procedure headers and function headers

- Comments

The package specification contains no other code. In other words, the actual source code of procedures and functions is never included in the package specification. The specification merely includes enough information to enable anyone who wants to use these constructs to understand their names, parameters, and their datatypes, and in the case of functions, their return datatypes, so that developers who want to write calls to these constructs may do so.

In other words, if any developer wants to create new programs that invoke your package constructs, all the developer needs to see is the package specification. That's enough information to create programs that employ the procedures and functions of your package. The developer does not need to have full access to the source code itself, provided that he or she understands the intent of the program unit.

Once the package specification has been successfully stored in the database, it will be given a status of VALID, even if the associated package body, containing the actual source code of any and all functions and/or procedures, has yet to be stored in the database.

Creating a Package Body

The following is a sample of a package body that correlates to the package specification we saw earlier:

```
CREATE OR REPLACE PACKAGE BODY pack_booking AS
  FUNCTION func_get_start_date
    (p_cruise_id IN CRUISES.CRUISE_ID%TYPE)
  RETURN DATE
  IS
    v_start_date CRUISES.START_DATE%TYPE;
  BEGIN
    SELECT START_DATE
    INTO   v_start_date
    FROM   CRUISES
    WHERE  CRUISE_ID = p_cruise_id;
    RETURN v_start_date;
  END func_get_start_date;
END pack_booking;
/
```

This package body defines the source code of the function func_get_start_date. Notice that the function header is completely represented here, even though it was already declared completely in the package specification. Also, notice that there are no provisions for the other declared constructs in the package specification. Only the functions and/or procedures that were declared in the package specification need to be defined in the package body. The package specification handles the full declaration of the other public constructs, such as variables, constants, cursors, types, and exceptions.

The package body is only required if the package specification declares any procedures and/or functions, or in some cases of declared cursors, depending on the cursor syntax that is used. The package body contains the complete source code of those declared procedures and/or functions, including the headers that were declared in the specification.

The package body can also include privately defined procedures and/or functions. These are program units that are recognized and callable only from within the package itself and are not callable from outside the package. They are not declared in the package specification, but are defined in the package body.

The procedures and/or functions that are contained in the package body are complete. In other words, although the package specification has already declared the headers, the package body must repeat those headers, as well as the code itself.

If you attempt to create a package body without a corresponding package specification, the code will be stored in the database, and the package body will be flagged with a status of INVALID. Then, once the corresponding package specification is created, the package body can be compiled to a VALID status using the ALTER PACKAGE . . . COMPILE statement.

Public versus Private Constructs

Constructs that are declared in the package specification are considered public constructs. However, a package body can also include constructs that aren't declared in the package specification. These are considered private constructs, which can be referenced from anywhere within its own package body but cannot be called from anywhere outside the particular package body. Furthermore, any developers with privileges to use the constructs of the package do not necessarily have to see the package body, which means that they do not necessarily know of the existence of the private constructs contained within the package body.

The following code is a sample of a package specification and its package body, where the package body contains private constructs. First, the package specification is shown:

```
PACKAGE general_ledger AS
  FUNCTION debit (p_book_id NUMBER, p_amt NUMBER)
  RETURN BOOLEAN;
  FUNCTION credit(p_book_id NUMBER, p_amt NUMBER)
  RETURN BOOLEAN;
END general_ledger;
```

Next, we show the package body:

```
PACKAGE BODY general_ledger AS
  c_pkg CONSTANT VARCHAR2(15) := 'general_ledger';
  PROCEDURE record_error(source VARCHAR2, message VARCHAR2)
  IS
  BEGIN
    INSERT INTO ERRORS (ERROR_ID, MESSAGE)
      VALUES (SEQ_ERROR_ID.NEXTVAL,
              c_pkg   || ': ' ||
              source  || ': ' ||
              message);
  END record_error;
  FUNCTION debit (p_book_id NUMBER, p_amt NUMBER)
  RETURN BOOLEAN
  IS
  BEGIN
    INSERT INTO ledger
      (ledger_id, book_id, amount)
       VALUES
      (SEQ_LEDGER_ID.NEXTVAL, p_book_id, p_amt);
```

```
      RETURN TRUE;
   EXCEPTION
     WHEN OTHERS THEN
       RETURN FALSE;
   END debit;
   FUNCTION credit(p_book_id NUMBER, p_amt NUMBER)
   RETURN BOOLEAN
   IS
   BEGIN
     RETURN debit(p_book_id, -(p_amt));
   EXCEPTION
     WHEN OTHERS THEN
       RETURN FALSE;
   END credit;
END general_ledger;
```

In the package body of general_ledger are two private constructs: the private constant c_pkg and the private procedure record_error. These constructs are declared with the package body and are referenced from within the package body itself. They cannot be referenced from outside the package body. The constant c_pkg is referenced from within the procedure, and the procedure record_error is called from the exception sections of both functions debit and credit.

There is no evidence of these private constructs in the package specification. By publishing only the package specification, the owner of this package can hide the private constructs from developers who, although empowered to make full use of the published package constructs, will never even know of the existence of the private constructs unless the package owner chooses to release that information.

Also notice that the function credit invokes the function debit. These are both public constructs but can be called elsewhere from within the package body.

If you make a reference within a package body to another construct within the package, that construct must already be declared in the code. In other words, the reference must follow the declared construct within the package body. More of this topic will be addressed under the "Invoking Packaged Constructs" section.

Global Constructs

Package constructs, such as variables, constants, cursors, types, and user-defined exceptions, are global to the user session that references them. Note that this dynamic is irrelevant for packaged procedures and packaged functions, but applies to all other packaged constructs. This is true for both public and private constructs in the package. In other words, the values for these constructs will be retained across multiple invocations within the user session.

For example, if an anonymous PL/SQL block references a public packaged variable and changes its value, the changed value can be identified by another

PL/SQL block that executes afterwards. Neither block declares the variable because it's declared as part of the package.

The user cannot directly access any private constructs, such as a variable, but imagine that a user invokes a packaged procedure, for example, that references its own private variable value and changes that value. If the user re-invokes that packaged procedure again within the same user session, the changed value will be recognized by the packaged procedure.

The value will be retained as long as the user session is still active. As soon as the user session terminates, the modified states of the packaged constructs are released, and the next time the user session starts up, the packaged constructs will be restored to their original state, until the user sessions modifies them again.

For example, consider the following package specification and package body:

```
PACKAGE PACK_TEST_GLOBALS IS
   v_public NUMBER := 0;
   PROCEDURE INCREASE_AND_DISPLAY;
END PACK_TEST_GLOBALS;
PACKAGE BODY PACK_TEST_GLOBALS IS
   v_private NUMBER := 0;
   PROCEDURE INCREASE_AND_DISPLAY
   IS
     v_local NUMBER := 0;
   BEGIN
      v_public  := v_public  + 1;
      v_private := v_private + 1;
      v_local   := v_local   + 1;
      DBMS_OUTPUT.PUT_LINE('Public  variable = ' || v_public);
      DBMS_OUTPUT.PUT_LINE('Private variable = ' || v_private);
      DBMS_OUTPUT.PUT_LINE('Local   variable = ' || v_local);
   END INCREASE_AND_DISPLAY;
END PACK_TEST_GLOBALS;
```

Notice that the package specification has a public construct, a variable called v_public. The variable is public because it's declared in the package specification, outside of a procedure or function. On the other hand, the package body declares a private construct, a variable called v_private. This construct is private because it's declared in the package body rather than the package specification, and it's also declared outside of a procedure or function. Finally, there's a local variable called v_local in the packaged procedure INCREASE_OR_DISPLAY. Variables are considered local when they are defined within a procedure or a function.

The procedure INCREASE_OR_DISPLAY changes the values of all three variables and prints them out. When executed from within SQL*Plus, the results might look like Figure 4-1.

```
Oracle SQL*Plus                                    _□×
File  Edit  Search  Options  Help
SQL> SET SERVEROUTPUT ON
SQL> EXEC PACK_TEST_GLOBALS.INCREASE_AND_DISPLAY;
Public   variable = 1
Private variable = 1
Local    variable = 1

PL/SQL procedure successfully completed.

SQL> EXEC PACK_TEST_GLOBALS.INCREASE_AND_DISPLAY;
Public   variable = 2
Private variable = 2
Local    variable = 1

PL/SQL procedure successfully completed.

SQL> EXEC PACK_TEST_GLOBALS.INCREASE_AND_DISPLAY;
Public   variable = 3
Private variable = 3
Local    variable = 1

PL/SQL procedure successfully completed.

SQL> |
```

FIGURE 4-1. *The packaged procedure INCREASE_OR_DISPLAY*

This figure shows a user session that has just begun and is invoking the packaged procedure INCREASE_OR_DISPLAY. (Notice the use of SET SERVEROUTPUT ON; this SQL*Plus statement sets the session parameter to ensure that the PUT_LINE packaged procedure prints successfully to the screen.) Notice that the procedure is executed three times in a row and that the results of each execution are remembered in each subsequent execution. This is what is global about the public and private constructs. The values are not forgotten when the program unit, such as the packaged procedure, completes execution.

Altering a Package

Packages, like procedures and functions, should be recompiled with the ALTER command if their referenced constructs are changed for any reason. This includes any referenced database objects, such as tables, views, snapshots, synonyms, and other PL/SQL packages, procedures, and functions.

The syntax to recompile a package with the ALTER statement is

```
ALTER PACKAGE package_name COMPILE;
```

This statement will attempt to recompile the package specification and the package body.

The syntax to recompile just the package body is

```
ALTER PACKAGE package_name COMPILE BODY;
```

Note that the package is listed in the data dictionary with two records: one record for the PACKAGE and another for the PACKAGE BODY. Both have their individual status assignments. The PACKAGE, meaning the package specification, can be VALID, while the PACKAGE BODY is INVALID. If this is the case, then an ALTER PACKAGE package_name COMPILE statement will attempt to restore the entire package, including the body, to a status of VALID.

If a change is made to the package body and it is recompiled, then the package specification does not demand that the package be recompiled. Even if the re-created package body results in a change that is inconsistent with the package specification, the package specification will still show a status of VALID in the data dictionary (assuming it was VALID to begin with), and the package body will be flagged with a status of INVALID. See Figure 4-2.

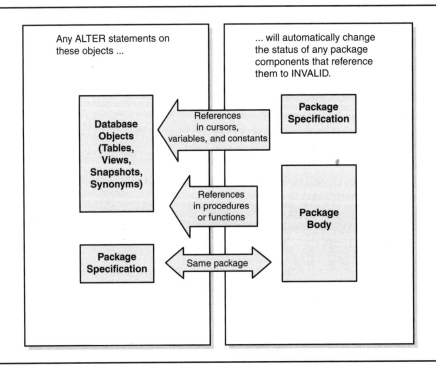

FIGURE 4-2. *Events that flag package components as INVALID*

Notice in the figure that there is no change you can make to a package body that will cause the package specification to be INVALID. Issuing an ALTER statement to the package body will either successfully compile the package body or not, but it will have no effect on the package specification.

On the other hand, any change to the code in a package specification always requires a recompilation of the entire package, both the package specification and the package body.

Furthermore, any changes to database objects that the package specification or the package body reference will always require an ALTER statement to recompile the INVALID package specification or package body.

For example, consider the following package specification:

```
PACKAGE reservations AS
  CURSOR cur_cruises IS
    SELECT CRUISE_ID, CRUISE_NAME
    FROM    CRUISES;
  v_guest_id GUESTS.GUEST_ID%TYPE;
  PROCEDURE book_cruise (p_cruise_id NUMBER, p_guest_id NUMBER);
END reservations;
```

Now see Figure 4-3. This figure demonstrates what happens when you do the following:

1. Create a package specification for reservations that references database objects—in this example, there are two: the table CRUISES and the table GUESTS.

2. Inspect the data dictionary and observe that the package specification is VALID.

3. Issue an ALTER statement on one of the referenced database objects in this example, a change that doesn't have any logical impact on the code of the package specification.

4. Inspect the data dictionary and observe that the package specification is now INVALID.

The reason the package specification is INVALID is not because of any problem with the specification. However, as is the case with procedures and functions, any package specification that references a database object that becomes the subject of an ALTER statement is flagged as INVALID. At this point, in order to restore the package specification to a status of VALID, issue the following command:

```
ALTER PACKAGE reservations COMPILE;
```

```
± Oracle SQL*Plus                              _ □ X
File  Edit  Search  Options  Help
SQL> CREATE OR REPLACE PACKAGE reservations
  2  AS
  3    CURSOR cur_cruises IS
  4      SELECT CRUISE_ID, CRUISE_NAME
  5      FROM   CRUISES;
  6    v_guest_id GUESTS.GUEST_ID%TYPE;
  7    PROCEDURE book_cruise
  8      (p_cruise_id NUMBER,
  9       p_guest_id NUMBER);
 10  END reservations;
 11  /

Package created.

SQL>
SQL> SELECT OBJECT_TYPE, STATUS
  2  FROM   USER_OBJECTS
  3  WHERE  OBJECT_NAME = 'RESERVATIONS';

OBJECT_TYPE        STATUS
------------------ -------
PACKAGE            VALID

SQL>
SQL> ALTER TABLE GUESTS
  2       MODIFY LAST_NAME VARCHAR2(30);

Table altered.

SQL>
SQL> SELECT OBJECT_TYPE, STATUS
  2  FROM   USER_OBJECTS
  3  WHERE  OBJECT_NAME = 'RESERVATIONS';

OBJECT_TYPE        STATUS
------------------ -------
PACKAGE            INVALID

SQL> |
```

FIGURE 4-3. *The impact of altering a package specification's dependent objects*

This will recompile the package specification. Now consider the following package body:

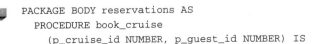

```
PACKAGE BODY reservations AS
  PROCEDURE book_cruise
    (p_cruise_id NUMBER, p_guest_id NUMBER) IS
```

```
  BEGIN
    INSERT INTO GUEST_BOOKINGS
      (GUEST_BOOKING_ID, GUEST_ID, CRUISE_ID, BOOKING_DATE)
      VALUES
      (SEQ_GUEST_BOOKING_ID.NEXTVAL,
       p_guest_id, p_cruise_id, SYSDATE);
    COMMIT;
  END book_cruise;
END reservations;
```

This is the package body for the reservations package specification we created earlier. Once this package has been successfully stored in the database, observe what happens next in Figure 4-4. In this figure, we do the following:

1. Inspect the data dictionary to observe that both the package specification and the package body are VALID.

2. Re-execute the same code that created with package specification, unchanged.

3. Inspect the data dictionary to observe that the package specification is VALID but that now the package body is INVALID.

No change has been made to the package specification that requires a change to the body. Nevertheless, the package body requires recompilation.

As is the case with procedures, a call to the package body's constructs will force an automatic attempt to recompile the package. If successful, the package body construct will be invoked successfully. If not, an error message will indicate that the package body has errors.

Note that simply issuing an ALTER statement on the package specification will not necessarily change the corresponding package body status to INVALID.

Dropping a Package

You have two options when dropping a package. The following statement will remove the package body reservations from the database:

```
DROP PACKAGE BODY RESERVATIONS;
```

This statement will remove the package body, but will leave the package specification in the database. Furthermore, the package specification for reservations will still be VALID.

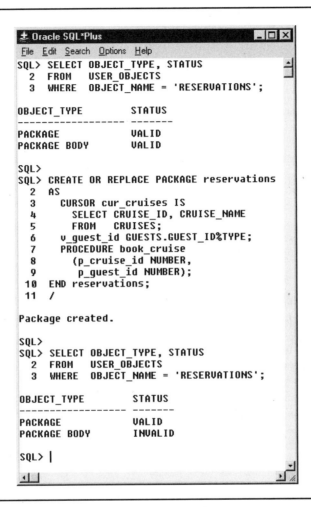

FIGURE 4-4. *The impact of altering a package body's dependent objects*

The following statement will remove the entire package:

```
DROP PACKAGE RESERVATIONS;
```

The result of issuing this statement to the database will be the complete removal of both the package specification and the package body from the database.

Dropping a package will cause any other program units that reference the package to be flagged with a status of INVALID.

Changes to a Package Specification that Require a Change to the Body

Some changes that you make to a package specification will require a corresponding change to the package body. These are changes to the constructs that must be identical in both parts. In a given package, the following constructs must be identical in both the package specification and the package body:

- Public procedure and public function names
- Parameter names, datatypes, and default values of public procedures and functions
- Public function return datatypes
- Cursor headers of public cursors whose SELECT statements are defined in the package body

In short, all information that is common between the package specification and the package body must be identical. The driving force in this relationship is the package specification. Any differences between the two parts of the package will result in the package body being flagged as INVALID.

For Review

1. To create a package body, use the CREATE . . . PACKAGE BODY statement. To create the package specification, use the CREATE . . . PACKAGE statement. The optional reserved words OR REPLACE may be used here as well. Note that there is no reserved word SPECIFICATION in this statement.

2. The package specification declares the minimum amount of information required for developers to invoke the constructs in the package. The package body includes the source code of all procedures and functions that were declared in the package specification.

3. To recompile a package, use the ALTER PACKAGE . . . COMPILE statement to recompile an entire package, or the ALTER PACKAGE . . . COMPILE BODY statement to recompile only the package body. Use the DROP PACKAGE or the DROP PACKAGE BODY statement to remove the entire package, or just the package body, from the database.

Exercises

1. **Consider the following package body:**

```
PACKAGE BODY maintenance AS
   c_starting_time CONSTANT CLEANING_SCHEDULE.START_TIME%TYPE := 9;
END maintenance;
```

Assuming that any referenced or related objects are valid, which of the following statements about this code is true? (Choose all that apply.)

A. The constant declaration is invalid.

B. The constant c_starting_time is a private construct.

C. The datatype for the constant is invalid.

D. The package body is invalid.

2. **You attempt to execute the following statements:**

```
CREATE OR REPLACE PACKAGE cleanup AS
  PROCEDURE purge_records;
END cleanup;
/
CREATE OR REPLACE PACKAGE BODY cleanup AS
  PROCEDURE purge_records IS
  BEGIN
    IF (TO_CHAR(SYSDATE,'DAY') = c_cleanup_day)
    THEN DELETE ERRORS;
    END IF;
  END purge_records;
  c_cleanup_day CONSTANT VARCHAR2(3) := 'SAT';
END cleanup;
/
```

Assuming that any referenced database objects are valid, which of the following statements is true? (Choose all that apply.)

A. The package will be stored in the database with a status of VALID.

B. The package body will not compile because you cannot have a CONSTANT declared outside of the procedure.

C. The package body will not compile because you cannot reference a private construct from within purge_records until after it's been declared.

D. The package body will not compile because the CONSTANT needs to be defined in the package specification, not the package body.

Answer Key

1. B. 2. C.

Invoking Packaged Constructs

Packages themselves are never directly invoked or executed. Instead, the constructs contained within the package are invoked. For example, procedures and functions within the package are executed. Other constructs in the package, such as constants and other declared constructs, can be referenced from within other PL/SQL programs, in the same manner that those program units could refer to their own locally declared PL/SQL program constructs.

This section addresses public constructs, meaning those constructs that are declared in the package specification. Constructs that are declared in the package body are private and are unavailable for reference from outside of the package.

Referencing Packaged Constructs

To call upon any construct of a package, simply use the package name as a prefix to the construct name. For example, to reference a procedure with no parameters called increase_wages that is stored in a package called hr, use this reference:

```
hr.increase_wages;
```

All packaged constructs are invoked in the same fashion: by including the package name as a prefix, with a period separating the package name and the construct name. This notation is often referred to as *dot notation*. It's the same format used to refer to database objects that are owned by a schema.

For example, if you have a package called assumptions that defines a public constant called tax_rate, you could use it this way in an expression:

```
v_full_price := v_pre_tax * (1 + assumptions.tax_rate);
```

Dot notation is required for references to any packaged constructs from outside of the package. However, although references to constructs from within the same package will accept dot notation, they do not require it.

Using Packaged Constructs

For the purpose of reviewing the rules of using packaged constructs, let's consider all constructs to be in either of two categories: packaged program units, meaning procedures and functions, and global constructs, meaning packaged variables, constants, cursors, exceptions, and types.

Packaged Program Units

The same rules apply to the use of packaged procedures and functions that apply to stand-alone procedures and functions. In other words, packaged procedures must be called from a single statement, whereas packaged functions must be called from within an expression, just like stand-alone PL/SQL stored functions. Parameters may be passed by positional notation or by named notation.

For example, the following PL/SQL block executes a packaged procedure:

```
BEGIN
  pack_finance.proc_reconcile_invoice(p_status => 'ACTIVE');
END;
/
```

The previous code sample executes a procedure called proc_reconcile_invoice in the package pack_finance. It also passes a parameter value using the by reference notation. If the package does not exist, then PL/SQL will produce the error message:

```
PLS-00201: identifier 'PACK_FINANCE.PROC_RECONCILE_INVOICE' must be declared
```

Furthermore, if the package exists but the procedure isn't stored within it, then PL/SQL will produce the error message:

```
PLS-00302: construct 'PROC_RECONCILE_INVOICE' must be declared
```

In short, valid packaged procedures and functions are invoked the same way as stand-alone stored procedures and functions.

Packaged Global Constructs

Packaged global constructs generally behave the same as their locally defined counterparts, with one dramatic difference: Their declaration is global to the user sessions.

Consider the following code sample:

```
PACKAGE rates AS
  bonus NUMBER(3,2);
END rates;
```

This package specification defines a single variable, bonus. Once this package is stored in the database, the variable rates.bonus is now a global variable to the user session. For an example of what can now be done with this global construct, see Figure 4-5.

In this figure, there are three separate autonomous PL/SQL anonymous blocks, each of which can reference the global construct without declaring anything. Furthermore, the global construct retains its value across blocks. This is, after all,

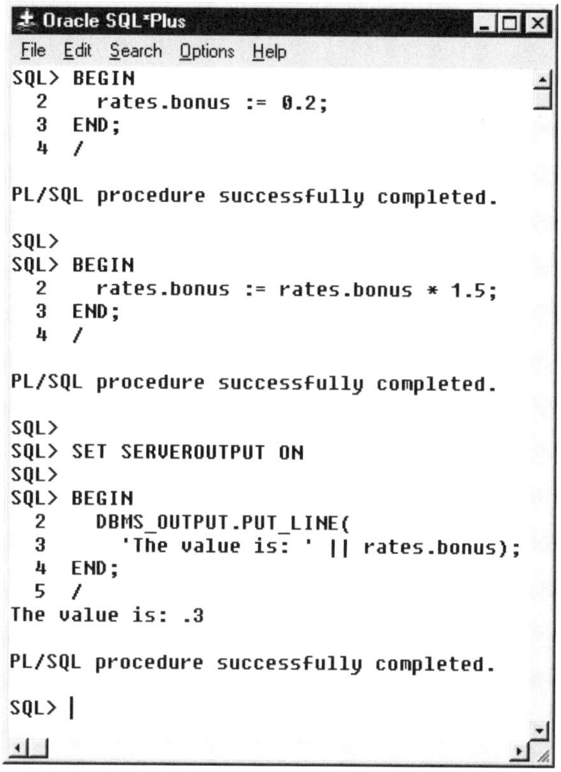

```
Oracle SQL*Plus                              _ □ ×
File  Edit  Search  Options  Help
SQL> BEGIN
  2     rates.bonus := 0.2;
  3   END;
  4   /

PL/SQL procedure successfully completed.

SQL>
SQL> BEGIN
  2     rates.bonus := rates.bonus * 1.5;
  3   END;
  4   /

PL/SQL procedure successfully completed.

SQL>
SQL> SET SERVEROUTPUT ON
SQL>
SQL> BEGIN
  2     DBMS_OUTPUT.PUT_LINE(
  3       'The value is: ' || rates.bonus);
  4   END;
  5   /
The value is: .3

PL/SQL procedure successfully completed.

SQL> |
```

FIGURE 4-5.   *Separate PL/SQL blocks referencing a global construct*

what a global construct does. Until the user session is terminated, the global construct will continue to retain its value. Once the user session is restarted, the global construct will restart at its value as declared in the package, which in this case is NULL.

This same global behavior is found in all of the other packaged constructs, such as constants, exceptions, and cursors. A globally declared cursor can be opened in one PL/SQL block, fetched in another, and closed in still another. User-defined exceptions that are declared in a package specification can be raised with the PL/SQL RAISE statement in any PL/SQL block and handled in the exception section of another calling block, without any declarations—the package specification has already declared the construct for the user session.

For example, consider the following package specification:

```
PACKAGE rates AS
  CURSOR cur_cruises IS
    SELECT CRUISE_ID, CRUISE_NAME
    FROM    CRUISES;
END rates;
```

This package specification declares a global cursor cur_cruises. Now consider Figure 4-6.

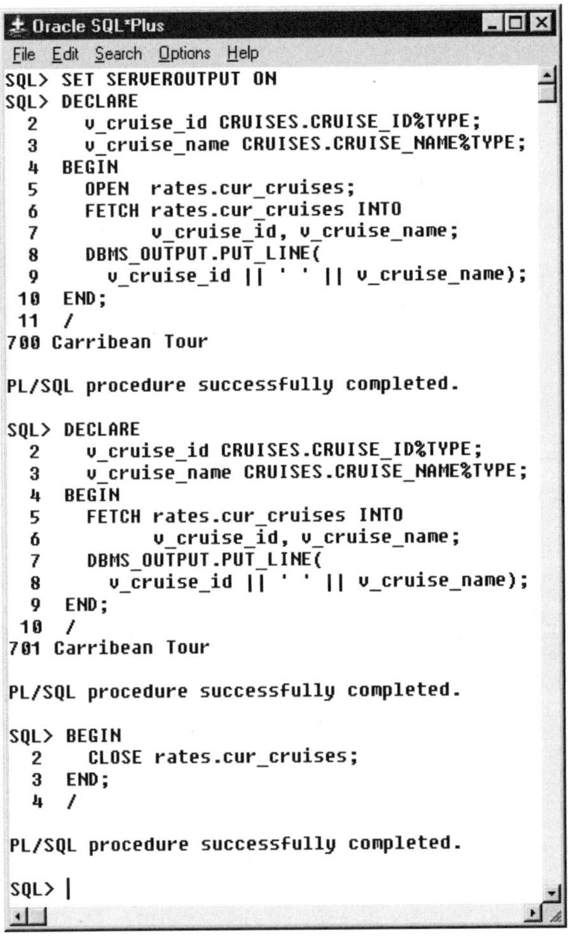

```
Oracle SQL*Plus                                    _ □ X
File  Edit  Search  Options  Help
SQL> SET SERVEROUTPUT ON
SQL> DECLARE
  2      v_cruise_id CRUISES.CRUISE_ID%TYPE;
  3      v_cruise_name CRUISES.CRUISE_NAME%TYPE;
  4  BEGIN
  5    OPEN  rates.cur_cruises;
  6    FETCH rates.cur_cruises INTO
  7          v_cruise_id, v_cruise_name;
  8    DBMS_OUTPUT.PUT_LINE(
  9      v_cruise_id || ' ' || v_cruise_name);
 10  END;
 11  /
700 Carribean Tour

PL/SQL procedure successfully completed.

SQL> DECLARE
  2      v_cruise_id CRUISES.CRUISE_ID%TYPE;
  3      v_cruise_name CRUISES.CRUISE_NAME%TYPE;
  4  BEGIN
  5    FETCH rates.cur_cruises INTO
  6          v_cruise_id, v_cruise_name;
  7    DBMS_OUTPUT.PUT_LINE(
  8      v_cruise_id || ' ' || v_cruise_name);
  9  END;
 10  /
701 Carribean Tour

PL/SQL procedure successfully completed.

SQL> BEGIN
  2      CLOSE rates.cur_cruises;
  3  END;
  4  /

PL/SQL procedure successfully completed.

SQL> |
```

FIGURE 4-6. *Separate PL/SQL anonymous blocks referencing a global cursor*

In the figure, one PL/SQL block opens and fetches the first row from the global cursor. A separate block performs another fetch, and a final block closes the cursor. Each reference to the cursor requires the package name prefix, using dot notation, but the continuity of the global cursor transcends each block.

We will explore this topic in more depth in the section "Persistent States" in Chapter 6.

For Review

1. Packaged constructs that are referenced from outside of the package must be called with the package name, followed by a period, followed by the construct name. The same dot notation works from within the package, but is not required—the construct name alone is sufficient from within the package.

2. Packaged program units, such as procedures and functions, behave the same as stand-alone program units.

3. Packaged global constructs, such as variables and cursors, are global to the user session.

Exercises

1. **You have created a package specification that declares a constant. Where can this constant now be referenced? (Choose all that apply.)**

    A. An anonymous block

    B. The same package where it's been declared

    C. A stored function

    D. A stored procedure

2. **You have created a package body that declares a variable. What can now be said of this variable? (Choose all that apply.)**

    A. It can be referenced from within another package.

    B. It is a global construct.

    C. Its value is retained throughout the user session.

    D. None of the above.

Answer Key

1. A, B, C, D. 2. D. (Trick question: Remember, variables declared in the package body are private.)

Data Dictionary Resources for Packages

The same data dictionary views that are used to monitor procedures and functions are used for packages. The most important factor to keep in mind when working with packages is that the data dictionary keeps track of a package as two objects: the package specification and the package body. Most data dictionary views have a column called TYPE, or something similar (the USER_OBJECTS view calls its column OBJECT_TYPE), where the type of object is indicated. A package specification is always identified with a type of PACKAGE, and a package body is always identified with a type of PACKAGE BODY.

The data dictionary views USER_DEPENDENCIES, USER_OBJECT_SIZE, USER_SOURCE, and USER_ERRORS all have a TYPE column, and USER_OBJECTS has the OBJECT_TYPE column.

When querying these data dictionary views for information about packages, be sure to include a WHERE clause like this:

```
WHERE TYPE = 'PACKAGE'
```

or like this

```
WHERE TYPE = 'PACKAGE BODY'
```

For example, consider the view USER_SOURCE. This view is where you will find the entire source code for both the package specification and the package body. To differentiate between them, consider the following query:

```
SELECT    TEXT
FROM      USER_SOURCE
WHERE     NAME = 'RATES'
   AND    TYPE = 'PACKAGE'
ORDER BY  LINE;
```

This query will produce the package specification code for a package called rates. Note that the value for NAME will always be stored in the database in uppercase, regardless of how it's created. (This is true for all data dictionary objects.)

To see the package body, use this query:

```
SELECT    TEXT
FROM      USER_SOURCE
WHERE     NAME = 'RATES'
   AND    TYPE = 'PACKAGE BODY'
ORDER BY  LINE;
```

The procedures and functions contained within the package are not recognized as separate objects. In other words, if you have created a set of stored procedures and functions, and then later choose to create a package that contains these procedures and functions, you will still have the old procedures and functions as separate objects in the database until you explicitly *drop* them. The individual procedures and functions that are stored within the package are not recognized as separate objects; instead, the data dictionary recognizes only the two objects of the package specification and the package body.

For Review

1. Package specifications are identified in the data dictionary with an OBJECT_TYPE of PACKAGE. Package bodies are identified with an OBJECT_TYPE of PACKAGE BODY.

2. The same data dictionary views used for procedures and functions are used with packages. Package names, as with all object names, are stored in the data dictionary in uppercase letters.

Exercises

1. **You have created a package, both the specification and the body, which contains three procedures and two functions. How many new entries exist in the USER_OBJECTS data dictionary view as a result?**

   A. 1

   B. 2

   C. 5

   D. 6

2. **Where can you find the source code for a package body?**

   A. USER_CODE

   B. USER_OBJECTS

   C. USER_SOURCE

   D. USER_TEXT

Answer Key

1. B. 2. C.

Chapter Summary

Packages are a type of PL/SQL program unit that lets you combine multiple constructs under a single name. Packages can contain procedures and functions, as well as variables, constants, cursors, exceptions, and types. These various constructs of the package can be either public or private. Public constructs are recognized by PL/SQL code outside of the package. Private constructs are only available for use from within the package and are generally used to support the procedures and functions.

The package has two parts: the specification and the body. In the specification, you declare the publicly known information about the package, such as the names of global constructs, or the procedure and function headers. In the body, you define the entire code for procedures and functions that are declared in the specification, as well as any private constructs you want to include. In order to create a package that's recognized by the database, you must define the specification as a minimum. You can even define a package as a specification and never create a corresponding body—for example, a collection of global constructs, such as variable and constants, does not require a package body.

Any reference to the package should include the package name as a prefix, followed by a dot, and then the name of the packaged construct. This is required for references to packaged constructs from outside of the package; from within the package, dot notation is optional.

When a package construct is invoked, the entire package is loaded into the SGA, which yields performance improvements for any future calls to other constructs that are contained within the same package. Compared to stand-alone stored procedures and functions, the use of packages is considered good design purely from a performance consideration. However, the benefit of being able to logically collect various constructs into one place is also considered good design. Finally, packages are the only mechanism that PL/SQL offers to create global constructs.

When any object upon which a package depends is altered, the package is flagged as INVALID and must be recompiled. However, note that the package specification and the package body are seen in the data dictionary as two different objects. The OBJECT_TYPE of the package specification is PACKAGE, and the OBJECT_TYPE of the package body is PACKAGE BODY. Both have their own STATUS values, and it's possible for the specification to be VALID while the body is INVALID. This can happen if the package body has been created and stored in the data dictionary, but the specification is re-created with the CREATE OR REPLACE PACKAGE . . . command. To recompile the package body, the ALTER PACKAGE . . . COMPILE BODY statement can be issued, or a simple invocation of any packaged construct can also automatically cause the package body to be recompiled. If the recompilation is successful, the packaged construct call will be able to successfully invoke the construct. Otherwise, it will require code modifications to the body.

The specification and the body of a package share the same procedure and function names, parameter names, parameter datatypes, and in the case of the function, the same return datatype. These must be identical for public procedures and functions; if they are not, then the package body will be flagged as INVALID.

Two-Minute Drill

- You create a package specification with the CREATE PACKAGE package_name AS statement. The statement ends with END and can optionally repeat the name of the package after the word END, as in END package_name.

- You can optionally use OR REPLACE.

- The reserved word AS is interchangeable with the reserved word IS.

- In the package specification, between the reserved words AS and END, are the declared constructs, which include variables, constants, cursors, user-defined exceptions, types, procedure headers, and function headers. No procedure or function code is included in the package specification; instead, the specification includes only enough information to enable developers using your package to know how to use the packaged procedures and functions.

- You create the package body with the CREATE PACKAGE BODY package_name AS statement with the option of OR REPLACE. Here, you can also optionally repeat the package name after the END word.

- Declared constructs in the package specification are considered public. Constructs that are only declared in the package body and not in the package specification are considered private.

- Either the package specification or the package body can have a status of VALID or INVALID. If either is INVALID, then the package needs to be recompiled with the ALTER PACKAGE . . . COMPILE statement and may require editing. If only the package body is invalid, you may recompile only the package body with the ALTER PACKAGE . . . COMPILE BODY statement.

- If the ALTER statement is issued against any database objects that the package references, then the package will be flagged as INVALID and must be recompiled.

- You can drop a package body with the DROP PACKAGE BODY command. You can drop the entire package with the DROP PACKAGE statement. You cannot drop the specification and keep the body.

- A global construct declared in a package specification can be referenced in other PL/SQL named program units and anonymous blocks. The constructs are global to the user session. For example, a variable that is assigned a value in one PL/SQL block will retain that value after the block concludes and another block executes. The value may be accessed in the subsequent autonomous PL/SQL blocks.

- Global cursors declared in a package specification can be opened in one block and fetched in another.

Chapter Questions

1. **The database contains a package called marketing, but it does not contain any program units called update_status. However, there is a procedure stored in the database called update_status that isn't part of any package. Now, consider the following code sample:**

```
CREATE OR REPLACE PROCEDURE daily_batch
IS
BEGIN
  marketing.update_status;
END;
/
```

   What will happen when you attempt to execute this code?

   A. PL/SQL will store the procedure, but it will produce an error message.

   B. PL/SQL will store the procedure and will not produce an error message. However, upon execution of daily_batch, an error message will display.

   C. PL/SQL will store the procedure and will not produce an error message. Furthermore, upon the attempt to execute the procedure daily_batch, PL/SQL will find the program unit update_status in the package marketing, and when it doesn't find update_status in marketing, it will execute the update_status procedure stored in the database.

   D. PL/SQL will store the procedure and will not produce an error message. Furthermore, upon execution of daily_batch, there will be no error message.

2. **What is the minimum required set of parts you must create to a build a valid package? (Choose all that apply.)**

   A. A package specification

   B. A package body

C. A package specification and a package body

D. A package construct

3. **Assume the following package is stored in the database:**

```
PACKAGE warehouse
AS
  CURSOR cur_inventory IS
    SELECT INVENTORY_ID, INVENTORY, QUANTITY
    FROM   INVENTORY;
  rec_inventory cur_inventory%ROWTYPE;
END warehouse;
```

Now consider the following anonymous PL/SQL block #1:

```
BEGIN
  OPEN warehouse.cur_inventory;
END;
```

Finally, consider the anonymous PL/SQL block #2:

```
BEGIN
  FETCH warehouse.cur_inventory INTO
        warehouse.rec_inventory;
END;
```

You execute the anonymous PL/SQL block #1. Assuming you stay logged in to the same user session, what is the result after you execute PL/SQL block #2? (Choose all that apply.)

A. ORA-01001: invalid cursor

B. ORA-06510: PL/SQL: unhandled exception

C. PL/SQL procedure successfully completed

D. ERROR at line 1

4. **Consider the following code sample:**

```
CREATE OR REPLACE PACKAGE SPECIFICATION acct
IS
  PROCEDURE make_entry(debit IN BOOLEAN, credit IN BOOLEAN, amt IN
NUMBER);
  PROCEDURE remove_entry(entry_id NUMBER);
  PROCEDURE balance_books;
END acct;
/
```

When you submit this code to the database, what will be the result?

A. The package specification will be stored in the data dictionary with a status of INVALID. The package will not be successfully created.

B. The package specification will be successfully created but unable to be used because of the BOOLEAN parameters in some of the procedures.

C. The package specification will be successfully created but unable to be used because the package body has not yet been created.

D. The package specification will be successfully created, and other program units that reference this package can now be successfully compiled.

5. **Consider the following package specification:**

```
PACKAGE budget_parameters
AS
  PROCEDURE SET_RATIO(ratio_id NUMBER, ratio_value VARCHAR2);
  FUNCTION  GET_RATIO(ratio_id NUMBER)
  RETURN VARCHAR2;
END budget_parameters;
```

You have already stored the complete package, including the previous specification and the appropriate package body, in the database and successfully created the package. You have logged off and logged back into the system. You then invoke the packaged function budget_parameters.get_ratio. Which of the following statements is now true? (Choose all that apply.)

A. The package specification is in the SGA but not the body.

B. The procedure set_ratio can now be executed, but it could not have been executed before the call to function get_ratio.

C. The portion of the package body containing the procedure set_ratio is in the SGA but not the rest of the package.

D. The call to the procedure set_ratio will now execute faster than it would have were the procedure set_ratio stored as a stand-alone procedure.

6. **Which of the following queries produces a listing of the package specification of mkt?**

A. SELECT TEXT FROM USER_SOURCE WHERE NAME = 'mkt' AND TYPE = 'PACKAGE SPECIFICATION' ORDER BY LINE;

B. SELECT TEXT FROM USER_SOURCE WHERE NAME = 'MKT' AND TYPE = 'PACKAGE SPECIFICATION' ORDER BY LINE;

C. SELECT TEXT FROM USER_SOURCE WHERE NAME = 'MKT' AND TYPE = 'PACKAGE' ORDER BY LINE;

D. SELECT TEXT FROM USER_SOURCE WHERE NAME = 'mkt' AND TYPE = 'PACKAGE' ORDER BY LINE;

7. Consider the following code:

```
PACKAGE accounting AS
  ex_overbooked EXCEPTION;
END accounting;
```

The exception accounting.ex_overbooked is a

A. Public local exception

B. Public global exception

C. Private local exception

D. Private global exception

8. Consider the following code:

```
BEGIN
  OPEN rates.cur_ledger;
END;
/
```

Assuming that rates is a valid stored package and that this code block successfully executes, which of the following statements is now true? (Choose all that apply.)

A. cur_ledger is a public local construct.

B. cur_ledger is opened, but closes automatically when the previous sample anonymous block concludes execution.

C. The cursor is now open and available for FETCH statements in other program units.

D. cur_ledger is a private global construct.

9. Consider the following code:

```
PACKAGE limits AS
  upper_bound NUMBER(3) := 10;
  PROCEDURE initialize;
END limits;
```

```
PACKAGE BODY limits AS
  PROCEDURE initialize IS
  BEGIN
    upper_bound := 25;
  END initialize;
END limits;
```

Assume the package specification and package body for limits is stored in the database. Now consider the following code block:

```
BEGIN
  DBMS_OUTPUT.PUT_LINE(limits.upper_bound);
END;
/
```

You have just logged into the database and issued a SET SERVEROUTPUT ON command. The next action you perform is to execute this block. What is the result?

A. 10

B. 25

C. NULL

D. PLS-00201: identifier 'LIMITS.UPPER_BOUND' must be declared

10. **Assuming you have a package called front_office, which of the following statements are valid? (Choose all that apply.)**

   A. DROP PACKAGE FRONT_OFFICE COMPILE

   B. DROP PACKAGE SPECIFICATION FRONT_OFFICE

   C. DROP PACKAGE BODY FRONT_OFFICE

   D. DROP PACKAGE FRONT_OFFICE CASCADE

Answers to Chapter Questions

   1. A.   PL/SQL will store the procedure, but it will produce an error message.

Explanation   The packaged construct marketing.update_status must exist in order for the CREATE . . . PROCEDURE daily_batch statement to execute successfully. As is always the case, the daily_batch procedure will be stored in the data dictionary regardless of the status of the daily_batch procedure. In this case, the daily_batch procedure will be given a status of INVALID. The existance of any stand-alone update_status procedure is irrelevant.

2. A. A package specification

Explanation To create a complete package, it is possible to simply create a package specification. As long as the specification doesn't declare any procedures or functions but instead declares constructs, such as variables, constants, user-defined exceptions, cursors, and the like, then a package body is not needed.

3. C. PL/SQL procedure successfully completed

Explanation The packaged cursor is a construct that is global to the user session. Provided that the same user is logged on, then when PL/SQL block #2 executes, it recognizes that the cursor is already open, even though it was opened as a result of the previous PL/SQL block #1's execution.

4. A. The package specification will be stored in the data dictionary with a status of INVALID. The package will not be successfully created.

Explanation The word SPECIFICATION is not acceptable in the header of the package and will produce a compilation error. However, the error will be misleading—the compiler will assume that SPECIFICATION is the name of your package and will fail to recognize the intended name of the package, which in this example is acct. Once the word SPECIFICATION is removed from this code, the package specification will compile accurately and can be used to write other program units that reference these packaged constructs. The other program units will compile correctly, but they will not successfully execute until the package body for acct is created.

5. D. The call to the procedure set_ratio will now execute faster than it would have were the procedure set_ratio stored as a stand-alone procedure.

Explanation Any call to any packaged construct has the effect of loading all the packaged constructs for that package into the SGA, thus causing all future calls to those constructs to execute faster than they would have if the individual procedures and functions were stored on their own as stand-alone program units.

6. C. SELECT TEXT FROM USER_SOURCE WHERE NAME = 'MKT' AND TYPE='PACKAGE' ORDER BY LINE

Explanation All object names are stored in the data dictionary in uppercase letters, and packages are indicated with a type of PACKAGE. There is no type of PACKAGE SPECIFICATION.

7. B. Public global exception

Explanation Because the exception is declared in a package as a separate construct (as opposed to being defined within the definition of a packaged procedure or packaged function), it is inherently public. Furthermore, because it is defined within the package specification, it is public. If it were declared in the package body, it would be private.

8. C.   The cursor is now open and available for FETCH statements in other program units.

Explanation   The cur_ledger construct is a public global construct and is a cursor. As such, it can be opened in one block, fetched in another, and closed in still another block.

9. A.   10

Explanation   Although the procedure initialize will change the value of the variable to 25, it will only do that once the procedure is executed. In the meantime, the public global variable upper_bound has the value of 10.

10. C.   DROP PACKAGE BODY FRONT_OFFICE

Explanation   There is no DROP PACKAGE SPECIFICATION command, and the reserved words COMPILE and CASCADE aren't relevant to the DROP statement. The command DROP PACKAGE BODY FRONT_OFFICE will remove the package body from the package front_office and leave the package specification alone.

CHAPTER
5

Triggers

riggers are one of the more unusual PL/SQL program units. A trigger is attached to a single database object, such as a table, view, schema, or the actual database. A trigger executes (or fires, as we say with triggers) in response to some predetermined event, such as an attempt to delete a record from a table, or a system event. Triggers can respond to a series of predetermined events on particular database objects in various combinations. They are not invoked by name. Triggers provide a tremendous power to enforce business rules right at the heart of the database, establishing something of a last line of defense for data, no matter who or what attempts to access the data from anywhere on the network.

In this chapter, you will review and understand the following topics:

- Uses of triggers

- Creating, altering, and dropping triggers

- Enabling and disabling triggers

- INSTEAD OF triggers

- Non-Data Manipulation Language (DML) triggers

- Data dictionary resources for triggers

Uses of Triggers

Triggers are the last line of defense in the database. With their ability to be associated directly with database objects, such as a table, triggers provide the capability of placing PL/SQL code between, for example, a table's data, and any user or process anywhere on the network that attempts to perform INSERT, UPDATE, or DELETE in that table. With their ability to intercept incoming data, triggers can actually be used to modify or filter changes to the database in real time and even stop attempts to modify data. Triggers can accomplish this without the knowledge or permission of the user or process that attempts the change. As such, we do not execute triggers by directly invoking them. Instead, triggers are fired automatically in response to other events that we cause to occur. Triggers can be designed to fire in response to (a) DML statements on tables or views, such as INSERT, UPDATE, or DELETE, (b) DDL statements and system events for a given schema, and (c) system events on the database.

By capturing incoming DML events on a table, a trigger can provide complex default values for one or more columns in a table. Triggers can perform validation checks that involve queries on other tables or any combination of PL/SQL statements for verification and validation. Triggers can block attempts to modify table data for any logical reason you choose, using the full power of PL/SQL processing to define the appropriate business rules you require. Triggers can be used to secretly track details of your choosing, by performing inserts into some audit table for every change performed on the trigger's assigned table.

Triggers can be attached to a database view for the purpose of transforming a view into an object that more closely resembles a table than it otherwise would. In other words, a trigger or a set of triggers attached to a given view can provide the view with custom-designed reactions to attempts to INSERT, UPDATE, or DELETE any record of the view. Non-updateable views can be made updateable with triggers. This is a powerful feature that opens up a tremendous potential with view objects that wouldn't exist otherwise.

Triggers can also be associated with system-level events, such as logging on or off the system, or an attempt to create a table within a given schema. These system-level triggers exist at a higher level than individual database objects; yet they still provide custom-defined performance capabilities that are tailored to business rules of your choosing.

Because triggers are designed to react to a variety of events in the database, the code you place in a trigger has a few restrictions to prevent it from conflicting with the events that may have fired the trigger. Triggers that are fired in response to a particular transaction, for example, may customize certain behaviors within that transaction, and even block the transaction from happening entirely, but are restricted from performing certain actions that run the risk of inadvertently compromising the integrity of the changes being performed by the transaction.

In short, triggers enable you to program a unique database environment that will respond to any process's attempt to interact with a given schema or database object, regardless of who or what on the network performs that interaction. This last line of defense provides powerful customization capabilities that don't exist anywhere else in the database.

For Review

1. Triggers can be associated with tables, views, or system level events.

2. Triggers are PL/SQL blocks that will fire in response to these events without any particular prompting from the user.

3. Triggers have some restrictions against what they can and cannot do, depending on what event fired the trigger.

Exercises

1. **Which of the following events can you not customize with a trigger?**

   A. INSERT statements on a given table

   B. SET PAUSE ON

    C. CREATE TABLE within a given schema

    D. DELETE . . . CASCADE CONSTRAINTS on a given view

2. **Which of the following statements is not true of a trigger?**

    A. Triggers can stop a DML statement from executing on a particular table.

    B. Triggers can include any valid PL/SQL statement at any time.

    C. Triggers can change incoming data in an UPDATE statement on a given table.

    D. Triggers can change a non-updateable view to an updateable view.

Answer Key
1. B. 2. B.

Creating, Altering, and Dropping Triggers

The ability to create triggers requires the procedural extension to the Oracle database installation in which you are working. If this hasn't been installed, then log into the SYS account and execute the file CATPROC.SQL from the SYS schema.

The syntax to create a database trigger is more involved than the syntax required for other program units. When you create a database trigger, you must declare (a) the name of the trigger, (b) the event or events that will fire the trigger, (c) the trigger timing, and (d) the trigger level.

The syntax to ALTER or DROP triggers is pretty straightforward and is similar to the syntax of other program units.

Note that triggers do not take parameters per se. However, triggers that are fired by INSERT or UPDATE statements have the ability to reference the new incoming data. By default, the :new prefix is used to reference new incoming data. In the case of UPDATE and DELETE statements, the trigger can reference the old information that is being updated or deleted using the :old prefix.

Each trigger you create must be less than or equal to 32K in size. Therefore, if your trigger requires a significant amount of code, you should create the bulk of your code in a separate program unit, such as a stored procedure, and call the procedure from within your trigger.

Creating Triggers

The syntax to create a trigger is as follows:

```
CREATE [OR REPLACE] TRIGGER trigger_name
  [BEFORE | AFTER | INSTEAD OF] database_event
  [REFERENCING [OLD AS old_name] [NEW AS new_name]]
  trigger_level
  [WHEN criteria]
BEGIN
  trigger_body
END;
```

As you can see, there is much more to creating a trigger than we've seen with other program units. Each trigger component requires some discussion and is addressed in the following subsections.

Trigger Names

This is a name you create for the trigger, which you must provide. The name must obey the rules for naming database objects. You must choose a name that will be unique within the schema—in other words, even though a trigger is attached to one and only one table, it cannot have the same name as a trigger attached to another table within the same schema. (Remember that a schema is the user ID.) Trigger names are used to identify the trigger in the data dictionary but are not used to invoke the trigger.

Triggers can be given the same name as an existing procedure, function, or package within the same schema, although this is not considered good design.

BEFORE, AFTER, INSTEAD OF, and the database_ event

This clause is required and will define the event that will fire the trigger, which means that the trigger will automatically execute in reaction to this event. The *database_event* must define a valid SQL event, such as INSERT ON CUSTOMERS, that names an SQL event and a specific database object by name.

Database events for DML triggers are either INSERT, UPDATE, or DELETE. A SELECT statement is not enabled; a SELECT statement will never fire a trigger. (Later in this chapter, we'll look at some new triggers that can be attached to DDL events.)

BEFORE database_event or AFTER database_event can be used only with database events on tables. For example, BEFORE INSERT ON CUSTOMERS or AFTER UPDATE OR DELETE ON EMPLOYEES. A single trigger can only use BEFORE or AFTER; you cannot use both BEFORE and AFTER in a single trigger. To create code that will fire in response to both events, you must create two triggers. On the other hand, a single trigger can apply to any or all of the three DML events of INSERT, UPDATE, or DELETE. Use the reserved word OR to separate the choices.

For example, BEFORE INSERT OR UPDATE OR DELETE ON GUEST_BOOKINGS. The database event must be for one and only one table.

In the case of UPDATE triggers only, you can optionally include a column list. This will cause the trigger to fire only in the event that a particular column from the list is updated, and if a column is updated that is not in the list, the trigger will not fire. Here is an example:

```
CREATE OR REPLACE TRIGGER trig_audit_bookings
BEFORE UPDATE OF GUEST_ID, PAYMENT ON BOOKINGS
BEGIN
   ... processing section here ...
END;
/
```

This trigger will only fire if an UPDATE is issued on the BOOKINGS table that attempts to update the columns GUEST_ID or PAYMENT. If an UPDATE tries to update any and all other columns, the UPDATF will not cause the trigger to be fired.

INSTEAD OF database_event is only used with database events on views. The same DML events that you can use with BEFORE and AFTER are available with INSTEAD OF: INSERT, UPDATE, and DELETE. As with BEFORE and AFTER, the INSTEAD OF will enable you to reference multiple DML events if you want, and again, you use the reserved word OR to separate the list. Just like the BEFORE and AFTER can only be applied to a single database table, the INSTEAD OF can only be applied to a single database view, for example, INSTEAD OF UPDATE ON VW_EMPLOYEES. The general purpose of the INSTEAD OF clause is to take a view that might otherwise be unable to receive DML statements and empower it for use with INSERT, UPDATE, and/or DELETE statements. Even views that join multiple tables together and that would not normally accept DML statements for changing data can have their capability to receive data defined with an INSTEAD OF trigger.

REFERENCING Clause

By default, incoming data can be referenced with the :new prefix, and data already in the database can be referenced with the :old prefix. This optional clause enables you to change the prefix. This is explained later in the section about the :old and :new qualifiers.

trigger_level Clause

You have one of two options here. Either leave this out, in which case you are automatically declaring the trigger as a FOR EACH STATEMENT type, or use the keywords FOR EACH ROW. The trigger level determines whether the trigger will fire once for the triggering SQL statement or once for each row affected by the triggering SQL statement. For example, an UPDATE statement can affect many rows in a single table. Should that UPDATE statement, when applied to a table with a BEFORE UPDATE trigger, cause the trigger to fire once (FOR EACH STATEMENT) or once for each row that is updated (FOR EACH ROW)? This is what the FOR EACH clause determines.

The following statement will create a database trigger:

```
CREATE OR REPLACE TRIGGER TRIG_EMPLOYEES_INSERT
BEFORE INSERT ON EMPLOYEES
FOR EACH ROW
BEGIN
  processing_statements;
END;
/
```

This trigger will automatically execute whenever an INSERT is performed on the EMPLOYEES table, and fire once for each row inserted. In the event of an INSERT that uses the SELECT option, which potentially could insert many rows at once, this trigger will fire once for each of those inserted records.

Again, note that there are no reserved words FOR EACH STATEMENT. To create a FOR EACH STATEMENT type of trigger, you don't have to do anything special in the declarative section. To achieve a FOR EACH ROW type of trigger, use the reserved words FOR EACH ROW.

This clause does not apply to INSTEAD OF triggers, which are always FOR EACH ROW triggers, and can never be FOR EACH STATEMENT triggers.

WHEN Clause

This optional clause defines the trigger condition. It is only valid for triggers with the FOR EACH ROW clause, in other words, for row-level triggers. It behaves much like a WHERE clause in a SELECT, UPDATE, or DELETE statement. The WHEN clause of a trigger must be an expression that evaluates to either TRUE or FALSE. The expression must be surrounded by parentheses; without them, you'll get a compilation error.

If the result of the WHEN clause is TRUE, the trigger body is executed, but if it's FALSE, then the trigger body is not executed. The WHEN clause can reference :new and :old qualifiers but does not use the colons, which are only required in the trigger body but are not used and will produce a compilation error in the WHEN clause.

For example, consider the following trigger declaration:

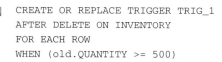

```
CREATE OR REPLACE TRIGGER TRIG_1
AFTER DELETE ON INVENTORY
FOR EACH ROW
WHEN (old.QUANTITY >= 500)
```

```
BEGIN
   ... trigger body ...
END;
/
```

The WHEN clause will ensure that this trigger will only fire for DELETE statements on records where the deleted record contains a QUANTITY value of 500 or more.

The Trigger Body

The trigger body can be any PL/SQL block. As a minimum, you must include the BEGIN and END reserved words, but if you declare anything, you must use the DECLARE statement, which isn't used in procedures, functions, or packages but is used in triggers.

For example, consider the following code sample:

```
CREATE OR REPLACE TRIGGER VALIDATE_SHIP_DATA
BEFORE INSERT OR UPDATE ON SHIPS
FOR EACH ROW
DECLARE
   too_many_cabins EXCEPTION;
   cabins          SHIPS.CABINS%TYPE;
   length          SHIPS.LENGTH%TYPE;
BEGIN
   cabins := NVL(:new.CABINS, :old.CABINS);
   length := NVL(:new.LENGTH, :old.LENGTH);
   IF FUNC_VALIDATE_SHIPS(cabins,length) THEN
     RAISE too_many_cabins;
   END IF;
END;
/
```

This trigger body declares three elements, including one exception and two variables. The variables use the %TYPE declaration method, and the exception is not only declared but raised in the trigger body. The trigger body calls the SQL function NVL and a user-defined function called FUNC_VALIDATE_SHIPS to determine if the cabins-to-ship-length ratio is realistic as a validation step to help prevent input errors. Finally, it raises a user-defined exception, which is not handled in the trigger body and will therefore have the effect of stopping the statement that fired the trigger to begin with. In other words, if an attempt to UPDATE the SHIPS table with data is inconsistent with the validation rules for ship LENGTH and CABINS, the UPDATE statement will fail when the too_many_cabins user-defined exception is raised, and the SHIP data will remain unchanged from the UPDATE statement.

The :old and :new Qualifiers

In any FOR EACH ROW trigger, the :old and :new qualifiers can be used as a prefix to any of the columns in the database object to which the trigger is attached. Remember that a trigger fires during the process of a database event—for example, during an UPDATE statement. Each column in the database has two states during an UPDATE—the state it is in before the UPDATE statement is executed and the changed state after the UPDATE is executed. The qualifiers can be used to identify which state of the column is intended to be referenced.

Consider the following UPDATE statement:

```
UPDATE EMPLOYEES
    SET SALARY = SALARY * 1.03
WHERE   SALARY < 100000;
```

This UPDATE statement will change the salaries for some of the records in the EMPLOYEES table. Now consider the following trigger:

```
CREATE OR REPLACE TRIGGER TRIG_RECORD_RAISE
BEFORE UPDATE ON EMPLOYEES
FOR EACH ROW
BEGIN
  IF (:new.SALARY > :old.SALARY)
  THEN
    :new.LAST_RAISE := SYSDATE;
  END IF;
END;
/
```

For each row that is updated, this trigger will make sure that the LAST_RAISE column in the EMPLOYEES table will be populated with the date of any actual increase performed on the SALARY column of that table. In this example, the database object is the EMPLOYEES table. For any UPDATE statement that is issued on the EMPLOYEES table, the LAST_RAISE column of the table will be automatically updated with the current system date but only if the SALARY column is being changed with an increase to the old value. This will override any incoming value for LAST_RAISE that may have been supplied in the UPDATE statement that fires the trigger.

The REFERENCING clause in the declarative section of the trigger can change the :old and :new qualifiers to something else, for the purpose of the trigger in which the REFERENCING clause is included. For example, consider the same code sample with the REFERENCES clause:

```
CREATE OR REPLACE TRIGGER TRIG_RECORD_RAISE
BEFORE UPDATE ON EMPLOYEES
REFERENCING OLD AS before_review NEW AS after_review
FOR EACH ROW
BEGIN
  IF (:after_review.SALARY > :before_review.SALARY)
  THEN
    :after_review.LAST_RAISE := SYSDATE;
  END IF;
END;
/
```

The qualifiers are defined according to the rules in Table 5-1. For example, in a trigger defined as a BEFORE DELETE trigger, if you reference a table column with the :new qualifier, the value will be NULL because there are no new values. However, you can reference a column with the :old qualifier, which will identify the values in the row that is about to be deleted.

The REFERENCING clause can redefine the qualifiers for use within the trigger. Their functionality doesn't change. You can change one or both in the REFERENCING clause.

Note that the WHEN clause in the trigger declaration header can reference these qualifiers but must not use the colon. For example

```
WHEN (new.SALARY > old.SALARY)
```

The colon is only used in the trigger body, not in the WHEN clause.

DML Statement	:old	:new
INSERT	Values are all NULL	Values in the INSERT statement
UPDATE	Values in the table	Values in the UPDATE statement
DELETE	Values in the table	Values are all NULL

TABLE 5-1. *:old and :new Values for Each DML Statement*

Conditional Predicates

As we have seen, it's possible to create a single trigger that will fire in reaction to an INSERT, UPDATE, and/or a DELETE statement. As a result, there may be occasions when your code in the trigger body needs to determine exactly which event it was that caused the trigger to fire. For this purpose, use the *conditional predicates*. There are three: INSERTING, DELETING, and UPDATING. Each is a BOOLEAN value, indicating a TRUE or FALSE according to the specific database event that has fired the trigger.

For example, the following code sample is of a trigger that will fire in response to either an INSERT or an UPDATE:

```
CREATE OR REPLACE TRIGGER TRIG_EMPLOYEES_AUDIT
BEFORE INSERT OR UPDATE ON EMPLOYEES
FOR EACH ROW
BEGIN
  IF INSERTING
  THEN
    :new.CREATE_DATE := SYSDATE;
    :new.CREATE_USER := USER;
  ELSIF UPDATING
  THEN
    :new.UPDATE_DATE := SYSDATE;
    :new.UPDATE_USER := USER;
  END IF;
END;
/
```

This code will fire in response to any INSERT or UPDATE statement on the EMPLOYEES table. The trigger will identify the current system date and the schema name (user ID) of the Oracle user causing the trigger to fire. If the triggering event is an INSERT, then the incoming values, if any, for CREATE_DATE and CREATE_USER (two columns in the EMPLOYEES table) will be assigned the values of the system date and user id, regardless of what the triggering INSERT statement may or may not have had defined for these columns. On the other hand, if the triggering event is an UPDATE, then the same data will be placed in the columns UPDATE_DATE and UPDATE_USER. The conditional predicates used here are INSERTING and UPDATING, and they are used in the IF statements.

Conditional predicates may be referenced in any place in the code and as frequently as necessary.

Firing Rules

Triggers that fire in response to a given DML statement will fire in a particular sequence. The sequence of firing for an INSERT statement on a given table is as follows:

1. BEFORE INSERT FOR EACH STATEMENT

2. BEFORE INSERT FOR EACH ROW

3. The INSERT statement itself

4. AFTER INSERT FOR EACH ROW

5. AFTER INSERT FOR EACH STATEMENT

This is the same pattern as the other DML statements. The FOR EACH STATEMENT triggers are fired first and last, and the FOR EACH ROW triggers are fired closest to the actual DML statement itself.

You can create multiple triggers for a single event. In other words, you can create a trigger named TRIG1 and another trigger called TRIG2 and make both of them a BEFORE INSERT ON EMPLOYEES FOR EACH ROW trigger. However, you have no control over which of these two triggers will fire first. The order is random and controlled by the database. Therefore, if the firing sequence is significant, your only choice is to re-create the two triggers as a single trigger and edit the code to achieve your desired result.

If constraints are present, the processing is the same, and constraints are processed within the trigger-processing pattern. As you will recall from SQL, constraints are simple standard rules you can apply to a given column or set of columns in a table, which can use a simple expression to accept, reject, or modify incoming data. There are two general categories of constraints: referential constraints, which protect primary key and foreign key relationships among tables, and integrity constraints, which can protect the data entered into one or more columns. Integrity constraints include NOT NULL, UNIQUE, and the CHECK constraint. Wherever you can use a constraint instead of a trigger, you should. Triggers exist to create the more complex error checking, data validation, and other purposes that referential and integrity constraints cannot address.

When a table has one or more constraints applied to it, the processing of constraints fits in to the trigger-processing model as follows:

1. Execute BEFORE . . . FOR EACH STATEMENT triggers.

2. For each row that is affected:

    A. Execute BEFORE . . . FOR EACH ROW triggers.

    B. Issue lock on the row and perform integrity constraint checking

      C. Execute the triggering DML statement.

      D. Execute AFTER . . . FOR EACH ROW triggers.

   3. Execute deferred integrity constraints.

   4. Execute AFTER . . . FOR EACH STATEMENT triggers.

Note that the lock on the row is released once a COMMIT is issued.

The integrity constraint checks are initiated as close to the actual DML statement as possible, more so than any triggers.

Restrictions

Because triggers fire within transactions, triggers themselves may not include any statements that perform transaction control. This means that you cannot include any COMMIT, SAVEPOINT, or ROLLBACK statements within the code of a trigger. The PL/SQL parser will enable you to create the trigger, but when the trigger is fired, it will produce a run-time error like this:

```
ORA-04092: cannot COMMIT in a trigger
```

Nothing the trigger does can cause a transaction control statement to execute. This includes calls to procedures or functions that contain transaction control statements—no calls to such program units are enabled. Once again, this will not yield a compilation error but will show up in execution.

Triggers also have restrictions against use of elements with large datatypes. Triggers may not declare or reference LONG or LONG RAW elements. This includes elements of the database object to which the trigger is attached—if the associated table, for example, has a column that has a LONG datatype, the trigger may not reference that column in any way, including references to incoming data, indicated with :new or :old. Triggers may not modify CLOB and BLOB elements, although triggers may reference these elements for read-only access.

Triggers have further restrictions involving concepts known as mutating and constraining tables. These restrictions are a little involved and are discussed in the next section.

Mutating and Constraining Tables

Triggers have restrictions against reading from or modifying data in tables that are mutating or are constraining tables relative to the action that has fired the trigger.

A *mutating table* is a table that is recognized by a trigger's firing process as a table that is in the midst of being modified at the time the trigger is fired. For example, if a table called EMPLOYEES has an AFTER UPDATE trigger attached to it and an update is performed on that table, then when the trigger is fired, the EMPLOYEES table is a mutating table for purposes of the trigger.

A trigger may not read from or modify any data in a table that is considered mutating relative to the event that fired the trigger. Specifically, this includes

■ The triggering table itself. There is an unusual exception: in the case of an INSERT trigger FOR EACH ROW, the triggering table will not be considered a mutating table unless the INSERT statement performed uses a subquery. If the INSERT . . . AS SELECT . . . variation of INSERT statement is the statement that fires the trigger, then the triggering table is considered a mutating table, regardless of what the subquery is. Otherwise, an INSERT trigger FOR EACH ROW does not recognize the triggering table as a mutating table.

■ In the case of a DELETE trigger FOR EACH STATEMENT that is fired by a DELETE statement, any tables with foreign key constraints that reference the triggering table and include the ON DELETE CASCADE option are considered mutating tables. This is in addition to the triggering table itself. For example, if a table called EMPLOYEES has a detail table called WORK_SCHEDULE with foreign key constraints that reference the EMPLOYEES table and include the ON DELETE CASCADE option in the foreign key, then a DELETE trigger FOR EACH STATEMENT on the EMPLOYEES table will recognize both the EMPLOYEES table and the WORK_SCHEDULE table as mutating tables when a DELETE statement is issued.

Statement triggers, that is, triggers that fire FOR EACH STATEMENT, are not restricted in this way. The issue of mutating tables only applies to triggers that fire FOR EACH ROW. The reason is that a FOR EACH STATEMENT trigger can enable the UPDATE or whatever process to complete before firing; whereas a FOR EACH ROW trigger fires once for each row affected, before the statement has completed processing.

Also, views are never considered mutating. For example, if an UPDATE statement fires an INSTEAD OF trigger on a view, the view is not considered mutating; whereas had the UPDATE statement been issued on a table, the table would be considered mutating.

A *constraining table* is a table that references, by a foreign key, the object that has fired the trigger. Constraining tables are considered tables that are being read from, and a trigger cannot modify these. However, note that restrictions on triggers with regard to constraining tables have been relaxed in Oracle8*i* and later versions. You are able to reference constraining tables with no restrictions in Oracle8*i* and later versions of the database.

Altering Triggers

The ALTER statement is used with triggers to recompile them, just like the ALTER statement is used to recompile procedures, functions, and packages. The syntax to recompile a trigger is

```
ALTER TRIGGER trigger_name COMPILE;
```

The same requirements apply when you compile triggers that we've seen with procedures, functions, and packages: If the trigger body references a database object that is altered for any reason, then the trigger is listed in the data dictionary's USER_OBJECTS view with a status of INVALID. The ALTER statement can be used to recompile the trigger and determine the impact of the database change. Or, as is the case with procedures, functions, and packages, the next action that invokes the trigger will force an automatic recompilation, and if successful, the trigger will fire as normal upon successful recompilation.

Although recompilation is the primary purpose of the ALTER statement with procedures, functions, and packages, there is an additional significant purpose for the ALTER statement when used with triggers. The ALTER statement is also used to enable and disable triggers. This is discussed in an upcoming section, "Enabling and Disabling Triggers."

Dropping Triggers

The syntax to drop a trigger is DROP TRIGGER, followed by the trigger name. For example, the following statement drops a trigger called archive_customers:

```
DROP TRIGGER ARCHIVE_CUSTOMERS;
```

This statement will permanently remove the trigger from the database.

In this sense, triggers can be dropped just like procedures, functions, and packages. However, unlike those program units, triggers can be disabled. Disabling a trigger renders it powerless, while leaving it in the database. Once a trigger has been disabled, it can be enabled again. For more information, see the discussion on disabling and enabling triggers.

If a table is dropped, then it's triggers are automatically dropped, too. This point cannot be overstated. When a procedure references a table, and the table is dropped, the procedure is kept in the data dictionary and given a status of INVALID. But when you create a trigger on a table, and the table is later dropped, the trigger is removed from the data dictionary.

For Review

1. The CREATE, ALTER, and DROP commands are used to create and modify triggers.

2. Triggers are created to automatically fire in response to database events, as defined in the trigger header. Triggers can identify incoming data or old data about to be replaced with the :old and :new qualifiers. Triggers are defined at one of two trigger levels: FOR EACH STATEMENT and FOR EACH ROW. If a trigger is FOR EACH STATEMENT, then it will fire once for the triggering statement; whereas a FOR EACH ROW will fire once for each row affected by the triggering statement. The trigger body is a complete PL/SQL block and uses the DECLARE keyword if it's necessary to declare any PL/SQL elements for the block. The block can include calls to other program units.

3. Triggers are fired in order according to their driving event; for example, the last set of triggers to fire in response to a DELETE statement will be all the AFTER DELETE FOR EACH STATEMENT triggers. However, if you define multiple triggers of the same type, such as more than one trigger for AFTER DELETE FOR EACH STATEMENT, you have no control over which of these will fire first.

4. Trigger bodies cannot modify a table that is in the process of being modified in response to the triggering event.

5. An ALTER statement can be used to recompile a trigger and to disable or enable a trigger. A DROP statement can be used to remove a trigger from the database. Dropping a table will result in that table's triggers also being dropped.

Exercises

1. **Assuming that any referenced database objects are properly declared, which of the following code snippets might be found in a trigger header? (Choose all that apply.)**

    A. BEFORE UPDATE ON EMPLOYEES

    B. FOR EACH STATEMENT

    C. REFERENCING NEW AS LATEST

    D. AFTER SELECT ON ORDERS

2. **Which of the following are valid in a trigger body? (Choose all that apply.)**

    A. An INSERT statement on the table to which the trigger is assigned

    B. A COMMIT statement

C. A call to a stored procedure with a COMMIT statement

D. CURSOR statements

Answer Key
1. A, C. **2.** D.

Enabling and Disabling Triggers

Unlike the other program units we have looked at, such as procedures, functions, and packages, triggers can be disabled. Disabling a trigger has the effect of rendering it powerless while leaving it in the database. This enables you to work in the database temporarily without the effect of the trigger, leaving you the option of enabling the trigger at some future date by entering a simple command. This is a highly desirable option when you need to perform some one-time operations on a table where a trigger or set of triggers may be irrelevant.

For example, a situation where you may want to disable triggers is when you need to perform an import of a large number of records into a table. The Oracle IMPORT utility will perform a series of INSERT statements to bring in the records into a given table. If the target table has a BEFORE INSERT or an AFTER INSERT trigger FOR EACH ROW, then the import will be relatively slow as each record fires the trigger. This is a good thing if you are bringing in data that has not been subjected to the business rules of the trigger, but what if this is data that was already sent through this trigger once before? If this is data that you previously exported for some reason and that you are confident is already consistent with the trigger logic, then why pass a large amount of records through this processing again if it is going to take an inordinate amount of time? You can choose to disable the appropriate triggers, perform the import relatively quickly, and then enable the triggers again for standard use.

There are two ways to disable and enable a trigger. One way is to disable or enable a specific trigger by name. Another is to disable or enable a set of triggers for a given table.

Disabling and Enabling a Named Trigger

The syntax to disable an individual trigger is

```
ALTER TRIGGER trigger_name DISABLE;
```

Once the trigger is disabled, it behaves as if it were dropped altogether—in other words, it has no effect.

The syntax to enable a trigger is

```
ALTER TRIGGER trigger_name ENABLE;
```

A trigger can only be enabled if it has been stored in the database and is valid.

Enabling and Disabling a Named Table's Triggers

There will be occasions when you attach several triggers to a single table, and you need to disable all of the table's triggers. The syntax is as follows:

```
ALTER TABLE table_name DISABLE ALL TRIGGERS;
```

For example

```
ALTER TABLE EMPLOYEES DISABLE ALL TRIGGERS;
```

To restore the triggers, use the ENABLE option:

```
ALTER TABLE table_name ENABLE ALL TRIGGERS;
```

For example

```
ALTER TABLE EMPLOYEES ENABLE ALL TRIGGERS;
```

These two statements, to DISABLE and ENABLE triggers, have the same result you would get if you disabled or enabled all of a particular table's triggers with individual commands.

For Review

1. Triggers can be disabled and enabled without removing them from the database.

2. You can enable and disable triggers by name, or you can reference a table's entire set of triggers.

Exercises

1. **Assuming the referenced database objects are properly declared, which of the following are valid statements? (Choose all that apply.)**

   A. ALTER TABLE PRODUCTS ENABLE TRIGGER TRIG_01

   B. ALTER TRIGGER TRIG_01 DISABLE

   C. ALTER TABLE PRODUCTS DISABLE ALL TRIGGERS

   D. ALTER TABLE PRODUCTS DISABLE TRIGGERS

2. **Assuming the CATALOG table's trigger MONITOR is disabled, which of the following statements is true? (Choose all that apply.)**

   A. The trigger code is still stored in the data dictionary.

   B. The table cannot be used.

   C. The trigger cannot be enabled until it is restored.

   D. The trigger will not have any effect on SQL statements applied to CATALOG.

Answer Key

1. B, C.   2. A, D.

INSTEAD OF Triggers

INSTEAD OF triggers, also known as *view triggers*, can only be assigned to database views. In contrast to BEFORE or AFTER triggers, which supplement the capability of DML statements, INSTEAD OF triggers replace the functionality of a DML statement for the view to which the trigger is assigned. INSTEAD OF triggers must always be FOR EACH ROW; they cannot be built as FOR EACH STATEMENT triggers, and they must be assigned to database views, not tables.

The purpose of the INSTEAD OF trigger is to enable DML statements that might be otherwise unavailable on a database view. Remember from SQL that database views are not always able to receive INSERT, UPDATE, or DELETE statements. Specifically, a database view may be built on a SELECT statement that contains one or more of the following features:

- A table join of two or more tables
- The GROUP BY clause
- The START WITH . . . CONNECT BY feature
- Any aggregate functions
- The DISTINCT function

- Set operations
- Columns based on expressions, such as concatenation, or pseudocolumns, such as SYSDATE (the view's other columns may still be updateable).

If any of these features are part of a view, then the view cannot accept INSERT, UPDATE, or DELETE statements—unless an INSTEAD OF trigger specifically enables the particular DML statement. INSTEAD OF triggers are available starting with Oracle version 8.

For example, consider the following two tables:

```
CREATE TABLE CRUISES
( CRUISE_ID      NUMBER(10)
, SHIP_ID        NUMBER(10)
, CRUISE_NAME    VARCHAR2(80)
, CONSTRAINT     PK_CRUISE_ID PRIMARY KEY (CRUISE_ID)
);
CREATE TABLE SHIPS
( SHIP_ID     NUMBER(10)
, SHIP_NAME   VARCHAR2(80)
, CONSTRAINT  PK_SHIP_ID PRIMARY KEY (SHIP_ID)
);
```

Now considering the following view, based on these tables:

```
CREATE VIEW CRUISES_AND_SHIPS AS
SELECT C.CRUISE_ID, C.CRUISE_NAME, S.SHIP_NAME
FROM    CRUISES C, SHIPS    S
WHERE   C.SHIP_ID = S.SHIP_ID;
```

This view selects some of the data from two database tables. Note, however, that the view does not include the primary key from the SHIPS table, only the ship name. The SHIP_ID column is not included. According to the rules of database views, this view will not accept INSERT statements because it is impossible to provide a SHIP_ID, which is required by the underlying table SHIPS.

However, an INSTEAD OF trigger can empower this view by giving it the capability to receive INSERT statements. The following code is an example of an INSTEAD OF trigger on the CRUISES_AND_SHIPS database view:

```
CREATE OR REPLACE TRIGGER TRIG_CRUISES_AND_SHIPS
INSTEAD OF INSERT ON CRUISES_AND_SHIPS
DECLARE
  v_ship_id SHIPS.SHIP_ID%TYPE;
BEGIN
  INSERT INTO SHIPS
```

```
    (SHIP_ID, SHIP_NAME)
    VALUES
    (SEQ_SHIP_ID.NEXTVAL, :new.SHIP_NAME);
  INSERT INTO CRUISES
    (CRUISE_ID, CRUISE_NAME, SHIP_ID)
    VALUES
    (:new.CRUISE_ID, :new.CRUISE_NAME, SEQ_SHIP_ID.CURRVAL);
END;
/
```

This trigger makes up for the lack of a SHIP_ID value by referencing the database sequence generator SEQ_SHIP_ID and using the sequence generator to generate a new value (NEXTVAL) in the INSERT INTO SHIPS statement then using the same value (CURRVAL) in the INSERT INTO CRUISES statement to ensure that the two records are properly related.

Any INSERT statement on this database view will fire this trigger. The trigger is automatically defined as a FOR EACH ROW trigger, whether that clause is included or not. The trigger body will replace the functionality of any INSERT statement that is executed against the CRUISES_AND_SHIPS view.

For Review

1. INSTEAD OF triggers are for database views only. They are automatically FOR EACH ROW and cannot be defined as statement-level triggers.

2. The INSTEAD OF trigger body will fire in the place of the DML statement that fires it.

Exercises

1. Which of the following trigger headers is valid for the PRODUCTS view? (Choose all that apply.)

A. CREATE TRIGGER TRIG_001
INSTEAD OF DELETE OR UPDATE ON PRODUCTS
FOR EACH ROW

B. CREATE TRIGGER TRIG_001
INSTEAD OF DELETE OR BEFORE INSERT ON PRODUCTS
FOR EACH STATEMENT

C. CREATE TRIGGER TRIG_001
INSTEAD_OF UPDATE ON PRODUCTS BEFORE INSERT

D. CREATE TRIGGER TRIG_001
INSTEAD OF INSERT ON PRODUCTS

2. **What database views can be assigned the INSTEAD OF trigger?**

   A. Any view

   B. Only views that join tables

   C. Views with missing primary key data

   D. Views that contain other triggers

Answer Key
1. A, D. **2.** A.

Non-DML Triggers

A feature that is new to Oracle is the capability to create triggers that fire on system events. These triggers are not built on a table or a view but instead are built ON SCHEMA or ON DATABASE. For example, you can build triggers that will fire on all CREATE, ALTER, or DROP events for a given schema or for all STARTUP and SHUTDOWN events for the database.

The DDL events you can work with are shown in Table 5-2.

DDL events that result from the use of PL/SQL, such as with the DBMS_SQL package, do not apply; no PL/SQL-initiated DDL events will fire a DDL trigger. (Creating DDL events with PL/SQL's DBMS_SQL package is addressed in Chapter 7.)

Also, CREATE will not ever fire in response to the CREATE DATABASE or CREATE CONTROLFILE statements.

CREATE	ALTER	DROP	GRANT	REVOKE
ASSOCIATE STATISTICS	DISASSOCIATE STATISTICS	AUDIT	NOAUDIT	COMMENT
RENAME	TRUNCATE	ANALYZE		

TABLE 5-2. *DDL Trigger Events*

LOGON	LOGOFF	STARTUP	SHUTDOWN	SERVERERROR

TABLE 5-3. *Database Trigger Events*

The database events that you can trigger are in Table 5-3. Note that you cannot create a BEFORE LOGON or AFTER LOGOFF trigger.

You can create a trigger for any of these DDL or database events and make the trigger fire ON SCHEMA or ON DATABASE with a few restrictions. Specifically, you can only create a trigger for STARTUP or for SHUTDOWN that is ON DATABASE; you cannot create it ON SCHEMA.

If you create a trigger ON DATABASE, the trigger will fire for all schemas. If you create a trigger ON SCHEMA, the trigger will fire for the schema in which you created the trigger, in other words, the trigger's owner. Therefore, to create a trigger for a particular schema, you don't actually name the schema in the trigger's creation statement but instead create the trigger ON SCHEMA and create the trigger while logged in as that schema.

A SERVERERROR trigger will fire when a server error is encountered. In the trigger's code, you can use the system defined built-in function IS_SERVERERROR (p_error_number), which returns a BOOLEAN, to identify a particular error message, as in

```
IF (IS_SERVERERROR(10562)) THEN
```

The syntax for these triggers is similar to DML triggers. They still require a PL/SQL block or a call to an existing stored program unit or both. There are some restrictions, however:

- You cannot use the REFERENCE clause with DDL triggers.

- You cannot use the WHEN clause, which is only available for ROW triggers.

DDL Triggers

DDL triggers fire in response to the statements CREATE, ALTER, and DROP. It's important to note that triggers will not fire until they are committed to the database and will continue to fire until they are disabled or removed. For example, if you create a trigger to fire before all DROP events in a given schema, then decide you want to drop that trigger, you will have to issue a DROP statement to remove the trigger. However, because the trigger is a BEFORE DROP trigger, then it will actually fire one more time immediately before being dropped by your DROP statement. A similar situation exists for AFTER CREATE triggers—the first time you create them, they will not fire because the trigger isn't considered committed to the database until after the CREATE statement has completed.

For Review

1. Non-DML triggers include triggers that fire in response to DDL events or database events.

2. You can create non-DML triggers to fire ON SCHEMA or ON DATABASE.

Exercises

1. **Which of the following database events cannot be created ON SCHEMA?**

   A. LOGON

   B. LOGOFF

   C. STARTUP

   D. SERVERERROR

2. **Which of the following are valid options for a trigger?**

   A. BEFORE CREATE OR DROP ON SCHEMA

   B. AFTER TRUNCATE ON DATABASE

   C. BEFORE OR AFTER CREATE OR ALTER ON SCHEMA

   D. AFTER SHUTDOWN ON DATABASE

Answer Key
1. C. 2. A, B.

Data Dictionary Resources for Triggers

When a trigger is created, it is stored in the data dictionary, just like the other program units. The USER_OBJECTS view shows a record for each trigger, just as it does for each stored procedure or function. If you attempt to store a trigger but encounter a parsing error, then the USER_ERRORS view will contain the errors until they are resolved. The USER_DEPENDENCIES view contains information we'll address in the chapter about interdependencies.

Unlike the other program units, you won't find the source code for the trigger in the USER_SOURCE view. Instead you'll find it in the USER_TRIGGERS view.

USER_TRIGGERS

Each trigger owned by a schema is stored in the USER_TRIGGERS view. Unlike the USER_SOURCE view, which consists of one record per each line of code in a program unit, there is only one record per trigger in the USER_TRIGGERS view. The entire set of code for a trigger is found in a single column with a LONG datatype, called TRIGGER_BODY, in the USER_TRIGGERS view.

The columns of the USER_TRIGGERS view are described in the following list:

- **TRIGGER_NAME**   This is the name you have assigned to the trigger.

- **TRIGGER_TYPE**   Contains a string identifying the trigger type, such as AFTER EACH ROW, or BEFORE EACH STATEMENT.

- **TRIGGERING_EVENT**   Identifies the triggering event, such as INSERT OR UPDATE, or DELETE.

- **TABLE_OWNER**   Identifies the owner of the database object, which is not necessarily a table, to which the trigger is attached. Note that a schema can create triggers on database objects owned by a different schema.

- **BASE_OBJECT_TYPE**   Identifies the type of database object to which the trigger is attached. This could be TABLE, VIEW, SCHEMA, or DATABASE.

- **TABLE_NAME**   Identifies the name of the database object, which could be a table or a view, to which the trigger is attached.

- **COLUMN_NAME**   The name of the nested table column—this only applies to nested table triggers. These are not addressed on the exam.

- **REFERENCING_NAMES**   This is the trigger's REFERENCING clause, such as REFERENCING NEW AS NEW OLD AS LAST_CHECKED.

- **WHEN_CLAUSE**   The trigger's WHEN clause, such as WHEN (new.QUANTITY > 500).

- **STATUS**   The trigger's status, which is either ENABLED or DISABLED.

- **DESCRIPTION**   This column repeats data from other columns to form the trigger's brief description. For example, VALIDATE_SHIP_DATA BEFORE INSERT OR UPDATE ON SHIPS FOR EACH ROW. The DESCRIPTION combines data from the TRIGGER_NAME, TRIGGER_TYPE, TRIGGERING_EVENT, and TABLE_NAME.

- **ACTION_TYPE** For PL/SQL triggers, this will be the string PL/SQL.

- **TRIGGER_BODY** The trigger's body. This is the PL/SQL block that defines what the trigger will actually do when fired.

If you want to look at any information in a column with a LONG datatype within the SQL*Plus interface, you don't automatically get to see it all unless you use the SET LONG command. For example, see Figure 5-1.

In Figure 5-1, the first query is run with the default settings in SQL*Plus and results in truncated output of the TRIGGER_BODY column. Then the SQL*Plus

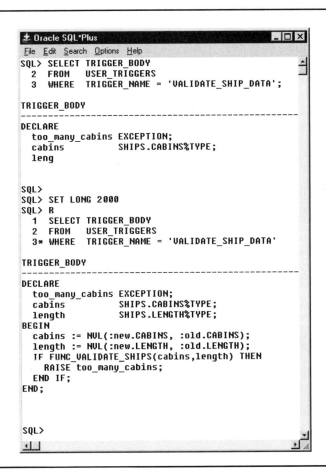

FIGURE 5-1. *Inspecting the LONG column TRIGGER_BODY*

session parameter LONG is reset to 2000, and the same query now produces the full output of the column.

Remember that in SQL*Plus, once you set a session parameter, it's set for the duration of your login session but needs to be reset for the next login session.

For Review

1. The USER_TRIGGER view shows information about the triggers owned by a schema.

2. There is one record per trigger in the USER_TRIGGER view.

Exercises

1. **Which column in the USER_TRIGGER view shows if the trigger is based on a table?**

   A. TRIGGER_TYPE

   B. TABLE_NAME

   C. BASE_OBJECT_TYPE

   D. TRIGGER_BODY

2. **In a brand new schema, you have created two triggers, the first consisting of 15 lines of PL/SQL code and the second consisting of 23 lines of PL/SQL code. The first trigger has parsed correctly, and the second has compilation errors. How many records are in the USER_TRIGGER view?**

   A. 15

   B. 38

   C. 2

   D. 0

Answer Key
1. C. 2. C.

Chapter Summary

A trigger is a PL/SQL program unit that is stored in the database and attached to a database object, such as a table. Triggers are not invoked by name and are not called directly but are automatically fired by the database when certain events occur in the database. You, as the developer, determine which event (or events) will cause the trigger to be fired, and you have a predetermined set of events from which to choose. The events include INSERT, UPDATE, and/or DELETE on a particular table. Triggers can be programmed to fire BEFORE or AFTER the event of an INSERT, UPDATE, and/or DELETE statement executed for a given table.

Triggers are used to attach business rules to a database object, so that any process that works on the table will be subject to the same rules. In other words, if a database object receives a DML statement and that database object has a trigger attached to it, then it doesn't matter if the source of the DML is an Oracle Form, Java program, or an ODBC call—they will all cause any appropriate database triggers to be fired.

Triggers can control incoming data to a table and can reference old data that is about to be deleted or updated just before the event actually occurs. Triggers can change the incoming data, record the old data, and even stop whatever DML statement that caused the trigger to fire from successfully completing.

Triggers are stored for one table. If the table is dropped, the trigger is dropped as well. You cannot create a single trigger for multiple tables. However, you are able to create a single trigger to respond to multiple events on a given table, such as BEFORE INSERT OR UPDATE. Also, triggers can be created to fire BEFORE or AFTER a database event but not both. A table can have more than one trigger attached to it and can even have multiple triggers for the same database event. In other words, you can create two different triggers with two different names that will both fire in response to the AFTER DELETE event on a given table.

Triggers can be assigned to one of two different levels. A row-level trigger will fire once for each row in the table that is processed. A statement-level trigger will fire once for each statement that is executed against the table. For example, a single DELETE statement may result in the deletion of 10 rows. If there is a statement-level AFTER DELETE trigger on the table, that trigger will fire once. If there is a row-level AFTER DELETE trigger on the table, that trigger will fire 10 times.

Because one database object can have multiple triggers and because a single DML statement can cause multiple triggers to be fired, then the order in which the triggers are fired needs to be considered. The firing order for a given set of triggers is determined by the level of each trigger, combined with the BEFORE and AFTER events. The firing order for a given DML statement is BEFORE STATEMENT, BEFORE ROW, AFTER ROW, AFTER STATEMENT. This is true for INSERT, UPDATE, and/or DELETE statements.

However, it's possible to create multiple triggers for a single database event. In other words, you can create two different triggers for the BEFORE DELETE FOR EACH ROW event. In that case, the firing order is random, and your only option to control the firing sequence is to edit the triggers into a single trigger.

Trigger bodies can include any valid PL/SQL statement but are restricted against using transaction control statements. The COMMIT, SAVEPOINT, and ROLLBACK commands will cause execution errors when the trigger is fired. No calls to procedures or functions that contain transaction control statements will work either. Again, you will get execution errors. You are also restricted against issuing DML statements to tables that are already in a state of change during the trigger-firing event. This generally means the table to which the trigger is attached. For example, if you have a BEFORE UPDATE ON EMPLOYEES FOR EACH ROW trigger, you cannot issue an UPDATE statement on the EMPLOYEES table. However, in row-level triggers, you can use the :old and :new prefixes to identify columns in the table and for the row being changed and thereby make changes to the specific record being referenced.

Trigger bodies can use the conditional predicates of INSERTING, UPDATING, and DELETING, which all have BOOLEAN values, to determine which particular event caused the trigger to fire. This is useful in a trigger such as AFTER INSERT OR UPDATE, where the trigger code may not know which event caused the trigger to fire.

Using the ALTER statement, triggers can be enabled and disabled. A disabled trigger remains in the data dictionary but will not fire. You can enable and disable triggers by name, or you can enable and disable all of the triggers for a given database object.

The USER_TRIGGERS data dictionary view is where you will find source code and other information about the triggers owned by a given schema.

Two-Minute Drill

- Use the CREATE TRIGGER statement to create a database trigger. The OR REPLACE option is accepted as well. You declare the name of a trigger in the CREATE statement.

- Trigger headers must include a database event. Triggers can either be BEFORE or AFTER (but one trigger cannot be defined for both) and can apply to any combination of INSERT, UPDATE or DELETE, separated by the word OR, as in BEFORE INSERT OR UPDATE.

- You may optionally redefine the :old and :new qualifiers with the REFERENCING statement, as in REFERENCING NEW AS UPDATED. By default, the REFERENCING NEW AS NEW OLD AS OLD is in force.

■ The WHEN clause is where you define business rules for when the trigger will fire. The trigger must have been fired to begin with for the WHEN clause to apply. In other words, only when the associated database event actually occurs is the WHEN clause even considered. The WHEN clause may reference the :old and :new qualifiers but without the colon, which is only used in the trigger body. The WHEN clause only applies to FOR EACH ROW triggers.

■ The trigger level can be omitted, in which case the trigger is assumed to be FOR EACH STATEMENT, or it can be specified as FOR EACH ROW. Note that you never actually declare a trigger with the words FOR EACH STATEMENT.

■ The trigger body is a PL/SQL block. If you declare variables, you must use the DECLARE keyword. You may declare any variable, constant, cursor, and other PL/SQL element.

■ Trigger bodies may raise exceptions. If the exception is not handled, you will effectively terminate the DML statement that fired the trigger to begin with.

■ Trigger bodies in FOR EACH ROW triggers may not issue DML statements to mutating tables, which are tables that are in the process of changing as a result of the database event that fired the trigger to begin with. Because the table is not yet changed, you are not allowed to issue any DML statements on the table. For example, you are restricted against a DELETE FROM EMPLOYEES statement in the trigger body of a BEFORE INSERT ON EMPLOYEES trigger.

■ Trigger bodies may not include transaction control statements, that is, COMMIT, SAVEPOINT, and ROLLBACK. The trigger will compile but not execute.

■ Any program units that the trigger calls, such as packaged procedures and functions, are subject to the same restrictions as the trigger itself. For example, a trigger body cannot call a procedure that has a COMMIT statement. This will produce an execution error.

■ The conditional predicates INSERTING, UPDATING, and DELETING can be used in the trigger body to determine which event fired the trigger. For example, the statement IF INSERTING THEN is enabled in a trigger body.

■ Triggers will fire in a predetermined order according to the trigger level and database event. The order is BEFORE STATEMENT, BEFORE ROW, AFTER ROW, AFTER STATEMENT.

- Triggers can be dropped with the DROP TRIGGER statement. They can also be disabled with the ALTER TRIGGER statement. Disabling a trigger leaves it in the data dictionary, where it can be enabled at some time in the future, but dropping the trigger removes it from the database altogether. A disabled trigger does not fire.

- The USER_TRIGGERS data dictionary view is where you will find one record of information for each trigger stored in the schema. The TRIGGER_BODY column is a LONG datatype column that contains the full text of the trigger body. Use the SET LONG command in the SQL*Plus interface to display the entire text of the trigger body when using a SELECT statement against the LONG datatype column TRIGGER_BODY.

- An INSTEAD OF trigger can be created for a database view to enable the view to process DML statements that it otherwise might not.

- You can create triggers BEFORE or AFTER DDL statements, such as CREATE, ALTER, or DROP. You can create these triggers ON SCHEMA or ON DATABASE to fire for the particular DDL statements within a particular schema, or within any schema in the database.

Chapter Questions

1. **You want to create a trigger that will store the name of the Oracle schema that issues any UPDATE statements against the PURCHASE_ORDERS table. You aren't concerned with the actual records changed, only with the fact that an UPDATE was issued. Which of the following is the best approach?**

   A. Create a BEFORE OR AFTER UPDATE trigger FOR EACH ROW.

   B. Create a BEFORE UPDATE trigger FOR EACH STATEMENT.

   C. Create a BEFORE OR AFTER UPDATE trigger, and use a WHEN clause to limit the firing.

   D. It cannot be done.

2. **Consider the following code sample:**

```
CREATE OR REPLACE TRIGGER GB_FLAG
BEFORE DELETE ON GUEST_BOOKINGS
DECLARE
   stop_it EXCEPTION;
BEGIN
   IF TO_CHAR(SYSDATE,'Dy') NOT IN ('Sat','Sun') THEN
      COMMIT;
```

```
    ELSE
      RAISE stop_it;
    END IF;
END;
/
```

Which of the following statements is true of this code?

   A. It will produce a compilation error because of the attempt to declare an exception.

   B. It will not compile because there is no FOR EACH statement.

   C. It will compile but will produce an execution error.

   D. There is nothing wrong with this trigger.

3. **An INSTEAD OF trigger can be used to: (Choose all that apply.)**

   A. Stop an UPDATE statement on a table according to the logic in the trigger body.

   B. Translate data on an INSERT statement to a table by using the REFERENCING qualifiers.

   C. Define how an INSERT statement will behave for a view.

   D. Fire once for each statement on a view.

4. **Which of the following can be included in the trigger body of an executable trigger? (Choose all that apply.)**

   A. A user-defined variable defined with the %ROWTYPE declarative

   B. A COMMIT statement

   C. Calls to a stored procedure that contains a SAVEPOINT statement

   D. An INSERT statement on the same table to which the trigger is assigned

5. **You have created triggers with the following headers:**

```
CREATE OR REPLACE TRIGGER PRODUCT_AUDIT
BEFORE DELETE ON PRODUCT
FOR EACH ROW

CREATE OR REPLACE TRIGGER PRODUCT_VALIDATE
AFTER DELETE ON PRODUCT
```

```
CREATE OR REPLACE TRIGGER PRODUCT_EDIT
BEFORE UPDATE OR DELETE ON PRODUCT
FOR EACH ROW
```

In which order will these triggers fire in response to a DELETE statement event?

A. PRODUCT_AUDIT, PRODUCT_VALIDATE, PRODUCT_EDIT

B. PRODUCT_VALIDATE, PRODUCT_AUDIT, PRODUCT_EDIT

C. PRODUCT_EDIT, PRODUCT_AUDIT, PRODUCT_VALIDATE

D. You cannot be sure of the order.

6. **Which of the following is a valid conditional predicate? (Choose all that apply.)**

   A. INSERTING

   B. SELECTING

   C. CREATING

   D. UPDATING

7. **You have created a trigger. Where will you find the trigger code in the data dictionary?**

   A. The TEXT column of the USER_SOURCE view

   B. The TRIGGER_TEXT column of the USER_TRIGGERS view

   C. The TRIGGER_BODY column of the USER_TRIGGERS view

   D. The TRIGGER_BODY column of the USER_SOURCE view

8. **Consider the following trigger:**

```
CREATE OR REPLACE TRIGGER MONITOR_INVENTORY
BEFORE INSERT ON INVENTORY
BEGIN
  PROC_MONITOR_INVENTORY(SYSDATE);
END;
/
```

Assume the procedure PROC_MONITOR_INVENTORY is a valid procedure, and it is properly called from this trigger. What is this trigger's level?

A. FOR EACH ROW

B. FOR EACH STATEMENT

C. FOR EACH ROW OR FOR EACH STATEMENT

D. This trigger won't compile.

9. **Which of the following are valid statements? (Choose all that apply.)**

A. ALTER TRIGGER TRIG_01 RECOMPILE

B. ALTER TRIGGER TRIG_01 ENABLE ALL

C. ALTER TABLE EMPLOYEES ENABLE ALL TRIGGERS

D. ALTER TABLE EMPLOYEES ENABLE TRIGGERS

10. **Which column of the USER_TRIGGERS data dictionary view displays the database event that will fire the trigger?**

A. TRIGGER_NAME

B. ACTION_TYPE

C. WHEN_CLAUSE

D. DESCRIPTION

Answers to Chapter Questions

1. B.   Create a BEFORE UPDATE trigger FOR EACH STATEMENT

Explanation   A is not true because you cannot create a BEFORE OR AFTER trigger. You can only use either BEFORE or AFTER but not both in a single trigger. C is not good because the WHEN clause is irrelevant here. D is just not true. C is the best answer because the FOR EACH STATEMENT is the best option to use when you're unconcerned with the actual data that is changed and are only concerned with issues related to whether the statement was issued or not, which is the case in this question.

2. C.   It will compile but will produce an execution error.

Explanation   A is not true; you are able to declare and use your own exceptions in triggers. B is not true because FOR EACH, if left out, will default to FOR EACH

STATEMENT. D is not true because there is something wrong. The problem that C alludes to is the use of the COMMIT statement. The trigger will compile and store, but the first attempt to fire it will produce an execution error because the use of COMMIT is not allowed.

3. C. Define how an INSERT statement will behave for a view.

Explanation Neither A or B can be true because the INSTEAD OF trigger only works with database views, not database tables. D is not true because the INSTEAD OF cannot work with FOR EACH STATEMENT triggers. C is the only answer that is true.

4. A. A user-defined variable defined with the %ROWTYPE declarative

Explanation B and C are not allowed because a trigger cannot include any transaction statements. D is not allowed because of the restrictions involving mutating tables—you cannot change a table that is already in the process of being changed, such as the very table that fired the trigger to begin with. Only A is allowed.

5. D. You cannot be sure of the order.

Explanation For a DELETE event, the firing order will be BEFORE DELETE FOR EACH STATEMENT, BEFORE DELETE FOR EACH ROW, AFTER DELETE FOR EACH ROW, AFTER DELETE FOR EACH STATEMENT. However, because two of these triggers apply to the BEFORE DELETE FOR EACH ROW event (namely, PRODUCT_AUDIT and PRODUCT_EDIT), then there is no way to know for sure which will be fired first. Ideally, those two triggers should be rewritten if the firing order is significant.

6. A. INSERTING and D. UPDATING

Explanation The conditional predicates are INSERTING, UPDATING, and DELETING.

7. C. The TRIGGER_BODY column of the USER_TRIGGERS view

Explanation Trigger code is always found in USER_TRIGGERS, never in USER_SOURCE. The LONG column TRIGGER_BODY contains the source code.

8. B. FOR EACH STATEMENT

Explanation Triggers are, by default, FOR EACH STATEMENT, unless specified as a FOR EACH ROW. Remember that the reserved words FOR EACH STATEMENT are never actually used.

9. C.   ALTER TABLE EMPLOYEES ENABLE ALL TRIGGERS

Explanation   A would be correct if the keyword COMPILE were used. B is incorrect; the ENABLE ALL phrase is used with tables. D is missing the ALL reserved word. C is correct.

10. D.   DESCRIPTION

Explanation   Don't get irritated at me, the exam really has questions like this! The DESRIPTION column combines information from many columns to display the trigger header, including the database event. TRIGGER_NAME is the name of the trigger, ACTION_TYPE only shows either PL/SQL or Call, and the WHEN_CLAUSE is the trigger's WHEN clause.

CHAPTER
6

Working with Program Units

here are a number of issues that are unique to program units that we discuss in this chapter. Where is the best place to execute a program unit—on the client or on the server? We'll look at the advantages and disadvantages of both. Other topics discussed here include some of the more unusual options of language syntax, including compiler directives and additional ways to declare procedures and functions. Finally, we look at packages in more detail, exploring how variables, constants, cursors, and other packaged constructs can be used to achieve effects that other declared program units' elements cannot achieve.

In this chapter, you will review and understand the following topics:

- Client-side versus server-side program units

- Local subprograms

- Overloading

- Initializing variables with a one-time-only procedure

- Functions and purity levels

- Persistent states

Client-Side versus Server-Side Program Units

For most of our review so far, we've considered program units that are stored in the database. In a typical client-server architecture, the database is stored on the server, while an end-user interface, such as an Oracle Form or Oracle Report, or a SQL*Plus window runs on the client. When we talk about Procedural Language/Structured Query Language (PL/SQL) program units that are running *on the server*, we mean that these program units are stored in the database, as either a stored procedure or function, or as a packaged procedure or function. Furthermore, stored program units not only reside in the database, but they execute there as well.

Program units may also be stored on the client side. Client-side programs can be stored in a variety of forms and in general have more limited accessibility than server-side program units.

See Figure 6-1 for a diagram that summarizes some of the different types of program units that we will look at in this section. Please note that in Chapter 7, we will examine examples of each of these program units in detail. This section addresses the general behavior of the different types of program units.

Program units are invoked in different ways, depending on where they are stored, and from where you are calling them. All of the examples we have looked at

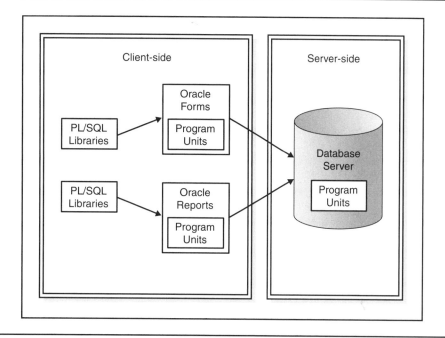

FIGURE 6-1. *Client-side and server-side program units*

so far have addressed the syntax of calling procedures, and the syntax you use to reference a program unit has nothing to do with whether the program unit is stored on the client or the server. Syntax is not the issue of this section. Our concern here is with whether the program unit will be located and identified by the code—you can be using the proper syntax to execute a procedure, but if the procedure cannot be located, then the program unit won't execute.

NOTE
For the purpose of this section's discussion, we are assuming that users attempting to reference the program units have already been granted the proper privileges to do so. The topic of privileges will be addressed in more detail in Chapter 10.

Invoking Server-Side Program Units

A stored program unit in the database can be invoked from anywhere on the network. If you issue a program unit call from within a SELECT statement or from any PL/SQL code in a client application, such as an Oracle Form, then any server-side program units to which the user has been granted privileges will be located and executed.

Server-side program units are much more accessible than client-side program units. Because they reside on the server, any client processes that execute the program unit will traverse the network to locate, execute, and return data from the program unit.

Invoking Client-Side Program Units

Program units that reside on the client are not as accessible as program units stored on the server. They are invoked in a variety of ways, but are not necessarily accessible to every user with access to the database. A program unit that is stored on the client can be any of the following:

- **Program units stored in a client-side module**   A *module* is generally an Oracle Form or Oracle Report. These program units include those that are stored in the module itself, such as procedures, functions, or packages. These program units are owned by the module and are only available for use within that particular module.

- **PL/SQL libraries attached to a client-side module**   Libraries are stand-alone files that reside on the client and may include procedures, functions, or packages. Libraries are attached to modules and enable the developer to create one set of program units that can be shared by multiple modules. The program units are only accessible to the modules to which the library is attached.

You could argue that stand-alone ASCII text files are client-side program units, but you'd have a hard time winning that argument. You can create any SQL code or PL/SQL code and store it in a text file, and then invoke that text file by filename from within a database session—provided that the machine you are using to access the database has access to the file. You can execute a text file from within SQL*Plus with the START filename command. PL/SQL blocks that are stored in text files are a crude alternative to stored program units. They can include anonymous blocks, or they can include CREATE OR REPLACE commands to store a program unit. You could even edit the file to include a command to execute the program unit after it has been created. However, these are not named program units.

In every example of client-side program units, it is required that the file containing the program unit be physically present on the client in order for the program unit to be accessible. Program units may be placed in the client-side module itself, or attached to it in the form of a separate library.

Once this is accomplished, the client can issue a call to a program unit (usually starting from a PL/SQL trigger), and the Oracle system will automatically locate the program unit. It will search, in order, the following:

1. The local module from within which the program unit call was made will be searched. This is a client-side search. If the program unit call was made from a form, then the form's own program units will be searched first.

2. Any attached libraries to the local module from which the program unit call was made will be searched. This is also a client-side search. For an Oracle Form or Report, if a program unit call is made and the program unit isn't owned by the module, then any attached libraries will be scanned for the program unit.

3. The current schema in the database will be searched. This is a server-side search. Any program units owned by the schema will be scanned.

4. Any program units stored elsewhere in the database that the schema has privileges for will be searched. This is also a server-side search.

In other words, when a program unit call is made, the Oracle system will try to find the closest program unit that matches the call, and it will execute the first one it finds. Once it finds a match, it will execute that program unit and stop looking any further. Therefore, if you have created a packaged function in your local Oracle Form with the same name as a packaged function stored in the database, the local packaged function will be the one that is executed from within your Oracle Form.

The Trade-off—Where to Put Them?

Where is the best place to store a program unit? It depends on what the program unit is intended to do. Generally, it is best to place a program unit closest to the objects with which it interacts the most. In many cases, that means the database—but not always. As we will see when we discuss prewritten database packages in Chapter 7, Oracle provides some database packages that work with objects that are not in the database, such as Oracle Form display elements like fields, checkboxes, and other screen components. Sometimes those program units have no interaction with the database at all, but instead interact with client-side form elements. In this case, it is not only silly to place them in the database, but it may be impossible if those program units invoke some of Oracle's prewritten packages that only reside in Oracle Forms. So although many examples, including most of what we will see in this book, are best stored in the database, that is not always the case. The rule of thumb: Place the program unit closest to the constructs with which the program unit interacts the most.

For Review

1. Program units stored in the database are known as *server-side* program units. Program units stored in an Oracle Form or an attached library are known as *client-side* program units.

2. When a call to a program unit is issued, the Oracle system will locate the closest match, execute that program unit, and not look any further across the network.

Exercises

1. **Which of the following is a client-side program unit? (Choose all that apply.)**

   A. A stand-alone function in a library file attached to an Oracle Report

   B. A stored function in the database schema LIBRARY that is called from an Oracle Form

   C. A procedure stored in a package that is stored in the schema CLIENT and executed from a Java application

   D. A procedure owned by an Oracle Form

2. **You have a PL/SQL program that executes in an Oracle Form stored on a client that is logged into the schema ACCOUNTING. The program calls the procedure BUDGET. Which one of the following program units is the one that will execute, at the exclusion of the others? (Choose one.)**

   A. The BUDGET procedure stored in the database in the schema ACCOUNTING

   B. The BUDGET procedure stored in a package in the database in the schema ACCOUNTING

   C. The BUDGET procedure stored in the library attached to the Oracle Form you are executing

   D. The BUDGET procedure owned by the Oracle Form you are executing

---

Answer Key
1. A, D.   2. D.

Local Subprograms

Local subprograms are procedures and functions that are declared in the declaration section within another procedure or function. The following is an example:

```
DECLARE
  v_discount NUMBER(3,2);
  v_price    NUMBER(3);
  PROCEDURE get_discounted_price (p_price NUMBER) IS
  BEGIN
    v_price := v_price - (p_price * v_discount);
  END;
BEGIN
  v_price    := 249.99;
  v_discount := .10;
  get_discounted_price(v_price);
  DBMS_OUTPUT.PUT_LINE('The discounted price is ' || v_price);
END;
```

This anonymous block includes a declaration section that declares two variables and a local subprogram, which is a procedure in this example. This procedure, get_discounted_price, is only accessible from within the processing section of this anonymous block. Note that the local procedure is able to take parameters and reference the variables v_discount and v_price.

Local subprograms can be defined within the declaration section of stored procedures, stored functions, and packaged procedures and functions. They are declared in the declaration section after all other declared constructs—they must be the last of the declared constructs. Once declared, a local subprogram can be invoked only from within the block that declares it, which means it can be called from the processing and/or exception sections. Local subprograms cannot be referenced outside the block in which they are declared.

Local subprograms can reference other declared elements, provided those declared elements precede them in the declaration section. Local subprograms can even call each other, again, provided the called subprogram is declared prior to the calling subprogram.

Forward Declarations

In the event that you need to create two local subprograms that both call each other, you can use a forward declaration to get around the issue of prior declaration. Here's an example:

```
PROCEDURE AUDIT_BOOKINGS IS
  v_bookings NUMBER(3) := 375;
```

```
FUNCTION GET_DISCOUNT(p_guest_id NUMBER DEFAULT 0)
RETURN NUMBER;

FUNCTION GET_REVENUE
RETURN NUMBER IS
BEGIN
  RETURN (v_bookings * (FINANCE.rate - GET_DISCOUNT));
END;

FUNCTION GET_DISCOUNT(p_guest_id NUMBER DEFAULT 0)
RETURN NUMBER IS
  v_discount NUMBER(3,2);
BEGIN
  IF (p_guest_id <> 0) THEN
    IF (GET_REVENUE > 1000000) THEN RETURN .05;
    ELSE                          RETURN .10;
    END IF;
  ELSE
    v_discount := .07;
    RETURN v_discount;
  END IF;
END;
BEGIN
  -- perform processing section statements here
END;
```

In the previous code sample, there are two local subprograms: GET_REVENUE and GET_DISCOUNT. Both contain calls to the other, but naturally only one can be defined before the other. Therefore, a forward declaration is used at the very beginning to declare the header for the function GET_DISCOUNT, yet the full declaration of GET_DISCOUNT is repeated in total later in the declaration section. Without that forward declaration, the procedure AUDIT_BOOKINGS won't compile successfully.

Forward declarations are not used with variables or constants, but they can be used with the TYPE statement. The TYPE statement is used to declare complex PL/SQL constructs. Sometimes one TYPE declaration is dependent upon another TYPE declaration. To make a forward declaration of a TYPE statement, declare the header of the TYPE and then repeat the entire TYPE declaration later when it can be declared. The following shows an example:

```
PROCEDURE PROC_BALANCE_LEDGER IS
  TYPE cpa_ptype;
  TYPE entry_ptype IS RECORD
    (entry_id NUMBER(3),
```

```
    cpa      cpa_ptype);
  TYPE cpa_ptype IS RECORD
    (cpa_id    NUMBER(3),
     name      VARCHAR2(30),
     firm      VARCHAR2(30));
BEGIN
  NULL;
END;
```

In this example, the header of type cpa_ptype is declared right away, so that the type entry_ptype, which is based on cpa_ptype, can be successfully declared. Finally, cpa_ptype is fully declared. The forward declaration of cpa_ptype at the beginning of the declarative section is what enables entry_ptype to be successfully declared.

Note that for this example, we could have done some editing and avoided the need for the forward declaration. However, you will find that this is sometimes not an option, especially with more complex examples. More often, you are likely to find that some program units have lengthy declarative sections. Although you may be able to cleverly juggle the sequencing of declarations to avoid forward declarations, the time involved may not be worth the effort from the standpoint of the initial development as well as the maintenance effort. Forward declarations are an option in such situations.

A Review: The PL/SQL TYPE Statement and PL/SQL Tables and Records

The TYPE statement is a PL/SQL syntax issue, which is the focus of the first certification exam, but you must be familiar with the TYPE statement and what it can do to fully understand some of the concepts that the second exam addresses, which is the focus of this book. The TYPE statement was first introduced in PL/SQL version 2.1, and its functionality has been extended significantly in Oracle8.

With the TYPE statement, you can create

■ Programmer-defined records (TYPE . . . IS RECORD . . .)

■ PL/SQL tables (TYPE . . . IS TABLE OF . . .)

A *programmer-defined record* is a combination of constructs similar to variables, using standard PL/SQL datatypes, collected under one single name. The process required to create a programmer-defined record is a two-step process. The first step is to define a unique type using the TYPE statement. The second step is to use that type to declare the programmer-defined record variable.

The following code sample demonstrates both:

```
PACKAGE PACK_VENDOR AS
  -- a record type
  TYPE vendor_ptype IS RECORD
    (vendor_id      NUMBER(3),
     company_name   VARCHAR2(30),
     url            VARCHAR2(80));
END PACK_VENDOR;
```

In this example, the TYPE statement is used to create the programmer-defined record type vendor_ptype, which can now be used to create programmer-defined record variables, as in the following example:

```
PROCEDURE MONTHLY_BILLING IS
  -- declare one PL/SQL record variable
  rec_leading_vendor PACK_VENDOR.vendor_ptype;
BEGIN
  ... processing statements here ...
END MONTHLY_BILLING;
```

In this example, the record variable rec_leading_vendor is a single declaration that creates, in essence, three variables:

- rec_leading_vendor.vendor_id
- rec_leading_vendor.company_name
- rec_leading_vendor.url

This record variable can now be used just like a variable declared with %ROWTYPE. In other words, use dot notation and the full name of the variable to reference each individual construct within the record variable.

A *PL/SQL table* is very similar to a single-dimensional array in other third-generation languages, such as COBOL, FORTRAN, C, or Java. A PL/SQL table is also created in two steps, just like programmer-defined records. The first step is to use the TYPE statement to declare a table type based on a standard PL/SQL datatype or record type. The second step is to use your newly created table type to declare the PL/SQL table variable. The following example builds on the PACK_VENDOR package we just examined:

```
PACKAGE PACK_VENDOR AS
  TYPE categories_ttype IS TABLE OF VARCHAR2(15);
  TYPE vendor_ptype IS RECORD
    (vendor_id      NUMBER(3),
```

```
          company_name    VARCHAR2(30),
          url              VARCHAR2(80));
    TYPE vendor_list_ttype IS TABLE OF vendor_ptype;
END PACK_VENDOR;
```

This example creates two PL/SQL table types. The first is called categories_ttype. It is a table of VARCHAR2(15), meaning that this single type represents a theoretically infinite set of rows, each consisting of one variable of the type VARCHAR2(15). The second PL/SQL table variable is vendor_list_ttype and is a table of vendor_ptype, which is the programmer-defined record that we looked at earlier. This second PL/SQL table type will declare a set of rows of the vendor_ptype. This is very similar to a database table object, except it's declared within a PL/SQL program unit.

Next, we create the actual PL/SQL tables based on these TYPE statements:

```
PROCEDURE MONTHLY_BILLING IS
  -- declare one PL/SQL record variable
  rec_leading_vendor       PACK_VENDOR.vendor_ptype;
  -- declare two PL/SQL tables
  table_approved_list      PACK_VENDOR.vendor_list_ttype;
  table_vendor_categories PACK_VENDOR.categories_ttype;
BEGIN
  ... processing statements here ...
END MONTHLY_BILLING;
```

The declared variables table_approved_list and table_vendor_categories are PL/SQL tables. The first, table_approved_list, represents a set of rows, each of which can contain a value for vendor_id, company_name, and url. The second, table_vendor_categories, represents a set of rows, each of which can contain one VARCHAR2(30) value.

In this example, the TYPE statement is used in a package PACK_VENDOR to declare the types as public global types, in other words, as persistent types. The TYPE statements and variable declarations could have been included in the same program unit, whether it was a package, procedure, function, or something else.

There is much more to the TYPE statement and programmer-defined records and PL/SQL tables. For example, the manner in which values can be assigned, the fact that two records cannot be compared in a BOOLEAN statement, or that one record variable can assign all of its values to another record variable of the same type in a single statement. There's also the issue of indexing in PL/SQL tables and how to iterate through the rows of a PL/SQL table. But all of these are issues for the first exam, not this one. For the subject matter of this book, we are more concerned with these complex types from the perspective of how they can be passed as parameters, how they behave as public globals, and other issues related to program units.

For Review

1. Local subprograms are procedures and functions that are declared in the declarative section of a PL/SQL block. They can be used in anonymous blocks, stored procedures or functions, and packaged procedures and functions. They can be called only within the block that declares them.

2. Any construct declarations in a PL/SQL block that references other declared constructs must be declared after the constructs they reference. However, forward declarations can be used with local subprograms as well as with declared types so that you can create mutually referential declarations.

Exercises

1. **Which of the following is true of a local subprogram? (Choose all that apply.)**

    A. It can be declared in a package specification.

    B. It must be declared with a forward declaration.

    C. It cannot be referenced outside the block that declares it.

    D. It is automatically global.

2. **Which of the following is true of forward declarations? (Choose all that apply.)**

    A. They can be used to declare constants that depend on values from another declared construct.

    B. Forward declarations of functions require the RETURN in the function header.

    C. They can only be used with procedures and functions.

    D. They use the keyword FORWARD.

Answers
1. C. 2. B.

Overloading

The concept of overloading, when applied to procedures and functions, is the concept of creating multiple program units with the same name but with different parameter lists. Parameter lists are considered different if the parameter list differs in number, order, and/or datatype family. Datatype families include DATE, character string (VARCHAR2, CHAR), and numeric (NUMBER, INTEGER, and so on). In other words, if a procedure has a single parameter of type NUMBER, you cannot overload it by making another procedure with the same name and with a single parameter of datatype INTEGER because that is considered the same datatype family. However, you could create another procedure of the same name with a single parameter with a datatype of DATE.

Overloaded program units are used frequently in the Oracle database; the SQL language already employs several. For example, consider the TO_CHAR function in SQL. TO_CHAR can be used to convert numeric values into character strings. If you were to attempt to create the function header for this function, you might start with this:

```
FUNCTION TO_CHAR(P_SOME_NUMBER NUMBER)
RETURN VARCHAR2
```

But after some thought, you would remember that TO_CHAR can also be used to convert DATE values into numeric strings, and you would need this function header for that purpose:

```
FUNCTION TO_CHAR(P_SOME_DATE DATE)
RETURN VARCHAR2
```

So which is correct? They both are. These are two different functions, both called TO_CHAR. The database enables you to create multiple procedures and functions with the same name within a schema as long as the parameters are different in number, order, and/or datatype and provided that the overloaded program units are contained in a package, or are local program units of the same PL/SQL block.

Creating Overloaded Modules

An *overloaded module*, also known as an *overloaded subprogram*, is a procedure or function that is created with the same name of another procedure but has a different parameter list. Specifically, you can overload procedures or functions within the same package, or you can overload local subprograms within the same declaration section of the same PL/SQL block.

For example, consider the following package specification:

```
CREATE OR REPLACE PACKAGE PACK_MARKETING AS
  PROCEDURE MKT_PROJECTION;
  PROCEDURE MKT_PROJECTION(MK_ID NUMBER);
```

```
    PROCEDURE MKT_PROJECTION(MK_NAME VARCHAR2);
    PROCEDURE MKT_PROJECTION(MK_ID NUMBER, MK_NAME VARCHAR2);
    PROCEDURE MKT_PROJECTION(MK_NAME VARCHAR2, MK_ID NUMBER);
END PACK_MARKETING;
/
```

This is a valid package that will compile successfully. The five procedures in the package have the same name, but different parameter lists. Parameter lists are considered different if they differ in the number of parameters, the order of the parameters, or the datatypes of the parameters. The first procedure has no parameters. The second procedure has a single parameter whose datatype is NUMBER. The third procedure also has a single parameter, but its datatype is VARCHAR2. The fourth and fifth procedures have two parameters, but the ordering, or sequencing, of the datatypes is different.

When identifying parameter lists as being unique, the actual names of the parameters themselves are irrelevant. Parameter names are only meaningful to the program unit to which the parameter is being passed. But for the purposes of comparing multiple parameter lists among a set of program units, the datatypes of the parameters and the number of parameters are all that matter.

This package specification could be given a corresponding package body to define each of these procedures. The package body should create each procedure individually because there are five different procedures.

Note that these procedures are included in a single package. You cannot create overloaded stored procedures outside of a package. If you issue a CREATE OR REPLACE PROCEDURE statement to build a procedure with the same name of an existing stored procedure but with a different parameter list, the result will be that the old procedure will be overwritten, not overloaded. If you issue the CREATE PROCEDURE statement without the OR REPLACE option to attempt the same thing, you'll get the error "ORA-00955: name is already used by an existing object."

You can overload packaged functions as well as packaged procedures. However, you cannot overload them in combination—in other words, you cannot name any function, in any situation, with the same name as any procedure in the same namespace. The opposite is true; you cannot create a procedure with the same name as any function, regardless of overloading. Also, note that when overloading functions in particular, the RETURN datatype can be different among the overloaded functions.

The code in your overloaded modules does not necessarily have to be identical or even remotely similar. However, the general reason for creating overloaded modules is to communicate through the common name that the business rules in each procedure or function are, in fact, similar in nature. For example, the TO_CHAR function we looked at earlier is meant to convert something to a character string. There are two different functions that were written to support the TO_CHAR feature: one that takes a NUMBER parameter and another that takes a

DATE parameter. These functions have their own processing sections, but they accomplish the same ultimate goal of conversion to a character string.

If you accidentally make a syntax mistake when you create your overloaded modules, you might not get an error message right away. Consider this example:

```
CREATE OR REPLACE PACKAGE MARKETING AS
   PROCEDURE MONTHLY_BUDGET(p_product_number IN VARCHAR2);
   PROCEDURE MONTHLY_BUDGET(p_product_name  IN VARCHAR2);
END MARKETING;
```

These two modules are improperly overloaded—the parameter names may be different, but that is irrelevant. The datatypes are identical, and the number in the list —one parameter per procedure—is also identical. This is a mistake.

However, the compiler will not complain when this code sample is submitted to the database:

```
Package created.
```

On the other hand, let's assume you've created a corresponding package body. When you attempt to actually use one of these procedures, you will receive the following execution error:

```
PLS-00307: too many declarations of 'MONTHLY_BUDGET' match this call
PL/SQL: Statement ignored
```

The block from which you call the improperly overloaded program unit will not execute. In this example, the package specification MARKETING, which compiled fine, needs to be edited in order for these procedures to be correctly overloaded.

Namespaces for Program Units

One topic that arises in a discussion of overloading is the topic of namespace. A *namespace* is a boundary within which you must choose distinct names for a particular type of database object. For example, as you probably know already, the namespace for a table is a schema (*schema* is the same as the user ID). You cannot create two or more tables with the same name in a single schema. However, you can create a table in one schema that has the same name as another table in another schema. Therefore, the namespace for a table is a schema.

Procedures, functions, and packages are collected into a single namespace for a given schema. In other words, it is illegal to create two procedures in a given schema that have the same name, and it is illegal to create a procedure that has the same name as a function in the same schema. You cannot name a package with the same name as a function or procedure in the same schema.

Note that the namespace for packaged procedures and packaged functions is the package itself. In other words, you can create a packaged procedure that has the same name as a stand-alone database procedure or function that is stored in the same schema.

Triggers have their own namespace within a given schema. You must create triggers with distinct names in a given schema. However, you are allowed to create a trigger that has the same name as a procedure, function, or package in the same schema.

For Review

1. Overloaded program units are those objects within the same namespace that share the same object name, but are allowed to do so provided they have a different set of parameters, as defined by the parameter datatype and the number of parameters. You can overload packaged procedures, and you can overload packaged functions.

2. Namespaces define the boundary within which you can create a database object. Nonpackaged procedures, nonpackaged functions, and packages are all in the same single namespace within a schema. Packaged procedures and packaged functions are in a single namespace within a given package. Triggers have their own namespace for a given schema.

Exercises

1. **Assume you already have a function with the following function header:**

```
FUNCTION CONFIRM_REC(book_id NUMBER)
RETURN BOOLEAN
```

   Which of the following headers would overload this function? (Choose all that apply.)

   A. FUNCTION CONFIRM_REC RETURN BOOLEAN

   B. FUNCTION CONFIRM_REC (book VARCHAR2) RETURN BOOLEAN

   C. FUNCTION CONFIRM_REC (acct NUMBER) RETURN BOOLEAN

   D. FUNCTION CONFIRM_REC (book VARCHAR2) RETURN NUMBER

2. **You have created a stored procedure in the package APPLICATION_TOOLS in the schema ENGINEERING with the following header:**

```
PROCEDURE ARCHIVE (p_archive_id NUMBER)
```

Which of the following procedure headers will be accepted in the package APPLICATION_TOOLS in the ENGINEERING schema? (Choose all that apply.)

A. PROCEDURE ARCHIVE (p_archive_id VARCHAR2)

B. PROCEDURE ARCHIVE (p_month NUMBER)

C. PACKAGE ARCHIVE

D. FUNCTION ARCHIVE(p_archive_id NUMBER) RETURN VARCHAR2

Answer Key
1. A, B, D. 2. A.

Initializing Variables with a One-Time-Only Procedure

One of the benefits of working with packages is the fact that an entire package is loaded into the System Global Area (SGA) when the first reference to a package construct is invoked within a schema session. This way, subsequent calls to any other package constructs are faster because the package is already loaded in the SGA, providing for a quick execution.

As the developer, you have an opportunity to execute code at the time the package is loaded. If you are familiar with Oracle Forms or recall the discussion about database triggers, you can think of this code as a *when-package-loaded* trigger. This initialization code consists of a PL/SQL block you include in the package body after the declaration of any program units within the package body. This code can include any valid PL/SQL statements and is often used to perform the complex initialization of package variables. Here is an example:

```
PACKAGE APPLICATION_SESSION AS
   session_id SESSIONS.SESSION_ID%TYPE;
   user_name  VARCHAR2(30);
   login_date DATE;
   PROCEDURE UPDATE_LAST_ACCESS (last_access_date DATE);
END APPLICATION_SESSION;

PACKAGE BODY APPLICATION_SESSION AS
   PROCEDURE UPDATE_LAST_ACCESS (last_access_date DATE) IS
```

```
BEGIN
  UPDATE SESSIONS
     SET LAST_ACCESS = last_access_date
   WHERE SESSION_ID  = APPLICATION_SESSION.session_id;
   COMMIT;
END UPDATE_LAST_ACCESS;
-- perform initialization
BEGIN
  SELECT SESSION_ID, USER, SYSDATE
   INTO   APPLICATION_SESSION.session_id,
          APPLICATION_SESSION.user_name,
          APPLICATION_SESSION.login_date
  . FROM   SESSIONS
   WHERE  USER_NAME = USER;
END APPLICATION_SESSION;
```

The initialization section is created in the package body and starts after the BEGIN statement in the package body. Note that in this example, the package body for APPLICATION_SESSION includes the full declaration of a procedure, and then the initialization section, starting with a BEGIN statement.

This initialization section of a package is executed only one time. That time is when the first package construct is invoked. This is true for any package construct— a packaged procedure, a packaged cursor, or whatever construct is first invoked will automatically cause the initialization section to execute.

Your package initialization may change the values of any package constructs, either constructs in this package or constructs in another. However, it is not considered good design to change the values in another package; this should only be done in the package in which the initialization appears.

For Review

1. The package initialization section is an optional section you can include in the package body. It must follow the declaration of any packaged constructs and starts with the BEGIN statement.

2. The package initialization section will load one time for a given schema session. That time is the first moment a packaged construct is referenced.

Exercises

1. **Where does the package initialization section appear?**

   A. Anywhere in the package specification if it is public

   B. Anywhere in the package body if it is private

    C. Anywhere in the package body regardless if it is private or public

    D. After all other declarations in the package body

  2. **When does package initialization execute? (Choose the single best answer.)**

    A. After the user logs into the schema session

    B. After the first packaged procedure is executed

    C. After the first packaged construct is referenced

    D. After the package body is executed

Answer Key
1. D. 2. C.

Functions and Purity Levels

Functions that are called from SQL statements have certain restrictions on what they can and cannot do. For example, a function that includes a SELECT statement in its processing section cannot be called from an UPDATE statement that attempts to update the same table that is being selected. You cannot call a function that mutates a particular table from an SQL statement that is also trying to perform a mutating SQL statement—an execution error will occur.

    Note that these restrictions do not apply to procedures because procedures are invoked with a single statement that calls the procedure directly. The issue we are addressing here is an issue of functions, because functions can be called from SQL statements that have the potential to reference the same tables that the function is also modifying at the same time the SQL statement is executing. Specifically, you have to be careful when a function engages in any of the following behavior:

- Changes data in a table

- Reads data from a table

- Changes data in packaged constructs

- Reads data from packaged constructs

For a function to be callable from a SQL statement, there are rules that the function must obey:

- Any function that is called from within any DML statements (SELECT, INSERT, UPDATE, or DELETE) cannot include any transaction control statements (COMMIT, SAVEPOINT, or ROLLBACK), nor can the function do anything to cause DDL statements to execute, since DDL statements automatically force a COMMIT to occur. No ALTER SYSTEM statements are allowed in the function.

- Any function that is called from within a SELECT statement is prohibited from issuing any INSERT. UPDATE, or DELETE statements on any tables.

- Any function that is called from within an INSERT, UPDATE, or DELETE statement is prohibited from referencing the table that is being modified with the INSERT, UPDATE, or DELETE statement. By "referencing the table," we mean that you cannot issue SELECT, INSERT, UPDATE, or DELETE statements on the table that is the subject of the DML statement that invokes the function.

- If a function is to be called from a remote database, it cannot read or write packaged constructs.

None of these behaviors will produce a compilation error in the function. The errors don't show up until execution. In other words, PL/SQL will let you create a valid packaged function that performs any and all of these behaviors. After all, none of them are completely problematic—if you were to call a function from the comparison expression in an IF statement, for example, you would not experience any of the problems we are describing. The only time that problems can occur is when you invoke the function from an SQL statement (such as the WHERE clause of a SELECT or an UPDATE statement), whether it's issued from within another PL/SQL program unit, or as a standalone SQL call in the database.

The reason why you never encounter a compilation error is simple: For the compiler to recognize when a function is crossing into these areas, the compiler must have access to the actual code of the function. With stored functions (functions that are stored in the database, but not in a package), this is not a problem; for packaged functions, this is very much a problem. Remember that you can create a package specification that simply declares the headers of procedures and functions without the body and produce a package that you can immediately start using. With a package specification alone, you can create other program units that make calls to your package specification's functions and procedures before you write the actual corresponding body.

So how does the package specification know what the function can and cannot do? The answer is it cannot know unless you tell it explicitly. You have the option to give the compiler some specific instructions as to what the function body will be doing, if you want to restrict the behavior of a function's processing section. This compiler instruction is declared with the PRAGMA RESTRICT_REFERENCES statement.

The PRAGMA statement is used for many things in PL/SQL. In the case of function warnings, it is used with the keyword RESTRICT_REFERENCES. For example, consider this package specification:

```
PACKAGE STOCK_SHIPS AS
  FUNCTION GET_SHIP_STATUS RETURN VARCHAR2;
  PROCEDURE STOCK_SHIP(p_ship_id NUMBER);
  PRAGMA RESTRICT_REFERENCES(GET_SHIP_STATUS, WNDS, WNPS, RNPS);
END;
```

This is a package specification that declares a function and a procedure. The PRAGMA RESTRICT_REFERENCES statement assures the compiler that the function GET_SHIP_STATUS will not write any database data, nor will it read or write any packaged constructs, such as variables. This declares to the world that this function can be depended upon to not perform any changes to the database or packaged constructs. How can it make this claim? Because the existence of the PRAGMA RESTRICT_REFERENCES in this package specification will force the compiler to analyze the corresponding package body when it is created. If the function that is restricted violates the restriction, the compiler will produce an error message like this:

```
PLS-00452: Subprogram 'GET_SHIP_STATUS'
           violates its associated pragma
```

The use of PRAGMA RESTRICT_REFERENCES in a package specification is optional, but very beneficial. It serves the purpose of clarifying what a function's processing code is doing with regard to the problem areas that might restrict the function's capability to be called from SQL statements and elsewhere. This clarification benefits the developer who creates the associated package body for the function, as well as those who call the function from outside the package.

There are four purity levels you can specify for a function:

- **Writes No Database State (WNDS)**   The function does not issue any INSERT, UPDATE, or DELETE statements to the database.

- **Reads No Database State (RNDS)**   The function issues no SELECT statements.

- **Writes No Package State (WNPS)**   The function makes no changes to packaged constructs.

- **Reads No Package State (RNPS)**   The function reads no packaged constructs.

You can specify any or all of these purity levels for a function. The order in which you specify the purity levels is up to you; it has no effect on the function's processing or functionality.

Note that the PRAGMA RESTRICT_REFERENCES applies to the function and any program units that the function may invoke. In other words, if you create a function that has the RNDS restriction, you are saying that the function and any program units it may call do not read any information from the database. Furthermore, if you do have a called packaged program unit from the function, the called program unit must also have a PRAGMA RESTRICT_REFERENCES declared as well, even if it is a procedure—unless the TRUST keyword is used, which is discussed in an upcoming section in this chapter.

Purity levels are frequently asserted for functions, but it is syntactically acceptable to assert purity levels for procedures, too. In addition, starting with Oracle8*i*, the PRAGMA RESTRICT_REFERENCES is an optional statement for program units in a package specification. Prior to Oracle8*i*, it was required for functions.

WNDS and RNDS

The WNDS purity level asserts that the function you name in the PRAGMA RESTRICT_REFERENCES statement will not issue any INSERT, UPDATE, or DELETE statements to the database. However, if you leave this assertion out, it will be in force anyway—the WNDS purity level is the default purity level for any PRAGMA RESTRICT_REFERENCES statement you include in your code. In other words, if you include the PRAGMA RESTRICT_REFERENCES statement, then WNDS will be in force as a minimum—even if you do not list it in your PRAGMA RESTRICT_REFERENCES statement.

The RNDS purity level asserts that the function will not issue any SELECT statements on the database. If you leave this out, it will not be in force.

Any attempt to create a package body that defines a function or procedure that violates its PRAGMA RESTRICT_REFERENCES assertions will produce a compilation error.

Note that it's possible for an INSERT, UPDATE, or DELETE to violate the RNDS purity level if the statement includes anything that reads from a column, such as an UPDATE statement's SET clause that uses one column to read from and assign a value to another column.

WNPS and RNPS

When a function is restricted with the PRAGMA RESTRICT_REFERENCES and the WNPS purity level, the function is guaranteed to never modify a packaged public construct. The RNPS purity level means the function is guaranteed to never read a packaged public construct. Remember that packaged public constructs are global to a schema session.

WNPS and RNPS do not apply to packaged functions that write to packaged constructs in their own package. They only are applicable to packaged constructs in other packages.

These purity levels are relevant for program units that want to call your package from another database via a database link. Program units that invoke your packaged functions from another database cannot ever call packaged functions that violate these purity levels; therefore, declaring these purity levels provides the assurances that program units in other databases require to successfully invoke your packaged function.

TRUST

In addition to asserting a purity level for a function, you can also use the keyword TRUST in the PRAGMA RESTRICT_REFERENCES statement. TRUST has the effect of enabling you to include the PRAGMA RESTRICT_REFERENCES statement, thus documenting the intended use of the function, but without invoking the parser to actually analyze the function code in the package body.

For example, the use of TRUST enables you to assert a purity level on a function that is stored in the database, but written in Java, and has been *wrapped* with a PL/SQL wrapper. The benefit is that you could now call this trusted function from another PL/SQL function that is, in fact, asserted at a given purity level without the TRUST keyword. Remember that when you assert a purity level, the parser will require that the function code and all program units that your function code calls must be at the same purity level. But what if your function calls a program unit whose purity level cannot be confirmed, such as a Java stored procedure? Then the parser will have no way of accepting the calling function. However, if you declare the called program unit with a PRAGMA RESTRICT_REFERENCES with the TRUST keyword and assert the required purity level, then the calling program unit will successfully compile.

Purity Levels for the Package Initialization Section

You may also assign a purity level to the initialization section of a package. To accomplish this, the same PRAGMA RESTRICT_REFERENCES is used in the package specification, but instead of naming a function, you name the package. This restriction will apply to only the initialization section of the package, not the packaged program units.

The following is an example of a package specification that includes a purity-level specification:

```
PACKAGE PACK_VALIDATION AS
  PRAGMA RESTRICT_REFERENCES(PACK_VALIDATION,WNDS,WNPS,RNDS,RNPS);
  PROCEDURE PROC_OPEN_ORDER;
  PROCEDURE PROC_CLOSE_ORDER;
END PACK_VALIDATION;
```

This package declared a couple packaged procedures, and the corresponding package body is assumed to have an initialization section. The PRAGMA at the beginning of the package declared the purity level for the initialization section. This PRAGMA statement can be issued anywhere within the package specification.

DEFAULT

You can assign a default purity level for a package. The following is an example:

```
PRAGMA RESTRICT_REFERENCES(DEFAULT, WNDS, RNDS);
```

This PRAGMA, included in a package specification, has the effect of declaring all packaged program units to be at this level, unless otherwise specified with its own PRAGMA. Here's another example:

```
PRAGMA RESTRICT_REFERENCES(get_revenue, WNDS);
PRAGMA RESTRICT_REFERENCES(DEFAULT, WNDS, RNDS);
```

These two PRAGMAs, included in a package specification, will assert that the purity level of the function get_revenue is WNDS and that all other packaged program units are WNDS and RNDS. The use of a DEFAULT PRAGMA is optional.

The Benefits of PRAGMA

In general, the benefit of the PRAGMA statement is that the compiler will ensure that the restricted entity (the packaged program unit or package initialization section) obeys the restrictions defined in the PRAGMA, so that anyone who works on this package in the future will understand the intentions for this package. This is important because the package may be invoked from various places that may or may not continue to work if the package is modified. Without the formally declared restrictions, it is possible that some developer in the future could modify the package and inadvertently make some change that will compile successfully and test correctly in some situations with no PRAGMA statement present. But if the package is invoked in those situations where the change would cause a problem, it runs the risk of complicating the testing process and permitting errors to slip through into production. By declaring your intent for a particular package with PRAGMA RESTRICT_REFERENCES statements, you can communicate your intentions clearly, and anyone modifying the package in the future will understand.

For Review

1. The PRAGMA RESTRICT_REFERENCES statement is a directive to the compiler that is declared in the package specification and that communicates to the compiler information about your intended coding restrictions for the package body. You can apply any of four purity levels: Writes No Database State (WNDS), Reads No Database State (RNDS), Writes No Package State (WNPS), and Reads No Package State (RNPS).

2. You can declare purity levels on packaged program units and also on a package initialization section. By making a purity-level declaration, you empower the compiler to protect the package body from violating the purity level and you clarify the intent of the restricted packaged function, packaged procedure, or package initialization for future developers.

Exercises

1. **You have created a function that must be called from a program unit in another database. Which of the following purity levels must you assert for the packaged function? (Choose all that apply.)**

    A. WNDS

    B. RNDS

    C. WNPS

    D. RNPS

2. **Where do you place the PRAGMA RESTRICT_REFERENCES statement for a packaged function that must not issue DELETE statements?**

    A. In the function's header.

    B. Anywhere in the package specification.

    C. In the package specification before the function header.

    D. You cannot do this.

Answer Key
1. C, D. **2.** B.

Persistent States

We first looked at the topic of persistent states when we reviewed global constructs in Chapter 4. We will discuss the concept in more detail in this section.

Persistence in PL/SQL refers to the capability of PL/SQL packaged public constructs to retain data beyond the execution of a single program unit. This is a feature of packaged public constructs; there is nothing you as the developer have to do over and above the declaration of a packaged public construct to achieve persistence.

The concept of persistence is not unique to PL/SQL. Persistence refers to the ability of a data store to retain information beyond the execution of a single program or process. In general, data that is stored in a database table is said to be persistent. The value of a variable declared in the declaration section of a PL/SQL program unit is not persistent—as soon as the program unit's execution is completed, any value the variable may have contained is lost. However, when you declare public constructs in a package, their existence is global to the session of the schema that invokes the package as opposed to local variable declarations within any program unit, which are not. Packaged public constructs are automatically persistent to the schema session. You can declare several types of persistent constructs in a PL/SQL package such as variables, constants, cursors, tables, and records.

Persistent Variables and Constants

The following is an example of a persistent variable and a persistent constant:

```
PACKAGE PACK_FINANCE AS
   v_interest_rate          NUMBER(3,2) := .09;
   c_loan_term     CONSTANT NUMBER(3)   := 60; -- in months
END PACK_FINANCE;
```

This package specification declares two constructs: a variable v_interest_rate and a constant c_loan_term. The construct v_interest_rate is a public variable, and c_loan_term is a public constant. Both are public because they are declared in the package specification. If both were declared in the package body instead, they would be private and only be access ible from within the same package body in which they were declared. They would not be global to the schema session however, they would still not be persistent. Packaged constructs, public or private, are persistent to each session of each schema that references them.

Figure 4-5, which we saw in Chapter 4, demonstrated how a packaged variable could be referenced from other PL/SQL blocks and how one PL/SQL block could set the value of a packaged global variable while another block referenced that changed value later on. Note, however, that the persistence found in packaged constructs, such as variables and constants, is global to the schema session. See

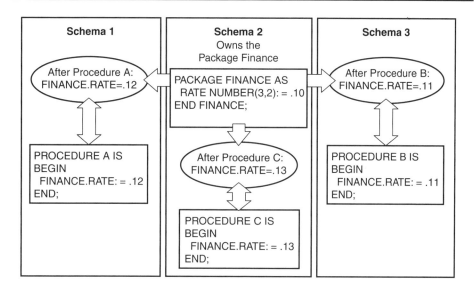

Note: This figure assumes the presence of a public synonym created with the statement
"CREATE PUBLIC SYNONYM FINANCE FOR SCHEMA2.FINANCE".

FIGURE 6-2. *One packaged global variable, changed by three different schemas*

Figure 6-2. Schema 2 owns a package with a public variable RATE. The variable is
initialized in the package to a value of .10. However, Schemas 1, 2, and 3 are all
able to modify the value of the package with their own procedures, and once
modified, they retain their own unique modifications within their own schema
sessions.

Any values set within a session are limited to that session alone and are lost
when the session terminates. If you want to enable values to persist beyond the
session, you must store the values in a database table.

The same is true for values you want to share across multiple schemas. Although
a single package can be invoked by many schemas, each schema recognizes its own
state for the packaged constructs.

See Figure 6-3. The schema FESTIVAL is logged in, and in a single session,
creates a package FINANCE that contains one public variable RATE initialized to the
value of .11. Then it grants execute privileges on the package to the schema
JBREWINGTON. (The topic of granting privileges will be explored in greater depth
in Chapter 10.) Then it runs two successive anonymous blocks. The first anonymous
block references the packaged variable RATE, adds .01 to the value, and then prints

```
Oracle SQL*Plus                                          _ □ ×
File  Edit  Search  Options  Help
SQL> SHOW USER              █
USER is "FESTIVAL"
SQL> CREATE OR REPLACE PACKAGE FINANCE AS
  2    rate NUMBER(3,2) := 0.11;
  3  END FINANCE;
  4  /

Package created.

SQL> GRANT EXECUTE ON FINANCE TO JBREWINGTON;

Grant succeeded.

SQL> BEGIN
  2    FINANCE.rate := FINANCE.rate + 0.01;
  3    DBMS_OUTPUT.PUT_LINE('rate=' || FINANCE.rate);
  4  END;
  5  /
rate=.12

PL/SQL procedure successfully completed.

SQL> BEGIN
  2    FINANCE.rate := FINANCE.rate + 0.01;
  3    DBMS_OUTPUT.PUT_LINE('rate=' || FINANCE.rate);
  4  END;
  5  /
rate=.13

PL/SQL procedure successfully completed.

SQL> CONNECT JBREWINGTON/PASSWORD
Connected.
SQL> SET SERVEROUTPUT ON
SQL> BEGIN
  2    FESTIVAL.FINANCE.rate := FESTIVAL.FINANCE.rate + 0.01;
  3    DBMS_OUTPUT.PUT_LINE('rate=' || FESTIVAL.FINANCE.rate);
  4  END;
  5  /
rate=.12

PL/SQL procedure successfully completed.

SQL>
SQL>
```

FIGURE 6-3. *The package FINANCE, as seen by two schemas*

the result, which is seen as .12. The second anonymous block does the exact same thing, and the result is seen as .13—in other words, the second anonymous block picked up where the previous block left off, remembering the last value of FINANCE.RATE.

Next, the session connects to a different schema, JBREWINGTON, from which we run the same anonymous block for a third time and get the result of .12. In other words, JBREWINGTON is starting over with the initialized value of .11 for FINANCE.RATE. The changes performed in the FESTIVAL schema's session are lost because that schema's session is completed.

If both schemas were logged on concurrently, the same result would occur. Changes made in one schema to a packaged variable are not seen in any concurrent schemas, which respect their own changes.

If Figure 6-3 were to continue with a reconnection to the original FESTIVAL schema, we would see that FINANCE.RATE is reinitialized to .11.

One item to note: You may have noticed in Figure 6-3 that JBREWINGTON references the packaged variable as FESTIVAL.FINANCE.RATE. This is the schema.package.construct naming convention that is required when no public synonyms have been created—more information on this topic appears in Chapter 10.

Persistent Tables, Records, and Types

Packaged public PL/SQL tables and records created with the TYPE statement behave the same way as variables and constants. In other words, when you declare a PL/SQL table or record, the construct is global to the schema and can be used in any PL/SQL code that executes during the course of the schema session.

One issue to be aware of, however, is the use of the same TYPE statement versus different TYPE statements that define the same structure. When you build a construct based on a programmer-defined record, as many PL/SQL tables and record variables are, you must recognize that one TYPE is not recognized as identical to another TYPE, even if they both use the same definition. This is an issue when passing parameters. The following shows an example:

```
PACKAGE GUEST_DEALS AS
  TYPE promotion_type IS RECORD
    (promotion_id NUMBER(3),
     promotion_name VARCHAR2(30));
END GUEST_DEALS;
```

This package declares a public TYPE that can be used to create a PL/SQL programmer-defined record variable. Now consider this procedure:

```
PROCEDURE SPECIAL_ORDER(p_promotion GUEST_DEALS.promotion_type) IS
  ... additional code here ...
END SPECIAL_ORDER;
```

This stand-alone procedure will accept an incoming parameter of a record variable defined with the packaged TYPE promotion_type.

However, now consider this code sample:

```
DECLARE
  TYPE promo_type IS RECORD
    (promotion_id NUMBER(3),
    promotion_name VARCHAR2(30));
  promo promo_type;
BEGIN
  ... populate values for "promo" ...
  SPECIAL_ORDER(promo);
END;
```

This code will not work. Because the record variable being passed is declared with a type that is technically different, even though the type is declared with the identical structure, it will not be recognized as the correct type for the procedure SPECIAL_ORDER, which is only expecting the packaged public type GUEST_DEALS.promo_type. The solution is as follows:

```
DECLARE
  promo GUEST_DEALS.promotion_type;
BEGIN
  ... populate values for "promo" ...
  SPECIAL_ORDER(promo);
END;
```

This code will be accepted by the procedure SPECIAL_ORDER.

Packaged public types can be used, therefore, to declare packaged public PL/SQL tables and records as well as other PL/SQL tables and records that must be recognized as the same type.

Persistent Cursors

Packaged public cursors are also persistent to a schema session. This means that a cursor can be opened in one program unit, fetched in another, and closed in still another. The following package contains public constructs:

```
PACKAGE BOX AS
  v_ship_id SHIPS.SHIP_ID%TYPE;
  CURSOR cur_cruises IS
    SELECT CRUISE_ID, CRUISE_NAME,
           CAPTAIN_ID, STATUS,
           START_DATE, END_DATE
    FROM   CRUISES
    WHERE  SHIP_ID = v_ship_id;
  rec_cruises cur_cruises%ROWTYPE;
END BOX;
```

In the package BOX, which is a toolbox of constructs for use elsewhere in our application, we now have the variable v_ship_id, the cursor cur_cruises, and the record variable rec_cruises. Note that the packaged cursor BOX.cur_cruises is based on the value of BOX.v_ship_id and that the cursor will parse based on the value of BOX.v_ship_id at the time the OPEN statement is issued. This package obviously doesn't issue an OPEN statement; this will be the job of some other program unit, which will have to define the value for v_ship_id first and then open the cursor.

Now that we have declared our packaged public constructs, let's start to use them. Consider the function FIND_SHIP:

```
FUNCTION FIND_SHIP
  (p_ship_name IN VARCHAR2)
RETURN BOOLEAN IS
  CURSOR cur_ships IS
    SELECT SHIP_ID
    FROM   SHIPS
    WHERE  SHIP_NAME = p_ship_name;
  v_found BOOLEAN;
BEGIN
  OPEN  cur_ships;
  FETCH cur_ships INTO BOX.v_ship_id;
  IF cur_ships%FOUND THEN
    v_found := TRUE;
  ELSE
    v_found := FALSE;
  END IF;
  CLOSE cur_ships;
  IF v_found THEN
  OPEN BOX.cur_cruises;
  END IF;
  RETURN v found;
END FIND_SHIP;
```

This function will receive a ship name as a string parameter and attempt to locate a corresponding SHIP_ID in the SHIPS table. The function returns a value of TRUE if it finds a SHIP_ID and a value of FALSE if it doesn't. When it locates the value for SHIP_ID, it assigns the value to the packaged public variable BOX.v_ship_id and opens the packaged public cursor BOX.cur_cruises.

The following procedure brings everything together. It uses the FIND_SHIP function to locate a ship, and if FIND_SHIP returns a value of TRUE, it fetches records from the cursor, which is already opened, and proceeds to analyze the cruise schedule records for the particular ship:

```
PROCEDURE REVIEW_CRUISE_SCHEDULE IS
BEGIN
  IF (FIND_SHIP('Tropical')) THEN
    LOOP
      FETCH BOX.cur_cruises INTO BOX.rec_cruises;
      EXIT WHEN BOX.cur_cruises%NOTFOUND;
      -- Process the ship's schedule here
      VERIFY_CRUISE_DATES(BOX.rec_cruises.CRUISE_ID);
    END LOOP;
  CLOSE BOX.cur_cruises;
  END IF;
END REVIEW_CRUISE_SCHEDULE;
```

The packaged public cursor BOX.cur_cruises is defined in one package, opened in a separate function, and fetched and closed in a separate stand-alone procedure. However, the fact that the cursor and the associated variables are packaged public constructs enables all of this to work.

One additional note: The cursor attribute %ISOPEN is very useful when using packaged public cursors. There may be occasions when you need a statement like the following:

```
IF BOX.cur_cruises%ISOPEN THEN
```

This sort of test may be required when working with packaged public cursors because they may have been opened—or may not have been opened—when a given program unit you are creating executes. This complication requires the use of the %ISOPEN attribute to check since any attempt to fetch or close a cursor that hasn't been opened will cause PL/SQL to raise an exception. Any attempt to open a cursor that is already open will also raise an exception.

Hiding Cursor Logic

You can choose to declare a packaged cursor in the package specification, but hide the actual SELECT statement in the package body. Here is an example:

```
PACKAGE PARMS AS
   -- the package specification declared the cursor header
   -- and the associated type declaration
   TYPE rec_payroll_type IS RECORD
     (EMPLOYEE_ID NUMBER(10),
      FIRST_NAME  VARCHAR2(20),
      LAST_NAME   VARCHAR2(30),
```

```
        GROSS_PAY    NUMBER(10,2));
   CURSOR cur_payroll RETURN rec_payroll_type;
END PARMS;

PACKAGE BODY PARMS AS
  -- the package body contains the full cursor declaration
  CURSOR cur_payroll RETURN rec_payroll_type
  IS
    SELECT    EMPLOYEE_ID, FIRST_NAME,
              LAST_NAME, (SALARY/26) GROSS_PAY
    FROM      EMPLOYEES
    ORDER BY EMPLOYEE_ID;
END PARMS;
```

When hiding cursor logic, you use the RETURN keyword in the cursor declaration statement. There is a very good reason for the RETURN keyword. Because the purpose of the package specification is to publish all of the information required to use the declared elements, declared cursors must provide information about what data is returned. This is the data that will be available for any FETCH statement that uses this cursor. However, even though you are allowed to fetch data into individual variables, the RETURN keyword only enables you to declare the following:

- A programmer-defined record type
- A database table record type declared with %ROWTYPE

Notice that the RETURN keyword defines the datatype, not the actual variable. You will need to declare a variable of the same type when you use the cursor. The following shows a procedure that uses the cur_payroll cursor we just declared:

```
PROCEDURE PROCESS_PAYROLL IS
  rec_payroll PARMS.rec_payroll_type;
BEGIN
  OPEN PARMS.cur_payroll;
  LOOP
    FETCH PARMS.cur_payroll INTO rec_payroll;
    EXIT WHEN PARMS.cur_payroll%NOTFOUND;
    PROC_PROCESS_PAYROLL(PARMS.cur_payroll);
  END LOOP;
  CLOSE PARMS.cur_payroll;
END PROCESS_PAYROLL;
```

This code declares the actual record type variable rec_payroll using the packaged type rec_payroll_type and fetches data into rec_payroll using the cursor. The developer of this procedure never had to see the package body that contained the full declaration of the cursor cur_payroll, only the package specification. In this example, the details of the calculation of gross_pay are kept hidden from the developer of this procedure, who only needs to know the final result of gross_pay, not the calculation.

This approach to declaring cursors yields the same benefits of persistence that any packaged cursor provides. In other words, this cursor with the hidden SELECT statement is just as global and persistent as if we had published the entire cursor declaration in the package specification.

For Review

1. Packaged constructs declared in the package specification are automatically public and global to the schema session that invokes them, regardless of which schema is the owner. All packaged constructs are persistent to the schema session.

2. Packaged cursors can be opened in one program unit, fetched in another, and closed in another. The %ISOPEN cursor attribute is useful in determining if a packaged public cursor is already open.

Exercises

1. **Consider the following code sample:**

```
PACKAGE PARMS
  c_project_duration CONSTANT NUMBER(3)  := 12;
  v_employee_count            NUMBER(3)  := 75;
END PARMS;
```

   Assuming the referenced schemas all have the necessary privileges, which of the following statements are true about this package? (Choose all that apply.)

   A. There are two public constructs in this package.

   B. If the schema JOHN changes the value for PARMS.v_employee_count to 125, then the schema KAREN will see the changed value of 125.

   C. If KAREN logs in, changes the value for PARMS.v_employee_count to 150, logs out, and then logs back in again, KAREN will see the value of PARMS.v_employee_count as 150.

   D. This package will not parse correctly.

2. **Assuming all referenced constructs are valid and properly declared, which of the following is a valid declaration of a CURSOR in a package specification?**

A. CURSOR cur_employees RETURN EMPLOYEES.LAST_NAME, EMPLOYEES.EMPLOYEE_ID;

B. CURSOR cur_employees RETURN EMPLOYEES.LAST_NAME%TYPE;

C. CURSOR cur_employees RETURN rec_employees;

D. CURSOR cur_employees RETURN EMPLOYEES;

Answer Key
1. A. **2.** C, D.

Chapter Summary

In this chapter, we reviewed various important topics dealing with program units and how to work effectively with them. Program units can execute on either the client side or server side. The choice of where to put them is up to the developer, with some limitations. Program units in the database are accessible everywhere on the network, provided the right privileges are granted, but program units stored on a client are only accessible from that client. However, calls to a program unit from a client will search the client before searching the database, and if the client executes a program unit on the server, then the network traffic must be considered in the performance of the overall application. On the other hand, when the program unit is located and executed, it will interact with other constructs and possibly perform database updates. If a program unit is on the client, but is updating the database, this also increases network traffic. A program unit executing on the server that is updating the database will execute more quickly. As the developer, you must consider these trade-offs when building your application.

Any PL/SQL block can declare procedures and functions in the declaration section of the block. These are called local subprograms and are only available for use within the block that declares them. Local subprograms can be declared in stand-alone procedures or functions, packaged procedures or functions, or anonymous blocks. Because any declared construct cannot reference another construct until after it is declared, the forward declaration mechanism is provided in the rare event that you need to create mutually referential local subprograms. The forward declaration also works for TYPE declarations.

When two or more packaged program units are created with the same name, you can still build them so that the system will differentiate among them by overloading them. Overloading refers to the ability to create multiple program units by giving them the same name, but making their parameter lists different. The parameter lists are considered different if the parameter datatype families are different, if the number of parameters is different, and/or if the order of parameters is different. The actual parameter names are irrelevant.

Package bodies have the option of including a one-time initialization section that will automatically execute when the first package construct is invoked. The initialization section is often used to initialize the packaged global constructs, but it can actually be used for anything. It must be defined after all other package body constructs are defined, and it is started with the BEGIN statement.

Since certain kinds of stored functions have certain inherent restrictions and potential problems, PL/SQL provides the capability to assert purity levels, prevent package bodies from violating your intended purpose and use of a given function or procedure, and declare to any future developers the intended use of a given packaged program unit. Purity levels can be used to restrict a function from reading or writing to the database or to other packaged constructs outside of their own package. The use of purity levels is optional, but can help prevent runaway processes or execution errors.

Packaged public constructs are global, and as a result, enable you to create persistent state in variables, cursors, and other packaged constructs to retain information within a given schema session across multiple program unit executions.

Two-Minute Drill

- Client-side program units include procedures, functions, and/or packages that are (a) created as part of an Oracle Form or Report or (b) stored in a library.

- Server-side program units are stored in the database.

- Server-side program units can be called from anywhere, assuming the right privileges are granted to the schema that calls them. Client-side programs can only be called from the client on which they are stored.

- Local subprograms are procedures or functions that are declared in a block. In the declaration section of any PL/SQL block, use the PROCEDURE or FUNCTION statement, much like you would in a package, to declare a procedure or function. The procedure or function header can be used on its own to forward-declare a procedure or function, provided that the full procedure or function declaration is repeated in its entirety later in the same declaration section.

- Local subprograms can only be called from the PL/SQL block that declares them.

- Program units that have the same name but different parameter lists are said to be *overloaded*. Parameter lists are considered different if they differ in datatype family, the number of parameters, and/or order of parameters.

- To execute an overloaded module, simply provide the appropriate set of parameters by datatype and number, and the run-time system will automatically invoke the appropriate module.

- Overloaded modules must be created in a package. Stand-alone procedures or functions cannot be overloaded.

- A package body can be given an initialization section that will execute one time for a given schema session when the first construct from the package is invoked. It must follow the declaration of all module code and start with the keyword BEGIN.

- Packaged functions may be assigned *purity levels* as a way of protecting applications from execution errors and runaway processes. Purity levels are assigned in the package specification with the PRAGMA RESTRICT_ REFERENCES statement, which ends with a set of parentheses that name the function, followed by any or all of the purity levels (WNDS, RDNS, WNPS, and RNPS) in any order.

- A packaged function with a purity level will not compile successfully if its code violates the purity level.

- A purity level can be asserted for a package's initialization section. You can also assert a default purity level for a package's procedures and functions.

- Packaged constructs are persistent, meaning that their values, if changed within a schema session, are retained beyond the execution of a single PL/SQL program unit.

Chapter Questions

1. **You have created a function called INVENTORY_QUEUE and stored it in the database in a schema called DEPOT. Which of the following may now be successfully created in the DEPOT schema? (Choose all that apply.)**

   A. A database trigger called INVENTORY_QUEUE

   B. A stored package called MAINTENANCE containing a function called INVENTORY_QUEUE

   C. A stored package called INVENTORY_QUEUE containing a function called MAINTENANCE

   D. A stored procedure called INVENTORY_QUEUE

2. **Consider the following code sample:**

```
PROCEDURE COMPUTE_BONUS
IS
  FETCH EMP.cur_employees INTO EMP.rec_employees;
  DISTRIBUTE_BONUS(EMP.rec_employees.EMPLOYEE_ID,
               EMP.v_bonus_rate);
END COMPUTE_BONUS;
```

Assuming all referenced objects are properly declared, which of the following can be said about this code sample? (Choose all that apply.)

A. EMP is a package specification, and there is no package body.

B. EMP.cur_employees is definitely open before this code executes.

C. Another program unit could also issue a FETCH on EMP.cur_employees.

D. The procedure will not compile.

3. **In the DEPOT schema, you have created a stored procedure with the following header:**

```
PROCEDURE BACK_ORDER(p_order_id IN NUMBER)
```

Which of the following procedures can now be stored in the DEPOT schema in addition to the procedure you have just stored? (Choose all that apply.)

A. PROCEDURE BACK_ORDER(p_order_id IN VARCHAR2)

B. PROCEDURE BACK_ORDER(p_order_number IN NUMBER)

C. PROCEDURE BACK_ORDER(p_order_id IN NUMBER, p_order_date IN DATE)

D. None of the above

4. **In the DEPOT schema, you have created the following stored package specification:**

```
PACKAGE WAREHOUSE AS
  FUNCTION RESTOCK(p_product_id NUMBER) RETURN BOOLEAN;
END WAREHOUSE;
```

You decide to add an additional program unit to this package specification. Which of the following function headers would be usable in the WAREHOUSE package as an overloaded function?

A. FUNCTION RESTOCK(p_product_number NUMBER) RETURN BOOLEAN;

B. FUNCTION RESTOCK(p_product_id VARCHAR2) RETURN BOOLEAN;

C. FUNCTION RESTOCK(p_product_id INTEGER) RETURN BOOLEAN;

D. FUNCTION RESTOCK(p_product_id NUMBER) RETURN VARCHAR2;

5. **Which of the following are valid purity levels? (Choose all that apply.)**

   A. WPNS

   B. WSDN

   C. RDSN

   D. WNDS

6. **Consider the following package body:**

```
PACKAGE BODY GUEST_TRACKING AS
  CURSOR cur_cruises RETURN rec_cruises IS
    SELECT CRUISE_ID, CRUISE_NAME
    FROM   CRUISES;
  BEGIN
    SELECT FIRST_NAME || ', ' || LAST_NAME GUEST_NAME
    INTO   GUEST_TRACKING.GUEST_NAME
    FROM   GUESTS
    WHERE  GUEST_ID = PARMS.guest_id;
END GUEST_TRACKING;
```

   Assuming all referenced constructs are properly declared, which of the following statements are true about this package body? (Choose all that apply.)

   A. It will not compile.

   B. It will not execute.

   C. It should be assigned the RNPS purity level.

   D. It cannot be assigned the RNPS purity level.

7. **Which of the following are acceptable to include in the RETURN statement of a CURSOR statement? (Choose all that apply.)**

   A. A programmer-defined record variable

   B. A set of variables, in the same order of the columns that are in the SELECT statement

    C. A set of variables, in any order, as long as it has the same number of columns in the SELECT statement

    D. A programmer-defined type

8. Consider the following code sample:

```
PACKAGE BODY PARM_LIST AS
  CURSOR cur_port RETURN rec_port_type
  IS
    SELECT   PORT_ID, PORT_NAME
    FROM     PORTS
    ORDER BY PORT_NAME;
END PARM_LIST;
```

  Assuming any referenced constructs are properly declared, which of the following statements are true about this code sample? (Choose all that apply.)

    A. This is a package body.

    B. The cursor cur_port is a public construct.

    C. The cursor cur_port is a private construct.

    D. The package body will not compile.

9. A stored procedure is able to execute which of the following program units, assuming the proper privileges have been granted? (Choose all that apply.)

    A. A packaged procedure stored in the database

    B. A stored procedure on the client

    C. A stored procedure in a library attached to an Oracle Form

    D. A stored function in an Oracle Form, provided that the function is included in a PL/SQL expression and not in a DML statement

10. Which of the following best describes PRAGMA RESTRICT_REFERENCES? (Choose one.)

    A. It empowers the function to perform operations it couldn't otherwise accomplish.

    B. It is an instruction to the PL/SQL run-time engine.

C. It documents a function's intended purpose.

D. It must be declared for all functions.

Answers to Chapter Questions

1. A, B.   A: A database trigger called INVENTORY_QUEUE. B: A stored package called MAINTENANCE containing a function called INVENTORY_QUEUE

Explanation   C and D are not legal because they will both be created in the same namespace as the function INVENTORY_QUEUE. A is allowed because triggers have their own namespace in a schema, and B is allowed because packaged components have their own namespace within the package.

2. C.   Another program unit could also issue a FETCH on EMP.cur_employees.

Explanation   A is not necessarily true; there's no way to tell from this example if there's a package body for EMP or not. B is not necessarily true; in fact, it would be better to check for the cursor status with an IF statement that checks to see if the cursor is open prior to issuing the FETCH, using something like IF EMP%ISOPEN THEN. D is not true; the syntax of the procedure is correct. C is true—the FETCH statement uses the packaged public cursor EMP.cur_employees, and other program units are able to issue FETCH statements on this same cursor.

3. D.   None of the above

Explanation   You cannot overload stand-alone procedures. You can only overload procedures that are stored in a package. If you issue a CREATE OR REPLACE PROCEDURE statement to create any of the procedures with the headers shown in answers A, B, or C, this will result in overwriting the original procedure.

4. B.   FUNCTION RESTOCK(p_product_id VARCHAR2) RETURN BOOLEAN;

Explanation   A is not acceptable because it merely renames the parameter name, and this accomplishes nothing. The parameter datatype is the same, and the number of parameters in the list—one—is the same. C is not acceptable because INTEGER is still a numeric datatype, and this is not considered a different datatype for the purposes of overloading. Because the existing function already has a single parameter with a numeric datatype, the overloaded module with a single parameter must use a datatype that is some sort of string or date. D is not acceptable because it changes the RETURN type, and this does nothing to differentiate the parameter list. B is correct because the single parameter has a string datatype of VARCHAR2.

5. D. WNDS

Explanation The four purity levels are WNDS, RNDS, WNPS, and RNPS. The answers for A, B, and C are all made up. But get ready for that—the exam asks questions like this.

6. D. It cannot be assigned the RNPS purity level.

Explanation The reference to PARMS.guest_id in the package initialization section is a packaged construct in another package. This package body would not compile successfully if the RNPS purity level were asserted for this package initialization section.

7. D. A programmer-defined type

Explanation Even though a FETCH statement will fetch into a set of variables, the RETURN statement doesn't accept them. A programmer-defined type or a %ROWTYPE declaration is required.

8. A. This is a package body.

Explanation This is clearly a package body, according to the first line that declares it. However, you cannot tell if the cursor is private or public from this declaration alone. You must see the package specification to know for sure. If the cursor header is included in the package specification, then it's public; otherwise, it's private. The package body syntax here is fine, so D is wrong.

9. A. A packaged procedure stored in the database

Explanation A procedure that is stored in the database cannot call any client-side program units.

10. C. It documents a function's intended purpose.

Explanation The PRAGMA RESTRICT_REFERENCES statement is a compiler directive and has no bearing on the actual execution of the program unit that is restricted. It is not required for any functions, but is highly recommended to avoid potential trouble with the execution of functions, especially functions that will be invoked from within SQL statements or remote databases.

CHAPTER
7

Working with Oracle's PL/SQL Packages

racle Corporation has already written a number of Procedural Language/Structured Query Language (PL/SQL) packages that are shipped with the Oracle database and are available for you to use in the development of your own PL/SQL code. These packages enable you to obtain functionality that you would otherwise have to work extensively to achieve. Various Oracle products come with their own unique packages—for example, Oracle Forms has its own set of built-in PL/SQL packaged procedures and functions that only work and have relevance in client-side Oracle forms. The PL/SQL web toolkit is a set of Oracle packages designed for use with web servers in the creation of web pages. Support for data warehousing, snapshots, and other special applications is found in a variety of special-purpose PL/SQL packages. Finally, third-party PL/SQL package products are available for sale from different sources.

In this chapter, you will review and understand the following standard PL/SQL packages that are shipped with every Oracle database installation. These are also the candidate subjects on the exam:

- DBMS_OUTPUT

- DBMS_JOB

- DBMS_DDL

- DBMS_PIPE

- DBMS_SQL

These packages come standard with the Oracle database and are created by running the utility script found in the file catproc.sql. This utility script should be located in the Oracle home directory in the rdbms/admin subdirectory.

One note about differences between Oracle's packages and database versions: several of these packages differ from one database release to another. The few differences that exist tend to be very minor and are generally found among the more obscure overloaded module options. Just be aware that as you look at the lists of overloaded modules for some of the packages in this section, you may find an additional module or two in your own installation that include a parameter option for an NCHAR datatype or something comparable to that. These variations are not addressed on the exam and have no impact on the knowledge you must have to pass.

Another important note: Oracle's prewritten packages execute with the privileges of the schema that calls them. These are known as *invoker rights*, which are addressed in Chapter 10. It is also contrary to the privilege scheme for packages that you create, which execute with *owner rights*, unless you specify otherwise.

DBMS_OUTPUT

The PL/SQL language does not have a reserved word or other built-in statement to support input/output (I/O). Instead, I/O is achieved through PL/SQL packages. The DBMS_OUTPUT package is a set of procedures that execute on the server side (not the client side) to print output to and read input from the output buffer. The DBMS_OUTPUT package includes several procedures, including the overloaded procedures PUT and PUT_LINE, which both execute with a single parameter of datatype NUMBER, DATE, or VARCHAR2. Those procedures are described in the sections that follow. The most frequent use of DBMS_OUTPUT is for debugging code because it can be used to easily print the contents of variables to the screen throughout the course of execution on any server-side program unit.

Note that all output sent to the output buffer is performed at the completion of the PL/SQL code's execution. There is no provision in DBMS_OUTPUT to send statements incrementally during the course of execution. In other words, you can't monitor output in real time or use DBMS_OUTPUT in combination with the STEP INTO feature of the Procedure Builder debugger. However, you can use DBMS_OUTPUT for printing statements for review upon the completion of the PL/SQL code block's execution and for printing out the contents of variables and other information to trace the path of execution and state of data within your PL/SQL code. This is the most frequent use of DBMS_OUTPUT.

SET SERVEROUTPUT ON

If you execute your PL/SQL code from within SQL*Plus or Enterprise Manager and want to see the results of DBMS_OUTPUT on the screen, then you need to pay attention to the SQL*Plus session parameter SERVEROUTPUT. This is an SQL*Plus session parameter that isn't a part of the DBMS_OUTPUT package, but is required to turn on the output buffer's capability to display to the screen. When you log into SQL*Plus, issue the SET SERVEROUTPUT ON statement in an SQL*Plus session in order for the output buffer contents to display to the screen. The SERVEROUTPUT parameter stays in force for the entire login session. If you don't do this, you will be able to execute PL/SQL code with DBMS_OUTPUT statements without experiencing any execution errors; however, you will also not see any results. The DBMS_OUTPUT procedures PUT and PUT_LINE will successfully print information to the output buffer and the output buffer will retain those statements; however, until the SERVEROUTPUT session parameter in SQL*Plus is set to ON, you won't see any of the output buffer contents on your screen display. For example, in a session of SQL*Plus, you can enter the following SQL*Plus command:

```
SET SERVEROUTPUT ON
```

or

```
SET SERVEROUTPUT ON SIZE 20000
```

By using the SIZE *n* option at the end of the statement, you can increase the output buffer size to accommodate larger amounts of data from the cumulative DBMS_OUTPUT statements.

This feature can be turned off within SQL*Plus as well with the following command:

```
SET SERVEROUTPUT OFF
```

Remember that these commands are not PL/SQL commands and cannot be issued from within a program unit or other PL/SQL block. They are session parameters and must be entered prior to the execution of your PL/SQL code in a SQL*Plus or Enterprise Manager session.

ENABLE and DISABLE

The ENABLE and DISABLE procedures turn on and off the ability to write data to the output buffer with the other procedures in this package. By default, DBMS_OUTPUT is already enabled, so you aren't necessarily required to issue an ENABLE statement. This is only necessary if some other procedure has disabled it prior to the execution of your procedure. It's more likely that SERVEROUTPUT is set to OFF and that's not something you can set from within your PL/SQL code, as we just discussed. You have to set it in SQL*Plus.

ENABLE has a single parameter that defines the buffer size and has a default value of 20000, so you can call it and pass no parameters, or you can call it with a single numeric parameter that specifies the size of the output buffer.

DISABLE takes no parameters and turns off the ability to issue the other procedures of the DBMS_OUTPUT package—namely, PUT, PUT_LINE, NEW_LINE, GET_LINE, and GET_LINES. This also purges the buffer of any data, which means that if you include this statement at the end of a series of PUT_LINE procedure calls, for example, all in the same block, no output will result.

PUT_LINE, PUT, and NEW_LINE

The PUT_LINE procedure takes a single parameter and puts it into the output buffer, along with a newline character at the end, which is automatically appended so that the line prints as a complete line. The newline character is the Unicode \n, which does not actually appear in output. The PUT procedure does the same thing, but without the newline. As a result, a series of calls to PUT print continuously on the same line, whereas PUT_LINE ensures that the next PUT or PUT_LINE starts on the beginning of the next line.

Both PUT and PUT_LINE are overloaded. There is a PUT_LINE procedure that takes a single parameter of VARCHAR2 or a single parameter of DATE, and another with a single parameter of NUMBER. The same is true for PUT. In other words, you can print anything and it will show up in the output buffer.

NEW_LINE doesn't print anything other than the Unicode newline character. This result forces a newline so that the next PUT or PUT_LINE starts on the next line.

There's an interesting dynamic that you might come across with PUT and PUT_LINE. Note that these procedures do not write directly to the output console, but write to the output buffer instead. Upon the successful completion of a transaction, the contents of the output buffer are released to the output console. However, there are occasions where you will get seemingly strange results. For example, say you create a database trigger BEFORE INSERT that includes a call to DBMS_OUTPUT.PUT_LINE. If the triggering INSERT statement is issued, it triggers the BEFORE INSERT trigger, which sends output to the output buffer. However, if the INSERT statement doesn't successfully parse, the output buffer won't be released to the screen. Furthermore, if you were to reissue the corrected INSERT statement, the BEFORE INSERT trigger would fire again and the DBMS_OUTPUT.PUT_LINE would send data to the output buffer in addition to what was there before. Assuming this second INSERT statement executes successfully, the contents of the output buffer display, including the information left over from the previous statement that did not successfully execute. This is as much a factor of the BEFORE INSERT trigger's successful execution even with a failed INSERT statement as it is a factor of the output buffer. However, it's a factor that must be considered when working with PUT_LINE more than other features and functions.

GET_LINE and GET_LINES

These procedures take data from the output buffer and bring that data into variables within your program unit. GET_LINE reads one line at a time and GET_LINES reads multiple lines at once.

GET_LINE has no IN parameters and two OUT parameters. The first OUT parameter is LINE and is a VARCHAR2. This is the actual data being read from the buffer minus the newline character. The second parameter is STATUS, which indicates if the GET_LINE was successful or not.

GET_LINES is similar, but its first parameter is LINES and is a parameter of type TABLE OF VARCHAR2(255), and the second parameter is NUMLINES and is of type NUMBER. This parameter is an IN OUT parameter. You can send in a requested number of lines and the response will represent the number of lines actually returned. If there's a difference, it will be the result of asking for a number of lines that is greater than the number actually found and the returning OUT value will indicate the number of lines actually found.

Note that GET_LINE and GET_LINES read from the output buffer—the same output buffer to which you write information with PUT, PUT_LINE, and NEW_LINE.

The advantage to GET_LINES over GET_LINE is that it reduces the number of calls to the server when you know you will need to retrieve multiple lines. You can use GET_LINE in one program unit to read data from the output buffer that was put there by another program unit.

For Review

1. The DBMS_OUTPUT package is good for debugging program units on the server side.

2. Once you've issued ENABLE, you can use PUT, PUT_LINE, and NEW_LINE to write output, or GET_LINE or GET_LINES to read from the output buffer. Use DISABLE when you want to close off the session. Use the SQL*Plus session command SET SERVEROUTPUT ON to enable the output buffer and see the results of DBMS_OUTPUT statements.

Exercises

1. **Which of the following PL/SQL statements will print something to the output buffer? (Choose all that apply.)**

   A. DBMS_OUTPUT.PUT_LINE(SYSDATE);

   B. DBMS_OUTPUT.PUT_LINE('Procedure Completed.');

   C. DBMS_OUTPUT.PUT((365/52) * 40);

   D. DBMS_OUTPUT.NEW_LINE;

2. **If this is not the first program unit executed in a schema's login session, what's missing?**

```
DECLARE
  v_answer VARCHAR2(30) := 'Anonymous block';
BEGIN
  DBMS_OUTPUT.PUT_LINE('The variable equals ' || v_answer);
END;
```

   A. The string should be concatenated first and then used as the PUT_LINE parameter.

   B. The LINES value is missing.

   C. SET

   D. ENABLE

Answer Key

1. A, B, C, D. 2. D.

DBMS_JOB

The DBMS_JOB package is designed to support batch job submissions. Batch jobs, as opposed to interactive jobs, are jobs that can execute in the background while you do other things, such as continuing with an SQL*Plus session, entering data in an Oracle Form, or even logging off altogether. Furthermore, DBMS_JOB can be used to schedule jobs in advance, so if you need to have some stored procedure execute automatically every night after midnight, for example, you can do so without having to log on each time to make it happen.

The DBMS_JOB package contains several procedures, as shown in Table 7-1.

The DBMS_JOB package executes based on certain database initialization parameters, as described in the next section.

JOB_QUEUE_PROCESSES and JOB_QUEUE_INTERVAL

There are two database initialization parameters that control the behavior of the DBMS_JOB package. The JOB_QUEUE_PROCESSES parameter defines how many

Procedure (P) or Function (F)	Name
P	BROKEN
P	CHANGE
P	INSTANCE
P	INTERVAL
P	ISUBMIT
P	NEXT_DATE
P	REMOVE
P	RUN
P	SUBMIT
P	USER_EXPORT (two overloaded)
P	WHAT

TABLE 7-1. *The DBMS_JOB Package Constructs*

processes will be started. If the JOB_QUEUE_PROCESSES initialization parameter is set to zero, jobs can be submitted and the DBMS_JOB packaged procedures can be invoked, but batch jobs won't actually execute. Set the JOB_QUEUE_PROCESSES initialization parameter to a number greater than zero to enable batch jobs.

The JOB_QUEUE_INTERVAL is also a numeric initialization parameter that defines the interval between times that the job queue checks for processes. This defaults to 60, meaning 60 seconds. You can set it as high as 3600. When a job is scheduled to execute at a specific time, it actually executes at some point at or after the scheduled time, depending on when the job queue process "wakes up" and checks to see if a job is scheduled. If the job queue has just completed the process of checking for scheduled jobs and then "goes to sleep," the JOB_QUEUE_INTERVAL determines when the job queue will wake up again to check for scheduled jobs. If a job is actually scheduled to execute before the job queue wakes up, the scheduled job does not execute until the job queue wakes up, finds the job, and processes it.

The SUBMIT Procedure

The most important procedure in the package is SUBMIT. The purpose of the SUBMIT procedure is to submit the PL/SQL code that you want to batch along with information about when the code should be executed. The procedure header looks like this:

```
PROCEDURE SUBMIT(job          OUT BINARY_INTEGER,
                 what       IN   VARCHAR2,
                 next_date  IN   DATE,
                 interval   IN   VARCHAR2,
                 no_parse   IN   BOOLEAN,
                 instance   IN   BINARY_INTEGER,
                 force      IN   BOOLEAN);
```

The parameters are as follows:

- **job**   This is an internal number that is assigned to your batch job and sent back out through an OUT parameter in case you need it for future procedure calls. Job numbers are unique for all schemas within a given instance and never change for the batch job—not after multiple executions and not even if you export the batch job and import it into a different database.

- **what**   This is a string that you want to submit as the batch job. This is not merely the name of the stored program unit you want to submit, although that is generally what is done. Instead, this is one or more PL/SQL statements, ending in semicolons, that define what you want to submit as batch.

- **next_date**   This is the date of when you want the job to execute.

- **interval**   This is the interval between the completion of the first batch submission and the subsequent submission. This value is passed in as a character string, but must actually define a DATE format. It can use SQL date functions to define this—for example, SYSDATE + .04.

- **no_parse**   This is a BOOLEAN value. If TRUE, then the code won't parse yet—this is useful for code you haven't written yet. If FALSE, then the code of the program unit you are submitting will parse right away.

- **instance and force**   These are both used for executing batch jobs in specific instances under the Oracle Parallel Server. They are outside the scope of the exam.

Consider the following example:

```
DBMS_JOB(BOX.v_job_number,
   'REVIEW_CRUISE_SCHEDULE;',
   (SYSDATE+1/24), FALSE, NULL, NULL);
```

This example submits a PL/SQL block with one statement that submits the procedure REVIEW_CRUISE_SCHEDULE to execute one hour from now. It returns the job number in the v_job_number variable.

The REMOVE Procedure

The REMOVE procedure has the following procedure header:

```
PROCEDURE REMOVE(job BINARY_INTEGER);
```

The purpose of this procedure is to remove a job from the queue altogether.

The RUN Procedure

The RUN procedure can be used to execute a batch job once right now. Its header is as follows:

```
PROCEDURE RUN(job BINARY_INTEGER, force BOOLEAN);
```

The RUN procedure uses the job number identified with SUBMIT and forces it to execute immediately.

The CHANGE, NEXT_DATE, WHAT, INTERVAL, and INSTANCE Procedures

The CHANGE, NEXT_DATE, WHAT, INTERVAL, and INSTANCE procedures can be used to change the parameters for any given batch job that has already been submitted. Their procedure headers are shown in the following:

```
PROCEDURE CHANGE    (job BINARY_INTEGER, what VARCHAR2, next_date DATE,
interval VARCHAR2, instance BINARY_INTEGER, force BOOLEAN);
PROCEDURE NEXT_DATE(job BINARY_INTEGER, next_date DATE);
PROCEDURE WHAT      (job BINARY_INTEGER, what VARCHAR2);
PROCEDURE INTERVAL (job BINARY_INTEGER, interval VARCHAR2);
PROCEDURE INSTANCE (job BINARY_INTEGER, instance BINARY_INTEGER, force
BOOLEAN);
```

Each of these procedures takes incoming parameters. Each one takes the job number, established with the SUBMIT procedure, to identify the particular job. Each procedure then takes various combinations of job parameters, which become the new value for the batch job you identify with job. For example, to change the batch job identified in the numeric variable v_job_number so that it now submits a stored packaged procedure called FINANCE.REFUND, use this call:

```
DBMS_JOB.WHAT(v_job_number,'FINANCE.REFUND;');
```

Each of the parameters is declared the same way it is declared in the SUBMIT procedure.

Other Procedures: USER_EXPORT, BROKEN, and ISUBMIT

The DBMS_JOB package includes a variety of other procedures:

```
PROCEDURE USER_EXPORT(job BINARY_INTEGER, mycall VARCHAR2);
PROCEDURE USER_EXPORT(job BINARY_INTEGER, mycall VARCHAR2, myinst VARCHAR2);
PROCEDURE BROKEN(job BINARY_INTEGER, broken BOOLEAN, next_date DATE);
PROCEDURE ISUBMIT(job BINARY_INTEGER, what VARCHAR2, next_date DATE,
interval VARCHAR2, no_parse BOOLEAN);
```

These procedures are summarized in the following section.
USER_EXPORT is a useful procedure for exporting the information necessary to recreate the batch submission. This is helpful for moving a batch job from one database to another. However, be aware of one complication. Job numbers are

generated with a sequence generator that creates sequential job numbers that are unique to a database instance. The USER_EXPORT procedure exports that exact job number, which may result in a creation error due to a duplicate job number when you import the job into a new database. If this is the case, you need to manually edit the code to recreate the batch job in the new database, enabling the new database to assign its own unique job number.

BROKEN can be used to deliberately mark a batch job as broken. You might want to do this for several reasons. If a batch job submission fails for any reason, the job queue automatically retries the job after a one-minute interval. If that attempt fails, it doubles the delay time and tries again. If this additional attempt fails, it doubles the delay again and retries, continuing until the job succeeds or 16 failed attempts are recorded. In the event that 16 failed attempts are reached, the batch job is flagged as broken. However, if you already know that the job is broken, you can force the issue and save the unnecessary attempts by using this procedure and work to resolve the problem.

ISUBMIT is intended for internal use and should never be directly invoked by your applications.

Monitoring Batch Jobs with USER_JOBS

The USER_JOBS data dictionary view is the source of information on batch jobs that have been submitted. Its column definitions include the following:

- **JOB**   The internally assigned job number for the batch job. This number stays constant for a batch job for all of its repeated executions and even if the job is exported and imported from one database to another.

- **LOG_USER**   The schema that submitted the batch job.

- **PRIV_USER**   The schema whose default privileges apply to the batch job.

- **SCHEMA_USER**   The default schema used to parse the batch job.

- **LAST_DATE**   The last date that the job was successfully executed as a batch.

- **LAST_SEC**   The same as LAST_DATE, as a VARCHAR2.

- **THIS_DATE**   If the job is currently executing, this column shows the date it was first started.

- **THIS_SEC**   Same as THIS_DATE, as a VARCHAR2.

- **NEXT_DATE**   The date of the next scheduled execution.

- **NEXT_SEC**   Same as NEXT_DATE, as a VARCHAR2.

- **TOTAL_TIME** Total execution time last required for the batch job (in seconds).

- **BROKEN** A VARCHAR2(1) datatype that, if set to Y, indicates that there is no attempt being made to execute this job. This can be set by the BROKEN procedure.

- **INTERVAL** A VARCHAR2(200) that shows a proper SQL date function, which is used to determine when each subsequent batch submission will occur.

- **FAILURES** If the batch job has not executed successfully in its most recent execution, this column shows the number of consecutive failures that have occurred.

- **WHAT** The PL/SQL code or block that this batch job is executing. This can be the name of a program unit, but it can also be a block of code.

- **NLS_ENV** Parameters describing the National Language Support (NLS) environment of the job.

- **MISC_ENV** Additional session parameters for the batch job.

- **INSTANCE** Identifies which instance can execute the batch job. If no instance is identified, the value is zero.

For Review

1. The DBMS_JOB package enables you to submit batch jobs to the database, scheduling them for delayed execution and optionally at regular intervals.

2. Several additional procedures exist to enable you to edit those batch jobs and remove them from the queue.

Exercises

1. **Which of the following procedures is used to remove a batch job with the job number 1 from the queue?**

   A. DROP BATCH_JOB 1;

   B. DBMS_JOB.DROP(1);

   C. DBMS_JOB.REMOVE(1);

   D. DBMS_JOB.DELETE(1);

2. **Which of the following parameters of the SUBMIT procedure identifies the PL/SQL block that you are submitting?**

   A. procedure

   B. program_unit

   C. what

   D. thatblock

Answer Key
1. C. 2. C.

DBMS_DDL

The DBMS_DDL package can be used to perform certain Data Definition Language (DDL) statements. The procedures are listed in Table 7-2.

The ALTER_COMPILE Procedure

The ALTER_COMPILE procedure can be used to issue an ALTER . . . COMPILE command from within a program unit. These are commands that you could issue from SQL*Plus or some other SQL interface, but as we've already discussed, DDL statements by themselves cannot be issued directly as PL/SQL statements. The header for the ALTER_COMPILE procedure is as follows:

```
PROCEDURE ALTER_COMPILE(type VARCHAR2, schema VARCHAR2, name VARCHAR2);
```

Procedure (P) or Function (F)	Name
P	ALTER_COMPILE
P	ANALYZE_OBJECT

TABLE 7-2. *The DBMS_DDL Package Constructs*

The following list describes the parts of this header:

- The type parameter identifies an object type of a program unit as you would find it listed in the USER_OBJECTS data dictionary view. The options are PROCEDURE, FUNCTION, PACKAGE, PACKAGE BODY, or TRIGGER.

- The schema value must be the name of an existing database schema.

- The name value is the name of an existing database object.

For example, the following ALTER_COMPILE procedure call

```
ALTER_COMPILE('PROCEDURE','FESTIVAL','RESCHEDULE_SHIP');
```

is the same as issuing the following statement from SQL*Plus:

```
ALTER PROCEDURE FESTIVAL.RESCHEDULE_SHIP COMPILE;
```

However, the difference is that you cannot issue the second statement from within a PL/SQL program unit.

The ANALYZE_OBJECT Procedure

The ANALYZE_OBJECT procedure produces a set of statistics for a given table. It is the PL/SQL alternative to the SQL DDL command ANALYZE TABLE/CLUSTER/INDEX. Its header is as follows:

```
PROCEDURE ANALYZE_OBJECT(type VARCHAR2, schema VARCHAR2, name VARCHAR2,
method VARCHAR2, estimate_rows NUMBER DEFAULT NULL, estimate_percent NUMBER
DEFAULT NULL, method_opt VARCHAR2 DEFAULT NULL, partname VARCHAR2 DEFAULT
NULL);
```

The following describes the parts of this header:

- The type parameter is either TABLE, CLUSTER, or INDEX.
- The schema is a valid schema name in the database.
- The name is the case-sensitive name of the object to be analyzed, which is provided as a string. (When in doubt, use uppercase letters in the string.)
- The method parameter is ESTIMATE, COMPUTE, or DELETE. If it is ESTIMATE, the parameter estimate_rows or estimate_percent must be something other than zero.

■ The estimate_rows is the number of rows to estimate.

■ The estimate_percent is the percentage of rows to estimate. This is an alternative to estimate_rows; if estimate_rows has a value, this is ignored.

■ The method_opt is either FOR TABLE, FOR ALL INDEXES, FOR ALL COLUMNS, or FOR ALL INDEXED COLUMNS. Both FOR ALL COLUMNS and FOR ALL INDEXED COLUMNS can be followed by the optional SIZE *s*, where *s* is the size.

■ The partname is the partition to be analyzed.

Monitoring the Results of ALTER_COMPILE and ANALYZE_OBJECT

To confirm that the ALTER_COMPILE and ANALYZE_OBJECT procedures have executed successfully, you can look at the entry in the USER_OBJECTS data dictionary view for the given object you are altering or analyzing. Note the value for the LAST_DDL_TIME or LAST_ANALYZED columns in the USER_OBJECTS view. These values, which are DATE values, should reflect the most recent date and time of the DDL action; therefore, you can use these values to determine if your calls to ALTER_COMPILE and/or ANALYZE_OBJECT properly executed.

For Review

I. The DBMS_DDL package enables you to submit DDL statements from within your PL/SQL programs.

2. The ALTER_COMPILE procedure is the PL/SQL alternative to the SQL command ALTER program unit COMPILE. The ANALYZE_OBJECT procedure is the PL/SQL alternative to the SQL command ANALYZE TABLE/CLUSTER/INDEX.

Exercises

I. **Which of the following statements can you effectively issue from within a PL/SQL procedure with the ALTER_COMPILE procedure? (Choose all that apply.)**

A. ALTER FUNCTION get_name COMPILE;

B. ALTER TABLE DISABLE ALL TRIGGERS;

C. ALTER PROCEDURE reschedule_ship COMPILE;

D. DROP PACKAGE BODY finance;

2. **Which of the following is a procedure in the DBMS_DDL package?**

   A. ANALYZE_TABLE

   B. ANALYZE_OBJECT

   C. ANALYZE_THIS

   D. ANALYZE_ALL

Answer Key
1. A, C. 2. B.

DBMS_PIPE

The DBMS_PIPE package enables you to create pipes that reside entirely within the Oracle database. Pipes are communication channels between specific login sessions on a single Oracle instance. They are separate from transactions—messages sent through pipes are unaffected by COMMIT, SAVEPOINT, or ROLLBACK.

Table 7-3 shows the full list of procedures and functions in the DBMS_PIPE package.

The PACK_MESSAGE Procedure

Before a message can be sent across a pipe, it must be packed. The PACK_MESSAGE procedure is overloaded as follows:

```
PROCEDURE PACK_MESSAGE(item VARCHAR2);
PROCEDURE PACK_MESSAGE(item NUMBER);
PROCEDURE PACK_MESSAGE(item DATE);
```

The PACK_MESSAGE procedure is related to other similar procedures: PACK_MESSAGE_RAW and PACK_MESSAGE_ROWID. All of these procedures accomplish the same goal: placing information into the message buffer.

The SEND_MESSAGE Function

Once the buffer contains information, the SEND_MESSAGE function sends it through a pipe. The SEND_MESSAGE function has the following header:

```
FUNCTION SEND_MESSAGE (pipename VARCHAR2, timeout INTEGER, maxpipsize
INTEGER)
RETURNS INTEGER
```

Procedure (P) or Function (F)	Name
F	CREATE_PIPE
F	NEXT_ITEM_TYPE
P	PACK_MESSAGE (overloaded)
P	PACK_MESSAGE_RAW
P	PACK_MESSAGE_ROWID
P	PURGE
F	RECEIVE_MESSAGE
F	REMOVE_PIPE
P	RESET_BUFFER
F	SEND_MESSAGE
F	UNIQUE_SESSION_NAME
P	UNPACK_MESSAGE (overloaded)
P	UNPACK_MESSAGE_RAW
P	UNPACK_MESSAGE_ROWID

TABLE 7-3. *The DBMS_PIPE Package Constructs*

The pipe name you define here is an original name you create and that you will need to reference in the separate session that reads the pipe.

The RECEIVE_MESSAGE Function

The RECEIVE_MESSAGE function is what you use in the receiving session, the other side of the pipe. Its header is as follows:

```
FUNCTION RECEIVE_MESSAGE(pipename VARCHAR2, timeout INTEGER) RETURNS
INTEGER;
```

The pipe name is the same string you define on the sending side. Once this function has executed, your session is ready to read information.

The NEXT_ITEM_TYPE Function

Once the RECEIVE_MESSAGE function has executed, you can use the
NEXT_ITEM_TYPE function to step or fetch through the list of items that were
packed on the sending side. The NEXT_ITEM_TYPE function header is as follows:

```
FUNCTION NEXT_ITEM_TYPE RETURN INTEGER;
```

There is no parameter list. This function sets the session to issue
UNPACK_MESSAGE procedure calls to extract the information that was sent.

The UNPACK_MESSAGE Procedure

Once the RECEIVE_MESSAGE function has executed, you can use a combination of
NEXT_ITEM_TYPE and UNPACK_MESSAGE calls to fetch through the set of packed
items for review. The overloaded UNPACK_MESSAGE procedure header is as
follows:

```
PROCEDURE UNPACK_MESSAGE(item VARCHAR2);
PROCEDURE UNPACK_MESSAGE(item NUMBER);
PROCEDURE UNPACK_MESSAGE(item DATE);
```

In the UNPACK_MESSAGE procedure, the item parameters are OUT parameters
and contain a single item of information that was packed on the sending side of
the pipe.

The two procedures UNPACK_MESSAGE_ROW and UNPACK_MESSAGE_
ROWID are related and accomplish the same basic goal, which is to extract
information from the piped message.

Other Procedures

The other procedures—CREATE_PIPE, REMOVE_PIPE, PURGE, RESET_BUFFER, and
UNIQUE_SESSION_NAME—are not addressed on the exam.

For Review

1. The DBMS_PIPE package contains procedures and functions for establishing
   communication pipes between sessions within an Oracle database
   instance.

2. Pipes are separate from transactions and can be used to pack items of
   information, send them to other sessions, and then unpack them.

Exercises

1. **Which of the following in the DBMS_PIPE package enables a reader session to advance to the next packed item?**

   A. PACK_MESSAGE

   B. PACK_ITEM

   C. NEXT_ITEM_TYPE

   D. NEXT_ITEM

2. **Which of the following in the DBMS_PIPE package sends the packed items to the reader?**

   A. PACK_MESSAGE

   B. SEND_MESSAGE

   C. SEND_ITEM

   D. PACK_ITEM

Answer Key
1. C. 2. B.

DBMS_SQL

As we have seen, PL/SQL lets you include Data Manipulation Language (DML) statements (SELECT, INSERT, UPDATE, and DELETE). However, PL/SQL does not let you include DDL commands as statements. In other words, you cannot have a PL/SQL block like this:

```
BEGIN
  CREATE TABLE IMPOSSIBLE_TO_DO (NOWAY NUMBER(3));
END;
```

However, although this code would produce an error message, there are ways in which you can execute DDL statements from within PL/SQL. These techniques offer an additional advantage: the ability to dynamically define at run time any SQL statement (both DDL and DML) so that the statement that executes can be created while the program executes, using parameters, variables, and string functions such as concatenation to build unique statements that are unknown at compilation time and can be defined based upon user input and other information available at run time. There are two primary ways to achieve this effect:

■ The DBMS_SQL package

■ A relatively new feature known as *native dynamic SQL*

We will address DBMS_SQL first and then look at native dynamic SQL.

The DBMS_SQL package consists of a few dozen procedures and functions, which are listed in Table 7-4.

Procedure (P) or Function (F)	Name	Overloaded
P	BIND_ARRAY	Yes
P	BIND_VARIABLE	Yes
P	BIND_VARIABLE_CHAR	Yes
P	BIND_VARIABLE_RAW	Yes
P	BIND_VARIABLE_ROWID	No
P	CLOSE_CURSOR	No
P	COLUMN_VALUE	Yes
P	COLUMN_VALUE_CHAR	Yes
P	COLUMN_VALUE_LONG	No
P	COLUMN_VALUE_RAW	Yes
P	COLUMN_VALUE_ROWID	Yes
P	DEFINE_ARRAY	Yes
P	DEFINE_COLUMN	Yes
P	DEFINE_COLUMN_CHAR	No
P	DEFINE_COLUMN_RAW	No
P	DEFINE_COLUMN_ROWID	No
P	DESCRIBE_COLUMNS	No
F	EXECUTE	No

Procedure (P) or Function (F)	Name	Overloaded
F	EXECUTE_AND_FETCH	No
F	FETCH_ROWS	No
F	IS_OPEN	No
F	LAST_ERROR_POSITION	No
F	LAST_ROW_COUNT	No
F	LAST_ROW_ID	No
F	LAST_SQL_FUNCTION_CODE	No
F	OPEN_CURSOR	No
P	PARSE	Yes
P	VARIABLE_VALUE	Yes
P	VARIABLE_VALUE_CHAR	No
P	VARIABLE_VALUE_RAW	No
P	VARIABLE_VALUE_ROWID	No

TABLE 7-4. *DBMS_SQL Package: Public Procedures and Functions*

Obviously, DBMS_SQL is an involved package, but you don't need all of the procedures all of the time. Generally, you use one set of procedure and function calls to build and execute a dynamic SELECT statement and an overlapping set of procedure and function calls for non-SELECT statements. The following is a sample of a procedure that uses DBMS_SQL to execute a SELECT statement:

```
PROCEDURE DO_QUERY (pTable   IN VARCHAR2,
                    pColumnA IN VARCHAR2,
                    pColumnB IN VARCHAR2)
IS
  vCursor NUMBER;
  vSQLStatement VARCHAR2(400);
  vResult    NUMBER;
  vColumnA VARCHAR2(30);
  vColumnB VARCHAR2(30);
BEGIN
```

```
        -- Build and parse the query
        vSQLStatement :=
            ' SELECT ' || pColumnA || ', ' || pColumnB ||
            ' FROM ' || pTable;
    vCursor := DBMS_SQL.OPEN_CURSOR;
    DBMS_SQL.PARSE(vCursor, vSQLStatement, DBMS_SQL.V7);
    -- Set up the columns and execute the query
    DBMS_SQL.DEFINE_COLUMN(vCursor, 1, vColumnA, 30);
    DBMS_SQL.DEFINE_COLUMN(vCursor, 2, vColumnB, 30);
    vResult := DBMS_SQL.EXECUTE(vCursor);
    -- Fetch the rows and print the results
    DBMS_OUTPUT.PUT_LINE('The results:');
    DBMS_OUTPUT.PUT_LINE('------------');
    LOOP
        EXIT WHEN DBMS_SQL.FETCH_ROWS(vCursor) = 0;
        DBMS_SQL.COLUMN_VALUE(vCursor, 1, vColumnA);
        DBMS_SQL.COLUMN_VALUE(vCursor, 2, vColumnB);
        DBMS_OUTPUT.PUT_LINE(vColumnA || ' ' || vColumnB);
    END LOOP;
    --
    DBMS_SQL.CLOSE_CURSOR(vCursor);
END DO_QUERY;
```

This procedure accepts three incoming parameters, each of which is a string. The first is the name of a table, and the second and third are columns in that table. This procedure accepts those parameters and builds the string vSQLStatement as a SELECT statement for that table. It uses the DBMS_SQL.PARSE procedure to parse the statement and then uses the DBMS_SQL.DEFINE_COLUMN procedure calls to associate the query's columns with locally declared variables. For example, the column in position 1 is associated with the variable vColumnA and is limited to a length of 30 characters. The DBMS_SQL.EXECUTE function actually executes the query and the DBMS_SQL.FETCH_ROWS function returns a single row of output, enabling DBMS_SQL.COLUMN_VALUE to grab individual values, transferring each value into the appropriate local variable, which we then print with the PUT_LINE procedure from the DBMS_OUTPUT package.

The following is an example of a call to this procedure from SQL*Plus:

```
EXEC DO_QUERY('PORTS','PORT_ID','PORT_NAME');
```

This procedure call generates the following query:

```
SELECT PORT_ID, PORT_NAME FROM PORTS
```

Here's an example of what the results might look like:

```
The results:
------------
1 Miami
2 Nassau

PL/SQL procedure successfully completed.
```

As you study this use of DBMS_SQL, it should become readily apparent that you could have built the string differently and included a WHERE or ORDER BY clause using string concatenation to create any SELECT statement you want.

The following is an example of how to use DBMS_SQL to issue an UPDATE statement:

```
PROCEDURE DO_UPDATE IS
  vCursor NUMBER;
  vSQLStatement VARCHAR2(400);
  vResult    NUMBER;
BEGIN
    -- Build and parse the statement
    vSQLStatement :=
      ' UPDATE PORTS ' ||
      ' SET PORT_NAME = "Paradise Island" ' ||
      ' WHERE PORT_ID = 2';
  vCursor := DBMS_SQL.OPEN_CURSOR;
  DBMS_SQL.PARSE(vCursor, vSQLStatement, DBMS_SQL.V7);
  -- Execute the query
  vResult := DBMS_SQL.EXECUTE(vCursor);
  DBMS_OUTPUT.PUT_LINE(vResult || ' rows were affected.');
  DBMS_SQL.CLOSE_CURSOR(vCursor);
END DO_UPDATE;
```

This statement contains fewer calls because there is no need to set up a looped series of FETCH statements. The UPDATE is executed with the DBMS_SQL.EXECUTE statement, and the number of rows updated is shown with in the DBMS_ OUTPUT.PUT_LINE statement.

The following sections look at how to use the package and what some of these public procedures and functions can do.

The OPEN_CURSOR Function and the CLOSE_CURSOR Procedure

The DBMS_SQL package works with cursors just like all other PL/SQL SQL statements. The first step in submitting a dynamically created SQL statement to the database using the DBMS_SQL package is to open a cursor. When you are done with a given cursor, you should close it. The headers for these program units are as follows:

```
FUNCTION OPEN_CURSOR RETURN INTEGER;
PROCEDURE CLOSE_CURSOR (c IN OUT INTEGER);
```

The OPEN_CURSOR function takes no parameters and returns an integer value representing the cursor. You need to save this number in a variable; this cursor integer is used by many other procedures and functions in this package, including the CLOSE_CURSOR procedure, which takes that same integer value as its only parameter to close the same cursor.

The PARSE Procedure

Once a cursor has been created with OPEN_CURSOR, you can use the PARSE procedure to submit a string containing a valid SQL statement for parsing. The headers for the two overloaded versions of PARSE are as follows:

```
PROCEDURE PARSE (c INTEGER, statement VARCHAR2, language_flag INTEGER);
PROCEDURE PARSE (c INTEGER, statement TABLE OF VARCHAR2, lb INTEGER, ub
INTEGER, lfflg BOOLEAN, language_flag INTEGER);
```

The first PARSE is used the most often. The first parameter is the integer of the cursor you created with OPEN_CURSOR. The second parameter is the string containing your SQL statement, which can be either DML or DDL. The SQL string should not include any semicolons at the end. However, it can include anything else you would submit in SQL. For example, if it's a SELECT statement, it can include GROUP BY, subqueries, functions, and so on.

Finally, the third parameter is a packaged constant indicating the version of PL/SQL that you want to use for the parse. Table 7-5 lists the three packaged constants you can reference from within this package to identify the appropriate language flag.

When in doubt, use DBMS_SQL.V7, which is fine for Oracle8*i* and higher applications as well as version 7. The big difference between version 6 and 7 has to do with the datatype change between Oracle6 and Oracle7 regarding CHAR, which was a variable character datatype in Oracle6, but became fixed length in Oracle7

Packaged Constant	Value
DBMS_SQL.V6	0
DBMS_SQL.V7	1
DBMS_SQL.NATIVE	2

TABLE 7-5. *DBMS_SQL Packaged Constants and Their Values*

when VARCHAR2 was introduced as the new variable character datatype. If you submit DDL to create CHAR columns with a version 6 flag, they will actually show up in your Oracle7 or higher database as a VARCHAR2 datatype. However, if you submit the same DDL with a version 7 flag, they will show up as CHAR columns.

If we were executing a DDL statement, PARSE would execute the statement immediately. For DML, the PARSE procedure would not actually execute the SQL statement, but it would parse for syntax and prepare it for execution. To actually execute the DML statement, we'll need another procedure. However, before we do that, we should bind some variables first.

NOTE
Because client-side PL/SQL programs cannot reference server-side packaged constants or variables, you'll need to know the values of those constants, as shown in Table 7-5, in the event that you create a client-side program unit that references them. In other words, a client-side statement that invokes the PARSE procedure that is working with the cursor cursor_id, submitting a string statement_string for parsing, and using version 7 should look like this:

```
DBMS_SQL.PARSE(cursor_id, statement_string,1);
```

This is only required from within client-side program units.

The DEFINE_COLUMN Procedure

The purpose of the DEFINE_COLUMN procedure is to associate local variables in your PL/SQL block with columns in a parsed—but as of yet unexecuted—query. The DEFINE_COLUMN must be called once for each column, and these calls must occur before the FETCH_ROWS procedure. The following are the procedure headers for DEFINE_COLUMN:

```
PROCEDURE DEFINE_COLUMN(c INTEGER, position INTEGER, column INTEGER);
PROCEDURE DEFINE_COLUMN(c INTEGER, position INTEGER, column VARCHAR2,
column_size INTEGER);
PROCEDURE DEFINE_COLUMN(c INTEGER, position INTEGER, column DATE);
PROCEDURE DEFINE_COLUMN(c INTEGER, position INTEGER, column BLOB);
PROCEDURE DEFINE_COLUMN(c INTEGER, position INTEGER, column CLOB);
PROCEDURE DEFINE_COLUMN(c INTEGER, position INTEGER, column BINARY FILE LOB);
```

The first parameter, c, is the cursor ID that is established with the OPEN_CURSOR function. The second parameter, position, is the number indicating which column in the query you are defining. The third parameter is the local variable that you are associating with the numbered column identified by position. If you are using a local variable that is a VARCHAR2, you must also provide a number indicating the maximum length that you will bring into the local variable.

In addition to DEFINE_COLUMN, there are also related procedures with similar names that perform the same basic purpose but with different datatypes. These include DEFINE_COLUMN_CHAR, DEFINE_COLUMN_RAW, and DEFINE_COLUMN_ROWID.

The EXECUTE Function

The EXECUTE function is very simple and takes only one parameter, which is the cursor ID. However, EXECUTE is a function that returns a number. This number is comparable to the %ROWCOUNT cursor attribute in PL/SQL—in other words, the returned number represents the number of rows affected. For example, with an UPDATE statement, the returned number represents the total number of rows updated. The following shows the header for the EXECUTE function:

```
FUNCTION EXECUTE (c INTEGER) RETURNS INTEGER
```

Once the EXECUTE is issued, the statement has been executed. For INSERT, UPDATE, or DELETE statements, this is all that is required. For SELECT statements, the EXECUTE statement sets the cursor up for the FETCH_ROWS function to step through the records that the SELECT returns.

The FETCH_ROWS Function

The FETCH_ROWS function is only used for SELECT statements and corresponds to the PL/SQL FETCH statements for explicit cursors. The only parameter is c, which is the cursor ID. FETCH_ROWS cannot be issued until after a SELECT statement has been set up appropriately with calls to program units such as PARSE, EXECUTE, and DEFINE_COLUMN, as described earlier. The function's header is as follows:

```
FUNCTION FETCH_ROWS(c INTEGER) RETURNS INTEGER;
```

One call to FETCH_ROWS generally returns a single row at a time. The procedure is generally called from inside a loop along with COLUMN_VALUE procedure calls to extract the fetched data from the row. The integer that is returned represents the number of rows returned. When no more rows remain, FETCH_ROWS returns a zero.

The COLUMN_VALUE Procedure

The COLUMN_VALUE procedure is intended for use after a FETCH_ROWS has been issued and moves data from the fetched row into the local variable that you've already defined with DEFINE_COLUMN.

The COLUMN_VALUE procedure is overloaded. There are several versions, including procedures with similar names that perform essentially the same purpose. The most commonly used versions of COLUMN_VALUE are shown here:

```
PROCEDURE COLUMN_VALUE(c INTEGER, position INTEGER, value INTEGER);
PROCEDURE COLUMN_VALUE(c INTEGER, position INTEGER, value VARCHAR2);
PROCEDURE COLUMN_VALUE(c INTEGER, position INTEGER, value DATE);
```

The others follow a similar pattern, where the third parameter is defined differently to accommodate different datatypes, including BLOB, CLOB, TABLE OF DATE, and others.

The BIND_VARIABLE Procedure

The BIND_VARIABLE procedure is something like a more powerful alternative to DEFINE_COLUMN. Whereas DEFINE_COLUMN can define a one-way channel of data transfer from the SQL column to a local variable, the BIND_VARIABLE procedure can be used to send data to the query. In many cases, you don't have to use BIND_VARIABLE because you can use simple string concatenation to build the SQL statement you want to use before you parse. However, BIND_VARIABLE enables you to insert placeholders in that query and then change the values for them after the statement has already been parsed as you reexecute it as required. Furthermore, BIND_VARIABLE empowers your code to programmatically change the values, rather than use string concatenation, which, although effective, can require more effort and demand careful coding.

To use a BIND_VARIABLE procedure, you must first create a placeholder in your query string. For example, consider the following code:

```
vSQLStatement := ' UPDATE SHIPS ' ||
                 ' SET CURRENT_PORT = :port_name ' ||
                 ' WHERE SHIP_ID = :ship_id ';
```

This query string contains two placeholders: :port_name and :ship_id. Both are given defined values later by BIND_VARIABLE procedures.

There are several BIND_VARIABLE procedures, including many procedures with similar names. The following are three of the most commonly used versions:

```
PROCEDURE BIND_VARIABLE(c INTEGER, name VARCHAR2, value VARCHAR2);
PROCEDURE BIND_VARIABLE(c INTEGER, name VARCHAR2, value INTEGER);
PROCEDURE BIND_VARIABLE(c INTEGER, name VARCHAR2, value DATE);
```

The first parameter, *c*, is the cursor ID that is established with the OPEN_CURSOR function. The second parameter, name, is the exact string used to identify the placeholder in the query. The third parameter is the local variable that you are associating with the numbered column identified by position. If you are using a local variable that is a VARCHAR2, you must also provide a number indicating the maximum length that you will bring to the local variable.

In keeping with our earlier example, consider the following BIND_VARIABLE procedure calls:

```
BIND_VARIABLE_CHAR(vCursor, ':port_name', 'Nassau');
BIND_VARIABLE(vCursor, ':ship_id',   1);
```

These BIND_VARIABLE procedures set up the UPDATE statement to be as follows:

```
UPDATE SHIPS SET CURRENT_PORT = 'Nassau' WHERE SHIP_ID = 1;
```

The BIND_VARIABLE procedure has some similarly named related procedures. I used BIND_VARIABLE_CHAR in the previous example. In addition, there are BIND_ARRAY, BIND_VARIABLE_RAW, and BIND_VARIABLE_ROWID.

Native Dynamic SQL

A new feature to PL/SQL is native dynamic SQL. At the time of this writing, the OCP exam doesn't address native dynamic SQL. Because native dynamic SQL is based on new statements and features of the language rather than prepackaged database objects like DBMS_SQL, it's likely to be included in the first exam when it is added instead of this one, but there's no guarantee of this.

The following shows a brief example of native dynamic SQL:

```
BEGIN
  EXECUTE IMMEDIATE 'CREATE TABLE NEW_TAB_1 (NT_ID NUMBER(3))';
END;
```

This PL/SQL block submits the string CREATE TABLE NEW TAB_1(NT_ID NUMBER(3)) as a SQL statement. As you might imagine, this could be a string based on concatenation as well.

The EXECUTE IMMEDIATE statement can be used for DML statements as well, but not for multirow queries.

There is much more to native dynamic SQL than this, but it's a subject that is beyond the scope of this book.

Compilation Errors

Regardless of whether you use DBMS_SQL or native dynamic SQL, any SQL statements submitted with either one will be parsed at execution time, not at compilation time. The SQL statements are merely recognized as strings at compilation time. If there is a parsing error in the SQL statement, the parser will never discover it because the statement is merely a string as far as the parser is concerned. It is not until execution time that you will discover if there is a problem with the SQL statement. Therefore, be aware that any PL/SQL program units that use DBMS_SQL or native dynamic SQL may parse correctly, but may still contain programming errors that you won't discover until execution time.

For Review

1. The DBMS_SQL package can be used to submit SQL statements that are defined at execution time. Using variables, parameters, string concatenation, and all other string functions, you can create programs that build SQL statements at run time for submission to the database.

2. Although PL/SQL does not permit the inclusion of DDL as executable statements, the DBMS_SQL package and native dynamic SQL feature enable you to submit any DDL you want.

Exercises

1. **Which of the following packaged program units in DBMS_SQL will cause a query to be executed?**

   A. PARSE

   B. EXECUTE

C. EXECUTE_QUERY

D. SUBMIT

2. **Which of the following packaged program units in DBMS_SQL creates and returns a cursor ID for your query?**

   A. GET_CURSOR_ID

   B. OPEN_CURSOR

   C. GET_CURSOR

   D. OPEN

Answer Key
1. B.   2. B.

Chapter Summary

Oracle Corporation provides many built-in prewritten PL/SQL packages. These packages contain procedures, functions, and other constructs, and follow the rules for constructing packages that we have been examining in this book. Oracle Corporation's packages support specific common job requirements.

The DBMS_OUTPUT package was originally designed to support the debugging of PL/SQL blocks. It provides procedures to send output to the screen in various forms and read data back from the output buffer. It can be enabled and disabled as required. To get the output buffer to display on the screen in SQL*Plus, the SERVEROUTPUT session parameter must be set to ON.

The DBMS_JOB package provides the ability to submit batch jobs for execution either immediately or at some later specified date. Batch jobs, by definition, execute in the background, meaning that you can continue in your interactive session without waiting for the batch job to complete. DBMS_JOB lets you schedule jobs for regular scheduled execution intervals, as controlled by and determined by the database initialization parameters JOB_QUEUE_PROCESSES and JOB_QUEUE_INTERVAL. Jobs are identified by a unique job number that are unique to a database instance. Job schedules can be exported to other databases.

The DBMS_DDL package is a special-purpose package that makes it convenient to submit two types of DDL statements: the ALTER . . . COMPILE statements and the ANALYZE . . . TABLE/CLUSTER/INDEX statements.

The DBMS_SQL package is a more complex alternative that enables you to submit any SQL statement to the database by using strings rather than parsed statements. The good news is that this provides more flexibility. The bad news is that compilation or parsing errors won't be discovered until execution time.

The DBMS_PIPE package enables multiple sessions to communicate directly with each other within a given instance without talking through database objects.

In addition to the packages that are described in this chapter, Oracle supplies many others within specific products. Oracle Forms has its own set of built-in packages that are unique to Oracle Forms. Similarly, Oracle Reports has its own set of packages and so on.

Two-Minute Drill

- The DBMS_OUTPUT package includes PUT_LINE, PUT, and NEW_LINE for printing complete lines, partial lines, and blank line feeds.

- The GET_LINE procedure obtains information from the output buffer.

- The DBMS_JOB package creates batch jobs for delayed submission and automatic submission at regular intervals. You can change the parameters that define the batch submission, force an immediate execution, and remove a batch job altogether from the job queue.

- The SUBMIT procedure establishes jobs in the queue and starts the process. Once submitted, you can REMOVE, RUN, CHANGE, and USER_EXPORT jobs, and use many other procedures.

- The JOB_QUEUE_PROCESSES database initialization parameter must be set to something other than zero for batch job work. The JOB_QUEUE_INTERVAL database initialization parameter defines how long the job queue will "sleep" before "waking up" to search the queue for schedule jobs; this influences when scheduled jobs actually execute.

- The DBMS_DDL package can be used to issue ALTER COMPILE and ANALYZE OBJECT DDL statements to the database from within PL/SQL procedures.

- The DBMS_PIPE package uses pipes between sessions within the same Oracle schema to PACK_MESSAGE and UNPACK_MESSAGE back and forth between writers and readers.

- The DBMS_SQL package empowers a PL/SQL application to dynamically define any SQL statement and submit it for processing. This includes the full range of DML and DDL. The OPEN_CURSOR function starts the process and PARSE submits your string for parsing. DEFINE_COLUMN lets you set up local variables to receive information so that when you EXECUTE, you can use FETCH_ROWS through your returned data and use COLUMN_VALUE to copy data from the database into local variables. You can also issue simple INSERT, UPDATE, or DELETE statements and determine how many rows were affected.

Chapter Questions

1. **Consider the following code sample:**

```
DBMS_OUTPUT.ENABLE;
DBMS_OUTPUT.PUT('Oracle ');
DBMS_OUTPUT.PUT_LINE('Press');
DBMS_OUTPUT.NEW_LINE;
DBMS_OUTPUT.DISABLE;
```

   After this block executes, what will the output buffer contain?

   A. Oracle Press

   B. The word "Oracle" on the first line and the word "Press" on the second line

   C. Oracle Press\n

   D. None of the above

2. **Which of the following is not possible with DBMS_SQL?**

   A. Submit ALTER statements.

   B. Issue SET commands to SQL*Plus to define a login session.

   C. Issue UPDATE statements.

   D. Issue CREATE TABLE statements.

3. **Which of the following packages enable you to submit DDL statements to the database? (Choose all that apply.)**

   A. DBMS_PIPE

   B. DBMS_SQL

   C. DBMS_OUTPUT

   D. DBMS_DDL

4. **Which of the following packages offers support for debugging?**

   A. DBMS_PIPE

   B. DBMS_SQL

    C. DBMS_OUTPUT

    D. DBMS_DDL

5. Which of the following packages lets you send information directly into the program unit of another user's login sessions without communicating directly with the database?

    A. DBMS_PIPE

    B. DBMS_SQL

    C. DBMS_OUTPUT

    D. DBMS_DDL

6. Which of the following is a procedure found in DBMS_PIPE?

    A. BIND_VARIABLE

    B. PACK_MESSAGE

    C. PACK_ITEM

    D. EXECUTE

7. Which of the following enables you to issue SELECT statements to the database? (Choose all that apply.)

    A. DBMS_SQL

    B. DBMS_DDL

    C. DBMS_SELECT

    D. A standard PL/SQL block

8. What can you *not* do with a batch job in the database?

    A. Remove it from the queue.

    B. Schedule it for a specific time and know that it will definitely execute at that specific time no matter what.

    C. Change its scheduled execution interval after it has already been submitted to the queue.

    D. Export it to another database.

9. **What command in SQL*Plus causes the SQL*Plus interface to get information that DBMS_OUTPUT sends to the output buffer and show it to the screen?**

   A. SET OUTPUT BUFFER ON

   B. SET SERVER ON

   C. SET SERVEROUTPUT ON

   D. SET BUFFER ON

10. **A pipe name created with DBMS_PIPE is unique to a**

    A. Procedure

    B. Stored database procedure

    C. Schema

    D. Instance

Answers to Chapter Questions

1. D.   None of the above

Explanation   Before the DBMS_OUTPUT.DISABLE procedure call, the output buffer contains the words "Oracle Press" on a single line followed by one blank line resulting from the NEW_LINE procedure call. However, the DISABLE procedure has the effect of purging the buffer and removing all of this information, which results in an empty buffer by the time the block concludes execution.

2. B.   Issue SET commands to SQL*Plus to define a login session.

Explanation   You cannot use DBMS_SQL to issue commands to set session parameters in SQL*Plus. You use it to issue SQL statements.

3. B, D.   B: DBMS_SQL
           D: DBMS_DDL

Explanation   The DBMS_PIPE package sends messages to other schemas, but sends nothing to the database. DBMS_OUTPUT sends output to the buffer. However, both DBMS_SQL and DBMS_DDL enable you to send DDL statements to the database for processing.

4. C.   DBMS_OUTPUT

Explanation   The original intent of the DBMS_OUTPUT package was to support debugging, and it isn't really set up for anything else—even though it prints output, its output buffer is limited, making it a poor choice for formal report presentation. However, using it to print statements of progress, the contents of variables, and such information provides standard, although crude, support in debugging efforts.

5. A.   DBMS_PIPE

Explanation   This is exactly what DBMS_PIPE is designed to do. Sending messages through pipes enables you to communicate directly with another session.

6. B.   PACK_MESSAGE

Explanation   BIND_VARIABLE and EXECUTE are DBMS_SQL procedures. PACK_ITEM is not real.

7. A, D.   A: DBMS_SQL D: A standard PL/SQL block

Explanation   DBMS_SQL enables you to send any SQL statement, including SELECT statements, to the database. Remember that you can do that with standard PL/SQL code anyway. There is no Oracle-Corporation-supplied package as DBMS_SELECT at the time of this writing, and DBMS_DDL only works with certain DDL statements.

8. B.   Schedule it for a specific time and know that it will definitely execute at that specific time no matter what.

Explanation   The scheduled execution time is influenced by when the job queue wakes up and looks for jobs to execute. This, in turn, is defined by the database initialization parameter JOB_QUEUE_INTERVAL.

9. C.   SET SERVEROUTPUT ON

Explanation   The DBMS_OUTPUT package sends information to the output buffer, but whether or not SQL*Plus displays this information on the screen depends on the SQL*Plus session parameter SERVEROUTPUT, which must be ON. You can set any session parameter value within SQL*Plus with the SET command; thus, it is SET SERVEROUTPUT ON.

10. D.   Instance

Explanation   The procedure UNIQUE_SESSION_NAME is specifically designed to assist in the process of making sure you come up with a pipe name that is unique to a given instance. Because multiple sessions within an instance can communicate with each other, the pipe name must be global to the entire instance in order for the sessions to locate the pipe.

PART
II

Development Tools

CHAPTER
8

Using Oracle
PL/SQL Tools

s you create PL/SQL program units, you will need to build source code, resolve compilation and execution errors, and possibly move code back and forth between the client and the server. You will inevitably work with a large number of program units, as you assemble them in various combinations for your applications. Oracle Corporation provides a set of tools for supporting these efforts, and those tools are the subject of this chapter.

In this chapter, you will review and understand the following topics as they relate to Procedural Language/Structured Query Language (PL/SQL) program units:

- SQL*Plus
    - The SQL*Plus buffer editor
    - Using text editors
    - Executing text files
    - PL/SQL blocks and the buffer
- Procedure Builder
    - The Object Navigator
    - The PL/SQL Editor

SQL*Plus

SQL*Plus is a popular command-line interface that can be used to communicate with an Oracle database. The SQL*Plus interface can be invoked on either the server or the client. One SQL*Plus interface can be used to connect to any database on the network to which the user has access. SQL*Plus can be used to submit SQL statements to the database, as well as SQL*Plus commands and PL/SQL program units. You can execute anonymous blocks, submit commands to store program units, and use SQL to inspect the data dictionary and observe the current status of PL/SQL program units in the database.

In general, PL/SQL program units have the capability to be executed on the client or on the server. However, when you use SQL*Plus to enter and/or execute PL/SQL program units, you are always running them on the PL/SQL engine in the server. It is not possible to use SQL*Plus to execute client-side PL/SQL program units. For that, you must use either Procedure Builder, or Oracle Forms or another client-side tool. Even if the SQL*Plus executable you are using is executing on the client, you are nevertheless executing server-side program units at all times.

Figure 8-1 is an example of the SQL*Plus command-line interface. The SQL> prompt indicates where keyboard typing will appear in the interface.

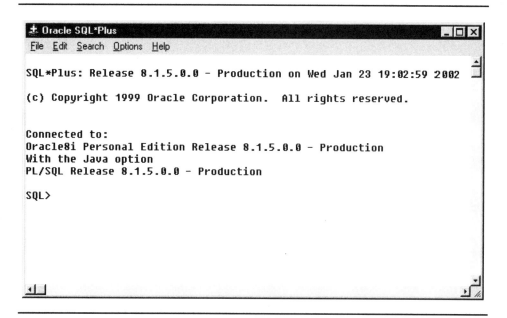

FIGURE 8-1.   *The SQL*Plus command-line interface*

The SQL*Plus interface can be used to submit any of the SQL commands we have reviewed for storing, executing, and manipulating PL/SQL program units, such as

- CREATE OR REPLACE PROCEDURE procedure_name;
- DROP PACKAGE procedure_name;
- EXECUTE procedure_name;

There is one important requirement in SQL*Plus: Any command involving a PL/SQL block must end with a slash (/) in order to execute. For example,

```
CREATE OR REPLACE FUNCTION GET_VERSION
RETURN VARCHAR2 IS
BEGIN
  RETURN 'Version 7.4';
END GET_VERSION;
/
```

Notice the slash at the very end—SQL*Plus requires the slash at the end in order to execute the PL/SQL block. This is true for all PL/SQL blocks. Even anonymous blocks require a slash:

```
BEGIN
  DBMS_OUTPUT.PUT_LINE('I will not execute without a slash!');
END;
/
```

Without the slash, the SQL*Plus command-line editor assumes you are continuing to enter more code, even though the PL/SQL block is ended. See Figure 8-2 for an example of what an editing session will look like if you type a PL/SQL block into the SQL*Plus interface, and instead of typing a slash, simply continue to press ENTER.

At this point, you can enter a slash and execute the command, provided that no other characters were typed and ENTER was the only key you continued to press. But what if you had typed some erroneous characters as part of the command? How can you edit the command without retyping everything?

The first thing to realize is that your typing hasn't just scrolled up through the screen. SQL*Plus retains the most recent SQL command you have entered in the *buffer*. This is true whether the command was entered correctly or not. Commands that are saved in the buffer include all SQL commands, including commands to create, alter, and drop PL/SQL program units. (Note: SQL*Plus commands, such as the EXECUTE program_unit command, are not retained in the buffer.)

You can edit the contents of the buffer using one of two general categories of editors available for use in SQL*Plus. One is the built-in SQL*Plus buffer editor. The

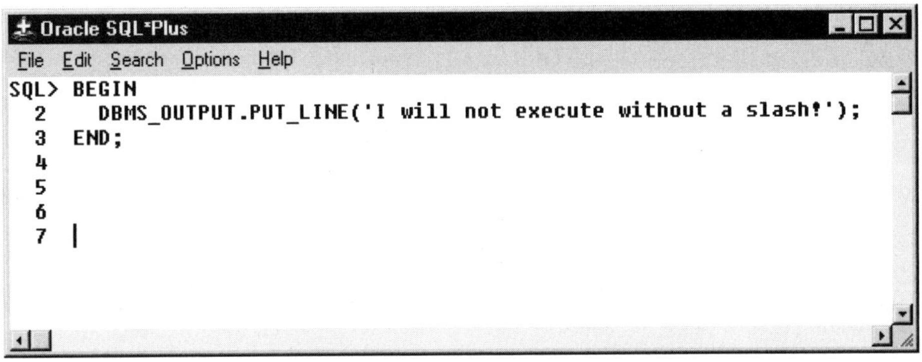

FIGURE 8-2. *Entering a PL/SQL block without the slash*

other category includes external text editors. We will examine both of these in the next two sections.

The SQL*Plus Buffer Editor

The SQL*Plus buffer editor is a crude command-line editor that requires you to remember a few brief editing commands that are unique to the buffer editor, but are similar to many traditional command-line editors. Using the buffer editor, you can edit the contents of the buffer—in other words, your most recently submitted SQL statement.

The buffer editor includes the following commands:

- **L or LIST**   This command displays the contents of the buffer, showing the line number for each line within the buffer. See Figure 8-3. In the figure, a function is created and stored in the database. After it is successfully stored, the L command is used to display the contents of the buffer.

- **n (a line number)**   Changes the buffer editor's current line to the line number indicated. This concept is important in understanding the buffer editor. Again, see Figure 8-3. Notice that the L command displays the contents of the buffer and shows the line number of each. However, notice line 5. There is an asterisk after line 5. This indicates that line 5 is the

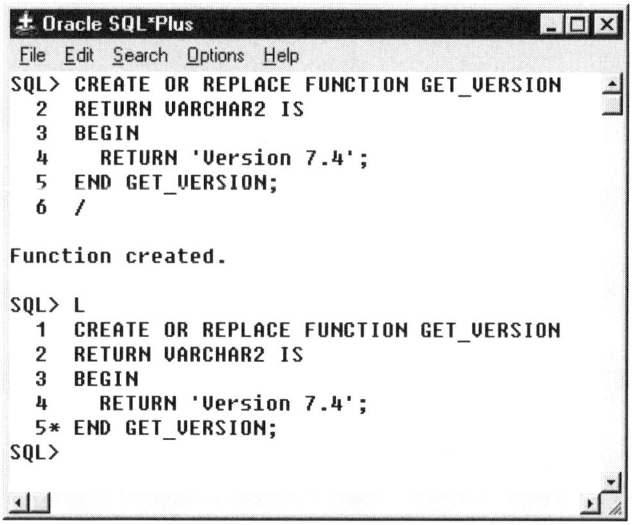

FIGURE 8-3.   *The LIST command in the SQL*Plus buffer editor*

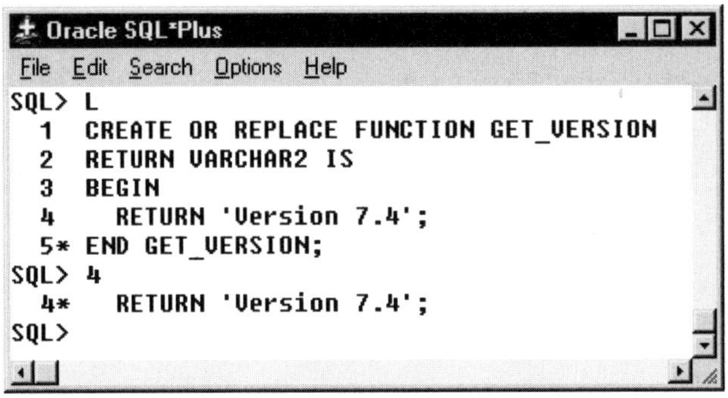

FIGURE 8-4. *The line number redirection command*

current line. The *current line* is the line upon which most of the commands that follow will affect. For example, when you delete a line, you are deleting the current line only. To make a different line become the current line, simply type the different line's line number by itself and press ENTER. This will refocus the buffer editor to the line number you have indicated. For example, after you reach the end of the display in Figure 8-3, you could type the number 4 and the current line would become line 4. See Figure 8-4 for an example of this.

- **C or CHANGE** Changes the contents of the current line in the buffer. The C command is followed by a character that will be interpreted as a delimiter, followed by the characters existing in the current line you want to change, followed by the delimiter, followed by the new characters that you want to replace the existing characters, and optionally followed by the delimiter. For example, "C/Tropical/Bahamas/" will change the first occurrence of the string "Tropical" to the string "Bahamas" within the current line. The command "C.Hawaii.LosAngeles ." will change the first occurrence of "Hawaii" to the string "Los Angeles". Notice that "Los Angeles " includes two blank spaces afterwards.

- **I or INPUT** Inserts a new line into the buffer after the current line. Just type **I** on a line by itself and press ENTER. The buffer editor will activate and display the line number of the next line, and wait for you to enter your additional SQL statement information. When you are done, you have two options of ending the INPUT session. You can type a period (**.**) on a line by itself, which will end the buffer editor session. Or, if you are at the end of your SQL command, you can enter a semicolon (**;**), which will not only end the buffer editing session, but it will also execute the command.

- **A or APPEND**   Appends additional typing at the end of the current line in the buffer. The APPEND command requires you to type **A** as well as the text you want appended at the end of the line. For example, A , CABIN_NUMBER will append the string , CABIN_NUMBER at the end of the current line.

- **DEL**   Deletes the current line in the buffer.

- **CLEAR BUFFER**   Clears the contents of the buffer.

- **/ (the slash character)**   Executes the contents of the buffer.

- **R**   Runs the contents of the buffer.

- **SAVE filename**   Saves the contents of the buffer to a filename you specify. If the file already exists, you must include the REPLACE keyword at the end, as in SAVE filename REPLACE.

- **GET filename**   Gets the contents of a text file and loads the entire file in the buffer. This command requires that the file contain one single SQL statement, as appropriate for the buffer. Files that contain a series of statements will not load correctly.

The buffer retains only the most recent SQL command, whether it was correctly entered or not. If you have something in the buffer already, but enter the beginning of a new command that is recognizable as an SQL command, then even if the command is not completed correctly, it will overwrite the old contents of the buffer and replace those contents with the new command you are typing.

The commands for the buffer editor are basic, but beneficial. The advantage to these commands is that they will operate anywhere. Remember that Oracle can run within any operating system. Not all operating systems support all forms of text editors, and even among those installations that share the same operating system, there is no guarantee that your favorite text editor will be available everywhere. However, knowledge of the buffer editor ensures that you can work with PL/SQL program units anywhere.

Using Text Editors

There is an alternative to the SQL*Plus buffer editor. The command ED, or EDIT, can be used in SQL*Plus to invoke the local text editor. The ED command will copy the contents of the buffer into the local editor and activate it, moving focus, or control, into that editor. If you type **ED** and the buffer contains anything, the next thing you will see is the local text editor, containing the contents of the buffer, ready for you to use the full capabilities of the local text editor to edit the buffer. When you are done, you can use the local text editor's feature to save the data, which will have the effect of saving the contents to a file called afiedt.buf, and using that file to overwrite the actual SQL*Plus buffer with your edited version from the afiedt.buf file and making it ready to execute. Control moves back into SQL*Plus, where you now have the option of executing the edited command or moving on to enter some new command altogether.

The following question arises: What is the local text editor? The answer is, it depends. First, it depends on the operating system in which you are running SQL*Plus. By default, the local text editor in Microsoft Windows is Notepad. In Unix systems, it's the legendary *vi editor*, which is powerful, but known for having a steep learning curve.

Note that the operating system we are talking about is the operating system in which SQL*Plus is operating, regardless of where the database might be. One popular architectural approach is to have the Oracle database run on a server with Unix, while the clients run on some variation of Microsoft Windows. If you start up SQL*Plus on the client in this situation, then you will get the default local text editor for Microsoft Windows, which means you'll get the Notepad editor. Notepad is a user-friendly, simple text editor that supports copy-and-paste, and full-screen editing.

To know exactly which editor is identified in SQL*Plus as the local text editor, you can use this command:

```
DEFINE _EDITOR
```

Note that no semicolon is required. If you run this from within an SQL*Plus installation in Microsoft Windows, you will probably see something like the display in Figure 8-5. The figure shows the results of the DEFINE _EDITOR command, which indicates that the local text editor is Notepad, meaning it's Notepad.exe. The .exe is assumed and not required.

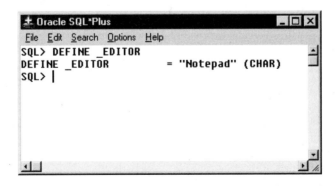

FIGURE 8-5. *The DEFINE _EDITOR command*

You can override the default local text editor by redefining the _EDITOR parameter. Here's an example:

```
DEFINE _EDITOR="C:\Program Files\Microsoft Office\Office\WINWORD"
```

This command will redefine the _EDITOR value to the fully qualified pathname of Microsoft Word in this particular installation. Your installation will probably vary. By providing the name of another executable file for a text editor, you can redefine the SQL*Plus local text editor.

Executing Text Files

The "GET filename" command will load a text file containing one single SQL statement, and execute it. If you have a text file that contains more than one SQL statement, each separated by semi-colons, then use the "START filename" command, or its alternative, the @ symbol. The following is an example of an SQL*Plus START command that loads and executes the contents of a text file called CREATE_PROCEDURES.SQL on the D: device:

```
SQL>START CREATE_PROCEDURES.SQL
```

The contents of the file will be loaded into the buffer and executed. You will see displayed on the screen any messages you would have seen had you typed the commands in yourself, such as "Procedure created" or "Warning . . . ." In other words, running the file is the same as typing each command yourself into the SQL*Plus interface except it's much more manageable.

PL/SQL Blocks and the Buffer

Those SQL developers who are used to working with the buffer know that the buffer only remembers the most recent SQL command. This is true with statements that you use to work with stored PL/SQL program units as well; however, there is one important dynamic that is very different from SQL. One single command to create a PL/SQL program unit could be hundreds or perhaps even thousands of lines long. If you submit a command to create a PL/SQL package body, with a few dozen procedures and another dozen functions, the entire set of code is considered one single SQL statement. The buffer will retain the entire statement in memory with line numbers assigned to each line. If you submit a statement that produces an error message and the error message indicates a line number on which the error occurred, it's relatively easy to list the contents of the buffer and identify the line number on which the error occurred.

For Review

1. The SQL*Plus interface can be used to enter in any SQL commands for working with program units. Commands are retained in the buffer and can be edited there with the built-in SQL*Plus buffer editor.

2. You can also choose to use a local text editor that is outside of SQL*Plus but defined within SQL*Plus with the _EDITOR value. When you use the ED command within SQL*Plus, the contents of the buffer are copied into the local text editor, where you can edit the command with the full power of the text editor and then save your changes back into the SQL*Plus buffer editor.

Exercises

1. **Which command is used to place a new line after the current line in the SQL*Plus buffer editor?**

   A. ADD

   B. APPEND

   C. INSERT

   D. INPUT

2. **What is the local text editor in Microsoft Windows? (Choose the best answer.)**

   A. The vi editor

   B. Notepad

   C. Whatever is contained in _EDITOR

   D. The SQL*Plus buffer editor

Answer Key
1. D.   2. C.

Procedure Builder

Procedure Builder is the graphical user interface (GUI) tool that Oracle provides for working with PL/SQL program units. It is an excellent tool with built-in support for compilation, error identification, and debugging. With search and replace features, the capability to navigate among a large number of program units on both the client and server, and the capability to easily move program units back and forth from the database to the local operating system, Procedure Builder is a powerful tool to support the creation of PL/SQL-based applications.

This section looks at the features that Procedure Builder provides for creating program units. Debugging will be analyzed in Chapter 9.

As we have observed many times already, PL/SQL program units have the capability to be executed on the client or server. While SQL*Plus can only be used to execute server-side PL/SQL, Procedure Builder can be used to execute either server- or client-side PL/SQL program units. The choice is up to you as the developer using Procedure Builder. When you run PL/SQL program units on the client, you are using the client-side PL/SQL engine; when you run PL/SQL program units on the server, you are using the server-side PL/SQL engine. There are some significant differences between the two. Server-side program units can call other server-side program units to which they have been granted access, but are unable to execute any client-side program units. Client-side program units, on the other hand, are able to execute both client-side and server-side program units to which they have been granted access. We will discuss how you can create and execute client- and server-side program units in this section.

When Procedure Builder is started, it is not connected to the database. In this state, Procedure Builder can be used to edit client-side libraries, but it cannot compile them, especially if they perform any interaction with the database, which most—if not all—program units will do. To connect Procedure Builder to the database, choose the File menu from the top left and choose the Connect option. You will be presented with a login screen. Enter a valid Oracle username and password, and if relevant, a database name. Upon the completion of a successful login, Procedure Builder will be connected to the database.

See Figure 8-6 for an example of what Procedure Builder looks like. On the left is the Object Navigator, which enables you to navigate among all of the program units known to Procedure Builder on both the client and server. You can create procedures, functions, and packages as stand-alone program units or collected in libraries. You can store your work on the client, the server, or both.

The PL/SQL Editor is on the right side of Figure 8-6. It displays one of the program units that is listed in the Object Navigator. The PL/SQL Editor lets you enter code with automatic color-coding assistance and text formatting to help create structured code. You can compile code and receive context-sensitive error messages in the PL/SQL Editor. (Note: This is the same PL/SQL Editor that is found in Oracle Forms and Oracle Reports.)

The next few sections describe the components of Procedure Builder in more detail.

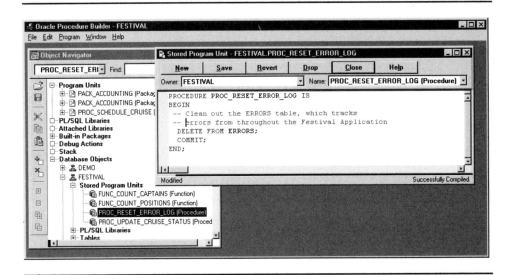

FIGURE 8-6. *Procedure Builder*

Object Navigator

The Object Navigator is the table of contents for Procedure Builder. It is a tree-structured listing of all of the program units known to Procedure Builder that you have access to work with on both the client and server.

The Object Navigator has a set of nodes and objects. A *node* is a standard category that the Object Navigator tracks, and you cannot change the text of a node. Nodes are displayed in bold font and in mixed case. *Objects* are the entities you create with Procedure Builder—entities such as program units and libraries. Each object will only appear as you create it, or add it, to Procedure Builder's Object Navigator. Object names appear in plain font (not bold) and in all uppercase letters (usually—it's actually possible to create library files with mixed case letters, too). Object names always have some sort of icon next to them, to the left, indicating the object's type. The icon is important—it not only provides a clue to what type of object you are seeing listed, but it is also where you will double-click to display an editor for the particular object.

Nodes never appear with an icon. A node is a placeholder that indicates the possible presence of objects, such as program units. Both nodes and objects may be expanded to reveal more nodes and/or objects contained within or subordinate to the particular node or object.

A box appears to the left of each node and some of the objects. If a box appears, it indicates that the node or object has the potential of owning more nodes or objects subordinate to itself. If the box is empty, then the node is empty for now—that is, there are no objects in that node, or category. However, the presence of the box indicates that it's possible to add additional nodes or objects within. If the node box contains a plus sign, this means that the node contains objects and that you can click on the plus sign to expand the list. When you click on the plus sign in the node box, the list of objects is displayed and the node box changes to display a dash (or minus) sign. This means that if you were to click on the box now, the list would collapse. For an example of what we're talking about, see Figure 8-7. The PL/SQL Libraries node is expanded to display one library FestivalDBUnits. The Attached Libraries node contains objects and is collapsed. The Program Units node is empty, indicating that there are no client-side program units included in this display.

Some nodes may display objects that have subnodes. See Figure 8-8 for an example. Figure 8-8 shows the Database Objects node expanded, exposing an alphabetic list of the schemas in the database. The FESTIVAL schema object is expanded, showing the first three of five nodes that display for each schema. The node for Tables is expanded, and one table in particular—the CRUISES table—is

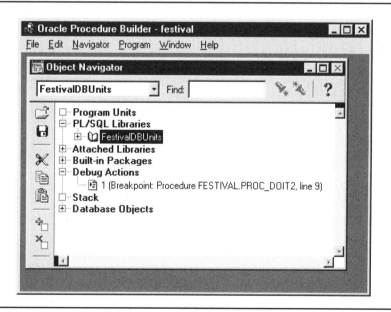

FIGURE 8-7.   *The Object Navigator up close*

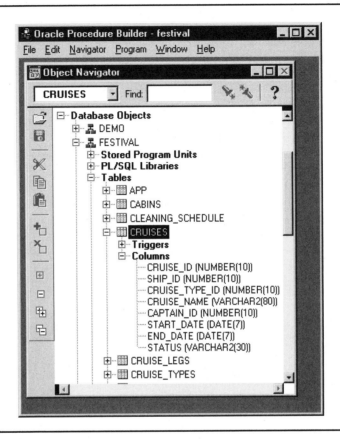

FIGURE 8-8. *The Object Navigator: nodes and subnodes*

expanded. Its node for Columns is also expanded, showing a list of the columns in the CRUISES table.

Because each node or object has the potential for displaying multiple levels of nodes and objects, the Procedure Builder menu enables you to *collapse all* or *expand all* nodes and objects to speed things up. When you highlight a particular node and choose the *expand all* option, you expand every subnode within the highlighted node, so that every possible node and object is displayed. Similarly, if you choose *collapse all*, you will collapse every node within the highlighted node. Otherwise, if you simply collapse a node that contains expanded nodes, then the next time you expand, the expanded subnodes will still display as expanded.

Here is a description of each node in the Object Navigator:

■ **Program Units**   This node refers to client-side procedures, functions, or packages. It's a temporary holding place where you can edit program units as you build them; however, program units edited here will not be saved when you terminate Procedure Builder. The Program Units node has three subnodes for each actual program unit you create:

    ■ **Specification**   Summarizes the program unit header information, including the name, parameter list, and return type (for functions).

    ■ **References**   Lists all other program units that this program unit references.

    ■ **Referenced By**   Lists all program units that make calls to this program unit.

■ **PL/SQL Libraries**   Libraries are a collection of one or more program units in a single client-side file structure. This node will list all of the libraries that you have opened with Procedure Builder so far. You can create new libraries or open existing libraries here. Each library will have its own set of subnodes:

    ■ **Program Units**   Lists the procedures, functions, and packages that make up the library.

    ■ **Attached Libraries**   Other libraries that have been attached to this one. (More information on attached libraries appears in the next few paragraphs.)

■ **Attached Libraries**   These are libraries just like the PL/SQL libraries in the previous node. However, these libraries have already been created and saved, and are now attached so that Procedure Builder can execute program units from within the library. The difference between this node and the previous node is that the PL/SQL Libraries node represents open libraries that can be edited, and the Attached Libraries node represents attached libraries that can be executed, but not edited.

■ **Built-in Packages**   These are prewritten Oracle package specifications. Under this node you will find package specifications such as STANDARD, which includes all of the standard SQL functions, like SUBSTR (substring) and ADD_MONTHS. The packages listed here are for reference only. Each package lists its program units and the corresponding parameter lists, and, in the case of functions, return datatypes.

- **Debug Actions** This is where debug actions, such as breakpoints, will be displayed if and when you create them. You create these debug actions elsewhere, and the Object Navigator lists them here to help you manage your work. This topic will be discussed in more detail in Chapter 9.

- **Stack** When debugging a program unit, this node automatically displays the stack of execution, including the values of declared constructs. This topic will be discussed in more detail in Chapter 9.

- **Database Objects** If Procedure Builder is not connected to the database, this node will be empty. However, when Procedure Builder is connected to the database, then—and only then—this node lists a hierarchical display of schemas in alphabetical order. Each schema has an identical set of subnodes, each of which lists objects owned by the respective schema:

  - Stored Program Units

  - PL/SQL Libraries

  - Tables

  - Views

  - Types

To create a new object in a given node, you can often highlight the node and click on the green plus sign to the left of the screen. This is the Create button. This is the same as choosing Navigator and then Create from the pull-down menu. Some objects, such as Stack and Debug Actions, are created through other means, which we will explore in Chapter 9. However, for program units, this method will work.

To help you navigate through the nodes, the Object Navigator provides a couple of features at the top. The Location Indicator is a pop list in the upper-left corner of the Object Navigator, which indicates where you currently are in the hierarchy and shows the enclosing (or owning) object, if applicable. See Figure 8-7.

Also, the upper-right corner of the Object Navigator has a Find field, which you can use to locate an object. Type in the name or partial name of an object in the Find field, and the Object Navigator will automatically jump to that particular object name, expanding and collapsing the hierarchy of nodes as required to display the object you are looking for.

Creating a Program Unit with Procedure Builder

To create a client-side procedure, use the Object Navigator to highlight one of the nodes for Program Unit, and then choose Create. You can choose Create in one of two ways. One is from the pull-down menu by selecting Navigator and then Create. The other way to choose Create is to click on the green plus sign button on the left side of the Object Navigator. Create will only be active when you have identified, with the Object Navigator, a valid node for program unit creation. Note, however, that you cannot "create" an object with every node in the Object Navigator; some nodes only list objects that are created elsewhere. See Table 8-1 for more information. Note that each "creatable" node supports the creation of multiple objects, one at a time, and will display each object's name under the node in the Object Navigator. Also note that Table 8-1 lists the first-order nodes that appear in the Object Navigator. As you create objects in the Object Navigator, additional nodes will appear automatically. For example, if you create a library under the PL/SQL Library node, then a new Program Units node will appear for each library you create. Under Database Objects, you will find a Stored Program Units node for each schema in the database, and so on.

When you choose Create with any Program Units or Stored Program Units node, you will end up with the display shown in Figure 8-9.

First-Order Node	Is Create Available	Effect of Create
Program Units	Yes	New Program Unit pop-up window (Figure 8-9).
PL/SQL Libraries	Yes	Add a new library object with a default system-assigned name, displayed as a node (Figure 8-10).
Attached Libraries	Yes	Attach Library pop-up window (Figure 8-11).
Built-in Packages	No	NA
Debug Actions	No	NA
Stack	No	NA
Database Objects	No	NA

TABLE 8-1. *Object Navigator Nodes and Create*

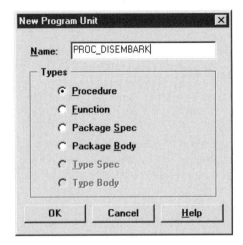

FIGURE 8-9. *New Program Unit pop-up window*

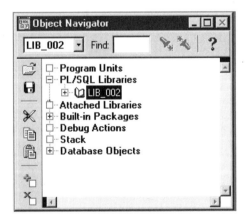

FIGURE 8-10. *Result of Create on the PL/SQL Libraries node*

In the display in Figure 8-9, type in the name of your program unit and highlight one of the radio buttons to indicate if you are creating a

- Procedure
- Function

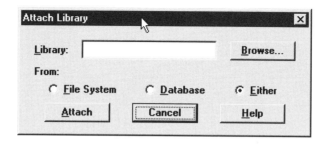

FIGURE 8-11.   *Attach Library pop-up window*

- Package Spec (specification)

- Package Body

- Type Spec (specification) (only available for Stored Program Units, that is, server side)

- Type Body (only available for Stored Program Units, that is, server side)

Once you've made your selection, click OK. The PL/SQL Editor will appear. See Figure 8-12 for an example.

The PL/SQL Editor is a powerful interface in Procedure Builder from which you can type PL/SQL code for procedures, functions, and packages. The editor will perform some automatic code formatting. It enables you to compile your program units and analyze compilation errors in context.

When you create a new program unit with the PL/SQL Editor, the name of your new program unit will appear in the Object Navigator and the PL/SQL Editor window. There will be an asterisk to the right of the name in both displays. This asterisk will remain until the program unit is successfully compiled, which will cause the asterisk to disappear. After that, as you make changes to program units, then whenever any program unit has a status of INVALID, the asterisk will reappear next to the name of the INVALID program unit until you successfully compile the code once again.

There are two versions of the PL/SQL Editor that are found in Procedure Builder. One version is the Program Unit version, which is used when working with client-side program units. The other version is the Stored Program Unit version, which is used when working with server-side program units—that is, database program units.

To display a program unit with the PL/SQL Editor, use the Object Navigator to locate the program unit you are looking for. When you locate the appropriate program unit, there should be an icon to the left of the program unit's name. Use the mouse to double-click the icon, and the PL/SQL Editor will appear on the screen.

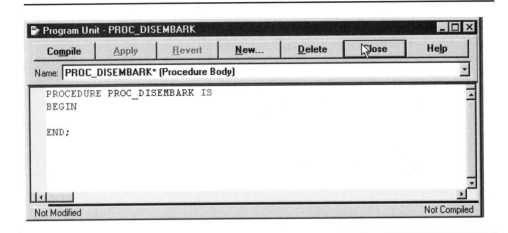

FIGURE 8-12. *The PL/SQL Editor—Program Unit version*

PL/SQL Editor—Program Units

See Figure 8-12 for an example of the client-side Program Unit version of the PL/SQL editor. Notice the set of buttons across the top. Each has a purpose, but not all buttons are activated all of the time. If a particular button is not activated, then it is not available for the node you are working in at the time.

- **Compile**   Once you have entered the code for your program unit, you can click the Compile button, and if there are any compilation errors, you will see them displayed on the screen.

- **Apply**   This saves your work, but it will not compile.

- **Revert**   This enables you to throw away any changes you've made and restore the last saved copy of your program unit.

- **New . . .**   This starts up the New Program Unit pop-up window, beginning the process of creating a new program unit.

- **Delete**   This removes the displayed program unit from the node and from memory.

- **Close**   This simply closes the PL/SQL editor, prompting you to save any unsaved work.

- **Help**   This displays the Procedure Builder help system.

Notice the bottom-left and bottom-right corners of the PL/SQL Editor in Figure 8-12. The bottom-left corner displays Not Modified, and the bottom-right corner displays Not Compiled. As soon as you start typing code into the window, Not Modified is replaced with Modified. Once you stop typing and compile the program unit by clicking the Compile button, for example, the bottom-left corner changes once again to Not Modified, and the bottom-right corner changes to Successfully Compiled. As soon as you start typing again, the Successfully Compiled message disappears and Not Compiled appears again.

Once you type in some code, you can click the Compile button and submit your code for parsing. If any compilation errors exist in your code, the error message (or messages) will display and the cursor in the code will move to the beginning of where the parser believes the error has occurred. See Figure 8-13 for an example.

Figure 8-13 shows the PL/SQL Editor as it displays some compilation errors. Notice that there are a couple of compilation error messages cited, but the first one

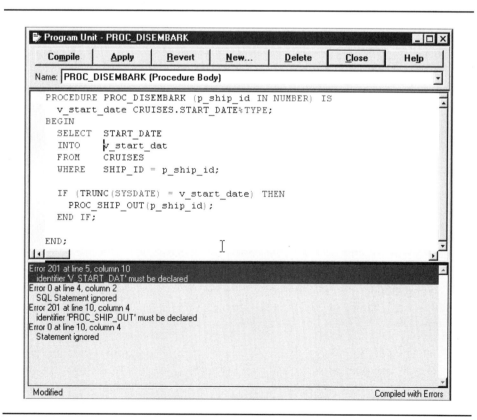

FIGURE 8-13. *The PL/SQL Editor with compilation error messages*

is noting that the variable v_start_dat has not been declared. Now look at the source code and note that the PL/SQL Editor has placed the cursor at the beginning of this undeclared variable, making it easier to fix the typo and move on to the next step.

PL/SQL Editor—Stored Program Units

The other version of the PL/SQL Editor is the Stored Program Units editor. This is the version that Procedure Builder uses for any server-side program units. An example of the Stored Program Units version of the PL/SQL Editor is shown in Figure 8-14.

The differences between this version and the client-side Program Units version are minor. Both share the same functionality with regard to code formatting and context-sensitive compilation error messages.The window title is Stored Program Units instead of Program Unit. Also, the buttons across the top of the screen are slightly different, as follows:

- **New** This is just like the Program Units version, but is located in a different place on the toolbar. This starts up the New Program Unit pop-up window, beginning the process of creating a new program unit.

- **Save** Unlike Apply, this commits the stored program unit to the database, which causes the code to be compiled and stored in the data dictionary.

- **Revert** Just like the Program Units version, this enables you to throw away any changes you've made and restore the last saved copy of your program unit.

- **Drop** This removes the stored program unit from the database.

- **Close** This simply closes the PL/SQL Editor window.

- **Help** This displays the Procedure Builder help system.

Finally, you can use the PL/SQL Editor to navigate from one program unit to the other. See Figure 8-15. Notice the pop-list menu options in the upper portion of the display. You can jump to another schema, and within a given schema, you can choose any of the available program units from the alphabetical list that appears in the upper-right pop list, as shown in the figure. When you navigate to a new program unit, the code of the target program unit will appear in the PL/SQL Editor. You can then use the PL/SQL Editor as you normally would to edit your code.

The client-side Program Units version of the PL/SQL Editor has a similar navigating feature, but it doesn't display a field for the schema. Instead, it merely displays one long pop list across the width of the editor window, showing the names of other program units. Furthermore, you can only navigate among other program

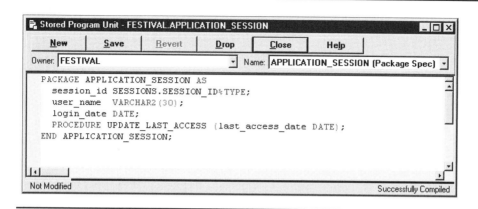

FIGURE 8-14.   *PL/SQL Editor—Stored Program Unit version*

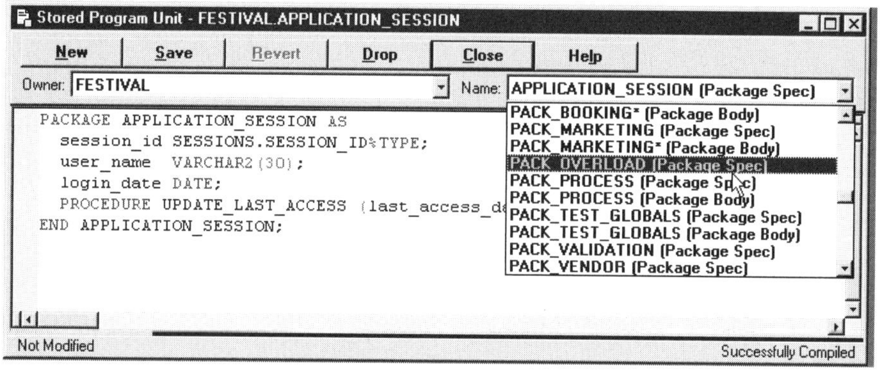

FIGURE 8-15.   *Navigating with the PL/SQL Editor*

units within the same PL/SQL library, attached library, or set of program units displayed in the Object Navigator node.

Executing a Program Unit

Once you have created a program unit, you frequently execute it outside of Procedure Builder—for example, from triggers in Oracle Forms, or from the

SQL*Plus command line interface, and so on. However, you can execute it within Procedure Builder using the PL/SQL Interpreter. To do this, follow these steps:

1. From the pull-down menu, choose Program and then PL/SQL Interpreter.

2. In the Interpreter Pane, which is the lower half of the PL/SQL Interpreter, type the name of the program unit you want to execute, followed by a semicolon. Do not use the EXEC keyword; that is a SQL*Plus requirement and is not understood here. Just type the single statement of the program unit's name. You can enter anonymous PL/SQL blocks here as well, if you need to create any variables or if you are testing a function and require some sort of PL/SQL expression.

We will discuss the PL/SQL Interpreter more in Chapter 9 when we discuss debugging.

Moving Program Units

One of the great advantages to Procedure Builder is its capability to easily copy and move program units from one location to another within the Object Navigator. To do this, display the program unit you want to move, highlight it, and then click and drag the program unit to the new location.

Figure 8-16 shows an example of how this works. In Figure 8-16, we have highlighted two Stored Program Units: the APPLICATION_SESSION package specification and its corresponding package body.

To highlight more than one object in the Object Navigator, hold down CTRL while clicking on each object; the first click on an object will select it, and a second click on the same object will deselect it. In other words, CTRL-MOUSECLICK will toggle each selection into your selection list. Or, as an alternative, you can highlight a series of objects by pressing SHIFT. First click a single object to anchor one end of your list, and then press and hold SHIFT while using the mouse to click on the single object on the opposite end of the list. This will result in highlighting all objects between the first and second objects you clicked.

Once the program units are highlighted, you can click and drag the entries to the location where you would like them to be copied—in Figure 8-16, the destination is the local client-side Program Unit node. A line will appear across the Object Navigator when you have dragged the object or objects to an acceptable destination.

This is an easy way to move program units from one library to another, from the database server to the client, or back. It's very powerful and easy. If you can display the two locations in the Object Navigator, then you can click and drag an object from one of those locations to the other.

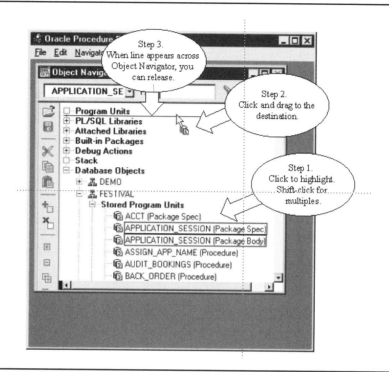

FIGURE 8-16.   *Clicking and dragging objects in the Object Navigator*

Working with Libraries

Libraries are collections of program units under one name. Unlike packages, which collect procedures, functions, and other constructs within PL/SQL code to create a single object, libraries allow program units to maintain their autonomy, but organize them for the purpose of moving them around, storing them together in files, and attaching them together to a client-side module such as an Oracle Form. Libraries do not provide the sort of benefits that packages do, in the sense of package initialization, automatic collective loading into the System Global Area (SGA), and others. Libraries are just a kind of box into which you can place your program units for easier manipulation. Their primary benefit is that they enable you to associate a set of program units—procedures, functions, and packages—with a client-side module such as an Oracle Form or an Oracle Report.

To create a library, choose the PL/SQL Library node, and click Create. The result will be the display we saw earlier in Figure 8-10. The new library will be automatically given two nodes: one for Program Units and one for Attached

Libraries. You can use the Program Units node to add procedures, functions, and packages to your library. You can use the Attached Libraries node to attach other libraries you might have created to this new library, which has the effect of including the program units contained in that library with this one.

Once you have created your library of program units, save the library. To save the library, highlight the library in the Object Navigator and choose File and then Save from the pull-down menu. The Save Library pop-up window will appear. See Figure 8-17 for an example.

Here is where you can change the system-defined name for your library to something more meaningful by typing the new name in the Library field. You also have the option of saving the file to the file system or the database. The file system is not necessarily the client—it means that you will save your library as a stand-alone binary file, named with your library name followed by the file suffix *.pll, anywhere on the file system that your computer has access. Presumably, this includes the client, but it could also theoretically include the computer that is set aside as the server. However, the file system is clearly not the database, so for all practical purposes, this is the client-side option; however, be aware that you may technically save the file on the same machine being used as the database server with this option.

The Database option enables you to save the library in the database on the server.

Creating Database Triggers

To create a database trigger in Procedure Builder, you must connect to the database (File | Connect), expand the Database Objects node, select the schema for which you want to create the database trigger, and then expand it to reveal its node for Tables. (Note that you cannot use Procedure Builder to create a schema; you must

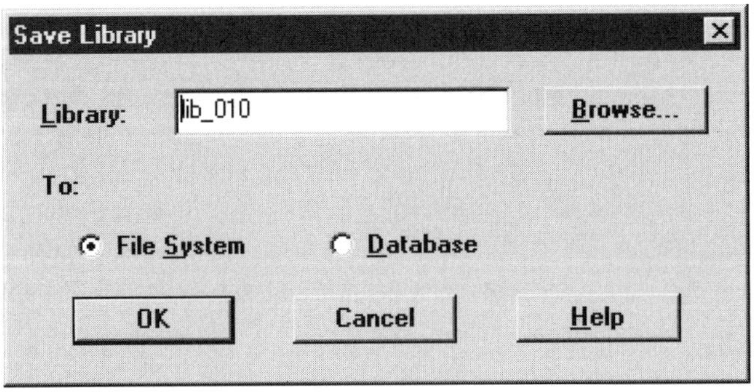

FIGURE 8-17. *The Save Library pop-up window*

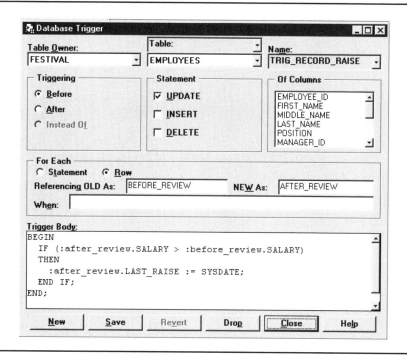

FIGURE 8-18. *The Database Trigger editor*

work with the existing schemas, or use a different tool to create the schema, such as
SQL*Plus.) Then you must expand the Tables node, select the table on which you
want to attach the trigger, and expand it. Then, at long last, you will locate the node
for Triggers. Highlight the node and choose Create. The Database Trigger editor will
display. See Figure 8-18 for an example.

The Database Trigger editor lets you define the entire database trigger. You will
find text fields and pop lists to create the database trigger, as we have already
discussed in Chapter 5. When you have entered the full definition of the trigger,
click the Save button to compile the trigger and save it to the database. If a
compilation error is encountered, it will be displayed on the screen so you can
correct the mistake and save again to recompile.

For Review

I. Procedure Builder is the Oracle GUI tool for building program units. You
   can use it for both client- and server-side program units.

2. In Procedure Builder, the Object Navigator is the interface for organizing and locating your various program units. You can create libraries of program units or click and drag to move program units back and forth between the client and the server.

3. The PL/SQL Editor in Procedure Builder lets you create, edit, and compile code, and get context-sensitive compilation error messages.

Exercises

1. **Which of the following is a node in the Procedure Builder Object Navigator? (Choose all that apply.)**

   A. Stored Program Units

   B. Attached Libraries

   C. Stack Actions

   D. Database Program Units

2. **In the PL/SQL Editor window, what does the Apply button do?**

   A. It saves your changes to the database.

   B. It compiles and saves your changes to the database.

   C. It saves your changes to the client, but it does not compile.

   D. It makes you work harder.

Answer Key
1. A, B. 2. C.

Chapter Summary

When creating PL/SQL code, you can use the SQL*Plus interface and/or Procedure Builder to create and debug program units. This chapter looks at creating your program units.

The SQL*Plus command interface includes a buffer editor that remembers your most recent SQL command. When creating a PL/SQL program unit, this includes the complete CREATE OR REPLACE . . . END statement that you issue to build a program unit, even if the statement consists of thousands of lines. The built-in

SQL*Plus buffer editor lets you issue simple commands to edit lines, delete lines, append to the end of lines, and input new lines to whatever the buffer contains. This buffer editor runs the same in whatever operating system your Oracle installation happens to be in. However, the option of using the local operating system's text editor may provide a more powerful alternative. By typing **ED** in SQL*Plus, you can automatically copy the contents of the buffer to the local text editor where the full power of the text editor is available for your use, and when you are done, you can save the file, which has the effect of copying your work back into the SQL*Plus buffer where you can now execute the results. You can change the local text editor from the default to whatever you choose.

Procedure Builder also lets you create program units, but with a more powerful set of tools. The Object Navigator provides a hierarchical display of program units in their various combinations on both the client and the server. Using the Object Navigator, you can expand and collapse lists of objects, and add new objects such as program units (procedures, functions, package specifications, and package bodies), libraries, and database triggers. You can navigate through schemas on the server, explore tables owned by schemas, and open and attach libraries on both the client and server.

The PL/SQL Editor in Procedure Builder lets you edit procedures and functions on the client (Program Units) and the server (Stored Program Units). You can compile your code and receive any compilation error messages in context with the cursor in the PL/SQL editor automatically moving to the beginning of the first error identified by the compilation error. You can also use the PL/SQL Editor to navigate to other program units, drop the program unit you are working with, and save your work for later, even if it's not completely compiled yet.

You can use the Object Navigator to move program units from one location to the other, between the client and server, or from one library to another—essentially, any location you can display in the Object Navigator.

Two-Minute Drill

- The SQL*Plus buffer editor automatically retains the most recent SQL statement. When you begin to type a new statement, the contents of the buffer will be overwritten with your new statement.

- To list the contents of the buffer, use the LIST command or L. The last line will automatically be the current line for all other commands. C or CHANGE lets you change the contents of the current line. A or APPEND adds whatever you type after the A to the end of the current line, extending the current line. I or INPUT followed by pressing ENTER will add a new blank line after the current line, enabling you to type your new line and continue typing until you type a single period on a line by itself. The DEL command will remove the current line from the buffer, causing the following line to become the new current line. To change the current line, type a single number that represents the line number in the buffer that you want to become the current line.

■ You can save the buffer's contents to a text file with the SAVE filename command, or get the contents of a previously saved text file and load them into the buffer with the GET filename command. However, note that GET will only load a file properly if it contains a single statement.

■ You can execute the contents of a text file that contains one or more sequential commands with the START filename command.

■ Instead of using the buffer editor, you can type **ED**, which will invoke the default local text editor. The contents of the buffer will be copied into the text editor. If you save the edited contents in the local text editor, the contents will be saved to a file called afiedt.buf and then automatically transferred back into the SQL*Plus buffer, where you can execute the contents and observe the results.

■ The Object Navigator in Procedure Builder is a hierarchical display, much like the Microsoft Windows Explorer display, and is similar to the Object Navigator found in Oracle Forms, Oracle Reports, Oracle Designer, and elsewhere. It displays nodes and objects, which you may expand and collapse to view at increasing levels of detail and drill down to observe objects nested (or contained) within larger objects.

■ The Object Navigator displays Program Units (client side), PL/SQL Libraries, and Database Objects such as Schemas, Tables, Database Triggers, and Stored Program Units.

■ You can use the PL/SQL Editor to create, compile, and store any program unit on the client side or the server side.

■ Compilation errors will appear in context and enable you to quickly edit and recompile your program units.

Chapter Questions

1. **Which of the following is an SQL*Plus buffer editor command? (Choose all that apply.)**

   A. LIST

   B. DELETE

   C. 1

   D. PUT

2. **Consider the following code sample:**

```
CREATE OR REPLACE PROCEDURE ASSIGN_APP_NAME
  (p_app_id IN VARCHAR2) IS
BEGIN
  SELECT APP_NAME
  INTO   PARMS.v_app_name
  FROM   APP
  WHERE  APP_ID = p_app_id;
  DBMS_OUTPUT.PUT_LINE('Done');
END;
/
```

You submit this code to the SQL*Plus interface. What are the contents of the buffer? (Choose the single best answer.)

A. It depends on whether this procedure compiled successfully or not.

B. SELECT APP_NAME INTO PARMS.v_app_name FROM APP WHERE APP_ID = p_app_id

C. DBMS_OUTPUT.PUT_LINE('Done');

D. The entire statement, from CREATE to END;

3. **You have used a text editor to save the CREATE ... PROCEDURE ASSIGN_APP_NAME statement from Question 2 in a single text file. Which of the following commands can be used from within SQL*Plus to load the contents of this file? (Choose all that apply.)**

A. EXEC

B. RUN

C. GET

D. START

4. **In the Object Navigator, when an asterisk appears to the right of the name of a program unit, what does it indicate? (Choose all that apply.)**

A. The program unit is on the client side.

B. The program unit is not valid, and needs to be compiled.

C. The program unit is a function.

D. The program unit includes parameters.

5. **In Procedure Builder's Object Navigator, what does the References node display for a given program unit?**

    A. Other program units that reference this program unit.

    B. Program units that this program unit references.

    C. A list of online help resources for programming in PL/SQL.

    D. There is no such node.

6. **In Procedure Builder's Object Navigator, you expand the Database Objects node and discover four subnodes. Which of the following statements are true? (Choose all that apply.)**

    A. There are four tables in the schema.

    B. There are four schemas in the database.

    C. Procedure Builder is not connected to the database.

    D. Procedure Builder is connected to the database.

7. **In the Procedure Builder Object Navigator, the difference between the nodes PL/SQL Libraries and Attached Libraries is that**

    A. You can edit PL/SQL Libraries, but you cannot edit Attached Libraries.

    B. You can execute PL/SQL Libraries, but you cannot execute Attached Libraries.

    C. PL/SQL Libraries are on the client and Attached Libraries are on the server.

    D. There is no difference.

8. **You can use Procedure Builder to move program units _____. (Choose all that apply.)**

    A. From one schema in the database to another schema in the database

    B. From one attached library on the client to a schema in the database

    C. From one attached library on the client to another attached library on the client

    D. From one schema in the database to an attached library on the client

9. **When Not Compiled in the lower-right corner of the PL/SQL Editor appears, this indicates that**

    A. The program unit in the editor has never been compiled.

    B. The code in the program unit cannot be compiled.

    C. You just attempted to compile the program unit, but the attempt was unsuccessful.

    D. None of the above.

10. **You can use Procedure Builder to create the following:**

    A. Database triggers

    B. Package specifications

    C. Stored functions

    D. Client-side procedures in a library

Answers to Chapter Questions

1. A, C.   LIST and 1

Explanation   The LIST command is correct; this will display the contents of the buffer. The DELETE command is oh so wrong—be very careful on this. DELETE, remember, is an SQL command. DEL is the buffer command. The answer 1 is correct; this will redirect the current line to the first line in the buffer editor. PUT is wrong.

2. D.   The entire statement, from CREATE to END;

Explanation   Even if the procedure doesn't compile correctly, the entire CREATE . . . PROCEDURE will overwrite whatever may have been in the buffer editor before and be completely retained in the buffer until another SQL statement is issued.

3. C, D.   GET and START

Explanation   EXEC is used to execute stored procedures that are already stored in the database. RUN can be used to run the contents of the buffer, but will not load a file into the buffer. GET will load a file and will perform successfully if the file contains one single statement, which this file will contain. START can be used to load and execute any file containing one or more SQL statements.

4. B.   The program unit is not valid, and needs to be compiled.

Explanation   The asterisk means that the program unit has a STATUS of INVALID. It doesn't matter if the program unit is a function or if it has parameters.

5. B.   Program units that this program unit references

Explanation   The References node shows program units that this particular program unit references, such as procedures and functions and packages that it invokes.

6. B, D.   B: There are four schemas in the database. D: Procedure Builder is connected to the database.

Explanation   The Database Objects node will not be activated at all unless Procedure Builder is connected to the database. When you expand Database Objects, you are first presented with an alphabetic list of schemas. You don't find tables until you expand the schema nodes.

7. A.   You can edit PL/SQL Libraries, but you cannot edit Attached Libraries.

Explanation   Any PL/SQL library can be included under either node. You can even open a single library under both nodes simultaneously. The PL/SQL Library is where a library appears that you have opened for editing. The Attached Libraries node is where a library appears that you have attached for execution.

8. A, B, C, D.   A: From one schema in the database to another schema in the database B: From one attached library on the client to a schema in the database C: From one attached library on the client to another attached library on the client D: From one schema in the database to an attached library on the client

Explanation   All are true—all can be displayed in the Object Navigator so they all will support the capability to copy a program unit from one location to the other.

9. D.   None of the above.

Explanation   The Not Compiled message means that the code has not been compiled since it was last changed. A change could consist of one blank space typed in a comment. If a compilation was just attempted and was unsuccessful, Compiled with Errors will appear.

10. A, B, C, D.   A: Database triggers B: Package specifications C: Stored functions D: Client-side procedures in a library

Explanation   You can create them all!

CHAPTER
9

Debugging PL/SQL

t's one thing to write a PL/SQL program. It's quite another to get it to execute successfully. No one writes error-free code all of the time. Debugging is the practice of analyzing existing software to identify errors, understand their causes, and fix them. This section looks at tools and techniques for debugging your program units.

In this chapter, you will review and understand the following topics:

- Debugging concepts
- Debugging with SQL*Plus
- Debugging with Procedure Builder

Debugging Concepts

There are two major categories of errors that you will encounter with any software program. The first category is *compilation errors*. Compilation errors are syntax errors that prevent your code from successfully compiling.

The second category is *run-time errors*, also known as execution or logic errors. These can occur after you've successfully compiled your program and you're able to execute it, but it's not performing as you intended. Compilation errors are manifested in poor or unexpected results, or even in an abnormal termination of the application during execution. The cause of these errors could be developer errors or even an Oracle bug.

Debugging is the science of identifying compilation and logic errors in an application, understanding the causes of the errors, and fixing them. The phrase "debugging techniques" refers largely to steps you can take in the process of writing your code that help minimize the occurrences of compilation and/or logic errors, and steps you can take to identify them. Debugging tools, on the other hand, are software systems, features, utilities, and other aids that are specifically designed to assist you in the process of debugging your programs. The tools will not magically debug your programs for you—you must understand the basic thought processes necessary to properly debug your code and use the tools where appropriate to assist you in your efforts.

Debugging Techniques

From a practical point of view, there are a number of common-sense techniques you should establish long before worrying about the debugging tools:

- *Develop a solid understanding of the PL/SQL language.* By establishing a solid and thorough understanding of PL/SQL language syntax, through the study of the Oracle Press book series on PL/SQL combined with hands-on work, many syntax errors and logical patterns will become increasingly obvious to you.

■ *Establish the habit of properly formatting your code.* You can avoid many compilation errors by lining up loops and indenting nested code. Some of the worst bugs that you will deal with in PL/SQL often involve a large IF/ELSIF/END IF statement that is missing the final END IF or a set of nested blocks where one of the END statements is not present. These errors can really throw the PL/SQL parser off the track of what your program is intended to do, which is why the parser will frequently provide misleading error messages. Proper code formatting techniques will minimize these problems.

■ *Make sure you understand the goal.* It's easy to get distracted with some problem that isn't really part of the project but instead is some sidetrack, a nice-to-have tangent that isn't really part of the application's purpose anyway. On the other hand, if you thoroughly understand the business process you're automating, you can more efficiently focus on the important issues.

■ *Start with what works.* If you've got a program that is producing errors, identify those portions of the code that you know are working correctly. Use comments to block out those portions that seem to be the source of the problem so you can narrow down the possible sources of the problem.

■ *Build your code incrementally and test incrementally.* Not even the Oracle database product itself was created completely perfect the first time. Develop a portion of your code and test it. If it's working, develop another small portion and test it. If it's suddenly not working, you'll have a much better idea of where the problem is coming from than if you'd created some complete, large application and found a problem from somewhere within it.

■ *PL/SQL compilation error messages do not necessarily tell you where the problem really is. They tell you where Oracle got confused.* These are two different things. Think of it like this: When you are driving somewhere, when do you first realize you are lost? Usually when you see something that you weren't expecting such as an unfamiliar landmark or something that's inconsistent with your directions. Is this where the error occurred? Probably not—it was probably before this, when you took some wrong turn that led you to this unfamiliar landmark. It's the same with PL/SQL (and for that matter, SQL), especially when it comes to compilation errors (more so than execution errors). The most difficult error messages you receive will often point to a place that is not really the error, but is somewhere after the error. See the next section entitled "Code Formatting: An Example" for an illustration of this.

Code Formatting: An Example

Consider the following code sample:

```
DECLARE v_today DATE := SYSDATE;
BEGIN IF TO_CHAR(v_today,'Dy') = 'Sat'
THEN DBMS_OUTPUT.PUT_LINE('Today is Saturday');
END;
```

Technically, this lack of indentation and placement of the IF statement on the same line as the BEGIN statement is acceptable to the PL/SQL parser, which completely ignores carriage returns and blank space between statements. However, this code sample will produce the following error message:

```
ERROR at line 4:
ORA-06550: line 4, column 4:
PLS-00103: Encountered the symbol ";" when expecting one of the following:
if
```

What does this mean? Is there something unacceptable about the semicolon? Of course not. But if you were to format the code, you may quickly discover the problem:

```
DECLARE
   v_today DATE := SYSDATE;
BEGIN
   IF TO_CHAR(v_today,'Dy') = 'Sat' THEN
      DBMS_OUTPUT.PUT_LINE('Today is Saturday');
END;
```

By lining up the components of nested statements, it's easier to identify the problem. In this case, the statement to declare a PL/SQL block, which is DECLARE ... BEGIN ... END, is lined up so that each part of the statement starts on the same column—the first leftmost column. The nested portions are indented by two spaces. The v_today declaration is indented two spaces to the right, as is the IF statement. However, the IF statement is also a nesting statement, so we line up each part of the IF statement and indent the nested portion. This is when it jumps out at us that we've left out the END IF portion of the IF statement, which is now obvious but was difficult to see before we reformatted our code. Furthermore, we now have a clue as to what the PL/SQL compilation error was trying to say to us—when it encountered the final END statement, it assumed we were typing END IF since it knows that we can't end the block until we end the IF statement. However, when the parser encountered the final closing semicolon, it got upset and said the following:

```
PLS-00103: Encountered the symbol ";" when expecting one of the following:
if
```

This makes perfect sense now. The parser encountered the final "END", and was expecting the corresponding "IF" to form the complete "END IF". But without proper formatting of code, this is difficult to understand. Furthermore, when we realize that the compilation error isn't really reporting the error, but instead is reporting where the parser realized it was lost, we can see that the actual error was probably right before the location that the parser is pointing us to. This is very common when dealing with compilation errors.

If there's a general theme to these techniques, it can be summed up in one phrase: Learn to think like PL/SQL. Get a thorough understanding of what it is doing and what it can do, as is explained in this book and others from the Oracle Press line, and you will dramatically improve your odds of successful and efficient software development.

Debugging Tools

No debugging tool can take the place of common sense, a solid understanding of the PL/SQL language, and professional coding practices. Debugging tools will build on these thought patterns, practices, and techniques to give you the arsenal you need to debug complex programs quickly.

Oracle provides several debugging tools, some of which are listed here:

- **Error message documentation**   Many errors, including all compilation errors and many execution errors, are reported by the PL/SQL system with assigned error codes, numbers, and some brief text describing the error. The Oracle Corporation publishes documentation that enables you to look up these error messages by number to gain some further explanation as to the possible cause of the problem as well as some suggested approaches on how to fix it.

- **The SQLCODE and SQLERRM functions**   The SQLCODE function is a PL/SQL function that returns the error message number as a negative number, and the SQLERRM function returns the entire three-part error message, including the prefix, number, and text. These functions can be used to trap system error messages and codes within your PL/SQL programs. By combining these functions with exception handlers, you can create programs that record error messages for you.

- **Data dictionary views**   When you submit a program unit for storage to the database, we have already seen that it will be compiled and either established as VALID, meaning it compiled correctly, or INVALID, meaning that it did not compile correctly. What we have not yet seen is that the actual compilation errors are recorded in the data dictionary. We will explore what that means and how we can leverage them in this chapter. These are excellent for fixing compilation errors.

- **SQL*Plus debugging features**   Some convenient built-in tools can assist in the display of detailed compilation errors that are stored in the data dictionary.

- **The Procedure Builder debugger**   One of the most powerful debugging tools in the Oracle universe, the Procedure Builder debugger, is the best way to peek into the inner workings of program units. This is excellent for fixing logic errors.

For Review

1. After you have created your application, you will have two categories of errors to contend with: compilation errors and execution errors. Debugging is the process of identifying these errors, understanding their causes, and fixing them. Oracle offers several tools to assist in this process.

2. The foundation of excellent PL/SQL debugging is a solid understanding of PL/SQL.

3. Remember that compilation errors are generally reported by the PL/SQL parser at the point the parser became confused, which is often a location in the source code that follows the actual error.

Exercises

1. **Which built-in function returns the error message number?**

    A. SQLERRNUMBER

    B. SQLERROR

    C. SQL_ERR

    D. None of the above

2. **How can the data dictionary assist in the debugging of PL/SQL program units? (Choose all that apply.)**

   A. It contains error messages from attempted but unsuccessful compilations.

   B. It contains source code of program units, even if the program unit didn't successfully compile.

   C. It can locate errors automatically and suggest ways to fix them.

   D. It contains the lookup master list of Oracle Corporation error messages.

Answer Key
1. D. 2. A, B.

Debugging with SQL*Plus

The SQL*Plus interface enables you to submit PL/SQL blocks for execution, as well as statements to create stored program units. When you are submitting anonymous blocks or creating stored program units, your code will be parsed first and then executed. On the other hand, once a stored program unit has been stored in the database, it is already parsed. As long as its status is VALID, it is ready for execution whenever it is invoked. However, remember that if you successfully compile and store a program unit that references database objects, such as a table, and if those database objects are altered at some point after the stored program unit was originally parsed, it will cause the program unit's status to change to INVALID; this indicates that the stored program unit will have to be parsed again before its next execution.

If everything parses correctly, the statement executes. If the statement is to CREATE a program unit, such as CREATE PROCEDURE, then once the code parses correctly, you should receive the *Procedure created* message on the screen. If the statement you submitted was an anonymous block and the compilation is successful, the block should execute right away. You can use SQL*Plus to analyze compilation errors as well as execution errors.

Debugging Compilation Errors with SQL*Plus

When you encounter compilation errors when attempting to run a PL/SQL block, the SQL*Plus screen will display one or more compilation error messages. For example, see Figure 9-1. The graphic shows a picture of an anonymous PL/SQL

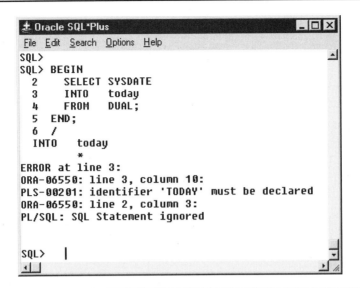

FIGURE 9-1. *Anonymous PL/SQL block with compilation error message*

block with a compilation error message. The following is the error message in the example:

```
    INTO    today
             *
ERROR at line 3:
ORA-06550: line 3, column 10:
PLS-00201: identifier 'TODAY' must be declared
ORA-06550: line 2, column 3:
PL/SQL: SQL Statement ignored
```

The error message includes the following parts:

- **Lines 1 and 2** The source code line on which the error occurred is repeated, in this case, INTO today. An asterisk is placed under the location in the line where the PL/SQL parser first became confused, in this case, the word "today."

- **Line 3** The message *ERROR at line n* indicates the source of the error within the PL/SQL block. The line number can be found by typing the SQL*Plus buffer editor command LIST or L while the PL/SQL block is still in the buffer. See Figure 9-2 for an example.

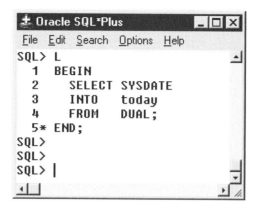

FIGURE 9-2. *The same block displayed with LIST to show line numbers*

- **Line 4 and continuing**   The first of the series of error messages from the Oracle error message system. The format of the Oracle error message is a three-part structure that is described in the next paragraph.

- **Final line**   The summary report from the PL/SQL error message system. In this example, it's *PL/SQL: SQL Statement ignored.*

Each Oracle error message is a three-part message:

- **The first part**   The error message prefix; a three-letter abbreviation showing which Oracle program issued the message. The prefixes most commonly encountered with PL/SQL program units include PLS (PL/SQL messages), ORA (Oracle server messages), and SQL (SQL run-time messages). Oracle error messages are documented in different places according to the program that produced the error, as indicated by the error message prefix.

- **The second part**   A five-digit number. This error code is what you use, combined with the error message prefix, to look up the error in the Oracle Corporation error message documentation. The documentation provides additional information, including a suggested cause of the problem as well as a suggested action to fix it.

- **The third part**   A descriptive but brief text message. This brief message is generally helpful, but much more information can be found by looking up the error in the Oracle Corporation error message documentation.

Our sample PL/SQL block has produced three error messages. Let's look at each message:

```
ORA-06550: line 3, column 10:
```

This first error message has the prefix ORA, indicating that the source of the error is the Oracle server and the code is 06550, followed by the message line 3, column 10. The source code listing, as displayed in Figure 9-2, shows that this is the location of the word "today" in the source code listing. The documentation for this error prefix and code is shown in Figure 9-3.

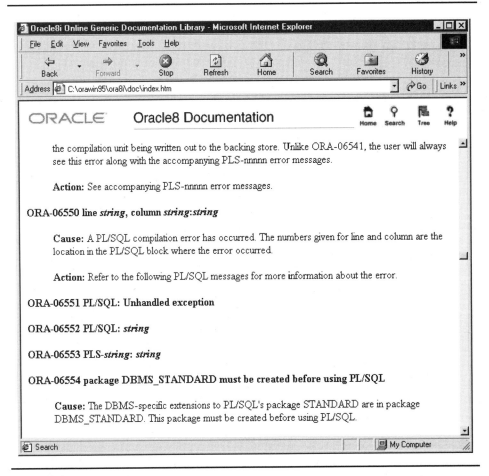

FIGURE 9-3. *Error message documentation: ORA-06550*

This standard message is indicating the source of the problem as the Oracle server sees it. However, the second error message gives us some further insight:

```
PLS-00201: identifier 'TODAY' must be declared
```

This error message is from PL/SQL, as indicated by the PLS error message prefix. The code 00201 points us to the documentation entry shown in Figure 9-4. Clearly, the identifier *today* needs to be declared. In other words, the error isn't that we're referencing *today* on line 3, but that we failed to declare it before this point in a declaration section.

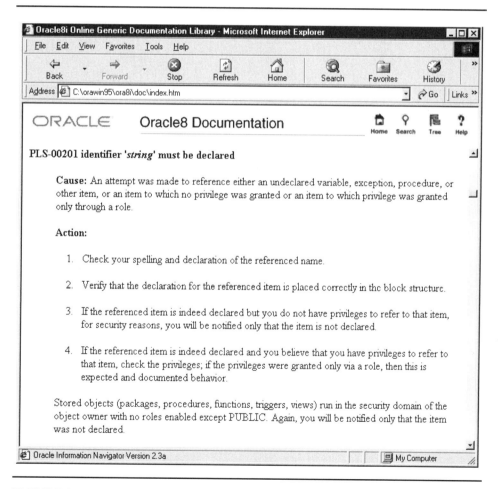

FIGURE 9-4. *Error message documentation: PLS-00201*

Finally, we have the third message:

```
ORA-06550: line 2, column 3:
```

This message points us to the SELECT statement on line 2. This SELECT includes the reference to the identifier *today* that we now know is undeclared. This third error message is letting us know that the SELECT statement is unable to parse correctly. This is redundant information in this example since we can tell by now that the correction of declaring the *today* variable will probably resolve the SELECT statement error as well. However, there is no guarantee that this will indeed be the case, and the error message is correct to inform us that we have a problem with the SELECT statement.

SHOW ERROR

SQL*Plus offers a built-in command that you can use to conveniently display compilation errors from the data dictionary view USER_ERRORS for any recently unsuccessful compilation attempt involving stored program units. This command does not work with anonymous PL/SQL blocks. The command is SHOW ERROR. The following are some examples:

```
SHOW ERR
SHOW ERROR
SHOW ERRORS
SHOW ERROR FUNCTION GET_CUSTOMER_NAME
```

As is true for all SQL*Plus commands, the semicolon is not required to end the command, but is optional. (Note: Do not confuse this with SQL commands, such as the CREATE OR REPLACE PROCEDURE command, which must close with a semicolon.) If you use the SHOW ERR or SHOW ERROR variations that do not name a specific program unit, then the output will automatically default to the error messages for the single most recently submitted and unsuccessful attempt to compile a stored program unit. If you include the name of a stored program unit, then you will see the error messages for that particular stored program unit's most recent unsuccessful compilation attempt. However, once the stored program unit has been successfully compiled, the error messages are removed from the data dictionary and can no longer be displayed.

For example, the SHOW ERROR command SHOW ERROR PROCEDURE PROC_INVOICE will query the data dictionary's USER_ERRORS data in the same way as the following SELECT statement:

```
SELECT    SUBSTR(LINE || '/' || POSITION,1,8) AS "LINE/COL",
          SUBSTR(TEXT,1,65) AS TEXT
FROM      USER_ERRORS
```

```
WHERE    TYPE = 'PROCEDURE'
  AND    NAME = 'PROC_INVOICE'
ORDER BY SEQUENCE
```

You are able to enter in SELECT . . . FROM USER_ERRORS commands yourself. SHOW ERROR is just easier to type. The USER_ERRORS data dictionary view is discussed in Chapter 2.

Debugging Execution Errors in SQL*Plus

SQL*Plus doesn't offer the same sort of built-in support for analyzing execution errors. Instead, the process of debugging execution errors in SQL*Plus usually involves clever use of the DBMS_OUTPUT.PUT_LINE procedure from within the processing section of your program units. By inserting PUT_LINE procedure calls in your code to print to the screen, displaying comments, loop counters, and the contents of other variables, you can narrow down the source of the error and fix it. When you have fixed your code, you'll have to remember to go back and remove the PUT_LINE calls.

Procedure Builder, on the other hand, offers some helpful tools to support the debugging of execution errors. These tools are more sophisticated and can save you a lot of time. We will look at Procedure Builder in the next section.

For Review

1. SQL*Plus provides compilation error messages and the SHOW ERR command to assist in the process of fixing compilation errors.

2. There are no debugging tools specifically designed for use with SQL*Plus. However, the use of DBMS_OUTPUT.PUT_LINE and other packages to trace the contents of variables and other aspects of program unit execution can be used to display output on the screen and observe stored program unit behavior.

Exercises

1. **You have just executed a command to create the stored function GET_PORT_CAPTAIN and encountered a compilation error. Which of the following SQL*Plus commands will present these errors on the screen?**

   A. SHOW ERR

   B. SHOW ERRORS

   C. SHOW ERR FUNCTION GET_PORT_CAPTAIN

   D. SHOW ALL ERRORS

2. **You have just submitted a PL/SQL block for compilation and encountered a compilation error. On the second line of the error messages, an asterisk has appeared on a line by itself. What does the asterisk indicate?**

   A. It's the generic symbol to indicate this is an error message.

   B. It's strategically placed under the name of the error.

   C. It's strategically placed under the location in the code where the parser first recognized that something was wrong.

   D. It marks the beginning of the list of error messages.

Answer Key
1. A, B, C. 2. C.

Debugging with Procedure Builder

Oracle's Procedure Builder tool offers a graphical user interface (GUI) that is very powerful and an effective alternative to SQL*Plus for analyzing both compilation and execution errors.

The same compilation error messages that are displayed in SQL*Plus are displayed in Procedure Builder. The difference is that the messages in Procedure Builder are displayed in the lower half of the two panel window that contains the source code in the upper panel, and you can double-click on an error message in the lower panel to cause the source code cursor to move immediately to the source of the error message within the source code listing itself in the upper panel. This context-based error-messaging system provides the same basic information that SQL*Plus provides, but in a vastly more user-friendly manner.

Procedure Builder really excels in its execution debugger. The Procedure Builder debugging system (which is also found in Oracle Forms) enables you to gain full control over an executing program unit during execution, gaining full insight into the inner workings of your program unit in real time. Procedure Builder's debugger enables you to create breakpoints, step execution through your code one line at a time, and observe the contents of variables, parameters, and other features of your code to determine the execution behavior of your program unit and identify possible sources of errors.

Starting Debugger: Setting Breakpoints

To start a debugging session with Procedure Builder, you will need the PL/SQL Interpreter window. This window automatically displays by default when you first start Procedure Builder, but you can invoke it at any time by choosing from the pull-down menu the Program | PL/SQL Interpreter . . . option. See Figure 9-5.

The PL/SQL Interpreter is composed of three panes: the Source Pane, which is in the upper half of the window, the Navigator Pane, which does not display by default, and the Interpreter Pane, which is in the lower half the window. You can toggle any of these panes on and off, including the Navigator Pane, by choosing View from the pull-down menu and checking any of the three panes. For example, Figure 9-6 shows the PL/SQL Interpreter with the Navigator Pane displayed.

Your first goal in debugging a program unit is to set a breakpoint in your code. A *breakpoint* is the location in your program unit that is a PL/SQL statement, and is where the program unit, when it executes, temporarily suspends execution and turns control over to the debugger. At this point, you can inspect the status of your program unit, including the value of variables. Furthermore, you will be able to step through your code, which means you will be able to cause your program unit to resume execution, but only one statement or one section at a time (according to

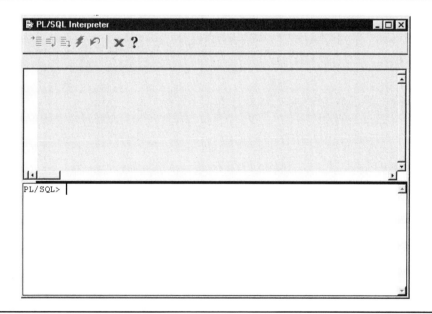

FIGURE 9-5. *Procedure Builder: PL/SQL Interpreter*

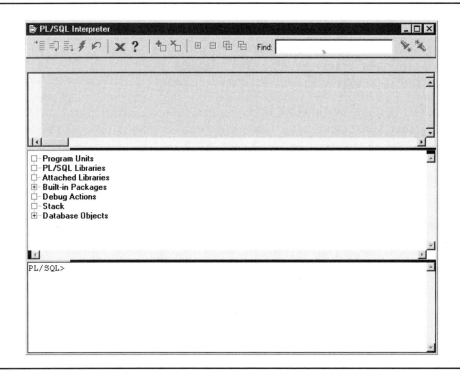

FIGURE 9-6. *PL/SQL Interpreter with Navigator Pane*

your instructions) while debugger is running. You can establish more than one breakpoint in your code.

To create a breakpoint, make sure the PL/SQL Interpreter window is displayed. Then, in the Object Navigator, click on the name of a program unit. See Figure 9-7. Here, Procedure Builder has been connected to the database, and the node for Database Objects has been expanded to view the FESTIVAL schema. We have expanded to see the APPLICATION_SESSION package body, which has been selected in the Object Navigator while the PL/SQL Interpreter window was open, causing the code for the APPLICATION_SESSION package body to display in the upper pane of the PL/SQL Interpreter window.

The full code listing for the package body APPLICATION_SESSION is shown in the following:

```
PACKAGE BODY APPLICATION_SESSION AS
  PROCEDURE UPDATE_LAST_ACCESS (last_access_date DATE) IS
  BEGIN
```

```
    UPDATE SESSIONS
       SET LAST_ACCESS = last_access_date
     WHERE SESSION_ID = APPLICATION_SESSION.session_id;
    COMMIT;
  END UPDATE_LAST_ACCESS;
  BEGIN
    -- perform initialization
    SELECT SESSION_ID, USER, SYSDATE
    INTO   APPLICATION_SESSION.session_id,
           APPLICATION_SESSION.user_name,
           APPLICATION_SESSION.login_date
    FROM   SESSIONS
    WHERE  USER_NAME = USER;
END APPLICATION_SESSION;
```

Now, to create the breakpoint, locate the line of source code in the Source Pane and identify the line numbers to the left of the source code. Using your mouse,

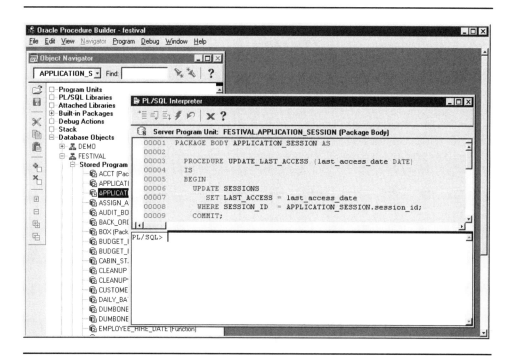

FIGURE 9-7. *PL/SQL Interpreter and package body APPLICATION_SESSION*

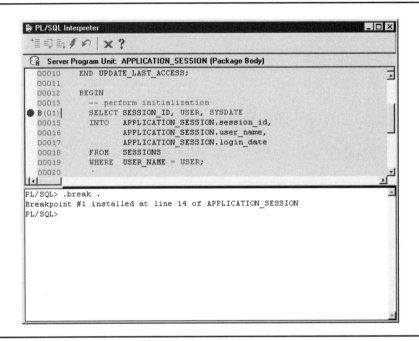

FIGURE 9-8. *Setting the breakpoint*

move the cursor so that it is over the line in the source code on which you want to suspend execution and double-click to create the breakpoint. See Figure 9-8.

A red circle will appear to the left of the line number, and the line number itself is replaced with a B(n), where *n* indicates the breakpoint number. The first breakpoint is 01, the second is 02, and so on. Furthermore, the Interpreter Pane now shows that "Breakpoint #1 is installed at line 6 of APPLICATION_SESSION".

You may continue setting additional breakpoints. When you have completed, click the red X in the upper area of the PL/SQL Interpreter Pane to dismiss the PL/SQL Interpreter window. The breakpoint will be preserved.

However, if you are ready to execute, you can begin program unit execution by typing the name of the program unit into the Interpreter Pane. See Figure 9-9. In this example, we are executing the program unit UPDATE_LAST_ACCESS in the package APPLICATION_SESSION.

Once you have typed the name of the program unit you want to execute, press ENTER, and the program unit will begin to execute. At the moment it encounters the breakpoint you entered, execution temporarily suspends and turns over control to the debugger, and awaits your next instruction. When this happens, the red circle in the Source Pane that indicates the location of your breakpoint should display a

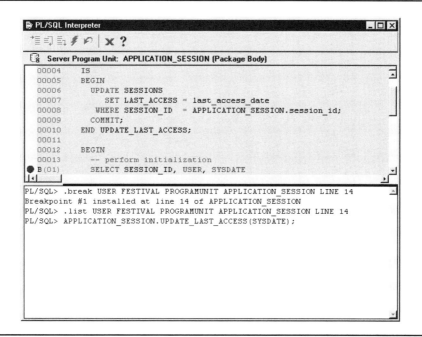

FIGURE 9-9. *Starting execution*

yellow arrow inside. This yellow arrow is the indicator for the location of debugger and indicates the next line of code that is expected to execute when you next instruct debugger to continue execution. In other words, this line has not yet executed, but it is about to. See Figure 9-10. Furthermore, in Figure 9-11, the navigator now displays a Stack node, showing the hierarchy of program unit calls, starting from the original command you typed that started execution of this program unit, which is listed as an anonymous block at level 0, and showing the call to package body APPLICATION_SESSION Line 14. As your program unit makes calls to other program units, the Stack node will display the structure of who called who, showing the line numbers of each program unit at the current execution point through the stack.

To continue execution, click the Step Into button, which is located in the upper-left corner of the PL/SQL Interpreter. See Figure 9-12. After one click of Step Into, the line at which execution was suspended will execute, and execution will suspend at the next executable line. The breakpoint will stay put, but the yellow arrow indicating the next executable line will move to that location in the Source Pane. The Interpreter Pane is updated with the Step Into command, which you could have

```
📇 PL/SQL Interpreter                                          _ □ X
⁺☰ ☴ ☶ ⚡ ↻ | X  ?
🗔 Server Program Unit: APPLICATION_SESSION (Package Body)
   00010     END UPDATE_LAST_ACCESS;
   00011
   00012     BEGIN
   00013        -- perform initialization
 ➡ B(01)  |    SELECT SESSION_ID, USER, SYSDATE
   00015     INTO     APPLICATION_SESSION.session_id,
   00016              APPLICATION_SESSION.user_name,
   00017              APPLICATION_SESSION.login_date
   00018     FROM     SESSIONS
   00019     WHERE    USER_NAME = USER;
   00020
 ◄
PL/SQL> .break USER FESTIVAL PROGRAMUNIT APPLICATION_SESSION LINE 14
Breakpoint #1 installed at line 14 of APPLICATION_SESSION
PL/SQL> .list USER FESTIVAL PROGRAMUNIT APPLICATION_SESSION LINE 14
PL/SQL> APPLICATION_SESSION.UPDATE_LAST_ACCESS(SYSDATE);

>> Entering Breakpoint #1 line 14 of APPLICATION_SESSION
(debug 1)PL/SQL>
```

FIGURE 9-10. *Execution suspended at breakpoint*

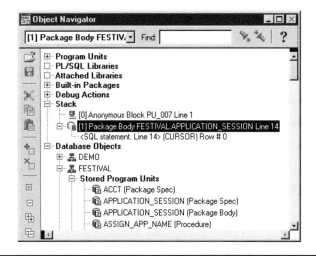

FIGURE 9-11. *The Stack*

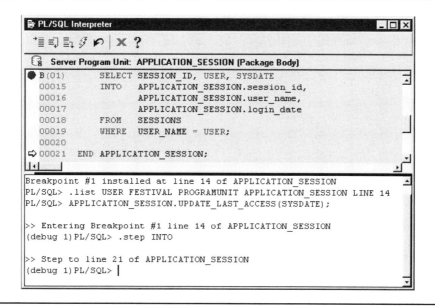

FIGURE 9-12. *Step Into: one execution statement past the breakpoint*

typed directly into the Interpreter Pane to achieve the same result. Also, the navigator now reflects that the current line number is 21.

To continue execution, click the Step Into button a second time. Execution now jumps to the beginning of the UPDATE_LAST_ACCESS procedure. Up to now, we've been executing the package's initialization section, but now we finally begin the execution of the actual program unit in question. Notice something significant in the navigator, though—the display of the parameter LAST_UPDATE_ACCESS, including its current value. See Figure 9-13. This is one of the most useful and powerful features of the debugger—the capability to inspect the values of parameters and variables during execution and observe their changes as the program unit executes. We could continue stepping through our code one line at a time, and as various lines of execution change the values of variables and parameters, we could witness the results in the navigator.

Once you have completed your work in debugger, click the yellow lightening bolt, which is the Go button, in the upper portion of the PL/SQL Interpreter. This will jump you out of the current breakpoint session and complete execution of the program unit. However, if a breakpoint is encountered along the way—even the same breakpoint you just processed—then debugger will start all over again.

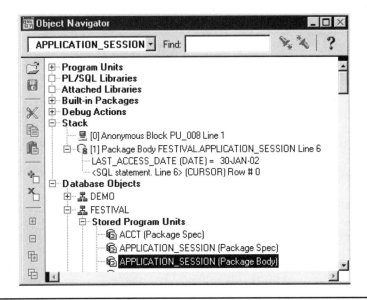

FIGURE 9-13.   *The Navigator Pane and LAST_UPDATE_ACCESS*

The PL/SQL Interpreter enables you to control execution through a program unit with action buttons in the upper portion of the screen, as follows:

- **Step Into**   Continues with program unit execution at the current line, executing the single line and returning control to the debugger. If the current line contains a call to a subprogram, then the stack reflects this fact, and the next line you see in debugger will be the first executable line within the subprogram.

- **Step Over**   The same as Step Into; however, if the current line contains an execution call to a subprogram of some sort, that call completes and control resumes at the next executable line within this same program unit.

- **Step Out**   This is useful if you find yourself within a nested subprogram. Step Out will complete execution of the subprogram and jump back up to the calling program, stopping at the next executable line in the calling program.

- **Go**   This completes the current debugging session and resumes uninterrupted program unit execution, unless, that is, a breakpoint is encountered again, in which case the debugger starts up all over again.

■ **Reset**   Exits the debug session and executes the program unit without interruption.

■ **Close**   Closes the PL/SQL Interpreter window.

For Review

1. Procedure Builder's debugger enables you to establish breakpoints, step execution of your program unit one executable line at a time, and observe the values of variables and parameters during execution.

2. The Stack node in the navigator displays a hierarchy of program unit calls, showing line numbers of one call to the other and providing a listing of declared elements and their values by program unit.

Exercises

1. **The stack displayed under the Stack node is best described as**
   _____.

   A. The listing of error messages produced by the program unit

   B. The hierarchy of calls from the originating invocation to the current line in the debugger

   C. The hierarchy of all possible program unit calls, regardless of the current line in the debugger

   D. The memory dump showing the trace of variables in the pipeline

2. **You have displayed the debugger to debug a procedure you have created called ISSUE_PAYMENT. This procedure calls CHECK_INVOICE at line 24, and you are currently looking at line 12 of CHECK_INVOICE in the debugger. You want to jump to the end and resume execution of ISSUE_PAYMENT with line 25 just after the call to CHECK_INVOICE. Which button do you click in the debugger?**

   A. Step Into

   B. Step Over

   C. Step Out

   D. None of the above

Answer Key
1. B. **2.** C.

Chapter Summary

Debugging is the process of identifying errors in your code, understanding the causes of the errors, and fixing them. You will encounter two types of errors in your code: compilation errors and execution errors. Compilation errors occur when your code contains errors in syntax; execution errors occur when your program contains logic errors.

The foundation of excellent debugging skills is based on a solid understanding of the PL/SQL language, good coding habits, such as formatting of your code, and working with a clear understanding of the goal in mind. Recognize that PL/SQL compilation errors often tell you where the PL/SQL parser was first confused, and that this is often not the actual source of the error, which frequently precedes the reported location of the error message.

The SQLERRM and SQLCODE built-in functions are excellent tools to use in combination with exception handlers to identify detailed information about exceptions that may get raised during execution of your program unit. Oracle's error message documentation provides suggested causes and actions to take when you encounter these messages.

The debugger that is built into Procedure Builder is a very powerful tool in which you can establish breakpoints and temporarily suspend the execution of any program unit to turn over control to debugger. This tool enables you to step through individual executable lines of code in your program unit, inspecting the values of variables and parameters along the way.

Two-Minute Drill

- Debugging is the practice of analyzing existing software to identify errors, understand their causes, and fix them.

- Compilation errors are language syntax problems that prevent your code from being compiled into executable form. Run-time errors include errors of logic, Oracle bugs, and other unexpected and/or unintended results that prevent your program from executing in a successful and intended manner.

- Compilation error messages in SQL*Plus repeat the code line where the parser experienced an error and print a three-letter error prefix, a five-digit error code, and an error text message.

- Remember that PL/SQL compilation error messages often indicate where the parser got confused—this is not necessarily where the error actually exists, but is often just after the actual coding error.

- The three-letter error prefix indicates which Oracle product is the source of the error. PLS indicates a PL/SQL error message, ORA indicates an Oracle server message, and SQL indicates a SQL run-time message.

■ The three-letter error prefix and the five-digit error code can be used to look up more information in the Oracle error message documentation.

■ Compilation errors resulting from attempts to store program units in the database are stored in the USER_ERRORS data dictionary view.

■ In SQL*Plus, the SHOW ERROR command can be used to present a printed display of error messages for the most recent program unit's unsuccessful compilation attempt.

■ Procedure Builder offers an excellent debugger for resolving run-time errors.

■ The Procedure Builder debugger lets you set breakpoints, which are locations in your source code that, when encountered during execution, will temporarily suspend and turn over control to the debugging interface via the PL/SQL Interpreter.

■ Once the PL/SQL Interpreter takes over, you can step through each executable line of code with the Step Into function. If the next executable line is a call to another program unit, then the Stack node shows the hierarchy of calls as the PL/SQL Interpreter enters the source code of the program unit and shows its execution, where you can continue to Step Into each individual line of code.

■ You can Step Out to get out of a called program unit or Step Over a program unit call without entering the program unit's code, but instead executing the entire program unit and simply moving to the next executable line within the same program unit you are already looking at.

■ You can use Go to jump out of the PL/SQL Interpreter altogether.

■ Procedure Builder can be used to debug client- and server-side program units.

Chapter Questions

I. **What is a breakpoint?**

   A. The location of any error where your program unit breaks

   B. An unrecoverable error where your program unit breaks

   C. A location in your code that you choose to suspend execution

   D. A bookmarked location where you choose to stop editing your code temporarily to take a break

2. **How many breakpoints can exist in a given program unit?**

   A. One

   B. Two

   C. As many as there are executable lines of code

   D. As many as there are program unit calls

3. **The PL/SQL Interpreter is capable of displaying how many panes?**

   A. One

   B. Two

   C. Three

   D. Four

4. **You have a procedure called PROCESS_PAYROLL, which calls another procedure PERFORM_AUDIT, which in turn calls a third procedure CHECK_ACCOUNT_RECORD. You place a breakpoint in the PROCESS_PAYROLL procedure and have stepped through to line number 56 of CHECK_ACCOUNT_RECORD. How many program unit nodes display in the stack?**

   A. One

   B. Two

   C. Three

   D. Four

5. **You have a procedure called PROCESS_PAYROLL, which calls another procedure PERFORM_AUDIT, which in turn calls a third procedure CHECK_ACCOUNT_RECORD. You place a breakpoint in the PROCESS_PAYROLL procedure and have stepped through to line number 56 of CHECK_ACCOUNT_RECORD. There is a line number displayed in the Stack node next to the entry for PERFORM_AUDIT. What does this line number represent?**

   A. The line number of the breakpoint in PERFORM_AUDIT

   B. The line number of the procedure call to CHECK_ACCOUNT_RECORD

   C. The total number of lines in PERFORM_AUDIT

   D. The line number of the procedure call to PERFORM_AUDIT

6. **Which built-in function displays the Oracle error message?**

    A. SQLERRM

    B. SQLERRORMESSAGE

    C. SQLERROR

    D. SQLERRMESSAGE

7. **How do you begin execution in the PL/SQL Interpreter?**

    A. Click on the lightening bolt button.

    B. Click on the Step Into button.

    C. Type the name of the program unit in the Interpreter Pane.

    D. Type **Go** in the Interpreter Pane.

8. **In the debugger, what does the yellow arrow represent?**

    A. A breakpoint

    B. The next executable line

    C. A line containing an error

    D. The line that just executed

9. **In the PL/SQL Interpreter Source Pane, what does the presence of a red dot next to a line number indicate?**

    A. An error

    B. A breakpoint

    C. The line that was just executed

    D. A call to a program unit

10. **You can create breakpoints on _____. (Choose all that apply.)**

    A. Stored procedures

    B. Packaged functions

    C. Client-side procedures

    D. Stored functions

Answers to Chapter Questions

1. C.   A location in your code that you choose to suspend execution

Explanation   You set the breakpoint during a debug session.

2. C.   As many as there are executable lines of code

Explanation   You can create breakpoints on any statement and can include as many as you want.

3. C.   Three

Explanation   The PL/SQL Interpreter shows the Source Pane and the Interpreter Pane when first displayed, but it can optionally display the Navigator Pane if you direct it do so, using the pull-down menu option View.

4. C.   Three

Explanation   The Stack node displays each program unit's call to the other. All three program units display in the Stack.

5. B.   The line number of the procedure call to CHECK_ACCOUNT_RECORD

Explanation   The line number displayed is the last line executed in that particular procedure, and given that we're currently in a subprogram, that last line executed had to have been the subprogram invocation.

6. A.   SQLERRM

Explanation   This built-in can be used in your code to obtain an error message, within an exception handler, to print to the screen or insert into your application's error tracking table. The other answers are all made up.

7. C.   Type the name of the program unit in the Interpreter Pane.

Explanation   The lightening bolt button is the Go button, which resumes execution after a debugging session. The Step Into button continues the statement-by-statement execution within a debug session. C is the answer.

8. B.   The next executable line

Explanation   The yellow arrow points to the current line, which is the next executable line in the debugger. This line has not yet executed, but if you click the Step Into button, the current line will execute right away.

9. B.   A breakpoint

Explanation   All breakpoints have a red dot to the left of the breakpoint and a B(n) overlaying the line number, where *n* represents the number of the breakpoint.

10. A, B, C, D.   A: Stored procedures B: Packaged functions C: Client-side procedures D: Stored functions

Explanation   You can create breakpoints on any PL/SQL program unit.

PART
III

Privileges and
Interdependence

CHAPTER
10

Managing Privileges

privilege is the right to perform some action in the database. Privileges are granted to schemas. There are two general categories of privileges: system privileges and database object privileges. As a developer, you must understand the general nature of system privileges and how they work. In order to create program units, you must understand the specific system privileges that are required to create the various program units. Regarding database objects, you must understand what it takes to grant specific privileges on program units to other schemas and roles so that others can properly invoke your program units, especially when logged in as a schema other than the program unit's owner. Finally, you must understand the circumstances and choices you need to make about granting privileges to the end users of your program units on the database objects that your program unit references.

In this chapter, you will review and understand the following topics:

- System privileges
- System and object privilege requirements for program units
- Owner and invoker rights
- Granting privileges
- Data dictionary resources

System Privileges

A system privilege is the right to perform a particular action in the database. There are over 100 different system privileges. Most system privileges involve the right to create, alter, or drop a particular type of database object. For example,

```
CREATE TABLE
CREATE PROCEDURE
CREATE ANY TRIGGER
```

Privileges are granted to a schema. They can also be granted to a role. Roles, in turn, are granted to one or more schemas. Either way, the schema is the ultimate intended recipient of any system privilege. Any schema must have some set of system privileges in order to be able to develop applications. All privileges and roles, whether they consist of system privileges or database object privileges, can be granted or revoked.

Any privilege can also be granted to PUBLIC. This has the effect of granting the privilege to all schemas in the database, present or future—in other words, when a privilege is granted to PUBLIC, even schemas that are not yet created will, when created, receive the privilege.

End users generally don't require many system privileges. The system privilege CREATE ANY SESSION, which is required for a schema to simply log in, may be all that is required. However, there is a large list of system privileges that are required for application developers and administrators to do their jobs.

System privilege expressions generally consist of three parts:

- The privilege keyword, such as CREATE, ALTER, DROP, SELECT, ADMINISTER, LOCK, and so on

- The optional word ANY

- The type of database object, such as TABLE, VIEW, PROCEDURE, and so on

Please note that this three-part breakdown is a simplification, and system privileges do not all conform to this format. However, for the purposes of the system privileges we are concerned with in this book, this format works well.

When a system privilege is granted to a schema, the schema is said to be the *grantee*. When the keyword ANY is left out of a system privilege, it means that the scope of the grantee's privileges is its own schema. For example, CREATE TABLE is the privilege for a grantee to create tables within its own schema, but CREATE ANY TABLE indicates that the grantee can create tables owned by any other schema.

Each system privilege can be granted the WITH ADMIN OPTION. When this is done, the grantee not only has the granted privilege, but it also has the capability to grant that same privilege to other schemas. Furthermore, those other schemas will receive and retain that granted privilege free of any dependence on the schema that issued it. In other words, if a grantee's system privileges are later revoked, any granted rights under the WITH ADMIN OPTION stay in force.

For example, if schema COTTON grants the CREATE ANY VIEW privilege WITH ADMIN OPTION to schema BOOTSY and schema BOOTSY grants that same CREATE ANY VIEW privilege to schema QNUT, but then schema COTTON revokes BOOTSY's privilege, QNUT will still have the CREATE ANY VIEW privilege. That privilege must be explicitly revoked from QNUT in order for it to be removed.

Roles

The topic of roles is not specifically tested on this exam and is generally considered part of a database administrator's curriculum. However, to fully understand system privileges, it is helpful to understand roles. They are simple to understand.

A role is an object in the database that represents a set of privileges. It serves the purpose of collecting a set of privileges under one name so that you can grant several privileges at once to a particular schema or to PUBLIC. Furthermore, you can add additional privileges to a role, and any schemas that already have been granted the role will automatically receive the additional privileges. A schema can be granted multiple roles, and a role can be granted to multiple schemas.

For example, if you know that a purchaser in the finance department needs to have SELECT, INSERT, and UPDATE on the LEDGER table as well as SELECT on the AUDIT table, you could do the following in SQL*Plus:

```
CREATE ROLE FINANCE_ROLE;
GRANT SELECT, INSERT, UPDATE ON LEDGER TO FINANCE_ROLE;
GRANT SELECT ON AUDIT TO FINANCE_ROLE;
```

Now that this is accomplished, you can grant the role to as many schemas as you want:

```
GRANT FINANCE_ROLE TO JOAN;
GRANT FINANCE_ROLE TO JEAN;
```

Roles are an easy and manageable approach to managing privileges. However, as we will soon see, although roles are very helpful and often used in Oracle applications, there is a potential problem involved in using roles with PL/SQL program units. Roles are disabled for program units that are granted with definer rights. As we will discuss laster in this chapter under Owner and Invoker Rights, if schema 1 grants privileges to schema 2 and schema 2 creates a program unit based on those privileges and then grants EXECUTE on the program unit to schema 3, schema 3 will be able to use the program unit—provided that schema 1 granted the original privileges to schema 2 directly and did not use a role. If a role is involved, schema 3 will be unable to use the program unit.

For Review

1. System privileges are required to perform various operations within the database for creating, altering, dropping, and otherwise building the components of an application. End users only require CREATE ANY SESSION to get into the system. Application developers and administrators require various privileges to perform their duties.

2. System privileges can be granted to schemas or roles. Roles are, in turn, granted to schemas. Privileges can be granted the WITH ADMIN OPTION, which enables the grantee to grant the same privilege to yet another schema. Privileges can be revoked as well.

Exercises

1. What keyword (or keywords) would have to be added to the privilege DROP TYPE to enable the grantee to drop TYPE objects in its own schema as well as other schemas?

   A. PUBLIC

   B. ALL

   C. ANY

   D. WITH ADMIN OPTION

2. What keyword (or keywords) would have to be added to the privilege DROP TYPE to enable the grantee to grant the same privilege to another schema?

   A. PUBLIC

   B. ALL

   C. ANY

   D. WITH ADMIN OPTION

Answer Key
1. C. 2. D.

System and Object Privilege Requirements for Program Units

When working with program units, you must first make sure you have the appropriate system privileges required for creating the various types of program units. Then, once you have created a database object, such as a PL/SQL program unit, you must issue privileges on that particular database object to the other schemas that you want to execute your program unit.

System Privileges for Program Units

Although there are over 100 different system privileges that exist in an Oracle database, there are only a few that concern program units. The following is a list of the system privileges that are relevant for developers of PL/SQL program units. The list isn't as straightforward as you might think. Some subtle generalizations are made with system privileges that are not consistent with other statements and PL/SQL syntax. For example, the CREATE PROCEDURE system privilege, when granted to a schema, enables that schema to create, alter, or drop any procedures, functions, or packages within their own schema. Note that there is no ALTER FUNCTION or DROP PACKAGE system privilege. The one system privilege CREATE PROCEDURE grants it all. On the other hand, CREATE ANY PROCEDURE is required for creating procedures, functions, and packages in other schemas, but it does not automatically have the capability to drop those program units. The privilege DROP ANY PROCEDURE is required to drop those program units. Finally, triggers have their own set of system privileges. The following lists the system privileges:

- **CREATE PROCEDURE**   The grantee can create, alter, and drop procedures, functions, and packages within its own schema.

- **CREATE ANY PROCEDURE**   The grantee can create procedures, functions, and packages within any schema—meaning that the grantee logs in with its own schema name, and from within its own schema, it can create procedures that are owned by any other schema. However, once created, the creating schema cannot alter or drop the program unit—and this includes the OR REPLACE clause in the CREATE statement, which is not usable under this privilege and requires the ALTER ANY PROCEDURE privilege to work.

- **ALTER ANY PROCEDURE**   The grantee can alter procedures, functions, and packages in any schema. This includes the OR REPLACE option of the CREATE statement.

- **DROP ANY PROCEDURE**   The grantee can drop procedures, functions, and packages in any schema.

- **EXECUTE ANY PROCEDURE**   The grantee can execute program units, meaning procedures, functions, and packaged procedures and functions, and reference other packaged constructs in any schema without being granted object privileges on those program units. Note that the alternative to the EXECUTE ANY PROCEDURE privilege is an object privilege, such as EXECUTE ON procedure_name, which is discussed in the section "Object Privileges for Program Units."

- **CREATE TRIGGER**   The grantee can create, alter, and drop triggers in its own schema on database objects within its own schema.

- **CREATE ANY TRIGGER**   The grantee can create triggers in any schema and/or on database objects within its own schema. For example, this is the privilege required for a schema to create a trigger in its own schema that fires on a database event on another schema's table.

- **ALTER ANY TRIGGER** The grantee can alter triggers in any schema and/or alter triggers that fire on database objects within any schema.

- **DROP ANY TRIGGER** The grantee can drop triggers in any schema.

- **ADMINISTER DATABASE TRIGGER** The grantee can create triggers ON DATABASE. This privilege must be granted along with CREATE TRIGGER or CREATE ANY TRIGGER.

Remember that any of these system privileges can be granted with the optional WITH ADMIN OPTION keywords.

For an application developer to be able to develop the program units that we have explored in this book, the application developer's schema must have the appropriate system privileges.

Revoking Privileges

After one of these system privileges has been granted to a schema, it can be revoked from the same schema. There is no negative impact to the existing objects that may have been created with the revoked system privilege. For example, if a schema is granted CREATE PROCEDURE and creates a procedure with the privilege, but then later has the CREATE PROCEDURE privilege revoked, the created procedures stay resident and are available within the schema. Furthermore, the schema can continue to issue CREATE OR REPLACE statements to change that existing procedure. However, the schema is unable to create any additional procedures.

Creating Program Units in Another Schema

Once a schema has been granted a system privilege, for example, CREATE ANY PROCEDURE, it can create a program unit in a different schema by using the schema.name notation in the CREATE statement. For example, say that schema JOAN has been granted the CREATE ANY PROCEDURE privilege. Now, consider this statement:

```
CREATE FUNCTION NOAH.CHECK_ARK ...
```

The schema JOAN can execute this statement to create a function CHECK_ARK in the schema NOAH. However, note that CREATE ANY PROCEDURE does not allow JOAN to make changes to the function—and this includes the OR REPLACE function of the CREATE statement. This is not to say that JOAN couldn't use the OR REPLACE option in the original statement. Technically, if the function does not yet exist, the OR REPLACE clause has no effect the first time it is executed:

```
CREATE OR REPLACE FUNCTION NOAH.CHECK_ARK ...
```

However, once the function has been created, if the same command were to be issued, the OR REPLACE clause would activate. However, CREATE ANY

PROCEDURE isn't enough for this to work. The ALTER ANY PROCEDURE system privilege would be required here. Without it, no changes of any kind—including the OR REPLACE option—will be accepted on a procedure, function, or package owned by another schema, even for a program unit you have just created. The error message "ORA-01031: insufficient privileges" will display.

Note that this is different from the CREATE PROCEDURE system privilege, which automatically has the capability to create, alter, and drop. When the ANY keyword is present, the schema is empowered to do much more—to create program units in any schema—and therefore this power is more selectively granted, requiring explicit ALTER ANY PROCEDURE and DROP ANY PROCEDURE system privileges to be issued if the schema is to perform those duties.

Object Privileges for Program Units

The schema that owns a program unit can always execute the program unit. But for other schemas to execute the program unit, the owning schema must grant the appropriate object privilege. There is only one object privilege for program units: EXECUTE. Object privileges are not the same as system privileges. An object privilege is the right to reference a particular created object in a given schema. Whereas system privileges are general in nature, object privileges are much narrower in scope, naming a particular database object.

For example, if the schema DHAMILL owns a procedure FIGURE_EIGHT and wants to grant the EXECUTE privilege on this procedure to the schema SHUGHES, the following statement issued from within the DHAMILL schema will do the trick:

```
GRANT EXECUTE ON FIGURE_EIGHT TO SHUGHES;
```

All object privileges, including EXECUTE, can also be granted to a role, which in turn can be granted to a schema. Finally, object privileges, just like system privileges, can be granted to PUBLIC.

To grant EXECUTE privileges on any packaged constructs, you must grant the entire package. For example, if the same schema DHAMILL owned a package CELEBRITY_ENDORSEMENT, containing multiple procedures, functions, and other package constructs, the following statement would grant EXECUTE on the packaged constructs:

```
GRANT EXECUTE ON CELEBRITY_ENDORSEMENT TO SHUGHES;
```

There is no way to selectively grant privileges on the individual package constructs; the only solution to that challenge is to restructure the package into multiple packages.

Note that triggers are exempt from the requirement to be granted by name. Because no schema ever invokes a trigger explicitly, no schema requires EXECUTE privileges on triggers. Instead, triggers are attached to other database objects, such as tables, and if a schema has privileges on a table, it indirectly has the appropriate privileges to fire whatever triggers are attached to the table. EXECUTE is only required for procedures, functions, or packages.

For Review

1. The CREATE PROCEDURE privilege enables a schema to create, alter, or drop procedures, functions, or packages within its own schema. The ANY option enables the schema to create program units owned by other schemas by including the schema name in front of the program unit, separated by a dot. However, when the ANY keyword is used, the privileges CREATE, ALTER, and DROP are all granted separately. Triggers are managed with a separate set of privileges, such as CREATE TRIGGER.

2. The only privilege required to execute a program unit is the EXECUTE privilege, which is granted by the schema that owns the program unit to the schema that requires the privilege.

Exercises

1. **Which of the following system privileges enables a schema to create a trigger on a table that it owns?**

   A. CREATE TRIGGER ON TABLE

   B. CREATE TRIGGER

   C. CREATE TABLE TRIGGER

   D. CREATE ALL TRIGGER

2. **What does the CREATE ANY PROCEDURE privilege enable a grantee to do?**

   A. Drop triggers that are owned by other schemas.

   B. Alter procedures owned by other schemas.

   C. Replace procedures that are owned by other schemas.

   D. Create packages that are owned by other schemas.

Answer Key
1. B. **2.** D.

Owner and Invoker Rights

Most program units contain statements that perform operations on various database objects. For example, a stored procedure might issue an UPDATE statement on a table owned by another schema, a DELETE statement on still another schema's table, or an INSERT on a table of its own. When this program unit is executed, a question arises: Who must have the UPDATE or DELETE privilege on the tables or any other privileges that are required for the program unit to execute successfully? Should it be the owner of the program unit? Should it be the grantee that is executing the program unit?

The answer is that it depends. Program units that execute with the rights of the owner are said to be *definer rights* program units, or *owner rights* program units. On the other hand, program units that execute according to the rights of the schema that is actually invoking, or executing, the program units are said to be *invoker rights* program units, or *caller rights* program units.

Owner Rights

A vast majority of program units execute with owner rights, meaning that they execute according to the privileges that the program unit owner has at the time of the execution. Owner rights are also known as definer rights. Consider the following procedure owned by the schema SNYDER:

```
PROCEDURE ADD_PORT(new_port_name VARCHAR2) IS
BEGIN
   INSERT INTO GREEN.PORTS (PORT_ID, PORT_NAME)
   VALUES (GREEN.SEQ_PORT_ID.NEXTVAL, new_port_name);
   COMMIT;
END;
```

The table PORTS and the sequence SEQ_PORT_ID are both owned by the schema GREEN. The assumption here is that GREEN has granted the necessary privileges to SNYDER, the owner of this program unit, with the following grants issued from GREEN:

```
GREEN> GRANT INSERT ON PORTS        TO SNYDER;
GREEN> GRANT SELECT ON SEQ_PORT_ID TO SNYDER;
```

If SNYDER, as the owner of this procedure, grants the EXECUTE privilege for this procedure to a third schema GIBBS, the statement would look like this:

```
SNYDER> GRANT EXECUTE ON ADD_PORT TO GIBBS;
```

This enables GIBBS to execute the procedure ADD_PORT, as follows:

```
GIBBS> EXEC SNYDER.ADD_PORT('Annapolis');
```

Under the owner rights model, the schema GIBBS does not require direct privileges on the PORTS table. In other words, this statement

```
GREEN> GRANT INSERT ON PORTS TO GIBBS;
```

need not be executed by GREEN or anyone else. GIBBS has EXECUTE privileges on the ADD_PORTS procedure, which will execute with definer rights, meaning that at the time GIBBS executes ADD_PORTS, the procedure executes with the privileges that SNYDER has at the time of execution. If SNYDER's privileges to the PORTS table are revoked after GIBBS has been given EXECUTE on ADD_PORTS, the procedure will fail. For example, see the following login session:

```
SYSTEM> CONNECT GREEN/GREEN
Connected.
GREEN> GRANT INSERT ON PORTS TO SNYDER;
Grant succeeded.
GREEN> GRANT SELECT ON SEQ_PORT_ID TO SNYDER;
Grant succeeded.
GREEN> CONNECT SNYDER/SNYDER
Connected.
SNYDER> GRANT EXECUTE ON ADD_PORT TO GIBBS;
Grant succeeded.
SNYDER> CONNECT GIBBS/GIBBS
Connected.
GIBBS> EXEC SNYDER.ADD_PORT('Savannah');
PL/SQL procedure successfully completed.
GIBBS> CONNECT GREEN/GREEN
Connected.
GREEN> REVOKE INSERT ON PORTS FROM SNYDER;
Revoke succeeded.
GREEN> CONNECT GIBBS/GIBBS
Connected.
GIBBS> EXEC SNYDER.ADD_PORT('Melbourne');
BEGIN SNYDER.ADD_PORT('Melbourne'); END;
              *
ERROR at line 1:
ORA-06550: line 1, column 14:
PLS-00905: object SNYDER.ADD_PORT is invalid
ORA-06550: line 1, column 7:
PL/SQL: Statement ignored
```

This issue of owner rights carries through to every database object that a given program unit references, including other program units. For example, if a procedure references a function, then the ultimate end user does not have to have EXECUTE privileges on the particular function if he or she has already been granted EXECUTE privileges to the procedure.

NOTE
When a schema executes another schema's program unit under the definer rights model, roles are disabled. The definer rights that are recognized do not include privileges granted via a role. The only rights recognized are those privileges that have been granted directly to the owner. However, roles are enabled for invoker rights, which are discussed in the next section.

Invoker Rights

The invoker rights model is the alternative to the owner rights model. When a program unit executes with invoker rights, it requires the invoker—that is, the schema that is executing the program unit—to have the necessary privileges to do whatever the program unit requires. Looking again at the example in the previous section, if the ADD_PORT procedure were defined with invoker rights, GIBBS could not successfully execute ADD_PORT unless GIBBS has the necessary privileges on the tables owned by GREEN.

Invoker rights are not the default and require the AUTHID CURRENT_USER keywords in the declaration. For example, see the following CREATE statement:

```
CREATE OR REPLACE PROCEDURE ADD_PORT(new_port_name VARCHAR2)
               AUTHID CURRENT_USER IS
BEGIN
  INSERT INTO GREEN.PORTS (PORT_ID, PORT_NAME)
  VALUES (GREEN.SEQ_PORT_ID.NEXTVAL, new_port_name);
  COMMIT;
END;
```

The keywords AUTHID CURRENT_USER are included just after the parameter list and before the keyword IS. The result is that this procedure will execute according to the rights of the invoker. In this example, if GIBBS executes this procedure, GIBBS will require INSERT privileges on the PORTS table owned by GREEN as well as SELECT privileges on the SEQ_PORT_ID sequence that is also owned by GREEN.

To create functions or packages with invoker rights, use the same keywords AUTHID CURRENT_USER just before the IS keyword, just as is shown with the ADD_PORTS previous example.

When the AUTHID clause is left out of a CREATE statement, the default of DEFINER is assumed. However, you can specify the AUTHID DEFINER if you want, as follows:

```
CREATE OR REPLACE PROCEDURE ADD_PORT(new_port_name VARCHAR2)
                AUTHID DEFINER IS
BEGIN
  INSERT INTO GREEN.PORTS (PORT_ID, PORT_NAME)
  VALUES (GREEN.SEQ_PORT_ID.NEXTVAL, new_port_name);
  COMMIT;
END;
```

In this example, the database objects in the procedure's code include the schema prefix. The table PORTS is specified as GREEN.PORTS and the sequence SEQ_PORT_ID is specified by GREEN.SEQ_PORT_ID. This leaves no doubt as to the owner of the object. However, one of the advantages to invoker rights program units involves the use of database object references that do not include the schema name. If several tables have their own local copies of a PORTS table, a single centrally stored ADD_PORTS procedure that issues an INSERT statement on the PORTS table can be granted with invoker rights to each of these schemas, enabling them to use one procedure for all of their respective local tables.

Note that roles are enabled for program units under invoker rights as opposed to definer rights, under which roles are disabled.

The program units we have created in this book have all been created with definer rights. However, Oracle Corporation provides many built-in packages, some of which we looked at in Chapter 7. Many of these packages, which are owned by the SYS schema, execute with invoker rights.

For Review

1. The definer rights model refers to the concept that a schema that has been given EXECUTE privileges on another schema's program unit will execute that program unit according to the privileges granted to the program unit's owner at execution time.

2. The invoker rights model refers to the concept that a schema that has been given EXECUTE privileges on another schema's program unit will execute that program unit according to the privileges granted to the calling schema, not the program unit's owner.

Exercises

1. Invoker rights refer to

   A. A schema's right to call another schema's program unit

   B. A schema's right to create a program unit

   C. The privileges that a called procedure will use when executed by a calling schema

   D. The system privileges required to create program units

2. A definer rights program unit will execute according to the privileges granted to the program unit's owner

   A. At the moment the program unit is created

   B. At the moment the EXECUTE privilege is granted

   C. At the moment the program unit is first executed

   D. At the moment the program unit is executed and each time it is executed

---

Answer Key
1. C. 2. D.

Granting and Revoking Privileges

The GRANT and REVOKE statements are SQL statements. GRANT is used to grant privileges to schemas. GRANT is also used to grant privileges to roles. A full discussion of the GRANT statement involves more than what we will address here; for the purpose of passing the exam, you will only need to be familiar with how system and object privileges are granted for database objects that program units reference as well as the program units themselves.

The syntax for GRANT is simple:

```
GRANT privilege TO schema name
```

For example, to give CREATE ANY PROCEDURE privileges to the schema DSTASCAVAGE, use

```
GRANT CREATE ANY PROCEDURE TO DSTASCAVAGE;
```

Alternatively, if you were to include the ability for DSTASCAVAGE to also issue the grant, use

```
GRANT CREATE ANY PROCEDURE TO DSTASCAVAGE WITH ADMIN OPTION;
```

You can replace the schema name with a role name or the keyword PUBLIC. You can also issue multiple grants with a single statement:

```
GRANT CREATE ANY TRIGGER, ALTER ANY TRIGGER TO DSTASCAVAGE;
```

Or you can choose to repeat the GRANT statement as required:

```
GRANT CREATE ANY TRIGGER TO DSTASCAVAGE;
GRANT ALTER ANY TRIGGER TO DSTASCAVAGE;
```

The format for issuing object privileges is similar. To grant the ability to execute the package BUNDLE to the DSTASCAVAGE, use

```
GRANT EXECUTE ON BUNDLE TO DSTASCAVAGE;
```

To revoke a previously granted privilege, use the REVOKE FROM command. For example,

```
REVOKE EXECUTE ON BUNDLE FROM DSTASCAVAGE;
REVOKE CREATE ANY PROCEDURE FROM DSTASCAVAGE;
```

NOTE
GRANT and REVOKE do not require a COMMIT. As Data Definition Language (DDL) statements, they automatically force a COMMIT.

For Review

1. Use the GRANT . . . TO statement to issue privileges and REVOKE . . . FROM to revoke privileges. You can manage both system and object privileges with these statements.

2. Both statements will, by default, force a COMMIT to be issued.

Exercises

1. Which of the following statements gives the CREATE TRIGGER privilege to the schema EROGERS?

    A. GRANT CREATE TRIGGER EROGERS;

    B. GRANT TO EROGERS CREATE TRIGGER;

    C. GRANT CREATE TRIGGER TO EROGERS;

    D. This cannot be done.

2. Which of the following statements will remove the CREATE TRIGGER privilege from EROGERS?

    A. REMOVE CREATE TRIGGER FROM EROGERS;

    B. REVOKE CREATE TRIGGER FROM EROGERS;

    C. ALTER GRANT CREATE TRIGGER TO EROGERS REVOKE;

    D. GET RID OF CREATE TRIGGER FROM EROGERS;

Answer Key
1. C. 2. B.

Data Dictionary Resources

The data dictionary is rich with details about the system and object privileges that your schema has granted to others and that other schemas have granted to you.

SESSION_PRIVS

The SESSION_PRIVS data dictionary view shows the complete list of the system privileges that are in effect for your schema. This includes all system privileges that have been granted either directly or indirectly to your schema. Indirectly granted privileges include those system privileges that have been granted to roles which, in turn, have been granted to your schema. The SESSIONS_PRIVS view only has one column. PRIVILEGE is a VARCHAR2 column showing the name of the system privilege.

SESSION_ROLES

The SESSION_ROLES data dictionary view shows the roles that are currently in force for the current schema. This includes all the roles granted directly or indirectly to the current schema. Roles can be granted indirectly to your schema by being granted to other roles, which, in turn, are granted to the current schema. It only has one column. ROLE is the name of the role that has been granted.

USER_SYS_PRIVS

This data dictionary view shows the system privileges that have been granted to the current schema. However, it does not include any privileges granted to the user via a role, so it doesn't show the complete picture. To get a complete picture of the privileges granted to this schema, inspect the SESSION_PRIVS view. Without it, you would have to do the following:

1. Query USER_SYS_PRIVS to get a list of system privileges that have been explicitly granted to this schema.

2. Query USER_ROLE_PRIVS to get a list of the roles that have been granted to the current schema.

3. Query the DBA_SYS_PRIVS, using the WHERE GRANTEE=RoleName for each role you listed in the USER_ROLE_PRIVS view. This produces a list of the privileges that have been granted via any roles to the current schema.

Each row in this USER_SYS_PRIVS view represents a system privilege that's been granted to the current schema:

- ■ **USERNAME**   The grantee of the privilege.

- ■ **PRIVILEGE**   The name of the granted privilege   for example, CREATE PROCEDURE or DROP ANY TRIGGER.

- ■ **ADMIN_OPTION**   This is a YES or NO column that indicates if the privilege was granted WITH ADMIN OPTION.

USER_ROLE_PRIVS

The USER_ROLE_PRIVS view shows the roles that have been granted to the current schema. Keep in mind that a role can represent a combination of system privileges, database object privileges, and other roles. This view only lists roles that were explicitly granted directly to the schema, but doesn't include roles within roles—in other words, the full list of roles that are actually in effect. For that, see SESSION_ROLES. Otherwise, you would have to look up each role in the

DBA_ROLE_PRIVS view and see if any roles have been granted to the roles listed here.

- ■ **USERNAME** The schema to which the role has been granted.

- ■ **GRANTED_ROLE** The name of the role.

- ■ **ADMIN_OPTION** YES or NO, indicating if the role was granted WITH ADMIN OPTION.

- ■ **DEFAULT_ROLE** YES if the role is the user's default role or NO if it is not.

- ■ **OS_GRANTED** YES if the operating system is being used to manage roles or NO if it is not. This is beyond the scope of the exam.

DBA_SYS_PRIVS

The DBA_SYS_PRIVS shows system privileges that have been granted to any schema in the database. By looking in this view, you can determine which system privileges have been granted to a particular role:

- ■ **GRANTEE** The name of the schema or role to which a system privilege has been granted

- ■ **PRIVILEGE** The name of the system privilege

- ■ **ADMIN_OPTION** YES if the privilege was granted WITH ADMIN OPTION or NO if it wasn't

USER_TAB_PRIVS, USER_TAB_PRIVS_MADE, and USER_TAB_PRIVS_RECD

These three views show basically the same information. Don't be fooled by the TAB portion of the name of these views. They are not limited to table privileges; they each show privileges to any database objects that are relevant, including PL/SQL program units.

These data dictionary views share a similar column structure. The only difference is that USER_TAB_PRIVS has one extra column: the OWNER column. The USER_TAB_PRIVS_MADE view shows all of the database object privileges that the current schema has granted to other schemas. The USER_TAB_PRIVS_RECD view shows all of the database object privileges that other schemas have granted to the current schema—in other words, privileges that have been received by the current schema. The USER_TAB_PRIVS view shows both sets of records combined.

Each row in these views represents one granted privilege on a database object. The privileges included here are not system privileges, but object privileges, such as a table privilege like INSERT or UPDATE ON PORTS, or a program unit privilege like EXECUTE ON PROC_FINANCE. A description of the columns follows:

- **GRANTEE**   This is the schema that has been granted the privilege.

- **OWNER**   This identifies the schema that owns the database object that is the subject of the privilege. (This is only present in the USER_TAB_PRIVS view.)

- **TABLE_NAME**   The name of the database object that is the subject of the privilege. This could be a table, view, sequence, or program unit, such as a procedure, function, or package.

- **GRANTOR**   The schema that granted the privilege. This is not necessarily the object owner. Remember that schemas other than the object owner may be capable of granting privileges. A grantee that's been given the privilege already WITH ADMIN OPTION could have, in turn, granted the same privilege to another schema.

- **PRIVILEGE**   This is the privilege that's been granted on the object named in TABLE_NAME. For tables, this could be SELECT, INSERT, UPDATE, or DELETE. For program units, this will be EXECUTE.

- **GRANTABLE**   This is a YES or NO column that indicates if the privilege was granted WITH ADMIN OPTION or not.

For Review

1. The data dictionary views SESSION_PRIVS and SESSION_ROLES show system privileges held by the current schema that are currently in force, regardless of how they were granted. The USER_SYS_PRIVS, USER_ROLE_PRIVS, and DBA_SYS_PRIVS show this same information, but show how they were granted, which means you may have to do some digging to find out what SESSION_PRIVS and SESSION_ROLES show. Many roles can be granted to roles and the level of grants can get a little deep.

2. The USER_TAB_PRIVS view in the data dictionary shows all grants made by and to the current schema, and USER_TAB_PRIVS_MADE and USER_TAB_PRIVS_RECD show a subset of that information, showing the privileges made by the current schema and privileges received by the current schema.

Exercises

1. Which data dictionary view can you query from within your own schema to list information about the privileges you have granted to other schemas for executing your program units?

   A. USER_TAB_PRIVS_MADE

   B. USER_TAB_PRIVS_GRANTED

   C. USER_PRIVS_MADE

   D. USER_PRIVS_GRANTED

2. Which data dictionary view shows all roles currently in effect for your current schema?

   A. ALL_ROLES

   B. USER_ROLES

   C. SESSION_ROLES

   D. ALL_ROLES_CURRENTLY_IN_EFFECT

Answer Key
1. A. 2. C.

Chapter Summary

There are two categories of privileges that an application developer must be concerned with and that are addressed on the exam: system privileges and object privileges. System privileges are the rights that a schema must possess in order to be able to perform various duties in the database of a general nature, such as the right to create tables or to alter program units owned by other schemas. Object privileges are the privileges on a named database object that has already been created, such as the right to SELECT from the SHIPS table or the right to EXECUTE the GET_CAPTAIN function.

There are over 100 system privileges. Of those that are of concern to developers of PL/SQL program units, the most important are CREATE PROCEDURE and/or CREATE TRIGGER.

The CREATE PROCEDURE system privilege enables a schema to create, alter, or drop any procedure, function, or package within its own schema. In addition, CREATE ANY PROCEDURE enables the schema to create program units owned by other schemas, but not alter or drop them. There are separate system privileges for ALTER ANY PROCEDURE and DROP ANY PROCEDURE.

The CREATE TRIGGER system privilege is similar, but is used for database triggers—it enables a schema to create, alter, or drop triggers within its own schema. There are separate CREATE ANY TRIGGER, ALTER ANY TRIGGER, and DROP ANY TRIGGER system privileges.

Any system privilege can be granted the WITH ADMIN OPTION to enable the grantee to grant the same privilege to another schema, but only as long as the grantee still retains the privilege. Any system privilege can be revoked. If it is revoked and the WITH ADMIN OPTION was issued with the grant, any privileges that the grantee has already granted stay in effect.

System privileges can be granted to roles and roles can be granted to schemas. Ultimately, the purpose of all privileges is to be granted to schemas, either directly or via roles.

Object privileges involve a schema's capability to reference and use named database objects that are owned by other schemas, such as the LEDGER table or the ACCOUNT_BALANCE procedure. A program unit owner must have the appropriate privileges to perform the statements in the program unit. For example, if the program unit includes an INSERT statement on the LEDGER table, the program unit owner must have the INSERT ON LEDGER privilege. If the program unit owner is also the LEDGER table owner, no privilege is required—object owners automatically hold all privileges for their own objects. If a schema needs to execute a program unit that it does not own, that schema must have EXECUTE privileges.

The calling schema does not have to have privileges on the objects within a program unit in order to execute the program unit, assuming the program unit is using definer rights, or owner rights, which means that the program unit will execute with the object privileges of its owner at the time of execution. If the program unit owner has, for example, INSERT ON LEDGER at the time some third schema is calling it, then the third schema will be able to execute the program unit, even if that third schema does not have INSERT ON LEDGER privileges.

The SESSION_PRIVS data dictionary view shows all system privileges currently in force for a schema and SESSION_ROLES shows all roles currently in force. This includes privileges that have been directly granted as well as indirectly granted. Indirect grants occur when a role is granted that, in turn, includes other roles. To identify the individual grants and the multiple levels of roles granted to roles, use the USER_SYS_PRIVS, USER_ROLE_PRIVS, and DBA_SYS_PRIVS views.

For information about object privileges, the USER_TAB_PRIVS view contains the entire set of privileges granted to and by the current schema, and the USER_TAB_ PRIVS_MADE and USER_TAB_PRIVS_RECD break out that list into object privileges that the current schema has granted to other schemas and the object privileges that other schemas have granted to the current schema.

Two-Minute Drill

■ System privileges are defined by Oracle Corporation and are a predetermined list of privileges. For any schema to be usable, it must have the CREATE SESSION privilege. Additional privileges like CREATE TABLE are required to build database objects. To create its own procedures, functions, or packages, a schema must have the CREATE PROCEDURE privilege. There is no CREATE FUNCTION or CREATE PACKAGE privilege. However, there is a CREATE TRIGGER privilege.

■ The CREATE PROCEDURE WITH ADMIN OPTION privilege, when granted to a schema, enables that schema to create procedures, functions, and packages, and grant that same system privilege to other schemas.

■ The ANY keyword, when present in the privilege, indicates that the privilege is extended to the ability to create program units in other schemas. CREATE ANY PROCEDURE only enables a schema to CREATE, but not alter or drop procedures, functions, or packages that are owned by other schemas. To alter, the ALTER ANY PROCEDURE must be granted and to drop, the DROP ANY PROCEDURE must be granted.

■ Once granted, a schema can create procedures in other schemas by prefixing the object name with the schema name in the CREATE statement —for example, CREATE PROCEDURE NEWSCHEMA.ACCOUNT_ BALANCE IS BEGIN . . . END;.

■ System privileges can be granted to schemas, roles, or PUBLIC.

■ A program unit can be owned by one schema, can reference objects by a second schema, and be executed by a third schema. When a program unit executes with definer rights, it means that the program unit owner must have the privileges required by the program unit. When the program unit executes with invoker rights, the executing schema must be the one to have the required privileges. Some of Oracle Corporation's built-in packages execute with invoker rights.

■ You can create program units with invoker rights with the AUTHID CURRENT_USER clause. The default is AUTHID DEFINER.

■ In the data dictionary, SESSION_PRIVS and SESSION_ROLES show the system privileges and roles that are currently in force, and USER_SYS_PRIVS, USER_ROLE_PRIVS, and DBA_SYS_PRIVS provide the background information showing the actual grants, but including the detailed roles-granted-to-roles layers of grants.

■ The USER_TAB_PRIVS view in the data dictionary shows all grants made by and to the current schema, and USER_TAB_PRIVS_MADE and

USER_TAB_PRIVS_RECD show the breakout of privileges made by the current schema and privileges received by the current schema.

Chapter Questions

1. **Which of the following best describes what the keywords WITH ADMIN OPTION mean?**

   A. A database administrator issued the grant.

   B. The granted privilege can be granted to another schema by the grantee.

   C. The system privilege has the capability to administer the database.

   D. The grantee has the option of becoming a database administrator by using the system privilege.

2. **Which of the following system privileges is required to create private packaged functions in another schema?**

   A. CREATE ANY FUNCTION

   B. CREATE ANY PACKAGE

   C. CREATE ANY PACKAGE BODY

   D. CREATE ANY PROCEDURE

3. **There is a function called BOOK_CRUISE in the schema KALORAMA. You want to issue a CREATE OR REPLACE FUNCTION KALORAMA.BOOK_ CRUISE statement from your own schema BOWIE. Which of the following system privileges is required by BOWIE to issue this statement?**

   A. CREATE ANY PROCEDURE

   B. ALTER ANY PROCEDURE

   C. CREATE ANY FUNCTION

   D. ALTER ANY FUNCTION

4. **The package MARKETING contains a procedure PRICING. You want to give the schema JSHEA the capability to execute this procedure. Which of the following statements will accomplish this?**

   A. GRANT SELECT ON MARKETING.PRICING TO JSHEA;

   B. GRANT EXECUTE ON MARKETING.PRICING TO JSHEA;

    C. GRANT EXECUTE ON MARKETING TO JSHEA;

    D. GRANT EXECUTE ON MARKETING TO JSHEA WITH PRICING OPTION

5. **Which of the following system privileges is required for a schema to create and drop its own triggers?**

    A. CREATE PROCEDURE

    B. CREATE TRIGGER

    C. CREATE PROCEDURE and DROP PROCEDURE

    D. CREATE TRIGGER and DROP TRIGGER

6. **SCHEMA1 owns table TAB1, and it grants SELECT ON TAB1 TO SCHEMA2, which uses it to build a procedure PROC2 that selects from TAB1. PROC2 is declared with definer rights. Next SCHEMA2 grants EXECUTE ON PROC2 to SCHEMA3. SCHEMA3 executes SCHEMA2.PROC2 with no problem, but then SCHEMA1 issues REVOKE SELECT ON TAB1 FROM SCHEMA2. What is now true?**

    A. SCHEMA3 can no longer execute SCHEMA2.PROC2.

    B. SCHEMA2 can no longer execute SCHEMA2.PROC2, but SCHEMA3 can still execute SCHEMA2.PROC2.

    C. SCHEMA3 can execute SCHEMA2.PROC2, but the code referencing SCHEMA2.PROC2 will just not work and those statements will be skipped over.

    D. None of the above.

7. **The schema PFLEMING has created a trigger TRIG1 on a table that the schema MKWAN already has privileges on. What GRANT statement must PFLEMING execute for MKWAN to invoke the trigger?**

    A. GRANT EXECUTE ON TRIG1 TO MKWAN;

    B. GRANT EXECUTE ON PFLEMING.TRIG1 TO MKWAN;

    C. GRANT TRIGGER TO MKWAN;

    D. None of the above.

8. **You are working with an application development team that has many developers working at various levels. The team leader has created several roles representing the different levels of system privileges required for building your application. You know that some roles are granted to other**

roles, and those roles are, in turn, granted to your schema. Which data dictionary view should you query to most easily obtain a list of all system privileges that are currently granted to your schema, regardless of whether it was granted directly or through a role?

A. SESSION_PRIVS

B. USER_ROLE_PRIVS

C. SYSTEM_PRIVS

D. DBA_ROLE_PRIVS

9. The schema TROBBINS has granted CREATE ANY TRIGGER to your current schema. Which of the following data dictionary resources can you inspect to confirm this?

A. USER_TRIGGERS

B. USER_OBJECTS

C. USER_SYS_PRIVS

D. USER_TAB_PRIVS

10. Your current schema has been granted the EXECUTE privilege on the package COMMITTEE owned by the schema MITT. If you wanted to find an entry for this privilege in the data dictionary from within your current schema, what WHERE clause would you use to complete the query SELECT * FROM USER_TAB_PRIVS?

A. WHERE TABLE_NAME = 'COMMITTEE'

B. WHERE OBJECT_TYPE = 'PACKAGE' AND NAME = 'COMMITTEE'

C. WHERE GRANTEE = 'MITT' AND NAME = 'COMMITTEE'

D. None of the above

Answers to Chapter Questions

 I. B.   The granted privilege can be granted to another schema by the grantee.

Explanation   A is not true—you cannot tell from the WITH ADMIN OPTION who issued the grant. B is definitely true. C is not true—the technical definition of the WITH ADMIN OPTION is that the grantee has been given the capability to administer the system privilege in question, but its capability is limited to only the privilege, not the entire database. D is not true.

2. D. CREATE ANY PROCEDURE

Explanation The CREATE ANY PROCEDURE system privilege grants the ability to create procedures, functions, and packages in any schema.

3. B. ALTER ANY PROCEDURE

Explanation Because the OR REPLACE portion of the statement is what will be used here, you must have the privilege ALTER ANY PROCEDURE. You don't need the CREATE ANY PROCEDURE privilege because the procedure already exists. Remember that there are no system privileges that contain the name FUNCTION or PACKAGE.

4. C. GRANT EXECUTE ON MARKETING TO JSHEA;

Explanation You cannot selectively grant privileges on a packaged program unit; you must grant privileges on the package as a whole.

5. B. CREATE TRIGGER

Explanation The CREATE TRIGGER system privilege is required for triggers and carries with it the capability to create, alter, and drop triggers in the schema that has been granted the privilege.

6. A. SCHEMA3 can no longer execute SCHEMA2.PROC2.

Explanation SCHEMA3 is executing the program unit with definer rights and cannot execute SCHEMA2.PROC2 unless SCHEMA2 continues to have the required privileges.

7. D. None of the above.

Explanation You never need to issue any grants regarding triggers. If the end-user schema already has privileges to the triggered table, no additional grants are required.

8. A. SESSION_PRIVS

Explanation The SESSION_PRIVS view presents a list of all system privileges in force for the current schema. This information can be pieced together out of a combination of queries on the views USER_SYS_PRIVS, USER_ROLE_PRIVS, and/or DBA_ROLE_PRIVS, depending on what is discovered in each query along the way. However, SESSION_PRIVS is meant to be a single source to easily query this information all at once.

9. C. USER_SYS_PRIVS

Explanation The CREATE ANY TRIGGER privilege is a system privilege, and if TROBBINS granted it explicitly to your current schema, it should be listed in the USER_SYS_PRIVS view.

10. A. WHERE TABLE_NAME = 'COMMITTEE'

Explanation The USER_TAB_PRIVS view uses the TABLE_NAME column to track the name of the database object, regardless of whether it is a table, view, or program unit.

CHAPTER
11

Managing
Interdependencies

ny serious PL/SQL application will be built on multiple program units that invoke each other and reference database objects such as tables and views. The more an application grows, the more the interdependencies of these program units grow, and the more crucial it becomes for you as the developer to have a strong command of the skills and tools at your disposal for tracking these interdependencies. This chapter looks at data dictionary resources, utilities, and design techniques to help you manage and monitor interdependencies. We will also discuss some issues involving remote databases and other issues involving interdependent program units.

In this chapter, you will review and understand the following topics:

- Tracking dependencies with the data dictionary

- Dependency issues within a single database

- Dependency issues across multiple databases

- Avoiding recompilation errors

Tracking Dependencies

Because program units can be created in one schema, reference tables and other database objects in a second schema, call program units in a third schema, grant EXECUTE privileges to a fourth schema, and so on, it's important to be able to monitor the dependencies among program units and other database objects that reference each other. There are data dictionary resources and utilities that you can use to monitor those dependencies. Some help you see direct relationships and others help you track indirect relationships. They are described in this chapter.

USER_DEPENDENCIES

The USER_DEPENDENCIES view in the data dictionary is where you will find the relationships that your program units have with database objects in the same schema as well as those database objects in other schemas. The following list describes its columns:

- **NAME** The name of the object, that is, the name of the procedure, table, and so on. This is the object that contains a reference or is dependent upon another database object. For example, if you have a procedure that calls a table in another schema, this column will show the name of the procedure.

- **TYPE** The object type that corresponds to the database object listed in the NAME column as found in the USER_OBJECTS view's OBJECT_TYPE column. Examples include PROCEDURE, PACKAGE, and TRIGGER.

- **REFERENCED_OWNER**   This is the schema name of the referenced object. Following our example, if you have a procedure listed under the NAME column that contains code that references another schema's table, this column will show that schema's name.

- **REFERENCED_NAME**   The database object in the other schema that the object listed under the NAME column is referencing.

- **REFERENCED_TYPE**   The type of object listed under REFERENCED_NAME.

- **REFERENCED_LINK_NAME**   If the schema listed under REFERENCED_NAME is being accessed via a database link, then that database link is listed in this column.

- **SCHEMAID**   The schema's internal ID assigned by the database.

- **DEPENDENCY_TYPE**   Either REF for REF-type dependencies or HARD for all other dependencies.

For an example of how this data dictionary view can be used, consider the following procedure:

```
PROCEDURE PROC_SCHEDULE_CRUISE
   ( p_start_date IN DATE    , p_total_days IN NUMBER
   , p_ship_id   IN NUMBER , p_cruise_name IN VARCHAR2) IS
   -- A procedure to schedule a cruise
   v_cruise_type_id CRUISE_TYPES.CRUISE_TYPE_ID%TYPE;
BEGIN
   -- Determine the type of cruise involved
   SELECT CRUISE_TYPE_ID
   INTO  v_cruise_type_id
   FROM  CRUISE_TYPES
   WHERE LENGTH_DAYS = p_total_days;
   -- Schedule cruise
   INSERT INTO CRUISES
     ( CRUISE_ID, SHIP_ID, CRUISE_TYPE_ID
     , CRUISE_NAME, START_DATE
     , END_DATE)
     VALUES
     ( SEQ_CRUISE_ID.NEXTVAL, P_SHIP_ID, v_cruise_type_id
     , p_cruise_name, p_start_date
     , (p_start_date + p_total_days));
   COMMIT;
EXCEPTION
   WHEN OTHERS THEN
     ROLLBACK;
     PROC_RECORD_ERROR('PROC_SCHEDULE_CRUISE');
END;
```

This procedure is owned by the schema FESTIVAL and contains several dependent objects. To find them in the USER_DEPENDENCIES table, use the following query:

```
SELECT REFERENCED_OWNER, REFERENCED_NAME, REFERENCED_TYPE
FROM   USER_DEPENDENCIES
WHERE  NAME = 'PROC_SCHEDULE_CRUISE'
```

See Figure 11-1 to see the results of this query.

In the figure, you can see that the procedure PROC_SCHEDULE_CRUISE references several objects. Four of the objects are owned by the schema FESTIVAL and three are owned by the schema SYS. The three SYS objects are common dependencies and are standard for all program units. STANDARD is the built-in Oracle package that contains all supporting built-in PL/SQL functions, such as SUBSTR, TO_CHAR, and others. For a full description of this package, you can use the same command that you would use to describe any PL/SQL program unit:

```
DESC SYS.STANDARD
```

This produces a list of the package's procedures and functions and the package specification headers for each.

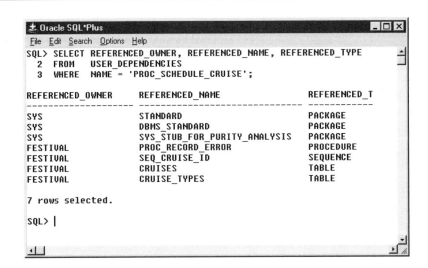

FIGURE 11-1. *The USER_DEPENDENCIES data dictionary view*

The DBMS_STANDARD package is similar, and the SYS_STUB_FOR_
PURITY_ANALYSIS is another Oracle-supplied built-in that supports purity analysis
for packages.

The objects owned by SYS are built-ins and are dependent objects that you
generally do not need to be concerned about. On the other hand, all other objects,
which in this example are owned by FESTIVAL, are theoretically under the control
of the developer. Furthermore, these objects are listed clearly in the source code of
the schema. In this example, there are four objects: one procedure, one sequence,
and two tables. Each object that could have a line entry in the USER_OBJECTS data
dictionary view of its owner's schema could be listed here. All database objects that
the PROC_SCHEDULE_CRUISE procedure references are listed in this data
dictionary view, even if the same schema that owns PROC_SCHEDULE_CRUISE
owns the database objects. Although you could identify these objects just by
scanning the source code of the procedure, the USER_DEPENDENCIES view
provides a queriable listing that clearly breaks out this information. Furthermore,
you cannot always determine the owner of a particular object from the source code
of the procedure. For example, if a schema SNYDER owns the procedure
PROC_RECORD_ERROR, then the PROC_SCHEDULE_CRUISE procedure could
reference PROC_RECORD_ERROR in the exception handler:

```
WHEN OTHERS THEN
   ROLLBACK;
   SNYDER.PROC_RECORD_ERROR('PROC_SCHEDULE_CRUISE');
```

However, it's possible that a DBA-privileged account may have created a public
synonym on this object, as follows:

```
CREATE PUBLIC SYNONYM PROC_RECORD_ERROR ON SNYDER.PROC_RECORD_ERROR
```

If this were the case, then we could remove the schema reference from the
source code:

```
WHEN OTHERS THEN
   ROLLBACK;
   PROC_RECORD_ERROR('PROC_SCHEDULE_CRUISE');
```

Assuming that SNYDER has granted the appropriate privilege to the current schema
by name or even to PUBLIC,

```
GRANT EXECUTE ON PROC_RECORD_ERROR TO PUBLIC;
```

the source code for PROC_SCHEDULE_CRUISE will execute and you will not be
able to tell from the PROC_SCHEDULE_CRUISE source code that the

PROC_RECORD_ERROR procedure is actually owned by SNYDER. The best source for information about these dependencies is the USER_DEPENDENCIES view.

The DBA_DEPENDENCIES view is just like the USER_DEPENDENCIES view but with one additional column: OWNER. This column can be used to see what other objects reference the program unit in question. Consider this query:

```
SELECT OWNER, NAME, TYPE
FROM   DBA_DEPENDENCIES
WHERE  REFERENCED_OWNER = 'FESTIVAL'
  AND  REFERENCED_NAME  = 'PROC_SCHEDULE_CRUISE'
  AND  REFERENCED_TYPE  = 'PROCEDURE';
```

This query lists all other program units and the names of their owners that have references to the procedure PROC_SCHEDULE_CRUISE.

DEPTREE and IDEPTREE

In our earlier figure, we listed the dependent objects of the procedure PROC_SCHEDULE_CRUISE. One of those objects is another PL/SQL program unit. What if that program unit has objects that it also references? In other words, what about the indirect dependencies? If these exist, you can requery the USER_DEPENDENCIES data dictionary view to see the dependent objects for that program unit. However, if that object is owned by another schema, you'll have to use the USER_DEPENDENCIES data dictionary view from within that schema or you can use the DBA_DEPENDENCIES view, which is the same as USER_DEPENDENCIES but adds the OWNER column to show all dependencies in the database.

Furthermore, the START WITH . . . CONNECT BY option in the SELECT statement cannot be used here. The START WITH clause in a SELECT statement enables you to create hierarchical queries on a single table. However, USER_DEPENDENCIES is not a database table—it is a database view and the START WITH . . . CONNECT BY feature will not work if attempted on the USER_DEPENDENCIES view to produce a hierarchical display.

The solution is the DEPTREE and IDEPTREE views, which will provide this information. However, these views are not automatically available for use. You must take some steps to set them up and populate them with the information you need:

1. First, execute a utility script called utldtree.sql, which should be installed in the Oracle home directory under the rdbms/admin subdirectory. This script will create the objects in Table 11-1.

   The utldtree.sql utility can be executed from within the SYS schema or from within any other schema. If it's executed while you are connected as INTERNAL, the utility creates a version of the DEPTREE view that shows information about shared cursors. If you execute the script while connected

Object Type	Object Name
SEQUENCE	DEPTREE_SEQ
TABLE	DEPTREE_TEMPTAB
PROCEDURE	DEPTREE_FILL
VIEW	DEPTREE
VIEW	IDEPTREE

TABLE 11-1.   *Database Objects Created by utldtree.sql*

to your own schema, a different version of DEPTREE that leaves out shared cursor information is created.

2. Once you have executed the utldtree.sql from within a schema, you must execute the DEPTREE_FILL procedure. This procedure deletes all records from the DEPTREE_TEMPTAB table and then populates it with information drawn from a series of SELECT and INSERT statements, including a START WITH . . . CONNECT BY query on the data dictionary view PUBLIC_ DEPENDENCY. To execute the procedure, you must provide three parameters:

- ■ **TYPE**   The type of object as listed in the OBJECT_TYPE column of the USER_OBJECTS view. This is case sensitive and must be in uppercase letters, for example, PROCEDURE.

- ■ **SCHEMA**   The name of the schema that owns the object you are analyzing, which should be in uppercase letters.

- ■ **NAME**   The name of the object you want to analyze, which should be in uppercase letters. This is the object whose dependencies you want to see.

For example, the following will execute DEPTREE_FILL for the procedure PROC_RECORD_ERROR in the schema FESTIVAL:

```
EXEC DEPTREE_FILL('PROCEDURE','FESTIVAL','PROC_RECORD_ERROR');
```

If you make a mistake, the procedure won't be able to locate the database object and will produce an execution error. However, once this procedure has executed successfully, the DEPTREE_TEMPTAB table will be populated and you can move to the next step.

3. Now you are ready to investigate the DEPTREE and/or IDEPTREE view. The DEPTREE view has the following columns:

■ **NESTED_LEVEL** This is the number taken from the value of LEVEL, which is computed as part of the underlying START WITH . . . CONNECT BY query, showing the hierarchical level of the nested calls. The parent object has a NESTED_LEVEL of 0, and all other objects are numbered according to their level relative to the parent object.

■ **TYPE** The type of object that is referenced, for example, PROCEDURE, PACKAGE, and so on.

■ **SCHEMA** The schema owner of the referenced object.

■ **NAME** The name of the referenced object.

■ **SEQ#** The sequence number of the row, which is useful when querying the view with an ORDER BY clause.

The DEPTREE view provides detailed information about program units that call your program unit, calls to those program units, and so on. The multiple levels in the hierarchy are indicated with the NESTED_LEVEL column.

For example, the following code listing shows a query and response of the DEPTREE view. It assumes that the DEPTREE_FILL procedure has already been executed for the procedure PROC_RECORD_ERROR in the schema FESTIVAL:

```
SELECT * FROM DEPTREE ORDER BY SEQ#;
NESTED_LEVEL TYPE                SCHEMA     NAME
------------ ------------------- ---------- ----------------------
           0 PROCEDURE           FESTIVAL   PROC_RECORD_ERROR
           1 PROCEDURE           FESTIVAL   PROC_SCHEDULE_CRUISE
           2 PACKAGE BODY        FESTIVAL   PACK_BOOKING
           1 FUNCTION            FESTIVAL   EMPLOYEE_HIRE_DATE
           1 PACKAGE BODY        FESTIVAL   GUEST_SURVEY
```

Remember that the NESTED_LEVEL of 0 indicates the root of this dependency tree. A NESTED_LEVEL of 1 indicates that the object is directly dependent on the root. A NESTED_LEVEL of 2 indicates that the object is dependent upon one of the objects listed with a NESTED_LEVEL of 1. If the ORDER BY SEQ# is used in the query, then you can look in the row above the NESTED_LEVEL 2 object's row for the first NESTED_LEVEL 1 record—that will be the object upon which the NESTED_LEVEL 2 object is directly dependent.

Both the DEPTREE and IDEPTREE views show basically the same information, but IDEPTREE is indented for a clearer presentation of the hierarchical levels. IDEPTREE also shows all of its information in a single column.

- **DEPENDENCIES** This shows a single string of information showing the dependent objects indented according to their level in the hierarchy.

See the following code listing for a sample of a query and response on the IDEPTREE view:

```
SQL> SELECT * FROM  IDEPTREE;
DEPENDENCIES
-------------------------------------------
PROCEDURE FESTIVAL.PROC_RECORD_ERROR
    PROCEDURE FESTIVAL.PROC_SCHEDULE_CRUISE
        PACKAGE BODY FESTIVAL.PACK_BOOKING
    FUNCTION FESTIVAL.EMPLOYEE_HIRE_DATE
    PACKAGE BODY FESTIVAL.GUEST_SURVEY
```

The results show an indented list and indicate that the procedure PROC_RECORD_ERROR is called by PROC_SCHEDULE_CRUISE, EMPLOYEE_HIRE_DATE, and GUEST_SURVEY. Furthermore, PROC_SCHEDULE_CRUISE is called by PACK_BOOKING.

The DEPTREE and IDEPTREE views display a hierarchical list of multiple calls among program units. The list includes all of the levels that exist in the hierarchy in a single query result—something you cannot get in the data dictionary. However, as we have seen, these views require some setup time that is not normally required with the data dictionary.

For Review

1. You can find direct dependencies in the USER_DEPENDENCIES view, which shows all dependent objects, including tables, views, and program units, regardless of schema owner, that are related to database objects within your own schema.

2. The script utldtree.sql can be executed to set up the DEPTREE and IDEPTREE views for looking at the indirect dependencies of your program units.

Exercises

1. What procedure must be executed before using the IDEPTREE view?

    A. IDEPTREE_FILL

    B. DEPTREE_FILL

    C. UTIL_DEPT

    D. PROC_DEPTREE

2. Which column in the USER_DEPENDENCIES view shows the owner of a referenced object?

    A. REFERENCED_SCHEMA

    B. REFERENCED_OWNER

    C. REFERENCED_NAME

    D. REFERENCED_USERNAME

Answer Key

1. B. 2. B.

Dependency Issues Within a Single Database

In previous chapters, we discussed a number of issues involving program unit compilation and interdependencies. We have already seen that if one program unit calls another program unit and the called program unit is recompiled, then the calling program unit is flagged as INVALID and must be recompiled. Furthermore, we've seen that this recompilation can be performed manually with the ALTER statement or will be performed automatically on the next execution of the INVALID program unit.

A database object privilege that has been granted directly to a schema enables that schema to use that database object in that schema's program units. For example, if schema 1 has a table, schema 1 can grant SELECT privileges on that table to schema 2. Schema 2 can then create program units that include SELECT statements on schema 1's table. If schema 1 grants additional privileges to schema 2, such as INSERT or UPDATE, then schema 2 can incorporate the additional Data

Manipulation Language (DML) statements in its program units. When completed, schema 2 can grant EXECUTE privileges on the program unit to schema 3, and assuming that the program unit was created with the default of owner rights, schema 3 can execute the program unit in schema 2 without having privileges on the table owned by schema 1. However, if schema 1 revokes the table privileges from schema 2, schema 3 will experience execution errors on the program unit the next time that schema 3 tries to execute schema 2's program unit.

A privilege that is granted via a role cannot be incorporated in a program unit, and in turn, cannot be granted to other schemas. In other words, if schema 1 grants SELECT privileges on a table to a role and the role is then granted to schema 2, schema 2 may be able to issue standard SQL SELECT statements from within SQL*Plus, but schema 2 cannot create program units with SELECT statements on that table. Schema 1 must grant SELECT privileges directly to schema 2 in order for schema 2 to successfully create program units that reference schema 1's table.

If schema 1 owns a table and schema 1 grants privileges on the table to schema 2, and if schema 2 has the CREATE ANY TRIGGER privilege, then schema 2 can create a database trigger on the table owned by schema 1. This is true even if the privileges to schema 2 are accomplished through a role. The result is that the table is still owned by schema 1 and the trigger is owned by schema 2. Furthermore, if schema 1 grants privileges on the table to schema 3, schema 3 issues a DML statement that causes the schema 2 trigger to fire and the trigger will fire. Even if the schema 2 trigger invokes additional program units that are not explicitly granted to schema 3, the trigger will successfully fire in response to schema 3's DML statements.

It is imperative that you are familiar with your program units that you create and the database objects that they invoke. The interdependencies can be tracked with the data dictionary and supporting utility files and procedures, and automatic recompilation will be invoked where appropriate. However, there is no substitute for your own familiarity with the program units and interdependencies you create.

For Review

1. Program units can reference database objects in other schemas if the other schema has granted the necessary privilege directly to the schema. Granting via roles does not work for program units.

2. Assuming that a schema has the CREATE ANY TRIGGER privilege, that schema can create a database trigger on a second schema's objects if privileges have been granted to the first schema on the database object, either directly with a GRANT statement or indirectly through a role.

Exercises

1. Schema 1 owns a table called CRUISES. Schema 2 wants to create a procedure that issues an UPDATE statement on schema 1's table CRUISES. What must schema 1 do in order for schema 2 to be able to create the procedure?

   A. It cannot be done.

   B. Schema 1 must grant UPDATE on the table to schema 2.

   C. Schema 1 must get a DBA to grant the right privileges.

   D. Schema 1 must create a role and grant privileges on the role to schema 2.

2. The schema MICHIE owns a table. The schema CRAIG has the CREATE ANY TRIGGER privilege and SELECT privileges on MICHIE's table. Which of the following is true? (Choose all that apply.)

   A. The schema MICHIE can create a trigger on the table.

   B. The schema CRAIG can create a trigger on the table.

   C. Once the schema MICHIE creates a trigger on the table, nobody else can.

   D. None of the above.

Answer Key
1. B. 2. A, B.

Dependency Issues Across Multiple Databases

As we have already seen, when one program unit invokes a second program unit and the second program unit is changed for any reason, the first program unit is automatically flagged with a status of INVALID and must be recompiled, otherwise it will be recompiled automatically at the next execution. This INVALID status is set immediately when the program units are located together in the same database. This is the standard behavior for program units that are located within the same database and cannot be changed.

However, when a remote database object is involved—that is, a database object, such as a table or program unit in a remote database connected to the local database via a database link—the INVALID status is not immediately set. Instead, when a local program unit that calls a remote database object is executed, the status of the remote database object is checked at execution to determine if a recompilation of the local program unit is required.

For example, say we have a procedure BALANCE that calls a procedure GENERAL_LEDGER that is located in a remote database. Both program units are VALID, but GENERAL_LEDGER is recreated in the remote database with a CREATE OR REPLACE PROCEDURE statement. If these two program units were in the same database, the BALANCE procedure would be flagged as INVALID. However, because the two program units are in separate databases, BALANCE will be left unchanged. The next time BALANCE is executed, the PL/SQL run-time engine checks the remote program unit call and does a quick comparison to determine if the local procedure needs to be recompiled before execution. If the initial comparison shows that the local program unit requires recompilation, the execution will fail. However, if the automatic recompilation succeeds, the second execution will succeed.

The PL/SQL engine uses two different ways to compare the local program unit and the remote database object to determine if BALANCE needs to be recompiled. These two different methods are referred to as *modes*: the *timestamp* mode and the *signature* mode. These modes are only relevant for remote database objects and have no impact on local database dependencies. In other words, regardless of which mode you use, an ALTER on a local program unit will still change local dependent program units to INVALID.

The initialization parameter REMOTE_DEPENDENCIES_MODE defines which mode is used. It can be set for the current session while the database is running from within a schema with the appropriate system privileges, or it can be added to the initialization file for database startup. To change it while the database is running, use the following command from a privileged account:

```
ALTER SESSION SET REMOTE_DEPENDENCIES_MODE = SIGNATURE;
```

This example of the ALTER SESSION statement does not modify the initialization file, but it changes the value for the REMOTE_DEPENDENCIES_MODE parameter immediately, if only for the current session.

As an alternative, you can use the ALTER SYSTEM statement:

```
ALTER SYSTEM SET REMOTE_DEPENDENCIES_MODE = SIGNATURE;
```

This example of the ALTER SYSTEM statement modifies the REMOTE_
DEPENDENCIES_MODE parameter, and the change takes effect the next time the
database is initialized.

To change the REMOTE_DEPENDENCIES_MODE parameter back to its default,
use the keyword TIMESTAMP. The mode only needs to be changed in the database
initiating the comparison. Both modes are described in the following sections.

The Timestamp Mode

The timestamp mode is the default. This mode compares the values in the data
dictionary for both objects by looking at the LAST_DDL_TIME column, which can
be found in the USER_OBJECTS data dictionary view. If these two times indicate
that the GENERAL_LEDGER program unit has been compiled after the last
compilation of BALANCE, the BALANCE procedure needs recompilation.

Unfortunately, there's a problem with this. What if the two databases are in
different time zones? After all, we're talking about two separate remote databases
and chances are that the GENERAL_LEDGER procedure really has been recompiled,
but because of time zone differences, the LAST_DDL_TIME column for GENERAL_
LEDGER in the remote database might not compare accurately with the LAST_DDL_
TIME column for BALANCE in the local database.

If this is the case—that is, if the remote database is in a different time zone—the
timestamp mode won't work. The signature mode must be used.

The Signature Mode

The purpose of the signature mode is to define a logical alternative to timestamp to
determine when a remote program unit has been changed and requires the
recompilation of a local program unit that invokes the remote program unit without
considering the timestamp of the change.

The signature mode compares the signature of the program units to determine
when a recompilation is required. The signature of any program unit consists of its
header information, that is, the parameter datatypes and their order. It includes the
following:

- **Parameter order**

- **Parameter datatype family**   For example, changing CHAR to VARCHAR2
  won't cause a change, nor will changing NUMBER to INTEGER. However,
  changing NUMBER to DATE will cause a change.

- **Parameter type**   In other words, IN, OUT, or IN OUT.

- **Function RETURN datatypes**

Notice what is not considered part of the signature: default values of parameters, changes to the name of the parameter, changes within a datatype family, or changes to source code itself.

When the signature is changed, the dependent program unit will be recompiled on the next execution of that dependent program unit.

The result is that it is possible for the dependent program unit to not be recompiled in every situation where the timestamp mode would otherwise require recompilation. The signature mode will require recompilation only when the signature is changed.

For Review

1. Changes to program units in remote databases do not automatically cause dependent objects in the local database to change to a status of INVALID.

2. The default timestamp mode of determining when a program unit is changed to INVALID can be problematic when working with remote databases in different time zones. The signature mode, the alternative to timestamp, can be used to overcome those problems.

Exercises

1. **Which of the following changes to a signature will cause a dependent program unit to be INVALID?**

    A. A change to the parameter's default value

    B. The addition of another parameter

    C. A change to the name of a parameter

    D. A change of the parameter datatype from FLOAT to INTEGER

2. **If a remote database function is recompiled, when is the local procedure that calls the remote function recompiled?**

    A. It never is.

    B. It depends on whether the timestamp or signature mode is used.

    C. It is immediately recompiled.

    D. It will definitely be compiled at execution time.

Answer Key
1. B. 2. B.

Avoiding Recompilation Errors

When the circumstances require that a program unit be recompiled, the automatic recompilation will either succeed or it will fail. You can increase the odds of success by taking certain steps in the creation of your program unit's structure and save yourself a lot of unnecessary maintenance. The following lists some recommended practices:

■ *Use %ROWTYPE to declare record variables and %TYPE to declare variables.* These powerful features dynamically declare variables with datatypes that are taken from the database at execution time. Each variable's datatype is taken from the database object's definition in the data dictionary. The result is that any changes to datatypes in the database are automatically reflected in your program unit. The good news is that you won't have to edit your program unit to change the datatype declaration of your variables. The bad news is that if you use the declared variable in ways that require it to have a particular datatype, your program unit may still need some editing. For example, if you use a variable as a numeric parameter in the absolute value (ABS) function but it is suddenly transformed into a DATE datatype by a dynamic database definition, you will still have compilation problems in your program unit because PL/SQL won't be able to compute the ABS of a date. However, in general, you will have less editing work and gain significant maintenance advantages by using these features as much as possible.

■ *The SELECT * notation.* To use it, or not to use it—that is the question . . . and the answer depends on who you ask. Oracle Corporation formally recommends that you use the SELECT * notation if your goal is to minimize recompilation errors due to changes in the database. The reason is obvious. The SELECT * notation will automatically select all columns as they exist in the table at the time the SELECT statement is executed. Therefore, any changes to the table will be picked up automatically by the SELECT statement and won't require a change to the SELECT statement. However, this is not where it ends. Any use of the SELECT statement in a PL/SQL block requires the use of a corresponding INTO clause, where you define the variables into which you are fetching your data. Even if you use %ROWTYPE variables, you must eventually name the columns in your PL/SQL block that you are selecting. If you haven't clearly documented them by naming them in the SELECT statement, then you must name them in the various places you use them later in your code. For this reason, there's another school of thought that says you *should not* use the SELECT * notation because you'll end up having to name your columns anyway and probably won't produce any recompilation advantage from it. You'll only make the intention of the SELECT statement less clear to anyone reading your code later, including yourself. However, for the purpose of the exam, you need to know that Oracle Corporation thinks SELECT * is a technique that will help avoid recompilation errors. So if you're asked, be sure to answer correctly.

■ *Include a column list with INSERT statements.* There are two forms of INSERT statements: the form that names columns and the form that does not. Use the form that names columns. If you use the INSERT statement that does not name columns, the syntax of that form assumes that your value list is in the exact order of the column descriptions in the database and represents the complete list of columns. If the column list changes as the result of an ALTER statement or a DROP and CREATE on the table, you will have unpredictable results. Perhaps the INSERT will fail in your program unit. For example, if a new column is added to the table, your INSERT will fail if it does not specify a value for this new column.

On the other hand, it might still work, but it could put the data in the wrong place, which is a worse problem than if it didn't work at all. The VALUES list in the INSERT statement only requires that the datatypes of the inserted data match the column list in order. For example, consider the following INSERT statement:

```
INSERT INTO SHIP_CAPTAINS VALUES ('Josh','Parreco');
```

If you use this statement, but the first column in the table's current data dictionary entry is LAST_NAME and the second column is FIRST_NAME, the INSERT will still succeed because the datatypes of both are in the VARCHAR2 family; however, the values are reversed in the table. The following is the better choice:

```
INSERT INTO SHIP_CAPTAINS (FIRST_NAME, LAST_NAME) VALUES
('Josh','Parreco');
```

Now there is no doubt about which value is meant for which column, and any changes to the structure of the SHIP_CAPTAINS table that affect the order of these columns or the addition of new columns will have no impact on this statement.

Taking care to structure your program units with the dynamic definitions listed here and simultaneously clarifying column lists where appropriate in INSERT statements are some steps you can take to avoid recompilation errors in your program units when database objects are changed after your program unit has already been compiled successfully.

For Review

1. There are programming steps that you can take to increase the chances of success if and when your program unit is automatically recompiled.

2. Use dynamic datatype declaration and carefully structure your SELECT and INSERT statements; as a result, any changes to the database objects that your program unit references are less likely to result in automatic recompilation errors.

Exercises

1. **Which of the following are benefits of the use of %TYPE?**

   A. It forces your program unit to be recompiled with every execution.

   B. It speeds up execution time.

   C. It is easier to type because it has the word "TYPE" in it.

   D. It makes sure that your program unit uses the correct datatype that is in the database for the corresponding table column.

2. **Why use the INSERT statement that names its column list?**

   A. So that if the columns are later removed from the table, your INSERT will still work.

   B. So that if unrelated changes to the table are made after your program unit is compiled successfully, automatic recompilation will succeed.

   C. It is more typing and makes it look like you are working harder.

   D. It is required.

Answer Key
1. D. 2. B.

Chapter Summary

The USER_DEPENDENCIES data dictionary view is the best source of information in the database for direct dependencies of objects in the database. The USER_DEPENDENCIES view includes information about program units and other objects, such as tables, views, and sequences. If you create a program unit that calls other program units, if those program units call other program units, and if all of your program units invoke various database objects such as tables and views, the USER_DEPENDENCIES view will provide information about these dependencies. However, a single query to this view will show the direct dependencies—in other words, if a procedure calls a second procedure that calls a third procedure, you will not see the indirect relationship between the first and third procedure without making multiple queries on the USER_DEPENDENCIES view. Furthermore, SQL does not allow the START WITH . . . CONNECT BY query on a view.

The DEPTREE and IDEPTREE views are good for showing these indirect relationships. However, these views are limited to showing program unit interdependencies and don't include database tables and views. Furthermore, they require explicit setup using the utldtree.sql utility script to set up the supporting database objects. You must execute the DEPTREE_FILL procedure for each individual program unit you want to analyze. When that's completed, the DEPTREE view will show detailed information about the dependent objects and the IDEPTREE view will show the same information in an indented list.

Multiple schemas within a single database can reference each other's program units and database objects, provided that their appropriate privileges are granted. However, privileges must be granted directly to support procedures, functions, and packages. Privileges granted through roles will not be recognized from within the code of your program units. Role-granted privileges will only authorize a schema to create a trigger on the indirectly granted object (assuming the CREATE ANY TRIGGER privilege is in force), but even the trigger's processing section cannot reference objects that are granted via roles. The privileges for those objects must be granted directly to the schema.

When one program unit is modified with an ALTER statement, other dependent program units in the same database are immediately flagged as INVALID and will therefore be recompiled at their next execution. When working with program units that are stored in remote databases, however, something different happens. Alterations to program units in remote databases will not cause local database program units to recompile. Instead, your local database program units will automatically look at remote database calls at execution time and check to see if recompilation is required. However, a problem may result when the remote database is in a different time zone because the mode that the local database will use, which is known as the timestamp mode, looks at the LAST_DDL_TIME of the local program unit and the remote program unit to determine if the remote program unit has been modified recently. When different time zones are involved, this approach could produce undesirable results. The signature mode is the alternative. However, the signature mode is more forgiving than the timestamp mode, and although it's a better choice when working with remote databases, it will not force recompilation as often as the timestamp approach will.

Two-Minute Drill

- The USER_DEPENDENCIES view contains information about program units and the objects they reference. You can use it to locate objects that your program unit calls and program units that call your object.

- The DEPTREE and IDEPTREE views can be set up to provide more detailed hierarchical lists of program units and their dependent objects. These can be as many levels deep as the levels of calls.

- Schemas within the same database can own program units that call objects in other schemas, but only if the privilege was granted directly and not via a role.

- Triggers can be created by a schema with the CREATE ANY TRIGGER privilege on database objects in another schema for which the first schema has privileges, even if the other schema's database object was granted to the current schema via a role.

- Your schemas can have database objects, such as program units, that call database objects in remote databases, and vice versa. However, when recompilation is required, remote databases may not always cause your local database to recompile when required. The two modes for determining recompilation across remote databases are timestamp and signature. Neither mode affects the recompilation of mutually local database objects.

- The timestamp mode is the default and compares the LAST_DDL_TIME of the two objects.

- The signature mode is the best choice for working with remote database in separate time zones. The signature mode will only cause recompilation when the signature of the called program unit is changed. The signature consists of the parameter datatype family, the parameter type, the parameter number, and the RETURN datatype (for functions).

Chapter Questions

1. **The difference between DEPTREE and IDEPTREE is**

   A. One is a view and the other is a table.

   B. One is interactive and the other is not.

   C. One is indented and the other is not.

   D. One is for a single schema and the other is for all schemas.

2. **The TYPE column of the USER_DEPENDENCIES view shows**

   A. The type of constraint that forms the dependency

   B. The type of object specified in the NAME column

   C. The type of object specified in the REFERENCED_NAME column

   D. The type of dependency

3. **Which is true of DEPTREE?**

   A. It is part of the data dictionary.

   B. It must be set up in advance in order to be used.

   C. It is owned by the SYS schema.

   D. It is a graphical user interface (GUI) object.

4. **Under the signature mode, which of the following changes to a function stored in a remote database will cause a local procedure to recompile?**

   A. A new SELECT statement in the processing section

   B. A change to the default value of the first parameter

   C. A change to the RETURN datatype of the remote function

   D. A change of one of the function's parameters from a NUMBER datatype to a REAL

5. **When one schema owns a table, who can trigger it? (Choose all that apply.)**

   A. The owner

   B. Any other schema with appropriate privileges

   C. Only the owner and SYSTEM

   D. PUBLIC

6. **The schema DGREEN grants SELECT on a table to a role FINANCE and then grants that role to schema JGIBBS, who has the CREATE ANY TRIGGER privilege. Which of the following is true? (Choose all that apply.)**

   A. JGIBBS can create a procedure that references the table.

   B. JGIBBS can create a function that references the table.

C. JGIBBS can create a packaged procedure that references the table.

D. JGIBBS can create a trigger on the table.

7. **Which initialization parameter must be changed to ensure that program units in remote databases and in separate time zones will properly recompile?**

   A. REMOTE_DEPENDENCIES_MODE

   B. USER_DEPENDENCIES_MODE

   C. DEPENDENCIES

   D. IDEPTREE

8. **The root object in IDEPTREE can include which of the following? (Choose all that apply.)**

   A. A called program unit

   B. Any database table

   C. A database view

   D. A function that calls other functions

9. **Under the timestamp mode, which value of the two program units is compared when determining if a recompilation is required?**

   A. LAST_DML_TIME

   B. LAST_TIME

   C. LAST_DDL_TIME

   D. LAST_DDL

10. **When working with program units in the same local database, what value should be assigned to the REMOTE_DEPENDENCIES_MODE initialization parameter to cause the database to best determine when recompilation is required?**

    A. TIMESTAMP

    B. INVALID

    C. SIGNATURE

    D. It doesn't matter.

Answers to Chapter Questions

1. C. One is indented and the other is not.

Explanation The IDEPTREE view shows the same basic information as DEPTREE, but shows it in a single column of concatenated information that is indented to clearly show the hierarchical relationships among the rows of information.

2. C. The type of object specified in the NAME column.

Explanation The TYPE column shows the object type of the referring object. The referenced type is listed in the REFERENCED_TYPE column.

3. B. It must be set up in advance in order to be used.

Explanation DEPTREE requires the use of the utldtree.sql utility and the execution of the DEPTREE_FILL procedure before it can be used. It is not necessarily owned by SYS—it can be created within any schema that runs the utldtree.sql utility script.

4. C. A change to the RETURN datatype of the remote function

Explanation The only change listed that causes the function to be flagged under the signature mode is a change to its RETURN datatype. The other changes might cause a recompilation under the timestamp mode, but not under the signature mode. The parameter datatype change from NUMBER to REAL is still within the same numeric family of datatypes.

5. A, B. A: The owner B: Any other schema with appropriate privileges

Explanation The owner can always create a trigger. However, other schemas with the appropriate privileges can also create a trigger on the table and retain ownership of the trigger.

6. D. JGIBBS can create a trigger on the table.

Explanation The granting of privileges via a role works for triggers, but not for procedures, functions, or packages.

7. A. REMOTE_DEPENDENCIES_MODE

Explanation The REMOTE_DEPENDENCIES_MODE initialization parameter can only be set by a schema with the appropriate privileges and is the parameter that you use to change from the default timestamp mode to the signature mode and back.

8. A, D.   A: A called program unit D: A function that calls other functions

Explanation   The root object can be any program unit, but the rest of the tree shows the objects that call the root object.

9. C.   LAST_DDL_TIME

Explanation   The LAST_DDL_TIME, which records the last time a SQL statement was issued on the objects to change their structure, is compared to determine if the referenced program unit has been changed since the referring program unit was last compiled.

10. C.   It doesn't matter.

Explanation   The REMOTE_DEPENDENCIES_MODE initialization parameter only controls remote dependencies. You cannot change the behavior of the database when it comes to automatic recompilation of mutually local database objects.

PART
IV

Practice Exams

CHAPTER
12

Practice Exams

ow it's time to see what you know! Before you take the Oracle Certification exam, take the exams here. Remember—if you don't pass the Oracle Certification exam, you'll have to wait for 30 days before being allowed to take it again, and you'll have to pay the test fee again, which at the time of this writing is $125. Take these exams first—there are three complete exams in this book, and if you fail one, you can take another right away, and reinforce your learning in the process.

The Oracle Certification exams are divided up into topic areas, and each exam has a specific number of questions on each topic. We've recreated that sort of exam structure with the exams in this chapter.

In this chapter, you have 3 full practice exams of 60 questions each. Each of the three exams asks a specific number of questions on each topic area that we've covered in this book.

The exams include questions in the following subject areas:

- Developing stored procedures and functions: 15 questions

- Managing stored procedures and functions: 6 questions

- Managing procedural dependencies: 9 questions

- Developing and using packages: 16 questions

- Developing database triggers: 14 questions

Each exam is followed by the answers to the questions along with an explanation of each answer.

Practice Exam #1

1. **You have stored a function called GET_STATUS in the database with the following header:**

```
FUNCTION GET_STATUS (p_order_id NUMBER, p_option VARCHAR2
DEFAULT NULL)
RETURN VARCHAR2
IS
```

Now you want to create a new procedure and store it in the database. Assuming you've declared all referenced variables, which of the following statements are syntactically acceptable for your new procedure? (Choose all that apply.)

A. v_status := v_priority || get_status(15, NULL);

B. v_status := get_status(15);

C. v_status := get_status(NULL);

D. v_status := get_status(ABS(v_order_id), 'FLAG');

2. **Which of the following statements creates a valid procedure? (Choose all that apply.)**

   A. CREATE OR REPLACE PROCEDURE PROC_TEST IS NULL; END;

   B. CREATE OR REPLACE PROCEDURE PROC_TEST AS BEGIN NULL; END;

   C. CREATE OR REPLACE PROCEDURE TEST IS NULL; END;

   D. CREATE OR REPLACE PROCEDURE TEST IS DECLARE BEGIN NULL; END;

3. **Assuming that the bodies of the following program units pose no problems, which of the following functions can be invoked from within a SQL statement?**

   A. FUNCTION LIST(CABIN_ID NUMBER) RETURN BOOLEAN;

   B. FUNCTION LIST(CABIN_ID CABINS.CABIN_ID%TYPE) RETURN VARCHAR2;

   C. FUNCTION LIST(CABIN_ID CABINS%ROWTYPE) RETURN VARCHAR2

   D. FUNCTION LIST(CABIN_ID CABINS.CABIN_ID%TYPE) RETURN CABINS%NOTFOUND

4. **Consider the following valid procedure header:**

```
PROCEDURE ASSIGN_PURCHASE_ORDER
  (purchase_order_id NUMBER DEFAULT 0,
   order_date        DATE   := SYSDATE,
   supplier_id       SUPPLIERS.SUPPLIER_ID%TYPE DEFAULT 0)
```

   Which of the following PL/SQL statements is *not* a valid call to this procedure? (Choose all that apply.)

   A. ASSIGN_PURCHASE_ORDER;

   B. ASSIGN_PURCHASE_ORDER(supplier_id => 700);

C. ASSIGN_PURCHASE_ORDER('01-JAN-2004');

D. ASSIGN_PURCHASE_ORDER(SEQ_PURCHASE_ORDER_ID.NEXTVAL);

5. **Consider the following function:**

```
FUNCTION ACTIVE_SESSION_COUNT RETURN NUMBER
```

This function does not write to the database or package constructs. You can invoke this function from which of the following? (Choose all that apply.)

A. The WHERE clause of an UPDATE statement

B. The left side of an assignment statement

C. The COLUMN list of an INSERT statement

D. The default value assignment of the parameter of a procedure

6. **Consider the following code sample:**

```
CREATE OR REPLACE FUNCTION BALANCE_LEDGER(account_id NUMBER)
RETURN NUMBER
IS
  v_result BOOLEAN;
BEGIN
  RECONCILE(account_id, v_result);
  IF (v_result) THEN    RETURN '1';
  ELSE                  RETURN '2';
  END IF;
END BALANCE_LEDGER;
```

Which of the following statements is true about this code sample? (Choose all that apply.)

A. It will not compile due to RETURN datatype conflicts.

B. It will compile, but it will not execute due to RETURN datatype conflicts.

C. It will compile, but it will not execute within SQL statements.

D. It will compile and execute.

7. **You submit a statement to the database that starts with the following:**

```
CREATE PROCEDURE PROC_AUDIT (AUDIT_ID AUDITS.AUDIT%TYPE) IS
```

Which of the following statements is guaranteed to be true?

A. The code for this program unit will definitely be stored in the data dictionary.

B. This procedure will definitely have a status of VALID.

C. This procedure will be callable from a SQL statement.

D. None of the above.

8. **The ALTER FUNCTION statement can be used to do which of the following? (Choose all that apply.)**

A. Modify the list of parameters for a function.

B. Change the program unit's processing section.

C. Recompile the program unit's code.

D. Create an overloaded function.

9. **You submit the following statement to the database:**

```
CREATE OR REPLACE FUNCTION CREDIT_CHECK (p_card_id NUMBER)
RETURN VARCHAR2
IS
  CURSOR cur_card_services IS
    SELECT APPROVAL_CODE
    FROM   CARD_SERVICE
    WHERE  CARD_ID = p_card_id;
  v_approval_code CARD_SERVICE.APPROVAL_CODE%TYPE;
BEGIN
  OPEN  cur_card_services;
  FETCH cur_card_services INTO v_approval_code;
  CLOSE cur_card_services;
  RETURN v_approval_code;
END CREDIT_CHECK;
```

Which of the following statements will successfully execute this function from SQL*Plus? (Choose all that apply.)

A. EXEC CREDIT_CHECK(4020);

B. SELECT CREDIT_CHECK(p_card_id=>101) FROM DUAL;

C. BEGIN DBMS_OUTPUT.PUT_LINE(CREDIT_CHECK(101)); END;

D. CREDIT_CHECK(4020);

10. **Which of the following statements describes a difference between a stored database procedure and a stored database function? (Choose all that apply.)**

    A. Procedures are easier to code and invoke than functions.

    B. Functions execute more quickly than procedures.

    C. Functions can be invoked from within a SQL statement; procedures cannot.

    D. Procedures can handle more parameters.

11. **Which of the following is an advantage of a stored database procedure? (Choose all that apply.)**

    A. It runs faster than a stored database function.

    B. It can be invoked by any privileged schema from anywhere on the network.

    C. It can be automatically invoked by any privileged client from anywhere on the operating system network configuration protocol adapter.

    D. When a stored database procedure is executed, all other stored database procedures are automatically loaded so future calls to those procedures will be faster.

12. **You have created a new schema that contains one database object—a table called LEDGER. Assuming that any references to LEDGER are syntactically correct, which of the following statements will successfully execute? (Choose all that apply.)**

    A. PROCEDURE NAME_LEDGER(p_name IN VARCHAR2, p_id IN NUMBER) IS BEGIN UPDATE LEDGER SET NAME = p_name WHERE LEDGER_ID = p_id; END;

    B. REPLACE PROCEDURE NAME_LEDGER(p_name IN VARCHAR2, p_id IN NUMBER) IS BEGIN UPDATE LEDGER SET NAME = p_name WHERE LEDGER_ID = p_id; END;

    C. CREATE PROCEDURE NAME_LEDGER(p_name IN VARCHAR2, p_id IN NUMBER) IS BEGIN UPDATE LEDGER SET NAME = p_name WHERE LEDGER_ID = p_id; END;

    D. CREATE OR REPLACE PROCEDURE NAME_LEDGER(p_name IN VARCHAR2, p_id IN NUMBER) IS BEGIN UPDATE LEDGER SET NAME = p_name WHERE LEDGER_ID = p_id; END;

13. **Assuming that any referenced database objects exist and are valid, which of the following will produce a compilation error? (Choose all that apply.)**

    A. CREATE OR REPLACE FUNCTION DEBIT (account_id NUMBER(3)) RETURN NUMBER IS BEGIN RETURN 1; END;

    B. CREATE OR REPLACE FUNCTION DEBIT RETURN NUMBER IS BEGIN RETURN 1; END;

    C. CREATE OR REPLACE FUNCTION DEBIT (account_id LEDGER.AMOUNT%TYPE) RETURN BOOLEAN IS BEGIN RETURN FALSE; END;

    D. CREATE OR REPLACE FUNCTION DEBIT (account_id BOOLEAN) RETURN VARCHAR2 IS BEGIN RETURN '1'; END;

14. **Consider the following procedure:**

    ```
    PROCEDURE ADD_PORT(new_port_name VARCHAR2)
    IS
    BEGIN
      INSERT INTO PORTS (PORT_ID, PORT_NAME)
      VALUES (SEQ_PORT_ID.NEXTVAL, new_port_name);
      COMMIT;
    END ;
    ```

    Which of the following is a valid call to this procedure from SQL*Plus?

    A. ADD_PORT('Miami');

    B. EXECUTE ADD_PORT('Miami');

    C. SELECT ADD_PORT('Miami') FROM DUAL;

    D. EXECUTE PROCEDURE ADD_PORT('Miami');

15. **You have already successfully compiled and stored a procedure called ADD_LINE_ITEM in the database. Now you want to make a change to the procedure's exception handling section. Which of the following statements will you use to make this change?**

    A. ALTER PROCEDURE

    B. DROP PROCEDURE

    C. CREATE PROCEDURE

    D. CREATE OR REPLACE PROCEDURE

16. Which of the following data dictionary views contains the source code for a stored packaged function?

    A. USER_TEXT

    B. USER_FUNCTIONS

    C. USER_SOURCE

    D. USER_PACKAGES

17. Where in the data dictionary can you find the status of a stored database procedure? (Choose all that apply.)

    A. USER_OBJECTS

    B. USER_PROCEDURES

    C. USER_STATUS

    D. USER_SOURCE

18. Which of the following queries will display the source code of a function called CANCEL_ORDER?

    A. SELECT TEXT FROM USER_SOURCE WHERE NAME = 'CANCEL_ORDER' ORDER BY TEXT;

    B. SELECT TEXT FROM USER_FUNCTIONS WHERE NAME = 'CANCEL_ORDER' ORDER BY LINE_NUMBER;

    C. SELECT TEXT FROM USER_SOURCE WHERE TYPE = 'FUNCTION' AND NAME = 'CANCEL_ORDER' ORDER BY LINE;

    D. SELECT TEXT FROM USER_SOURCE WHERE OBJECT_TYPE = 'FUNCTION' AND NAME = 'CANCEL_ORDER' ORDER BY LINE;

19. You have stored the following procedure in the database schema PROD:

```
PROCEDURE DISEMBARK (p_cruise_leg_id IN NUMBER)
IS
  UPDATE CRUISE_LEGS
    SET STATUS = 'Disembarked'
  WHERE CRUISE_LEG_ID = p_cruise_leg_id;
END;
```

Which of the following statements must be executed from within PROD so that the schema LAUREN can definitely execute the procedure?

    A. GRANT UPDATE ON CRUISE_LEGS TO LAUREN;

    B. GRANT EXECUTE ON DISEMBARK TO LAUREN;

C. Both A and B

D. GRANT PROCEDURE TO LAUREN;

20. **You want to debug a stored database procedure, but temporarily halt the execution in order to inspect the value of some of the variables. Which of the following actions should you take?**

A. Use STEP INTO.

B. Insert a stack.

C. Insert a breakpoint.

D. Use STEP OUT.

21. **You attempt to compile the package body RETRIEVAL_DATA in SQL*Plus and encounter some compilation errors. You log off of the schema and then log back on again in SQL*Plus. Which of the following queries will definitely give you the correct number of errors for this compilation?**

A. SELECT COUNT(SEQUENCE) FROM USER_ERRORS WHERE NAME = 'RETRIEVAL_DATA';

B. SELECT SUM(SEQUENCE) FROM USER_ERRORS WHERE NAME = 'RETRIEVAL_DATA' AND TYPE = 'PACKAGE BODY';

C. SELECT COUNT(*) FROM USER_ERRORS WHERE TYPE = 'PACKAGE BODY' AND NAME = 'RETRIEVAL_DATA';

D. None of the above

22. **In a schema CEMERICK, you create a stored database procedure as follows:**

```
PROCEDURE SETUP IS
BEGIN
   INITIALIZE_RATIOS;
END;
```

This procedure calls another procedure called INITIALIZE_RATIOS, which is a synonym for a procedure stored in another schema. Which of the following data dictionary views will provide you with the name of the schema that owns INITIALIZE_RATIOS?

A. USER_DEPENDENCIES

B. USER_OBJECTS

C. USER_SOURCE

D. USER_ERRORS

23. You have stored the following procedure in your schema:

```
PROCEDURE INITIALIZE_RATIOS IS
BEGIN
  UPDATE RATIO_LIST
    SET A = 100,
        B = 200
  WHERE RATIO_LIST_ID = 1;
END INITIALIZE_RATIOS;
```

With this procedure stored in the database with a status of VALID, you issue the following DDL statement:

```
ALTER TABLE RATIO_LIST ADD C NUMBER(3);
```

What is the status of the procedure after this DDL is executed?

A. VALID

B. INVALID

C. CHANGED

D. NEW

24. In a schema JNELSON, you have created the following procedure:

```
PROCEDURE PURGE_AUDIT IS
BEGIN
  DELETE FROM AUDIT;
END;
```

The schema JNELSON has granted EXECUTE privileges on this procedure to the schema JBAUCHSPIES. Next, in the schema JBAUCHSPIES, you have created the following procedure:

```
PROCEDURE PURGE_ALL IS
BEGIN
    JNELSON.PURGE_AUDIT;
END;
```

Finally, you want to grant the ability to run the procedure PURGE_ALL to a third schema CJONES. Which of the following is the best solution to achieve this result?

A. (From JNELSON) GRANT EXECUTE ON PURGE_AUDIT TO CJONES;

B. (From JBAUCHSPIES) GRANT EXECUTE ON PURGE_ALL TO CJONES;

C. Both A and B

D. (From JBAUCHSPIES) GRANT EXECUTE ON PURGE_ALL TO CJONES CASCADE;

25. **You have created two procedures and stored them in two different schemas. One is called ADD_PORT, which is stored in the schema YACOSTA, and the other is called ASSIGN_CRUISE, which is stored in the schema GWBUSH. The ADD_PORT procedure calls the procedure ASSIGN_CRUISE. What is the easiest way to recompile both of these procedures?**

A. (From YACOSTA) ALTER PROCEDURE ADD_PORT COMPILE;

B. (From GWBUSH) ALTER PROCEDURE ASSIGN_CRUISE COMPILE;

C. Both A and B

D. Neither A or B

26. **Your schema owns a stored procedure with a status of VALID, as follows:**

```
PROCEDURE BACK_PAY (p_paycheck_id IN PAY_HISTORY.PAYCHECK_ID%TYPE,
                    p_amount       IN NUMBER)
IS
BEGIN
  INSERT INTO CK_REGISTER VALUES (p_paycheck_id, p_amount);
END BACK_PAY;
```

Next, you issue the following statement from within your schema:

```
ALTER TABLE PAY_HISTORY ADD STUB VARCHAR2(30);
```

No other change is made to the database. Finally, you attempt to execute your procedure from within SQL*Plus with the following statement:

```
EXEC BACK_PAY(101,5000);
```

What is the result of this attempted execution?

A. The procedure BACK_PAY fails because the procedure has a status of INVALID.

B. The procedure BACK_PAY is recompiled and attempts to execute.

C. The syntax to execute the procedure is wrong.

D. It is impossible to determine from this information.

27. Your schema owns a procedure called ADD_PORT. You know that the procedure references a table in your schema, but you don't know which one. Which of the following data dictionary views can identify the table? (Choose all that apply.)

    A. USER_DEPENDENCIES

    B. USER_SOURCE

    C. USER_OBJECTS

    D. USER_ERRORS

28. Assuming all referenced constructs are valid, which of the following is a valid declaration of a cursor in a package specification?

    A. CURSOR cur_suppliers RETURN SUPPLIERS.LAST_NAME, SUPPLIERS.SUPPLIER_ID;

    B. CURSOR cur_suppliers RETURN SUPPLIERS.LAST_NAME%TYPE;

    C. CURSOR cur_suppliers RETURN SUPPLIERS %ROWTYPE;

    D. CURSOR cur_suppliers RETURN 'SUPPLIER';

29. Consider the following code sample:

```
CREATE OR REPLACE PACKAGE SALES
AS
   PRAGMA RESTRICT_REFERENCES(GET_SALES_RANK,WNDS,RNDS,WNPS,RNPS);
   FUNCTION GET_SALES_RANK(product_number NUMBER) RETURN NUMBER;
END SALES;
```

    Which of the following statements about this code sample is true?

    A. It will not compile.

    B. It will require that the function GET_SALES_RANK does not read or write to the database or other packaged constructs.

    C. This is a package body.

    D. The function cannot be overloaded.

30. You have created a new schema and have only created a stored database package called SUPPLIER_TOOLS, including one function in the package called INCREASE_PRODUCT_PRICE. Which of the following are valid queries against the data dictionary for locating information about your new package?

A. SELECT * FROM USER_PACKAGES WHERE PACKAGE_NAME = 'SUPPLIER_TOOLS';

B. SELECT * FROM USER_SOURCE WHERE NAME = 'INCREASE_PRODUCT_PRICE' AND TYPE = 'FUNCTION';

C. SELECT * FROM USER_OBJECTS WHERE OBJECT_NAME = 'SUPPLIER_TOOLS' AND OBJECT_TYPE = 'PACKAGE SPECIFICATION';

D. SELECT * FROM USER_OBJECTS WHERE OBJECT_NAME = 'SUPPLIER_TOOLS' AND OBJECT_TYPE = 'PACKAGE BODY'

31. **You are creating a package to be stored on the client called GUEST_BOOKING. It contains three public procedures, one private procedure, and a public function. You want to create a single constant called DISCOUNT for use by all of these procedures and functions, and no other package will ever reference DISCOUNT directly. Where is the best place to declare the constant?**

A. In the declaration section of each procedure and function

B. In the package body of a package stored on the database

C. In the package specification of the same package

D. In the package body of the same package

32. **You have created a cursor that is declared in a package specification. Which of the following statements is now true for this cursor? (Choose all that apply.)**

A. You can open the cursor in one PL/SQL block and fetch it in another within the same schema session.

B. The cursor is automatically opened when any package construct is invoked.

C. The cursor name is unique to the schema and cannot be repeated in any other cursor in the schema.

D. The cursor is never closed until the schema session is disconnected.

33. **You have created a stored database package called INVOICING. Which of the following statements will remove the package from the database?**

A. DROP PACKAGE INVOICING;

B. DROP PACKAGE SPECIFICATION INVOICING; DROP PACKAGE BODY INVOICING;

C. DROP PACKAGE BODY INVOICING;

D. DROP PACKAGE SPECIFICATION INVOICING;

34. **Consider the following package specification:**

```
PACKAGE BILLING AS
  PROCEDURE STATUS_ORDERS;
  PROCEDURE PREPARE_INVOICES;
  FUNCTION  GET_INVOICE_STATUS(invoice_id NUMBER) RETURN VARCHAR2;
  PRAGMA RESTRICT_REFERENCES(GET_INVOICE_STATUS, WNDS, RNDS);
END BILLING;
```

How many local functions does this package contain?

A. Cannot be determined

B. Zero

C. One

D. None of the above

35. **Which of the following is a valid purity level? (Choose all that apply.)**

A. WNNS

B. WINS

C. WRPS

D. WNDS

36. **You create a package specification ASSET_MGT with a status of VALID. Next, you create a package body ASSET_MGT with a status of VALID. Finally, you make a change to the package body with a CREATE OR REPLACE PACKAGE BODY ASSET_MGT statement. The result, however, is unsuccessful, and the status of the package body is INVALID. No other statements have been sent to the database. What is the status of the package specification?**

A. VALID

B. INVALID

C. You cannot determine from this question.

D. There is no way to know for sure.

37. **What is the benefit of asserting a function's purity level as WNPS and RNPS?**

A. It assures other schemas that package privileges aren't required.

B. It prevents a function from running local procedures.

C. It depends on the function.

D. It assures schemas in the remote database that they can execute the function.

38. **Assume the existence of a valid table with no records called WORK_SCHEDULE. You submit the following code to the database:**

```
CREATE OR REPLACE PACKAGE STAFFING AS
  p_start_date DATE;
  p_end_date   DATE;
  PROCEDURE SCHEDULE_WORK
    (p_employee_id NUMBER,
     p_ship_id   NUMBER);
END STAFFING;
CREATE OR REPLACE PACKAGE BODY STAFFING AS
  PROCEDURE SCHEDULE_WORK
    (p_employee_id NUMBER,
     p_ship_id   NUMBER) IS
  BEGIN
    INSERT INTO WORK_SCHEDULE
      VALUES (SEQ_WORK_SCHEDULE_ID.NEXTVAL,
              p_employee_id, p_ship_id,
              p_start_date,  p_end_date);
  END SCHEDULE_WORK;
  BEGIN
  p_start_date := SYSDATE;
  p_end_date   := SYSDATE + 7;
END STAFFING;
```

Next, you issue the following statement:

```
EXEC STAFFING.SCHEDULE_WORK(101,12);
```

Which of the following statements is now true? (Choose all that apply.)

A. The packaged construct p_start_date is a private variable.

B. The value of p_start_date is equal to SYSDATE.

C. The code won't work.

D. None of the above.

39. Which of the following program units share the same namespace? (Choose all that apply.)

   A. Database triggers and stored functions

   B. Stored packages in one schema and stored procedures in another schema

   C. Stored procedures and stored functions within the same schema

   D. Local procedures and local functions

40. You are creating a package called PURCHASING and want to make sure that every procedure and function in this package is restricted to never making any changes to the database unless explicitly authorized. Which of the following statements in the package specification will help ensure this?

   A. PRAGMA RESTRICT_REFERENCES(DEFAULT,WNDS);

   B. PRAGMA RESTRICT_REFERENCES(PURCHASING,WNDS);

   C. PRAGMA RESTRICT_REFERENCES(WNDS);

   D. PRAGMA RESTRICT_REFERENCES(ALL,WNDS);

41. You decide to create a package called SHIP_MAINTENANCE. As your first step, you issue the following statement:

```
CREATE OR REPLACE PACKAGE BODY SHIP_MAINTENANCE AS
  PROCEDURE CHECK_SUPPLIES IS
  BEGIN
    SUPPLIERS.SUPPLY_CHECK;
  END CHECK_SUPPLIES;
END SHIP_MAINTENANCE;
```

Assuming that this code compiles successfully, which of the following statements is definitely true? (Choose all that apply.)

   A. The procedure CHECK_SUPPLIES is public.

   B. The procedure CHECK_SUPPLIES is private.

   C. The package body SHIP_MAINTENANCE has a status of VALID.

   D. The package body SHIP_MAINTENANCE has a status of INVALID.

42. Your current application demands that you create a set of global PL/SQL variables for your schema. These variables need to be initialized, but the logic required is rather complex. Which of the following is the best solution?

A. Create a package initialization section.

B. Create a packaged procedure that is always called first by your application.

C. Create a database trigger.

D. Create a default value for each variable.

43. You have created a stored database package with the following specification:

```
PACKAGE BILLING AS
  PROCEDURE STATUS_ORDERS;
  PROCEDURE PREPARE_INVOICES;
  FUNCTION  GET_INVOICE_STATUS(invoice_id NUMBER) RETURN VARCHAR2;
  PRAGMA RESTRICT_REFERENCES(GET_INVOICE_STATUS, WNDS, RNDS);
END BILLING;
```

This package is owned by the schema JWATERS. Another schema LRUSS needs to execute the procedure PREPARE_INVOICES in this package. Which of the following statements issued by JWATERS will grant LRUSS the necessary privileges? (Choose all that apply.)

A. GRANT EXECUTE ON BILLING TO LRUSS;

B. GRANT EXECUTE ON BILLING.PREPARE_INVOICES TO LRUSS;

C. None of the above—you need more information.

D. It cannot be done.

44. Assuming that any referenced database objects are properly declared and properly referenced, which of the following is *not* a valid statement? (Choose all that apply.)

A. CREATE OR REPLACE TRIGGER TRIG_SUPPLIER_AUDIT BEFORE OR AFTER INSERT ON SUPPLIERS BEGIN INSERT INTO SUPPLIER_AUDIT VALUES (AUDIT_ID.NEXTVAL, SYSDATE, USER); END;

B. CREATE OR REPLACE TRIGGER TRIG_SUPPLIER_AUDIT BEFORE INSERT OR UPDATE ON SUPPLIERS BEGIN INSERT INTO SUPPLIER_AUDIT VALUES (AUDIT_ID.NEXTVAL, SYSDATE, USER); END;

C. CREATE OR REPLACE TRIGGER TRIG_SUPPLIER_AUDIT BEFORE SELECT OR UPDATE ON SUPPLIERS BEGIN INSERT INTO SUPPLIER_AUDIT VALUES (AUDIT_ID.NEXTVAL, SYSDATE, USER); END;

D. CREATE OR REPLACE TRIGGER TRIG_SUPPLIER_AUDIT BEFORE INSERT OR UPDATE OR DELETE ON SUPPLIERS BEGIN INSERT INTO SUPPLIER_AUDIT VALUES (AUDIT_ID.NEXTVAL, SYSDATE, USER); END;

45. **You have created the following database triggers:**

```
CREATE OR REPLACE TRIGGER TRIG_01
  BEFORE INSERT ON CRUISE_TYPES
  BEGIN
    AUDIT_CRUISE_TYPES;
  END;
CREATE OR REPLACE TRIGGER TRIG_02
  BEFORE INSERT ON CRUISE_TYPES
  BEGIN
    VALIDATE_USER;
  END;
```

When an INSERT statement is issued on the CRUISE_TYPES table, which trigger is fired first?

A. TRIG_01, because it was created first.

B. TRIG_02, because it was created last.

C. TRIG_01, because it is alphabetically first.

D. The answer cannot be determined.

46. **Consider the following trigger header:**

```
TRIGGER AUDIT_SCHEDULE BEFORE INSERT ON WORK_SCHEDULE
```

Which of the following commands will remove this trigger from the database?

A. DROP TRIGGER AUDIT_SCHEDULE;

B. DELETE TRIGGER AUDIT_SCHEDULE;

C. ALTER TABLE WORK_SCHEDULE DROP ALL TRIGGERS;

D. ALTER TABLE WORK_SCHEDULE DISABLE ALL TRIGGERS;

47. You have already created a trigger called AUDIT_SCHEDULE on the table WORK_SCHEDULE. You decide to modify the code in this trigger. Which of the following commands will you use?

    A. ALTER TRIGGER AUDIT_SCHEDULE

    B. ALTER TABLE WORK_SCHEDULE MODIFY AUDIT_SCHEDULE

    C. CREATE TRIGGER AUDIT_SCHEDULE

    D. CREATE OR REPLACE TRIGGER AUDIT_SCHEDULE

48. You have created the following two triggers:

```
TRIGGER AUDIT_SCHEDULE
BEFORE INSERT ON WORK_SCHEDULE
FOR EACH ROW
BEGIN
  INSERT INTO AUDIT_RECORD VALUES
    (SEQ_AUDIT_RECORD_ID.NEXTVAL, USER);
END AUDIT_SCHEDULE;

TRIGGER AUDIT_CHANGES
BEFORE INSERT ON WORK_SCHEDULE
BEGIN
  INSERT INTO AUDIT_CHANGES VALUES
    (SEQ_AUDIT_CHANGE_ID.NEXTVAL, USER);
END AUDIT_CHANGES;
```

    You then issue the following valid DML statement to the database:

```
INSERT INTO WORK_SCHEDULE VALUES
  (SEQ_WORK_SCHEDULE_ID.NEXTVAL, 101, SYSDATE);
```

    Which trigger fires first?

    A. AUDIT_SCHEDULE

    B. AUDIT_CHANGES

    C. Both triggers fire simultaneously.

    D. You cannot know for sure.

49. Which of the following data dictionary views contains the source code for a database trigger?

    A. USER_TEXT

    B. USER_TRIGGERS

C. USER_SOURCE

D. USER_OBJECTS

50. **Which of the following statements is permitted in a trigger? (Choose all that apply.)**

A. SELECT

B. CREATE TABLE

C. COMMIT

D. SAVEPOINT

51. **You have created a trigger called TRIG1 that is a BEFORE CREATE ON SCHEMA trigger and is owned by a schema ADESOLLAR. When does it fire?**

A. On all CREATE events that occur within the schema ADESOLLAR

B. On most CREATE events that occur within the schema ADESOLLAR

C. On all schema-level CREATE events that occur within any schema in the database

D. On most schema-level CREATE events that occur within any schema in the database

52. **For which of the following database events can you create a trigger? (Choose all that apply.)**

A. SQLERROR

B. STARTUP

C. CONNECT INTERNAL

D. CREATE DATABASE

53. **You log onto the schema SSMITH and create the following trigger:**

```
TRIGGER AUDIT_SCHEDULE
BEFORE INSERT ON WORK_SCHEDULE
FOR EACH ROW
BEGIN
  INSERT INTO AUDIT_RECORD VALUES
    (SEQ_AUDIT_RECORD_ID.NEXTVAL, USER);
END AUDIT_SCHEDULE;
```

This is the only trigger in the schema. How many records are in the USER_TRIGGERS data dictionary view for SSMITH?

A. One

B. Seven

C. You cannot tell from this information.

D. None of the above

54. **Which of the following are conditional predicates?**

A. :NEW, :OLD

B. BEFORE and AFTER

C. INSERTING, UPDATING, and DELETING

D. There is no such thing.

55. **You have created a trigger with the following header:**

```
TRIGGER TRIG1
AFTER DELETE ON PURCHASE_ORDER
FOR EACH ROW
```

For the purpose of this trigger's processing section, PURCHASE_ORDER is considered

A. A view

B. A trigger target

C. A mutating table

D. A constraining table

56. **You have created a trigger that fires BEFORE INSERT OR UPDATE ON EMPLOYEES. Which of the following IF statements will be TRUE only when an INSERT statement fires the trigger?**

A. IF INSERT = TRUE THEN

B. IF INSERTING THEN

C. IF :NEW = TRUE THEN

D. IF :NEW.INSERTING THEN

57. **Consider the following trigger header:**

```
TRIGGER TRACK_CHANGES
AFTER UPDATE OF END_DATE ON CRUISE_LEGS
```

What is END_DATE?

A. A mutating table

B. A conditional predicate

C. A database table column

D. A database table

58. **Consider the following trigger:**

```
TRIGGER EMP_AUDIT
BEFORE UPDATE ON EMPLOYEES
FOR EACH ROW
BEGIN
  :NEW.UPDATE_DATE := SYSDATE;
  :NEW.UPDATE_USER := USER;
END;
```

Now consider the following UPDATE statement:

```
UPDATE EMPLOYEES SET SALARY = 100000 WHERE EMPLOYEE_ID = 123;
```

At the end of this statement, what is the value for the UPDATE_DATE column in the EMPLOYEES table for the record where EMPLOYEE_ID = 123?

A. The system date as defined on the server at the time of the UPDATE statement

B. NULL

C. Unchanged from what it was before the UPDATE statement

D. The system date as defined on the client at the time of the UPDATE statement

59. **You are logged into the schema JCONNELLY with the privilege CREATE ANY TRIGGER. On which of the following can you create a BEFORE UPDATE trigger? (Choose all that apply.)**

A. A table in the same schema

B. A table in another schema for which JCONNELLY has the UPDATE privilege

C. A table in another schema, regardless of what privilege for that table has been granted to JCONNELLY

D. A view in the same schema

60. **You are logged into the schema PICABO. On which of the following can you create an INSTEAD OF trigger? (Choose all that apply.)**

   A. A table in the same schema

   B. A table in another schema for which PICABO has the SELECT privilege

   C. A table in another schema, regardless of what privilege has been granted to PICABO

   D. A view in the same schema

Answers to Practice Exam #1

  1. A, B, C, D. A: v_status := v_priority || get_status(15, NULL);
                              B: v_status := get_status(15);
                              C: v_status := get_status(NULL);
                              D: v_status := get_status(ABS(v_order_id), 'FLAG');

Explanation   All of the answers are acceptable.

  2. B. CREATE OR REPLACE PROCEDURE PROC_TEST AS BEGIN NULL; END;

Explanation   The keyword BEGIN is required in a procedure. The keyword IS normally follows the procedure name, but the keyword AS is also accepted. The name of the procedure can be any valid identifier name. The inclusion of a prefix to differentiate this program unit as a procedure as opposed to a function or something else is strictly a design choice. Of the other choices, A and C are both missing the keyword BEGIN. D includes the keyword DECLARE, which is never accepted in a procedure. Instead, if you have elements that must be declared, simply declare them after the keyword IS (or AS) and before the keyword BEGIN.

  3. B. FUNCTION LIST(CABIN_ID CABINS.CABIN_ID%TYPE) RETURN VARCHAR2;

Explanation   Only B can be validly invoked from within a SQL statement. A cannot because it returns a BOOLEAN value, which is not recognized in SQL. C cannot because of the %ROWTYPE variable, which does not exist in SQL. D is unacceptable because of the use of %NOTFOUND, which is nonsense in this context. %NOTFOUND is a cursor attribute, and no cursor is allowed in this context.

4. C.   ASSIGN_PURCHASE_ORDER('01-JAN-2004');

Explanation   Because the procedure has declared default values for each parameter, none of the parameters are required. A is an acceptable statement. B is valid because it uses the pass-by reference format and supplies a valid value for the supplier_id parameter. D is valid because it provides a sequence-generated number as the parameter value of the first parameter, which is PURCHASE_ORDER_ID. However, the correct answer is C, which is not a valid call due to the single value of a string containing a date value. This value is assumed to be the first parameter value, which requires a numeric value, and even an automatic datatype conversion will fail on this parameter value.

5. A, D.   A: The WHERE clause of an UPDATE statement D: The default value assignment of the parameter of a procedure

Explanation   B is wrong because function calls cannot be the target of an assignment statement. Function calls could, however, be on the right side of an assignment statement. C is not acceptable because an INSERT statement's column list must list columns, not functions. A is acceptable—any WHERE clause of a Data Manipulation Language (DML) statement is a valid location for a function call. D is valid—the function will resolve and return its value as the default value.

6. D.   It will compile and execute.

Explanation   This function will compile and execute fine. Although it's true that it's returning string values when it's declared to return numeric values, Procedural Language/Structured Query Language (PL/SQL) will be able to successfully perform an automatic datatype conversion on these string values to numeric values. Furthermore, because the parameters and return datatypes are all valid SQL datatypes, there is no reason why this function can't execute from within SQL statements.

7. D.   None of the above.

Explanation   This procedure does not use the OR REPLACE option of the CREATE PROCEDURE statement. If it did, you could have selected A because the program unit would definitely be stored in the data dictionary. However, without OR REPLACE, the attempt may be rejected altogether in the event that an existing program unit of the same name in the same namespace happens to exist. B is incorrect since the code of the procedure influences whether or not the procedure is assigned a status of VALID or INVALID. C is not true since no procedure is callable from a SQL statement.

8. C.   Recompile the program unit's code.

Explanation   The ALTER FUNCTION is used with the COMPILE clause to recompile code that is already stored in the data dictionary. To change the parameter list of a processing section, you must use the CREATE OR REPLACE FUNCTION statement. You cannot create an overloaded stored function; you can only create overloaded packaged functions or local functions.

9. C.   BEGIN DBMS_OUTPUT.PUT_LINE(CREDIT_CHECK(101)); END;

Explanation   A is not valid because the EXEC, or EXECUTE, statement is for procedures, not functions. B isn't correct because passing parameters by reference doesn't work from within SQL statements. D is wrong—this is the syntax for invoking procedures, but only from within a PL/SQL block, not as a stand-alone SQL*Plus command-line statement. C is correct.

10. C.   Functions can be invoked from within a SQL statement; procedures cannot.

Explanation   Functions can be called as part of an expression. This includes several of the clauses of various SQL statements, such as the WHERE clause of a SELECT, UPDATE, or DELETE statement, or a SELECT statement's column list or ORDER BY clause.

11. B.   It can be invoked by any privileged schema from anywhere on the network.

Explanation   A is wrong—procedures have no inherent speed advantage over stored database functions. C is wrong—I'm not even sure what that means and I'm the one who made it up! D is only true for program units stored within a single package—the entire package is loaded when a single package construct is invoked, but this doesn't apply to stand-alone stored database procedures. B is true.

12. C, D.   C: CREATE PROCEDURE NAME_LEDGER(p_name IN VARCHAR2, p_id IN NUMBER) IS BEGIN UPDATE LEDGER SET NAME = p_name WHERE LEDGER_ID = p_id; END;
D: CREATE OR REPLACE PROCEDURE NAME_LEDGER(p_name IN VARCHAR2, p_id IN NUMBER) IS BEGIN UPDATE LEDGER SET NAME = p_name WHERE LEDGER_ID = p_id; END;

Explanation   A does not work as an executable statement. It could be used within a package specification, but not as a stand-alone statement. B is syntactically incomplete. C works as long as there is not a procedure named NAME_LEDGER already in place, which the question clarifies to be true. D is acceptable even if NAME_LEDGER already exists.

13. A.   CREATE OR REPLACE FUNCTION DEBIT (account_id NUMBER(3))
RETURN NUMBER IS BEGIN RETURN 1; END;

Explanation   A produces a compilation error because of the parameter datatype
NUMBER(3), which should simply be NUMBER. The other statements are all valid.

14. B.   EXECUTE ADD_PORT('Miami');

Explanation   A is wrong because the procedure name on a line by itself doesn't
work within SQL*Plus—that only works as a part of a PL/SQL block. C is wrong for
procedures, but would be correct if this were a function. D includes the incorrectly
placed keyword PROCEDURE. B is correct.

15. D.   CREATE OR REPLACE PROCEDURE

Explanation   The ALTER PROCEDURE statement can be used to recompile the
code that already exists in the database, but if you want to change that code, you
must use the CREATE OR REPLACE PROCEDURE statement and include the entire
procedure code, including the modified portion you want to include. DROP
PROCEDURE can be used to remove the procedure from the database. CREATE
PROCEDURE does not work on this program unit because it already exists in the
database.

16. C.   USER_SOURCE

Explanation   All source code for stored procedures, functions, and packages are
stored in USER_SOURCE and can be found in the TEXT column of that data
dictionary view. The other answers are fictitious views that don't exist.

17. A.   USER_OBJECTS

Explanation   There is no data dictionary view called USER_PROCEDURES or
USER_STATUS. USER_SOURCE contains the source code for stored database
procedures, functions, and packages, but it doesn't contain any information about
status, which is kept in the USER_OBJECTS view.

18. C.   SELECT TEXT FROM USER_SOURCE WHERE TYPE = 'FUNCTION'
AND NAME = 'CANCEL_ORDER' ORDER BY LINE;

Explanation   A is incorrect because there is no provision in the WHERE clause to
limit the search to functions. The USER_SOURCE data dictionary view also contains
source code for procedures and packages. B is incorrect because there is no column
called LINE_NUMBER. D is incorrect because the column OBJECT_TYPE is not in
the USER_SOURCE view (it is in the USER_OBJECTS view). C is correct.

19. B. GRANT EXECUTE ON DISEMBARK TO LAUREN;

Explanation Only B is required. When you grant EXECUTE privileges on a procedure, the grantee does not need additional privileges in order for the procedure to execute successfully. In this example, the grantee does not need separate privileges to update on the table CRUISE_LEGS, but it also does not receive those separate privileges either. LAUREN will be able to execute the procedure successfully and nothing more. D is not a valid statement.

20. C. Insert a stack.

Explanation The PL/SQL debugger enables you to insert a breakpoint to temporarily halt execution and inspect variables and other aspects of the program unit's execution. The STEP OUT or STEP INTO operations can be performed once the breakpoint is encountered, and the stack, which cannot be inserted, is how you can see the hierarchical display of program unit calls.

21. C. SELECT COUNT(*) FROM USER_ERRORS WHERE TYPE = 'PACKAGE BODY' AND NAME = 'RETRIEVAL_DATA';

Explanation A would work if and only if the package specification didn't produce an error message—because the query doesn't include WHERE TYPE = 'PACKAGE BODY', the package specification might accidentally be included in that query. B is wrong because of the use of SUM on the SEQUENCE column. The SEQUENCE column shows the number of the error message for the program unit, starting with 1, continuing with 2, 3, and so on until the complete list of error messages is numbered. D is wrong because the answer is C, which counts the number of records in the view, and there is one record per error in the view.

22. A. USER_DEPENDENCIES

Explanation The USER_DEPENDENCIES view displays one row for each dependent relationship for this procedure and includes a column called REFERENCED_OWNER, which indicates which schema owns the dependent reference. The other data dictionary views exist, but do not provide this information.

23. B. INVALID

Explanation Once any dependent object is altered, even if the change doesn't materially affect the procedure, the procedure is nevertheless marked as having a status of INVALID. The only other option for status is VALID.

24. B.   (From JBAUCHSPIES) GRANT EXECUTE ON PURGE_ALL TO CJONES;

Explanation   The procedure PURGE_ALL resides in a schema that has all of the privileges it requires to execute this procedure. Therefore, the granting of EXECUTE privileges on this procedure automatically grants all the required privileges that are required to go with this procedure—no more and no less.

25. A.   (From YACOSTA) ALTER PROCEDURE ADD_PORT COMPILE;

Explanation   The action of issuing an ALTER statement on one procedure automatically invokes an attempt to compile all called program units, even those owned by other schemas.

26. B.   The BACK_PAY procedure is recompiled and attempts to execute.

Explanation   Even though the ALTER statement changed the procedure's status to INVALID, the next attempt to execute the procedure will automatically recompile the procedure. Given that the ALTER statement has no logical impact on the procedure, the recompilation will be successful and the procedure will execute.

27. A, B.   A: USER_DEPENDENCIES
B: USER_SOURCE

Explanation   The USER_DEPENDENCIES view shows all objects referenced by your procedure, including tables. The USER_SOURCE view contains the entire source code of your procedure, which you could scan for the table references. The other views won't help you locate the referenced table.

28. C.   CURSOR cur_ suppliers RETURN SUPPLIERS %ROWTYPE;

Explanation   The requirement of a RETURN clause in a publicly declared cursor is that it must return a %ROWTYPE variable or a programmer-defined record type. Only C does this.

29. A.   It will not compile.

Explanation   The PRAGMA RESTRICT_REFERENCES specifically names the function GET_SALES_RANK. Therefore, the PRAGMA declaration must follow the function header, and this code sample produces the error "PLS-00115: this PRAGMA must follow the declaration of GET_SALES_RANK." However, once the code sample is edited so that the PRAGMA properly follows the function, B will be true.

30. D.   SELECT * FROM USER_OBJECTS WHERE OBJECT_NAME = 'SUPPLIER_TOOLS' AND OBJECT_TYPE = 'PACKAGE BODY';

Explanation A is incorrect because there is no data dictionary view called USER_PACKAGES. B is incorrect because the packaged function is not recognized as a separate entry in the data dictionary; only the package specification and the package body are recognized. C is incorrect because the object type of PACKAGE SPECIFICATION is never used in the data dictionary; instead, a package specification is identified as PACKAGE. D is correct because the package body is shown with the type of PACKAGE BODY.

31. D. In the package body of the same package

Explanation Because the constant will never be referenced from outside of the package, it should be made private, which means that you should define it within the package body of the same package. A is not entirely wrong—it's just not the best approach. B won't work at all because putting the constant declaration in the package body of a different package has the effect of making the constant private to that other package, and your GUEST_BOOKING package won't be able to reference it. C would work, but it isn't the best choice because it would make the DISCOUNT constant public and thereby accessible to other packages— you don't need that. You should always declare package constructs at their lowest necessary level.

32. A. You can open the cursor in one PL/SQL block and fetch it in another within the same schema session.

Explanation The cursor is a public global cursor and can be invoked across multiple PL/SQL blocks within the same schema session. B is not true; this would only be true if the cursor were explicitly opened in the package initialization section. C and D are not true at all.

33. A. DROP PACKAGE INVOICING;

Explanation The package consists of two parts, the package specification and the package body, both of which are dropped with the statement in answer A. There is no DROP PACKAGE SPECIFICATION statement. There is, on the other hand, a DROP PACKAGE BODY statement, but that statement leaves the package specification in place.

34. A. Cannot be determined

Explanation Local functions are defined in the declaration section of a procedure or function, which is included in the package body, not in the package specification.

35. D. WNDS

Explanation The only answer that is valid is D, which is the purity level for Writes No Database State (WNDS). The other answers are made up.

36. A.   VALID

Explanation   Because the package specification was valid to begin with, it is still valid. No change to a package body can result in a change to the package specification status.

37. D.   It assures schemas in remote database that they can execute the function.

Explanation   The WNPS is the Writes No Package State and the RNPS is the Reads No Package State. Remote database objects that are granted EXECUTE privileges on the function are not automatically granted the appropriate privileges for packaged constructs that the function might reference. These purity levels assure the user of the function that there are no packaged constructs involved.

38. B.   The value of p_start_date is equal to SYSDATE.

Explanation   The package is fine and will compile with a status of VALID. Then, when the EXEC statement is issued, the act of invoking a packaged construct— which is the procedure SCHEDULE_WORK in this case—has the effect of executing the package initialization section in the package body, which initializes the public packaged constructs p_start_date and p_end_date to SYSDATE and SYSDATE+7, respectively. This initialization completes before the procedure SCHEDULE_WORK is executed so that the INSERT statement executes after p_start_date is initialized to SYSDATE.

39. C.   Stored procedures and stored functions within the same schema

Explanation   A is wrong because database triggers have their own namespace. B is wrong because the namespaces for program units do not cross schemas, but instead are contained within schemas. C is correct because stored procedures, functions, and packages within a single namespace all share a single namespace together. D is wrong. You can name a local procedure the same as a local function within the same block; they do not share the same namespace.

40. A.   PRAGMA RESTRICT_REFERENCES(DEFAULT,WNDS);

Explanation   The DEFAULT keyword sets the default purity level for the package. You can also issue explicit PRAGMA RESTRICT_REFERENCES statements that name any individual procedure or function to override the default. B establishes the purity level for the package initialization section, not the procedures or functions. C is not valid, and D would only establish the purity level for a procedure or function named ALL. The keyword ALL is not in the PRAGMA RESTRICT_REFERENCES statement.

41. D.   The package body SHIP_MAINTENANCE has a status of INVALID.

Explanation   Without the package specification, no package body can be compiled with a status of VALID. Also, without a package specification, it's impossible to know if any procedure or function in the package body is public or private.

42. A.   Create a package initialization section.

Explanation   The package initialization section automatically executes whenever any package construct is invoked and is ideal for performing a complex initialization of any packaged variables. B would technically work, but it places a burden on the developers and is not dependable. C isn't relevant here and D is limited to simple logic. Complex initialization cannot be accomplished with this approach.

43. A.   GRANT EXECUTE ON BILLING TO LRUSS;

Explanation   You cannot selectively grant privileges on one portion of a package. You grant the entire package to a schema.

44. A, C.   A: CREATE OR REPLACE TRIGGER TRIG_SUPPLIER_AUDIT BEFORE OR AFTER INSERT ON SUPPLIERS BEGIN INSERT INTO SUPPLIER_AUDIT VALUES (AUDIT_ID.NEXTVAL, SYSDATE, USER); END;
C: CREATE OR REPLACE TRIGGER TRIG_SUPPLIER_AUDIT BEFORE SELECT OR UPDATE ON SUPPLIERS BEGIN INSERT INTO SUPPLIER_AUDIT VALUES (AUDIT_ID.NEXTVAL, SYSDATE, USER); END;

Explanation   A is wrong because of the BEFORE OR AFTER clause—you can only create a trigger BEFORE, or AFTER, but you cannot create a single trigger for both. C is not valid because of BEFORE SELECT. Triggers cannot be created on SELECT statements.

45. D.   The answer cannot be determined.

Explanation   For two or more triggers at the same database event, which in this case is BEFORE INSERT, the firing order is randomly assigned at execution time.

46. A.   DROP TRIGGER AUDIT_SCHEDULE;

Explanation   B and C are syntactically incorrect. D disables the trigger, but leaves it in the database. A is correct.

47. D.   CREATE OR REPLACE TRIGGER AUDIT_SCHEDULE

Explanation   Just like with procedures, functions, and packages, triggers are modified with the CREATE OR REPLACE TRIGGER command.

48. B.   AUDIT_CHANGES

Explanation   The AUDIT_CHANGES trigger is a FOR EACH STATEMENT trigger by default, whereas the AUDIT_SCHEDULE trigger is declared as a FOR EACH ROW trigger instead. Both are BEFORE INSERT so the FOR EACH STATEMENT trigger fires first, which is the AUDIT_CHANGES trigger.

49. B.   USER_TRIGGERS

Explanation   The source code for triggers is stored in the database dictionary view USER_TRIGGERS. Each individual trigger is a single record in that view. The USER_SOURCE view is for procedures, functions, and packages, and USER_OBJECTS contains a single line entry for each program unit, including triggers, but it does not contain the source code.

50. A.   SELECT

Explanation   Data Definition Language (DDL) statements cannot be issued from within PL/SQL program units. (However, the DBMS_SQL package can be used to achieve the same result without issuing explicit DDL statements.) Transaction controls, including COMMIT, SAVEPOINT, and ROLLBACK, are also not permitted. DML statements are allowed so A is correct.

51. B.   On most CREATE events that occur within the ADESOLLAR schema

Explanation   The trigger option ON SCHEMA is appropriate for DDL events that occur within the specific schema. The alternative to ON SCHEMA is ON DATABASE, which is how you would trigger DDL events in any schema within the database. However, BEFORE CREATE does not trigger on the CREATE DATABASE or the CREATE CONTROLFILE events.

52. B.   STARTUP

Explanation   The only event in this list that is valid is STARTUP. Although it's possible to write a trigger that fires on CREATE statements, the CREATE DATABASE statement never fires a trigger. Other valid options for triggers on database events include SHUTDOWN, LOGON, LOGOFF, and SERVERERROR.

53. A.   One

Explanation   The USER_TRIGGERS view contains one row per trigger you create.

54. C.   INSERTING, UPDATING, and DELETING

Explanation   The conditional predicates are BOOLEAN values defined by the system to identify the event that fires the trigger. They can be very helpful in a single trigger that is fired by two or more events so that you can determine which event fired the trigger, for example, in an IF statement.

55. C.   A mutating table

Explanation   PURCHASE_ORDER is a table, not a view—you can create INSTEAD OF triggers on views, but not AFTER DELETE triggers. Because the trigger is a FOR EACH ROW trigger, the PURCHASE_ORDER table is considered as mutating for the trigger's processing section, which means that it is in the midst of being changed. The change isn't done yet and therefore the trigger's processing section cannot read to or write from this table.

56. B.   IF INSERTING THEN

Explanation   The conditional predicate INSERTING is TRUE if the triggering event is an INSERT statement. The other options are all invalid.

57. C.   A database table column

Explanation   The END_DATE column of the CRUISE_LEGS table specifically is being triggered in this situation. Only UPDATE statements that modify the END_DATE column fire this trigger. Any other UPDATE statements do not fire this trigger, even if they're on the CRUISE_LEGS table.

58. A.   The system date as defined on the server at the time of the UPDATE statement

Explanation   Even though the UPDATE statement doesn't explicitly set the value of CREATE_DATE, nevertheless the :NEW.UPDATE_DATE reference forces the UPDATE statement to modify the UPDATE_DATE column with a new incoming value. The SYSDATE will definitely be drawn from the server because database triggers are, by definition, stored and executed on the server, regardless of where the UPDATE statement may be sent from.

59. A, B.   A: A table in the same schema B: A table in another schema for which JCONNELLY has the UPDATE privilege

Explanation   The BEFORE UPDATE trigger is intended for use with tables, not views. Because the schema has the CREATE ANY TRIGGER privilege, any table to which the schema has the appropriate DML privileges is a candidate for a BEFORE UPDATE trigger.

60. D.   A view in the same schema

Explanation   The INSTEAD OF trigger can only be created for a view.

Practice Exam #2

1. **Consider the following code sample:**

```
CREATE OR REPLACE FUNCTION GET_SHIP_COUNT
RETURN NUMBER IS
  v_ships NUMBER;
BEGIN
  RETURN v_ships;
  SELECT COUNT(*) INTO v_ships FROM SHIPS;
END;
```

   Which of the following statements best describes what will happen when this statement is executed in SQL*Plus?

   A. It will create a function called GET_SHIP_COUNT with a status of INVALID because of the SELECT statement.

   B. It will not compile because the RETURN statement is not the last statement.

   C. It will create a function called GET_SHIP_COUNT and overwrite any preexisting function or procedure of the same name.

   D. It will create a function called GET_SHIP_COUNT and overwrite any preexisting function of the same name.

2. **You create a stored database function with the following header and declaration section:**

```
FUNCTION LEADING_PRODUCT (mon_of_sale VARCHAR2)
RETURN VARCHAR2 IS
  tot_sales NUMBER(5);
  prod_name VARCHAR2(30);
BEGIN
```

   Which of the following is a valid RETURN statement to include in the processing section of the function? (Choose all that apply.)

   A. RETURN tot_sales;

   B. RETURN prod_name;

   C. RETURN TRUE;

   D. RETURN CRUISES%ROWTYPE;

3. Assume that the database has a table called **CRUISES** with a column called **SHIP_ID**. Which of the following is a valid datatype for a parameter in a stored database function? (Choose all that apply.)

   A. NUMBER

   B. VARCHAR2(30)

   C. CRUISES.SHIP_ID%TYPE

   D. CRUISES%ROWTYPE

4. In a stored database procedure, which of the following can you *not* call?

   A. Another stored database procedure

   B. A stored database function

   C. A client-side procedure

   D. A variable declared in a stored database package specification

5. You have created a client-side function in an Oracle Form that returns a value of datatype VARCHAR2. From where can you call this function?

   A. From a SQL statement in a client-side procedure in the same Oracle Form

   B. From an IF comparison expression in a stored database procedure

   C. From the right side of an assignment statement in a client-side procedure in the same Oracle Form

   D. From the processing section of a client-side function in a different client

6. Which of the following statements will remove the stored database function **PORT_STATS**?

   A. DROP OR REPLACE FUNCTION PORT_STATS;

   B. CREATE OR REPLACE FUNCTION PORT_STATS NULL;

   C. DROP FUNCTION PROT_STATS;

   D. DELETE FUNCTION PROT_STATS;

7. Assume the following function header:

```
FUNCTION PROCESS_REQUEST(guest_id NUMBER, cruise_name VARCHAR2)
RETURN VARCHAR2 IS
```

Assuming that any referenced variables are properly declared, which of the following is a valid call to this function?

A. v_result := process_request(cruise_name =>'Tropical', guest_id => 77);

B. process_request(77, 'Tropical');

C. SELECT process_request(guest_id => 77, 'Tropical' FROM DUAL);

D. None of the above

8. **You have created a procedure with the following header:**

```
PROCEDURE SHIPMENTS (SHIP_DATE OUT DATE);
```

Assuming that any referenced variables are properly declared, which of the following is a valid call to this procedure?

A. ship_date := shipments();

B. shipments(SYSDATE);

C. shipments('24-MAY-2004');

D. None of the above

9. **Which of the following is *not* a valid parameter declaration?**

A. parm1 NUMBER(3)

B. parm1 OUT VARCHAR2 := 'DeSollar'

C. parm1 VARCHAR2 DEFAULT 'DeSollar'

D. parm1 IN BOOLEAN;

10. **You have a stored function called SHIP_DOCK with no parameters that returns BOOLEAN in a schema MSALZBERG, which owns no stored procedures. Next, you issue this command:**

```
CREATE OR REPLACE PROCEDURE SHIP_DOCK(p_ship_id NUMBER) IS
BEGIN
  UPDATE SHIPS SET STATUS = 'DOCK' WHERE SHIP_ID = p_ship_id;
END SHIP_DOCK;
```

Which of the following statements best describes the result?

A. The procedure is created, stored in the data dictionary, and given a status of INVALID. The function remains in the data dictionary.

B. The procedure is created, stored in the data dictionary, and given a status of VALID.

C. The ORA-00955 message "name is already used by an existing object" appears.

D. The procedure is created, stored in the data dictionary, and given a status of INVALID. The function no longer exists in the data dictionary.

11. **The schema SSMITH owns a procedure SEND_NEWSLETTER with no parameters. SSMITH has granted privileges to this procedure to MAPPLEGATE. No synonyms exist for this procedure. Which of the following is a valid call to this procedure from a PL/SQL block in the schema MAPPLEGATE?**

A. SSMITH.SEND_NEWSLETTER;

B. MAPPLEGATE.SSMITH.SEND_NEWSLETTER;

C. SEND_NEWSLETTER;

D. PROCEDURE.SSMITH.SEND_NEWSLETTER;

12. **Which of the following statements about an IN parameter is true?**

A. It cannot be modified in its program unit's processing section.

B. It stores data in the database.

C. It is a public construct.

D. It is global to the schema session.

13. **Which of the following is a valid name for a procedure?**

A. 1FUNCTION

B. PROCEDURE

C. PR_HEADER$

D. ALL RESULTS

14. **A local function is**

A. A function within the same schema of another function

B. A client-side function

C. A function defined in the declaration of a PL/SQL block

D. None of the above

15. Consider the following function headers:

```
FUNCTION guest_name(guest_id VARCHAR2) RETURN VARCHAR2
FUNCTION register(signee VARCHAR2) RETURN VARCHAR2
```

Which of the following is not a valid statement?

A. guest_name := register('Larry');

B. register(guest_name('Larry'));

C. guest_name(register('Larry'));

D. BMS_OUTPUT.PUT_LINE(register('Larry') || guest_name('Bill'));

16. How do you execute a client-side procedure in Procedure Builder?

A. Locate the node of the procedure in the Object Navigator and double-click it.

B. Locate the node of the procedure in the Object Navigator and click the green traffic light.

C. In the PL/SQL Interpreter Pane, type in the name of the procedure followed by a semicolon and press ENTER.

D. Right-click the procedure node in the Object Navigator and choose RUN.

17. Which of the following statements is *not* a feature of Procedure Builder?

A. It enables the developer to move program units from the client to the server and back.

B. It provides a navigator display of database objects, including tables, columns, and triggers.

C. It includes context-sensitive compilation error messages.

D. It limits your visibility to objects owned by the schema you use to connect Procedure Builder to the database.

18. In the USER_ERRORS data dictionary view, the LINE column shows

A. The error message text

B. The line number in the program unit where the error was found

C. The line number of the error message text that spans multiple lines

D. The error message number

19. Which of the following data dictionary views shows the size of the compiled version of the source code?

   A. USER_SOURCE

   B. USER_OBJECTS

   C. USER_OBJECT_SIZE

   D. USER_SOURCE_COMPILED

20. Which of the following statements will grant privileges on the procedure ACCOUNT_BALANCE to the schema NYUN?

   A. GRANT SELECT ACCOUNT_BALANCE TO NYUN;

   B. GRANT SELECT ON PROCEDURE ACCOUNT_BALANCE TO NYUN;

   C. GRANT EXECUTE ON ACCOUNT_BALANCE TO NYUN;

   D. GRANT EXECUTE ON PROCEDURE ACCOUNT_BALANCE TO NYUN;

21. Using Procedure Builder, you have created a breakpoint, executed a program unit, and used the PL/SQL Interpreter to inspect the current state of some of your program unit's variables. The debugger's current line indicator shows that the next executable statement is a call to a packaged procedure. How can you instruct the debugger to execute this line and enter the procedure's code so that you will be able to continue to control the statement execution within that packaged procedure?

   A. STEP INTO

   B. STEP OVER

   C. STEP OUT

   D. STEP ENTER

22. You have a function DEFINE_ROUTE that calls a procedure WEATHER_RPT. The procedure WEATHER_RPT performs an UPDATE on the table STATS. All three objects have a status of VALID when you perform an ALTER statement on the STATS table. What is the result?

   A. The function and procedure are both INVALID.

   B. The procedure is INVALID, but the function is VALID.

   C. The function and procedure are both VALID.

   D. There is not enough information here to determine.

23. You have a function DEFINE_ROUTE that calls a procedure CLEAR_VARS that is owned by another schema. Which of the following data dictionary views can you query to identify the schema that owns CLEAR_VARS?

    A. USER_OBJECTS

    B. USER_SOURCE

    C. USER_DEPENDENCIES

    D. USER_PROCEDURES

24. Where is it possible to find an indented hierarchical list of dependent objects?

    A. DEPTREE

    B. IDEPTREE

    C. USER_DEPENDENCIES

    D. Nothing like this exists.

25. You have created a package BENEFITS in the schema LINSLEY that declares a variable DEDUCTION in the package specification. What must you do to make this variable available for use by the schema TNELSON?

    A. GRANT EXECUTE ON BENEFITS TO TNELSON;

    B. GRANT EXECUTE ON BENEFITS.DEDUCTION TO TNELSON;

    C. GRANT EXECUTE ON PACKAGE.BENEFITS.DEDUCTION TO TNELSON;

    D. GRANT SELECT ON BENEFITS.DEDUCTION TO TNELSON;

26. You have a procedure PLAN that selects from the table SCHEDULE. You want to grant privileges to the schema LEOGREEN, who has no privileges yet on anything, to use this procedure. Which of the following is required?

    A. GRANT SELECT ON PLAN TO LEOGREEN;

    B. GRANT EXECUTE ON PLAN TO LEOGREEN;

    C. GRANT EXECUTE ON PLAN TO LEOGREEN; GRANT SELECT ON SCHEDULE TO LEOGREEN;

    D. GRANT EXECUTE ON PLAN TO LEOGREEN; GRANT SELECT ON SCHEDULE TO PUBLIC;

27. **What query will locate all stored procedures owned by the current schema that are invalid?**

    A. SELECT * FROM USER_SOURCE WHERE STATUS = 'INVALID';

    B. SELECT * FROM USER_ERRORS WHERE TYPE = 'PROCEDURE' AND STATUS = 'INVALID'

    C. SELECT * FROM USER_OBJECTS WHERE OBJECT_TYPE = 'PROCEDURE' AND STATUS = 'INVALID'

    D. SELECT * FROM USER_STATUS WHERE OBJECT_TYPE = 'PROCEDURE' AND STATUS = 'INVALID'

28. **The schema SKEET owns a table INVENTORIES and the schema MRUN owns a trigger TRIG_INV defined as BEFORE UPDATE ON SKEET.INVENTORIES. SKEET issues the following statement:**

    ```
    DROP TABLE INVENTORIES;
    ```

    What is the result?

    A. The TRIG_INV trigger is given a status of INVALID.

    B. The TRIG_INV trigger is given a status of DISABLED.

    C. The TRIG_INV trigger is dropped.

    D. None of the above.

29. **The package PARM_INIT contains a set of public constants, and the package FIN_UTILITIES includes procedures and functions that reference those public constants in PARM_INIT. With both packages having a status of VALID, you issue the following statement:**

    ```
    DROP PACKAGE PARM_INIT;
    ```

    What is the result?

    A. The FIN_UTILITIES package has a status of INVALID.

    B. The FIN_UTILITIES package has a status of DISABLED.

    C. The FIN_UTILITIES package is dropped.

    D. The FIN_UTILITIES package has a status of VALID.

30. **What is the script file that must be executed to create the required dependency objects and PL/SQL blocks that DEPTREE will need for analyzing dependencies in your program units?**

    A. create_deptree.sql

    B. deptree_fill.sql

    C. fill_ideptree.sql

    D. utldtree.sql

31. **In a client-side function stored within an Oracle Form, which of the following can you not call?**

    A. A constant declared in a stored database package body

    B. A cursor declared in a stored database package specification

    C. A stored database function

    D. A client-side procedure in the same client Oracle Form

32. **You have a package called PRODUCT_TRIALS consisting of a package specification and package body. How can you remove the package body from the database and leave the package specification?**

    A. ALTER PACKAGE PRODUCT_TRIALS DROP BODY;

    B. ALTER PACKAGE BODY PRODUCT_TRIALS DROP BODY;

    C. DROP PACKAGE BODY PRODUCT_TRIALS;

    D. None of the above

33. **You have created a stored database procedure. From where can you call this procedure?**

    A. A SQL statement in SQL*Plus

    B. A SQL statement in a client-side program unit

    C. After the BEGIN statement in a package body's initialization section

    D. In a parameter declaration

34. **You have a stored package called PARMS that contains a procedure called RUN_STATUS. How do you remove the RUN_STATUS procedure from the package and leave the package intact?**

    A. DROP PROCEDURE PARMS.RUN_STATUS;

    B. ALTER PACKAGE PARMS DROP PROCEDURE RUN_STATUS;

    C. DELETE PROCEDURE PARMS.RUN_STATUS;

    D. None of the above

35. **The schema LDEMERY owns a package FINANCE that contains a procedure DEBIT. How can the schema LDEMERY grant the necessary privileges on the DEBIT procedure to the schema JADAMS?**

    A. GRANT EXECUTE ON FINANCE.DEBIT TO JADAMS;

    B. GRANT EXECUTE ON FINANCE TO JADAMS;

    C. GRANT EXECUTE(FINANCE) ON DEBIT TO JADAMS;

    D. None of the above

36. **As a minimum, what must you create to have a valid package in a schema?**

    A. A package body

    B. A package specification

    C. At least one packaged procedure

    D. At least one packaged procedure or function

37. **What must be identical in both the package body and the package specification of the same package? (Choose all that apply.)**

    A. The package name

    B. The initialization section

    C. The parameter list of public functions

    D. The parameter list of private functions

38. **Consider the following specification of a package owned by KLGIFFORD:**

```
PACKAGE VENDOR_SUPPORT AS
  PROCEDURE MANAGE_AUDIT(u_date DATE DEFAULT SYSDATE, u_id NUMBER);
END VENDOR_SUPPORT;
```

    Assuming that the appropriate privileges have been granted and assuming there are no synonyms, which of the following statements will execute the packaged procedure shown previously from SQL*Plus in the schema MMADER?

    A. EXEC VENDOR_SUPPORT.MANAGE_AUDIT(77,'15-APR-2004');

    B. EXEC KLGIFFORD.VENDOR_SUPPORT.MANAGE_AUDIT(u_id=>77, u_date=>'15-APR-2004');

C. EXECUTE KLGIFFORD.VENDOR_SUPPORT;

D. None of the above

39. **You want to make the procedure AUDIT_TAB in the package MISC executable by any other user in the database. Which of the following accomplishes this?**

    A. GRANT EXECUTE ON MISC TO PUBLIC;

    B. GRANT EXECUTE ON MISC TO DATABASE;

    C. GRANT EXECUTE ON MISC TO ALL;

    D. Put the procedure in the package body.

40. **You want to create a procedure that creates a table by concatenating two incoming VARCHAR2 parameters together to build the table name. What package will you use?**

    A. DBMS_OUTPUT

    B. DBMS_DDL

    C. DBMS_SQL

    D. This cannot be done.

41. **Consider the following package represented by this package specification:**

```
PACKAGE GUEST_SURVEY AS
   PROCEDURE SCORE_EMPLOYEE(EMP_ID   NUMBER);
   PROCEDURE SCORE_EMPLOYEE(WORK_DAY DATE);
END GUEST_SURVEY;
```

    Next, consider this statement:

```
EXEC GUEST_SURVEY.SCORE_EMPLOYEE(77);
```

    What happens when you submit this statement in SQL*Plus?

    A. The procedure SCORE_EMPLOYEE(EMP_ID NUMBER) is executed.

    B. The procedure SCORE_EMPLOYEE(WORK_DATE DATE) is executed.

    C. Both A and B.

    D. None of the above.

42. **You are creating a package specification. You decide to create the following package constructs: one function, one procedure, one variable, and one cursor. In which order must you declare these constructs in the package specification? (Choose the best answer.)**

    A. Variable, cursor, procedure, and function.

    B. Cursor and variable in any combination, and procedure and function in any combination.

    C. Alphabetical order according to the names of the constructs.

    D. The order doesn't matter.

43. **Where can you put a package initialization section? (Choose all that apply.)**

    A. At the beginning of a package specification

    B. At the end of a package specification

    C. At the beginning of a package body

    D. At the end of a package body

44. **How do you create a public packaged procedure?**

    A. Declare and define it in the package specification.

    B. Declare and define it in the package body.

    C. Declare it in the package specification and define it in the package body.

    D. Declare it in either the package specification or the package body, and define it in the package body.

45. **You have created a package specification and a package body for a package called PKG_GUIDES. You want to create a constant that will only be used for two procedures in the package. Where should you declare this constant?**

    A. In the package specification as a packaged construct

    B. In the declaration sections of the two procedures

    C. In the package body as a packaged construct

    D. In the package initialization section

46. Consider the following package represented by this package specification:

```
PACKAGE GUEST_SURVEY AS
  PROCEDURE SCORE_EMPLOYEE(EMP_ID    NUMBER);
  PROCEDURE SCORE_EMPLOYEE(EMP_ID    NUMBER, WORK_DAY DATE DEFAULT
SYSDATE);
END GUEST_SURVEY;
```

Next, consider this statement:

```
EXEC GUEST_SURVEY.SCORE_EMPLOYEE(77);
```

What happens when you submit this statement in SQL*Plus?

A. The procedure SCORE_EMPLOYEE(EMP_ID NUMBER) is executed.

B. The procedure SCORE_EMPLOYEE(EMP_ID NUMBER, WORK_DATE DATE DEFAULT SYSDATE) is executed.

C. Both A and B.

D. Neither A nor B.

47. You create two triggers on the same table—one as a BEFORE UPDATE FOR EACH ROW trigger and another as a BEFORE UPDATE OR DELETE FOR EACH ROW trigger. Which will execute first in response to an UPDATE statement?

A. The BEFORE UPDATE trigger.

B. The BEFORE UPDATE OR DELETE trigger.

C. Neither—you cannot create both of these triggers.

D. The order will be random.

48. Which of the following is not an acceptable triggering event?

A. INSERT

B. UPDATE

C. SELECT

D. DELETE

49. Which of the following triggers cannot modify a mutating table?

A. FOR EACH STATEMENT triggered directly by an INSERT

B. INSTEAD OF

C. FOR EACH ROW

D. None of the above

50. **Which column in USER_TRIGGERS can you query to determine if a particular trigger is FOR EACH STATEMENT or FOR EACH ROW?**

   A. STATUS

   B. TRIGGERING_EVENT

   C. ACTION_TYPE

   D. TRIGGER_TYPE

51. **You have created a trigger with the following header:**

   ```
   TRIGGER TRIG_SS_AUDIT AFTER UPDATE ON SHIP_ENGINES FOR EACH ROW
   ```

   You want to include a statement that will capture the resulting SHIP_STATUS value from any UPDATE statement as well as the current server system date and put them in a separate table for future reference. How will you reference these values?

   A. :old.SHIP_STATUS and :old.SYSDATE

   B. :new.SHIP_STATUS and :new.SYSDATE

   C. Query the SHIP_STATUS table to get the latest information and use SYSDATE.

   D. None of the above

52. **A FOR EACH STATEMENT trigger cannot include**

   A. An UPDATE statement of any kind

   B. A REFERENCING clause

   C. A WHEN clause

   D. A packaged cursor reference

53. **Which of the following is a conditional predicate? (Choose all that apply.)**

   A. INSERTING

   B. DROPPING

   C. SELECTING

   D. LOGGING

54. **Consider the following trigger header:**

   ```
   TRIGGER TRIG_A BEFORE UPDATE ON GUESTS FOR EACH ROW
   ```

   During the triggering event, which of the following statements is true?

   A. GUESTS is a constraining table.

   B. GUESTS is a referencing table.

   C. GUESTS is a mutating table.

   D. GUESTS is a trigger table.

55. **Which of the following statements will cause the triggers on table CRUISE_SCHEDULE to stop working yet remain in the database?**

   A. ALTER TRIGGERS (CRUISE_SCHEDULE) DISABLE;

   B. ALTER TABLE CRUISE_SCHEDULE DISABLE TRIGGERS;

   C. ALTER TABLE CRUISE_SCHEDULE DISABLE ALL TRIGGERS;

   D. This cannot be accomplished in a single statement.

56. **You have a table called WORK_SCHEDULE that can receive records from multiple program units in multiple schemas and a Java program using JDBC. For every record inserted into WORK_SCHEDULE, you want to insert another record in another table called WS_AUDIT. What should you do?**

   A. Create a database trigger on WS_AUDIT.

   B. Create a database trigger on WORK_SCHEDULE.

   C. Create a package initialization section.

   D. Create a client-side function.

57. **Consider the following statement:**

   ```
   CREATE OR REPLACE TRIGGER TRIG_AUDIT
   BEFORE INSERT ON WORK_SCHEDULE
   FOR EACH ROW
   BEGIN
     INSERT INTO WS_AUDIT VALUES
       (SEQ_WS_AUDIT_ID.NEXTVAL, SYSDATE, USER);
   END;
   ```

What must be changed in this trigger to make it execute FOR EACH
STATEMENT?

A. Change FOR EACH ROW to FOR EACH STATEMENT.

B. Change FOR EACH ROW to FOR EACH ROW, STATEMENT.

C. Add FOR EACH STATEMENT after FOR EACH ROW.

D. Remove FOR EACH ROW.

58. **Consider the following statement:**

```
CREATE OR REPLACE TRIGGER T_CHECK_LEDGER
BEFORE UPDATE ON LEDGER
FOR EACH ROW
```

What would have to be changed to make this trigger only fire when the
LEDGER'S AMOUNT column is updated?

A. Change ON LEDGER to OF AMOUNT ON LEDGER.

B. Change ON LEDGER to ON LEDGER.AMOUNT.

C. Change ON LEDGER to ON LEDGER(AMOUNT).

D. Change FOR EACH ROW to FOR EACH AMOUNT.

59. **Which of the following is a valid trigger header? (Choose all that apply.)**

A. CREATE TRIGGER TRIG1 BEFORE INSERT ON PORTS, SHIPS FOR
EACH ROW

B. CREATE TRIGGER TRIG1 BEFORE INSERT ON PORTS WHEN
(TO_CHAR(SYSDATE,'DY') = 'SUN')

C. CREATE TRIGGER TRIG1 BEFORE UPDATE ON PORTS REFERENCING
NEW AS LATEST

D. CREATE TRIGGER TRIG1 BEFORE INSERT OR AFTER UPDATE ON
PORTS FOR EACH ROW

60. **The STATUS column in the USER_TRIGGERS can be queried to reveal**

A. If a trigger is VALID or INVALID

B. If a trigger is a BEFORE or AFTER trigger

C. If a trigger is ENABLED or DISABLED

D. If a trigger is NEW or MODIFIED

Answers to Practice Exam #2

1. D.   It will create a function called GET_SHIP_COUNT and overwrite any preexisting function of the same name.

Explanation   Although it's true that stored database procedures, functions, and packages share the same namespace within a single schema, the CREATE OR REPLACE FUNCTION only overwrites a function of the same name. If a procedure of the same name already exists within the same schema, you will see the message "ORA-00955 error: name is already used by an existing object." Finally, the RETURN statement is syntactically acceptable where it is. Ideally, however, it should be the last executable statement, although the function will still compile and execute.

2. A, B.   A: RETURN tot_sales;
B: RETURN prod_name;

Explanation   The declared RETURN datatype is VARCHAR2 so B is correct. However, the PL/SQL parser allows for the potential of an automatic datatype conversion with A, which is a candidate for a successful datatype conversion, not a VARCHAR2. C is unacceptable because BOOLEAN values are not automatically converted to VARCHAR2. D is also unacceptable, which is a datatype declaration, not a variable.

3. A, C, D.   A: NUMBER
C: CRUISES.SHIP_ID%TYPE
D: CRUISES%ROWTYPE

Explanation   All are valid datatypes for a parameter except for B. Remember that parameter datatype declarations cannot have precision, scale, or length. However, C is considered valid and has the effect of assigning the datatype found in the CRUISES table's SHIP_ID column, identifying this datatype at run time, and defining the parameter accordingly. Finally, the record type defined in D is acceptable for a record-type variable.

4. C.   A client-side procedure

Explanation   You cannot call any client-side code from a stored database program unit of any kind. D is a public package construct, and A, B, and D are callable from anywhere on the network, assuming the executing schema has the right privileges.

5. C.   From the right side of an assignment statement in a client-side procedure in the same Oracle Form

Explanation A is wrong because the SQL statement will look to the database to be parsed and executed, even though the SQL statement is included in a client-side program unit. The result is that the SQL statement does not locate the client-side function. B is also wrong because no server-side code can invoke a client-side program unit. D is wrong because code running on one client cannot invoke a program unit on another client. C is correct because a program unit on the same client running in the same client tool, which is an Oracle Form in this case, can reference a client-side function in a PL/SQL expression—not a SQL statement, but a PL/SQL expression.

6. C.   DROP FUNCTION PROT_STATS;

Explanation The command to remove a stored function from the database is DROP FUNCTION, followed by the name of the function.

7. A.   v_result := process_request(cruise_name =>'Tropical' ,
    guest_id => 77);

Explanation In A, the function is the expression on the right side of the assignment statement and uses the pass-by reference notation, which is acceptable. However, you cannot mix the pass-by reference and pass-by position as is done in C, which is why C is unacceptable. B is a procedure call, not a function call.

8. D.   None of the above

Explanation The presence of the OUT parameter requires that a variable be declared to receive the parameter value that is sent back out. A is not correct, however, because that is the format for functions, not procedures with OUT parameters. B is not correct because of the system-defined SYSDATE, which cannot receive the OUT value. C is obviously wrong because of the literal value. D is the correct choice here.

9. A.   parm1 NUMBER(3)

Explanation Parameter declarations cannot have scale, precision, or length, which is why A is the correct answer. B and C are two acceptable ways to assign a default value, and D is a valid PL/SQL datatype.

10. C.   The ORA-00955 message "name is already used by an existing object" appears.

Explanation In a single schema, procedures, functions, and packages are all in the same namespace. As a result, you cannot create a procedure in a schema that has the same name as a function in the same schema. The use of the OR REPLACE option in the CREATE PROCEDURE command only works to replace another procedure, not a different kind of program unit of the same name. As a result, in this situation, the error prevents any compilation attempt, and the procedure's source code is not even stored in the data dictionary.

11. A. SSMITH.SEND_NEWSLETTER;

Explanation The proper and full reference to the schema SEND_NEWSLETTER is with the schema name appended to the beginning, separated from the procedure name with a dot, which is A. D is not valid syntax. C works from within the schema SSMITH. Also, in practice, it's not uncommon for a public synonym to be created for the database that equates the procedure name with the schema.procedure name syntax—in this example, SEND_NEWSLETTER would be a public synonym for SSMITH.SEND_NEWLSETTER. However, the question specifically said that no synonyms exist for this procedure. Finally, B has bad syntax.

12. A. It stores data in the database.

Explanation Incoming parameters behave like constants. They cannot be changed in their program unit's processing section.

13. C. PR_HEADER$

Explanation You must start a program unit name with a letter. Numbers can be included in any character after the first one. You cannot use reserved words, such as PROCEDURE, as the name of your program unit. Spaces are also not allowed. However, dollar signs are allowed as long as they are not the first character. The correct answer is C.

14. C. A function defined in the declaration of a PL/SQL block

Explanation Any PL/SQL block can include, among other declared elements, any number of functions or procedures defined in the declaration section. These local functions and procedures are only callable from within the PL/SQL block that declares them.

15. A. guest_name := register('Larry');

Explanation A function cannot be the target of an assignment statement, which is why A is the correct answer. The other statements are valid uses of functions, which can be passed as parameter values to each other or treated as variables of the same datatype as their RETURN declaration states.

16. C. In the PL/SQL Interpreter Pane, type in the name of the procedure followed by a semicolon and press ENTER.

Explanation   The PL/SQL Interpreter Pane is where you can execute a procedure by typing the name of the procedure.

> **17.** D.   Limits your visibility to objects owned by the schema you use to connect Procedure Builder to the database

Explanation   Although it's true that you must connect Procedure Builder to the database, once connected, you are able to inspect other schema's objects, according to the privileges of the schema you are using. A schema with database administrator (DBA) privileges, for example, can see and change program units throughout the database using Procedure Builder.

> **18.** B.   The line number in the program unit where the error was found

Explanation   The LINE column is the number of the line in the original program unit source code and can be combined with the value of the POSITION column, which shows the column in that line where the error occurred, to identify the specific location where the PL/SQL parser became confused.

> **19.** C.   USER_OBJECT_SIZE

Explanation   The USER_OBJECT_SIZE view includes a column CODE_SIZE that shows the size of the compiled version of the code. A is incorrect because it only includes the source code. B does not have this data, and D is a fictitious name.

> **20.** C.   GRANT EXECUTE ON ACCOUNT_BALANCE TO NYUN;

Explanation   The statement to grant privileges on a procedure is GRANT EXECUTE. The keyword PROCEDURE is not required or allowed, but the name of the procedure is required, followed by the keyword TO and the schema name.

> **21.** A.   STEP INTO

Explanation   The STEP INTO feature tells the debugger to execute the next statement, showing that statement in the PL/SQL Interpreter. If the next statement is a call to another program unit, the PL/SQL Interpreter shows that program unit's statements and the stack in the Object Navigator indicates the current program unit call hierarchy. B and C and valid debugger instructions, but they accomplish different things. D is not a valid debugger instruction.

> **22.** A.   The function and procedure are both INVALID.

Explanation   Any program unit that references an INVALID object is itself INVALID. The status automatically changes as the status of other program units changes. In the case of the alteration to the STATS table, even if the change doesn't affect the logic of the procedure and the resulting state of the STATS table is VALID, the change causes the procedure to be changed to INVALID no matter what and the function is also changed to INVALID.

23. C. USER_DEPENDENCIES

Explanation The USER_DEPENDENCIES view contains a record for every object referenced from within your program units. One of the columns in the view is REFERENCED_OWNER. This tells you the owner of the referenced object. USER_OBJECTS doesn't have this information, and although USER_SOURCE contains the full text of a program unit, the schema name might not be included. For example, if a public synonym has been created to replace the name of another schema's program unit with a simpler name and your stored source code uses that synonym, the text won't indicate the object's owner. Finally, there is no view called USER_PROCEDURES.

24. B. IDEPTREE

Explanation IDEPTREE is the data dictionary view that shows an indented version of DEPTREE. Objects are listed with their referred objects indented at subsequent levels within the calls.

25. A. GRANT EXECUTE ON BENEFITS TO TNELSON;

Explanation You cannot grant privileges on a particular construct within a package. Instead, you grant EXECUTE privileges on the package, making sure to declare those elements you want to make public in the specification and those you do not want to make available in the package body. B, C, and D are all syntax errors.

26. B. GRANT EXECUTE ON PLAN TO LEOGREEN;

Explanation The only thing that is required is the granting of EXECUTE privileges to the LEOGREEN schema. The fact that the table selects from SCHEDULE does not require an additional grant, but it does not result in LEOGREEN having SELECT privileges on the table either. The procedure has the privileges it requires every time it executes and is able to fully function, but without requiring LEOGREEN to be separately granted direct privileges on the table PLAN.

27. C. SELECT * FROM USER_OBJECTS WHERE OBJECT_TYPE = 'PROCEDURE' AND STATUS = 'INVALID'

Explanation All objects owned by the current schema are listed in the USER_OBJECTS view, which includes the STATUS column showing if the object is VALID or INVALID.

28. C.   The TRIG_INV trigger is dropped.

Explanation   When a table is dropped, its triggers are also dropped, even if those triggers are owned by another schema.

29. A.   The FIN_UTILITIES package has a status of INVALID.

Explanation   If any changes are made to any objects that are referenced from within a program unit, the program unit is given a status of INVALID.

30. D.   utldtree.sql

Explanation   The utldtree.sql utility is located, by default, in the Oracle home directory in the rdbms80/admin subdirectory and must be executed prior to working with DEPTREE or IDEPTREE.

31. A.   A constant declared in a stored database package body

Explanation   Any construct, including a constant, that is declared in a package body is private by definition and cannot be called by any program unit outside of the package body, especially a client-side function.

32. C.   DROP PACKAGE BODY PRODUCT_TRIALS;

Explanation   The DROP PACKAGE BODY statement, followed by the name of the package, removes the package body and leaves the package specification. A and B are not valid statements.

33. C.   After the BEGIN statement in a package body's initialization section

Explanation   Stored procedures cannot be called from within an SQL function or parameter declaration. However, they can be called from within executable statements of other program units, including those that are executing on the client side.

34. D.   None of the above

Explanation   The only way to accomplish this feat is to edit the original source code of the package and recompile it with the CREATE OR REPLACE statement. There is no single statement that removes a program unit from within a package.

35. B.   GRANT EXECUTE ON FINANCE TO JADAMS;

Explanation   To grant privileges on a packaged procedure or function to another schema, you must grant privileges on the entire package. B is an example of how to do this. A and C cannot be done because both are syntactically unacceptable.

36. B.   A package specification

Explanation   You must create at least a package specification to have a valid package. Although you are able to create and store a package body before the specification, it is given a status of INVALID until the appropriate package specification is created. A package does not have to have any procedures or functions; a package specification can be created with other constructs, such as variables, and still be considered valid and complete.

37. A, C.   A: The package name C: The parameter list of public functions

Explanation   A is definitely required to be the same; this is the mechanism that causes the body and specification to recognize that they are a part of the same package. B is not included in both locations; it's found in the package body. C is true because any public procedure or function must declare the same parameter list in the specification and the body. However, private procedures or functions are only found in the body, so D is not true.

38. B.   EXEC KLGIFFORD.VENDOR_SUPPORT.MANAGE_AUDIT(u_id=>77, u_date=>'15-APR-2004');

Explanation   To call the packaged procedure from another schema, use the format of schema.package.procedure and include the parameter list. The call from SQL*Plus accepts the named parameter notation.

39. A.   GRANT EXECUTE ON MISC TO PUBLIC;

Explanation   This GRANT statement assures that anyone can execute and have access to anything in the package MISC, including the procedure AUDIT_TAB. Answers B and C are not valid syntax. D has the opposite of the desired effect; it will make the procedure private instead of public.

40. C.   DBMS_SQL

Explanation   The DBMS_SQL package enables you to issue any SQL statement, including DDL statements that are otherwise not allowed in PL/SQL, by building a string that contains the complete and (hopefully) valid SQL statement and then issuing it to the database SQL engine via packaged procedures and functions within the DBMS_SQL package. DBMS_OUTPUT is used for sending written output to the screen, and DBMS_DDL doesn't exist.

41. A.   The procedure SCORE_EMPLOYEE(EMP_ID NUMBER) is executed.

Explanation   This is an example of overloaded modules. The two different procedures, which have the same name, are different in their parameter lists. The execution resolves to the correct procedure according to the number, order, and datatypes of the parameters in the parameter list.

42. D.   The order doesn't matter.

Explanation   You can declare the elements in any order. This isn't always true of everything, however—for example, if you include a package initialization section in a package body, it must be declared after all other elements. But these constructs listed in the question can be declared in any order.

43. D.   At the end of a package body

Explanation   The package initialization section must be at the end of the package body after all other constructs, public or private.

44. C.   Declare it in the package specification and define it in the package body.

Explanation   Any public constructs must be defined in the package specification. All program unit code must be defined in the package body. Program units that are declared and defined in the package body are accepted, but are considered private, not public.

45. C.   In the package body, as a packaged construct

Explanation   If the constant is used by more than one procedure and/or function, then declaring it as some sort of packaged construct is ideal. The question is whether the constant should be made public or private—that is, should it be in the package specification, which makes the construct public and therefore accessible outside of the package, or should it be declared in the package body, which makes the construct private and therefore not accessible outside of the package? The question clearly states that the construct is only required inside the package, and you should always create only the minimal level of accessibility required, which means the construct should be private and therefore declared in the package body.

46. D.   Neither A nor B.

Explanation   The result is the error "PLS-00307: too many declarations of 'SCORE_EMPLOYEE' match this call." This is an example of when overloaded modules can get you into trouble. What's curious is that the package is acceptable and you can create this package successfully. The reason for this is that the overloaded modules, which are what the two SCORE_EMPLOYEE procedures are, follow the syntax for overloaded modules, which is to say that their parameter lists are different in order, number, and/or datatypes. However, the default value in the second overloaded module introduces a loophole into the use of these procedures, and the EXEC statement walks right into it. The presence of the default value in the second procedure sets up a scenario whereby the first procedure cannot be invoked without a doubt as to which procedure is intended. The procedure call cannot be resolved, resulting in the error message.

47. D.   The order will be random.

Explanation   You are able to make these two different triggers, but you cannot control which will be fired first, or in the event of an UPDATE statement, which will fire both of them.

48. C.   SELECT

Explanation   SELECT is the only DML that does not fire a trigger.

49. C.   FOR EACH ROW

Explanation   A mutating table is one that is in the midst of changing during the trigger event that fires the trigger. During a FOR EACH STATEMENT trigger, this does not apply because the triggering event has an opportunity to complete the change—unless the FOR EACH STATEMENT is fired indirectly as the result of a DELETE CASCADE constraint. The INSTEAD OF trigger fires on a view, and mutating tables aren't relevant during VIEW events. FOR EACH ROW is the sort of trigger that can be fired during the midst of a table change and before the change is completed.

50. D.   TRIGGER_TYPE

Explanation   The TRIGGER_TYPE indicates BEFORE or AFTER, followed by the expression STATEMENT (when the trigger is FOR EACH STATEMENT) or EACH ROW (when the trigger is FOR EACH ROW). There is no STATUS column in the USER_TRIGGERS view, and ACTION_TYPE indicates PL/SQL as opposed to Java. The TRIGGERING_EVENT column tells if the trigger is an INSERT, UPDATE, and/or DELETE trigger.

51. D.   None of the above

Explanation   You cannot use the conditional predicates, which default to :new and :old, as prefixes to SYSDATE. However, note that you would use the :new.SHIP_STATUS reference to determine the resulting value of the SHIP_STATUS column.

52. C.   A WHEN clause

Explanation   A trigger's WHEN clause acts much like a WHERE clause to determine which individual rows affected by a query in a FOR EACH ROW trigger should fire the trigger. It serves the purpose of providing a finer level of detail than the trigger event information in the trigger header (BEFORE or AFTER or INSERT/UPDATE/DELETE) in filtering which events cause the trigger's code to execute. However, it is only available in FOR EACH ROW triggers; you cannot use the WHEN clause in the FOR EACH STATEMENT trigger.

53. A. INSERTING

Explanation   The conditional predicates are INSERTING, UPDATING, and DELETING. These are BOOLEAN system-defined values that indicate the triggering event and can be referenced within your trigger's processing section.

54. C. GUESTS is a mutating table.

Explanation   During the triggering event, GUESTS is mutating. Constraining tables would be other tables with foreign key relationships on this table. Answers B and D are fictitious answers.

55. C. ALTER TABLE CRUISE_SCHEDULE DISABLE ALL TRIGGERS;

Explanation   The keyword ALL TRIGGERS can be used as an alternative to naming each trigger you want to disable.

56. B. Create a database trigger on WORK_SCHEDULE.

Explanation   A database trigger on the WORK_SCHEDULE table gives you the option of monitoring transactions on the WORK_SCHEDULE table from any source, including Java programs.

57. D. Remove FOR EACH ROW.

Explanation   Any trigger is FOR EACH STATEMENT automatically unless otherwise specified with the FOR EACH ROW clause. There is no actual FOR EACH STATEMENT clause.

58. A. Change ON LEDGER to OF AMOUNT ON LEDGER.

Explanation   You can narrow a trigger's focus by providing a column list prior to the table name, with each column separated by commas, to make sure that the trigger only fires when updates to the specified columns are processed. The other answers have invalid syntax.

59. B, C. B: CREATE TRIGGER TRIG1 BEFORE INSERT ON PORTS WHEN (TO_CHAR(SYSDATE,'DY') = 'SUN')
C: CREATE TRIGGER TRIG1 BEFORE UPDATE ON PORTS REFERENCING NEW AS LATEST

Explanation   A is not acceptable because you cannot create a single trigger on more than one table. D is not acceptable because you cannot have a single trigger that is both BEFORE and AFTER. B is fine—the WHEN clause is acceptable to further restrict the circumstances under which the trigger fires. C is also acceptable —it declares a new keyword to indicate new incoming data with the prefix of LATEST.

60. C.   If a trigger is ENABLED or DISABLED

Explanation   Although the STATUS column in the USER_OBJECTS view shows if a program unit is VALID or INVALID, the USER_TRIGGERS view uses its STATUS column to show if a trigger is currently ENABLED or not.

Practice Exam #3

1. Where can you store a named PL/SQL procedure? (Choose all that apply.)

   A. In a database

   B. As part of a client-side library

   C. In a text file

   D. In a network packet

2. The declaration section of a stored database function can declare

   A. Global constants

   B. Local procedures

   C. Table constraints

   D. Public synonyms

3. You have created a stored function called TICKET. Next, you execute the following statement:

```
CREATE OR REPLACE PROCEDURE TICKET AS
BEGIN
  DBMS_OUTPUT.PUT_LINE('The procedure has been executed.');
END;
```

What is the result of this statement?

   A. The procedure is not created.

   B. The procedure is created, but not executed.

C. The procedure is created and executed.

D. This is not a valid statement.

4. **The procedure TICKET has no parameters. Which of the following is a valid call from a PL/SQL block to this procedure? (Choose all that apply.)**

   A. EXEC TICKET();

   B. TICKET;

   C. TICKET();

   D. TICKET(NULL);

5. **How many OUT parameters can be declared in a function header?**

   A. None

   B. One

   C. Any number

   D. It depends on what the RETURN datatype is.

6. **You have already created a stored database procedure with the following header:**

```
PROCEDURE ACCT_BAL(account_id IN NUMBER);
```

   Next, in the same schema, you submit the following statement to the database:

```
CREATE OR REPLACE PROCEDURE ACCT_BAL(account_id IN NUMBER) IS
BEGIN
  DBMS_OUTPUT.PUT_LINE('Account balanced.');
END;
```

   What is the result?

   A. The first ACCT_BAL procedure is overwritten, and the code from the second ACCT_BAL is placed in the data dictionary.

   B. The attempt to create the second procedure is rejected because the parameter list is the same as the first.

   C. Both procedures coexist in the database.

   D. None of the above.

7. **What is true of a stored database function? (Choose all that apply.)**

A. It can be passed as a value to an OUT parameter of another function.

B. It can be invoked in a statement on a line by itself.

C. It can be referenced in the WHERE clause of a SELECT statement in a client-side procedure.

D. It can be defined as part of a table.

8. **You have a stored procedure COMPUTE_BENEFITS. You want to render it unable to be executed, but leave it in the database. How can you accomplish this?**

A. ALTER PROCEDURE COMPUTE_BENEFITS DISABLE;

B. UPDATE USER_OBJECTS SET STATUS = 'INVALID' WHERE OBJECT_NAME = 'COMPUTE_BENEFITS';

C. DISABLE PROCEDURE COMPUTE_BENEFITS;

D. None of the above

9. **Consider the following procedure header:**

```
PROCEDURE SCHED_TRIP
   (p_cruise_id   IN      NUMBER DEFAULT 0,
    p_customer_id IN OUT NUMBER,
    p_start_date  IN OUT DATE)
```

Assume any referenced variables are properly declared. Which of the following is a valid call to this procedure from a PL/SQL block? (Choose all that apply.)

A. SCHED_TRIP(p_start_date => SYSDATE, p_customer_id => 1018);

B. SCHED_TRIP(NULL, NULL, NULL);

C. SCHED_TRIP(1018, 177, '26-NOV-2004');

D. SCHED_TRIP(1018, v_cust_number, v_start);

10. **What will be the compilation error resulting from the following statement?**

```
CREATE OR REPLACE PROCEDURE ORDER_SUPPLIES
   (p_ship_id     IN      SHIPS.SHIP_ID%TYPE,
    p_port_id     IN OUT NUMBER DEFAULT 0,
    p_guest_count    OUT VARCHAR2,
    p_supply_list IN      BOOLEAN) IS
```

```
BEGIN
  DBMS_OUTPUT.PUT_LINE('Procedure has executed.');
END;
```

    A. The BOOLEAN datatype is not allowed in a parameter datatype.

    B. The %TYPE declaration is invalid.

    C. The DEFAULT value cannot be used with an OUT parameter.

    D. All OUT parameters must follow any IN parameter declarations.

11. **You need to create a function to be called from an IF statement of an Oracle Form's PL/SQL trigger and nowhere else. Where is the best place to store this function?**

    A. In the database as a stored function

    B. In a text file on the client

    C. In the form of a program unit

    D. In a common library to be shared by several Oracle Forms

12. **Assume that any referenced tables and columns are properly declared. Which of the following is *not* a valid datatype for a local function parameter?**

    A. VARCHAR2(30)

    B. BOOLEAN

    C. NUMBER

    D. CRUISES.CRUISE_NAME%TYPE

13. **You want to create a stored procedure that includes a local procedure FLIP and another local procedure FLOP. Neither local procedure takes any parameters. FLIP includes a call to FLOP and FLOP includes a call to FLIP. You declare FLIP before you declare FLOP. Which statement must precede the declaration of FLIP in the declaration section?**

    A. FORWARD PROCEDURE FLOP;

    B. PROCEDURE FLOP;

    C. PROCEDURE FORWARD FLOP;

    D. None of the above

14. **You attempt to execute a CREATE OR REPLACE FUNCTION statement and receive a compilation error. Where is the best source of information about what went wrong with your statement?**

    A. USER_OBJECTS

    B. USER_ERRORS

    C. USER_COMPILATION

    D. USER_STATS

15. **Which of the following statements best describes what the RETURN statement in the processing section of a function does?**

    A. It declares the value that will be returned at the end of the function.

    B. It declares the datatype of what the function will return.

    C. It stops processing the function.

    D. It sends data back out through any OUT parameters the function might have.

16. **The schema CPOWELL owns a procedure PURCHASING, which calls a procedure BAL_ACCT. The procedure BAL_ACCT has an INSERT on a table called ACCOUNTS. The schema CPOWELL needs to grant privileges on the procedure PURCHASING to the schema AGREENSPAN. Which of the following will achieve the desired result?**

    A. GRANT INSERT ON ACCOUNTS TO AGREENSPAN; GRANT EXECUTE ON BAL_ACCT TO AGREENSPAN; GRANT EXECUTE ON PURCHASING TO AGREENSPAN;

    B. GRANT EXECUTE ON PURCHASING TO AGREENSPAN; GRANT EXECUTE ON BAL_ACCT TO AGREENSPAN;

    C. GRANT EXECUTE ON PURCHASING TO AGREENSPAN;

    D. GRANT EXECUTE CASCADE ON PURCHASING TO AGREENSPAN;

17. **Which column should you ORDER BY to query the data dictionary and display the source code of a procedure in the proper order?**

    A. The LINE column of the USER_SOURCE view

    B. The NUM column of the USER_PROCEDURE view

    C. The LINE column of the USER_OBJECTS view

    D. None of the above

18. **What feature in Procedure Builder can you use to execute a procedure?**

    A. The PL/SQL Interpreter

    B. The Object Navigator

    C. The PL/SQL Editor

    D. The Stack

19. **The schema CANDERSON owns a procedure SCHEDULING that performs a SELECT on the CRUISES table. CANDERSON grants privileges on SCHEDULING to the schema CJONES who doesn't have DBA or any other privileges on any database objects. What is now true?**

    A. CJONES can issue SELECT statements on CRUISES.

    B. CJONES can change the code in the procedure SCHEDULING.

    C. CJONES can execute SCHEDULING.

    D. CJONES can create triggers on CRUISES.

20. **You would like to run a single query to identify all functions that are invalid. What data dictionary view should you query?**

    A. USER_SOURCE

    B. USER_OBJECTS

    C. USER_ERRORS

    D. USER_DEPENDENCIES

21. **What tool in Procedure Builder gives you compilation error messages in context for your program units?**

    A. The PL/SQL Interpreter

    B. The Object Navigator

    C. The PL/SQL Editor

    D. The Stack

22. **Your schema contains packaged procedures that call other procedures, which, in turn, call other procedures. You'd like to see a single report that shows a hierarchical listing of these procedure calls. Which data dictionary view should you query?**

    A. USER_OBJECTS

    B. USER_OBJECT_REFERENCE

   C. USER_REFERENCES_TREE

   D. DEPTREE

23. **You want to query the data dictionary to determine if the program units in your schema make any calls to program units owned by other schemas, and if so, you'd like to know what those schemas are. Where will you query?**

   A. USER_OBJECTS

   B. USER_OBJECT_SIZE

   C. USER_SOURCE

   D. USER_DEPENDENCIES

24. **To create a function that doesn't change any database object values, such as records in a table, what PRAGMA RESTRICT_REFERENCES can you assert?**

   A. WDNS

   B. WNDS

   C. WNNS

   D. WDDS

25. **You have created a stored database procedure INITIALIZE that is owned by the schema HEATHER and declares a local procedure SET_PARM. How can you grant privileges on the local procedure so that any schema can execute it?**

   A. GRANT EXECUTE ON SET_PARM TO PUBLIC;

   B. GRANT EXECUTE ON INITIALIZE.SET_PARM TO PUBLIC;

   C. GRANT EXECUTE ON HEATHER.INITIALIZE.SET_PARM TO PUBLIC;

   D. It cannot be done.

26. **You have created a stored database procedure COMPUTE_TAX that includes a call to a stored database function GET_TAX_RATE that is stored in a remote database. Everything is VALID, but then someone recompiles the GET_TAX_RATE function in the remote database. What will happen the next time you execute COMPUTE_TAX?**

   A. It will execute fine.

   B. It will automatically recompile.

   C. You will get an error message.

   D. None of the above.

27. Which of the following data dictionary views contains information about batch submissions?

   A. USER_SUBMISSIONS

   B. USER_OBJECTS

   C. USER_JOBS

   D. USER_BATCH

28. The schema DHAMILL owns a package FIGURES that contains a procedure EIGHTS with no parameters. Assuming that appropriate privileges are granted, how would PFLEMING invoke the EIGHTS procedure from within a function that PLFEMING owns?

   A. FIGURES.EIGHTS;

   B. DHAMILL.EIGHTS;

   C. DHAMILL.FIGURES.EIGHTS;

   D. It can't be done.

29. In Procedure Builder's Object Navigator, client-side program units can be expanded to show which of the following? (Choose all that apply.)

   A. Subprograms

   B. Local subprograms

   C. Referenced by

   D. References

30. The presence of the reserved word TRUST in PRAGMA RESTRICT_REFERENCES indicates

   A. The highest level of purity is being asserted.

   B. The most trusted level of purity is being asserted.

   C. The developer must trust that the purity levels asserted are actually in force because the compiler isn't checking for them.

   D. The purity levels have been successfully validated and can now be trusted.

31. **You want to create a package that contains two procedures with the same name, but with different parameter lists. This is known as**

    A. Making a mistake

    B. Overdriving

    C. Overloading

    D. Overbearing

32. **How do you declare a private cursor?**

    A. Declare it in a package specification.

    B. Declare it in a package body.

    C. Declare it in a private procedure or private function.

    D. Use the keyword PRIVATE.

33. **You want to create a public function. Where must you specify the RETURN datatype?**

    A. In the package specification only.

    B. In the package body only.

    C. In both the package specification and the package body.

    D. It depends on whether you hide the function's code or not.

34. **You want to create a variable that can be referenced from several procedures within a stored database package as well as a few functions in another package. Where should you declare this variable? (Choose all that apply.)**

    A. A database trigger

    B. A package specification on the client

    C. A package specification in the database

    D. A package body in the database

35. **Consider the following package owned by the schema TSTOTTLEMYER:**

```
PACKAGE MARKETING AS
  PROCEDURE PRICE_PRODUCT(set_price IN OUT NUMBER);
END MARKETING;
```

```
PACKAGE BODY MARKETING AS
  PROCEDURE PRICE_PRODUCT(set_price IN OUT NUMBER
  BEGIN
    set_price := VALIDATE_PRICE(set_price);
    INSERT INTO CATALOG VALUES (S_PRICE_ID.NEXTVAL, set_price);
  END PRICE_PRODUCT;
  FUNCTION VALIDATE_PRICE(p IN NUMBER) RETURN NUMBER
  IS
    IF (p <= 100) THEN RETURN p;
    ELSE              RETURN 100;
    END IF;
  END VALIDATE_PRICE;
END MARKETING;
```

If the schema DWISE wants to directly invoke the VALIDATE_PRICE function, what must be done from within TSTOTTLEMYER?

A. GRANT EXECUTE ON MARKETING TO DWISE;

B. GRANT EXECUTE ON MARKETING.VALIDATE_PRICE TO DWISE;

C. GRANT EXECUTE ON VALIDATE_PRICE TO DWISE;

D. It cannot be done.

36. **You need to create a stored procedure that issues a statement to drop an archive table from the database. Which of the following packages could you use?**

A. DBMS_DROP

B. DBMS_OUTPUT

C. DBMS_SQL

D. DBMS_JOB

37. **How can you create two functions that are overloaded?**

A. As two local functions within the same stored database procedure

B. As two stored database functions in the same schema

C. As public functions in different packages, but in the same schema

D. As stored database functions in separate schemas

38. Which of the following will drop the package specification for STAT_TRACKING, but leave the package body?

   A. DROP PACKAGE BODY STAT_TRACKING;

   B. DROP PACKAGE STAT_TRACKING BODY;

   C. DROP PACKAGE(BODY) STAT_TRACKING;

   D. This cannot be done.

39. To create a public global cursor,

   A. Declare the cursor in the package specification and GRANT EXECUTE TO PUBLIC on the package.

   B. Declare the cursor with the PUBLIC GLOBAL keywords.

   C. Declare the cursor in the package specification.

   D. It cannot be done.

40. You have created a VALID stored database procedure AUDIT with no parameters. You decide to place this procedure in a package ACCOUNTING. You begin by creating the package specification with the following statement:

```
CREATE OR REPLACE PACKAGE ACCOUNTING AS
  PROCEDURE AUDIT;
END;
```

Assuming that this statement executes successfully, what is the status of the original stored database procedure PROCEDURE_AUDIT?

   A. VALID

   B. INVALID

   C. The procedure AUDIT has been removed from the database.

   D. PACKAGED

41. Which statement will recompile the package body AP_LEDGER without recompiling the package specification?

   A. ALTER PACKAGE AP_LEDGER COMPILE BODY;

   B. ALTER PACKAGE BODY AP_LEDGER COMPILE;

   C. ALTER PACKAGE AP_LEDGER COMPILE;

   D. COMPILE PACKAGE BODY AP_LEDGER;

42. **Which of the following must be declared and defined in the package specification?**

    A. A public cursor with a hidden SELECT statement

    B. A public procedure

    C. A public global constant

    D. A private function

43. **Which of the following is a valid package name?**

    A. SELECT

    B. 1BIGPACKAGE

    C. The same name of an existing procedure in the same schema

    D. The same name of an existing trigger in the same schema

44. **Where do you put a stored packaged procedure's PL/SQL processing section?**

    A. In the package specification for private procedures only

    B. In the package specification for all procedures

    C. In the package body for private procedures only

    D. In the package body for all procedures

45. **You have created a package that has a package initialization section. You would like to monitor the values of the packaged constructs that are initialized during the execution of the package initialization section. Which of the following can you do? (Choose all that apply.)**

    A. Use the SHOW ERRORS feature in SQL*Plus.

    B. Use the Procedure Builder's debugger to set a breakpoint and step into the package initialization section's execution.

    C. Insert some DBMS_OUTPUT.PUT_LINE statements in the package initialization section to print the contents of the variables.

    D. Put the package initialization section in the package specification so that it is public.

46. You want to set up a stored program unit so that it automatically executes every night after midnight. Which of the following packages can you use to achieve this result?

A. DBMS_PIPE

B. DBMS_SQL

C. DBMS_JOB

D. DBMS_BATCH

47. You want to create a trigger that monitors activity on a particular table, and based on certain values inserted or updated in a particular column, you want to insert a record in a separate auditing table. You don't want to audit the record unless it was, indeed, processed. Which event will you trigger?

A. ON SCHEMA

B. BEFORE

C. FOR EACH STATEMENT

D. AFTER

48. How many DML triggers can be created for a single table?

A. BEFORE INSERT, BEFORE UPDATE, BEFORE DELETE, AFTER INSERT, AFTER UPDATE, AFTER DELETE, for a total of six triggers

B. As many as you want

C. No more than 10

D. Only one

49. What is wrong with the following statement?

```
CREATE OR REPLACE TRIGGER LOG_ACTIVITY
AFTER UPDATE ON WORK_SCHEDULE
BEGIN
   INSERT INTO CHANGE_LOG VALUES (:new.WORK_SCHEDULE_ID, USER);
END;
```

A. The reference to USER is not accepted.

B. The reference to :new is not allowed here.

C. You cannot perform an INSERT in an AFTER UPDATE trigger.

D. Nothing is wrong with this statement.

50. **You have a table CRUISES with a trigger CRUISE_AUDIT. The trigger inserts records in the table AUDIT_TAB. You drop the CRUISES table from the database. Which of the following statements is true?**

    A. The CRUISE_AUDIT trigger and AUDIT_TAB table are also dropped.

    B. The CRUISE_AUDIT trigger is dropped.

    C. The CRUISE_AUDIT trigger is INVALID.

    D. There is no change to CRUISE_AUDIT and AUDIT_TAB.

51. **You want to create a trigger that captures any attempt to DELETE a record in the PORTS table, and based on logic in the trigger, stop the DELETE from being successful or allow it to complete. What do you do?**

    A. Make an INSTEAD OF DELETE trigger to replace what the DELETE functionality will do.

    B. Use a RAISE statement to raise a user-defined exception and handle the exception in the trigger to stop the DELETE.

    C. Use a RAISE statement to raise a user-defined exception and do not handle the exception in the trigger to stop the DELETE.

    D. This cannot be done.

52. **A CREATE trigger will fire on which of the following events? (Choose all that apply.)**

    A. CREATE TABLE

    B. CREATE DATABASE

    C. CREATE CONTROLFILE

    D. CREATE VIEW

53. **You want to create a trigger that will fire in response to any DROP statement from any schema in the database. What do you do?**

    A. Create an ON SCHEMA trigger for the SYS schema.

    B. Create an ON SCHEMA trigger for the PUBLIC schema.

    C. Create an ON DATABASE trigger.

    D. Create an ON SCHEMA ALL trigger.

54. A conditional predicate is

    A. BEFORE

    B. INSERTING

    C. :new

    D. INSTEAD OF

55. To inspect the source code of the processing section of a trigger, you can query

    A. USER_OBJECTS

    B. USER_SOURCE

    C. USER_TRIGGERS

    D. USER_PROCESSING_SECTION_OF_THAT_TRIGGER_YOU_WANT

56. You have a table CRUISES with a BEFORE UPDATE FOR EACH ROW trigger CRUISE_AUDIT. The trigger performs an INSERT on a table AUDIT_TAB. Someone has performed an ALTER on the AUDIT_TAB table in such a way that the trigger is not working any more, and other users are unable to perform UPDATE statements on the CRUISES table. What's the best step can you take to allow those developers to continue working while you investigate and solve the problem with the trigger?

    A. Drop the trigger from the database.

    B. Redefine the trigger to be on a different table temporarily.

    C. Disable the trigger.

    D. Create a duplicate CRUISES table.

57. Database triggers can be created to fire on which of the following events? (Choose all that apply.)

    A. COMMIT

    B. GRANT

    C. RENAME

    D. DROP

58. Assuming that any referenced database objects are properly created and available, what is syntactically wrong with the following statement that

creates an INSTEAD OF trigger on the database view GUEST_SUMMARY_VIEW?

```
CREATE OR REPLACE TRIGGER GSV_AUDIT
INSTEAD OF INSERT ON GUEST_SUMMARY_VIEW
FOR EACH ROW
BEGIN
  STATISTICS.PERFORM_AUDIT(:new.GUEST_ID);
END;
```

A. The call to the package STATISTICS is invalid because you cannot reference packages from within a trigger.

B. The call to PERFORM_AUDIT is invalid because you cannot pass a value to a procedure with the :new prefix.

C. The FOR EACH ROW clause is not present, making this a FOR EACH STATEMENT trigger, which is not acceptable with an INSTEAD OF trigger.

D. Nothing is wrong.

59. **You want to create a database trigger that contains an unusually large amount of code in the processing section. What's the best way to achieve this?**

A. Create a separate stored procedure containing the code and call the procedure from the trigger.

B. Create a set of triggers that all have the same trigger header so that they are called in succession and each individual trigger is relatively small.

C. Create the trigger using Procedure Builder.

D. Place the trigger in a package.

60. **The WHEN clause of a trigger**

A. Determines if a trigger fires BEFORE or AFTER a particular event

B. Can optionally specify the time of day that a trigger will fire

C. Determines if a trigger fires on an INSERT, UPDATE, or DELETE event

D. Doesn't exist in triggers

Answers to Practice Exam #3

I. A, B.   A: In a database B: As part of a client-side library

Explanation   Although you can store PL/SQL code in a text file, you cannot store a named program unit in a text file. However, you can definitely store named program units in the database or as part of a client-side library.

2. B.   Local procedures

Explanation   You can declare local procedures and/or functions within the declaration section of any stored program unit.

3. A.   The procedure is not created.

Explanation   The statement is valid, but the problem is that functions, procedures, and packages share the same namespace within a single schema. In other words, you cannot create any function that has the same name as a procedure within the same schema. The complication here is that the CREATE OR REPLACE statement will replace another procedure of the same name, but not a function. An attempt to execute this statement results in the error "ORA-00955: name is already used by an existing object."

4. B, C.   B: TICKET;
C: TICKET();

Explanation   A is a valid call from SQL*Plus, but not from a PL/SQL block. B is a standard call, but C is actually acceptable. D, however, is not an empty parameter list; it is an attempt to pass a single parameter value of NULL, and that's not acceptable for a procedure that takes no parameters.

5. C.   Any number

Explanation   You can technically declare as many OUT parameters as you want when you declare a function. However, the usefulness of these OUT parameters is another story—they are not really useful, nor recommended. However, syntactically, they are acceptable.

6. A.   The first ACCT_BAL procedure is overwritten, and the code from the second ACCT_BAL is placed in the data dictionary.

Explanation   This is not an overloaded procedure because you can't do that with stored database procedures. The attempt to CREATE OR REPLACE the original ACCT_BAL procedure results in the new procedure overwriting the first procedure, but not overloading it.

7. C.   It can be referenced in the WHERE clause of a SELECT statement in a client-side procedure.

Explanation   A is not true—if the parameter were an IN parameter, it would be true, but it's not true for OUT parameters. B is not true for functions, but it is true for procedures. D seems to describe a database trigger, but is not relevant for stored database functions. C is the correct answer.

8. D.   None of the above

Explanation   It would be incorrect to say that this is completely impossible. Technically, if you introduced a single compilation error into the procedure's code through a CREATE OR REPLACE PROCEDURE statement, you would theoretically achieve this effect. However, this is really stretching it—there is no way to disable a procedure in the same manner that you disable a trigger. If you attempt B, you run the risk of creating some very serious problems in your database, assuming you had the privileges to do so—any direct changes to the data dictionary are extremely ill advised and run the risk of irrevocably damaging your database.

9. D.   SCHED_TRIP(1018, v_cust_number, v_start);

Explanation   The OUT parameters require that a variable be provided as the parameter so that the data value assigned to the OUT parameter within the procedure can be passed back out to the calling statement. D is the only valid option here. A, B, and C would work if the second and third parameters were both IN parameters.

10. C.   The DEFAULT value cannot be used with an OUT parameter.

Explanation   You cannot have a DEFAULT value assigned to an OUT or an IN OUT parameter. Syntactically, this is never accepted and prevents the procedure from compiling successfully.

11. C.   In the form as a program unit

Explanation   This is a subjective question, but not unlike OCP exam questions. Ideally, you should store a program unit where it has only the exposure it requires and no more. In this scenario, the function should be stored in the Oracle Form that is calling it because no other program unit will require it. B wouldn't work because you can't store a named program unit in a text file. (You can store the code that creates a named program unit in a text file, but the named program unit cannot be invoked from within the text file.) A and D would technically work, but C is ideal.

12. A. VARCHAR2(30)

Explanation You cannot specify length, precision, or scale in parameter datatypes for procedures or functions, whether they are local or not.

13. B. PROCEDURE FLOP;

Explanation The call in FLIP to the as-yet-undeclared procedure FLOP requires a forward declaration, and B is the syntax for it. The forward declaration is simply the program unit header, much like the declaration of a program unit in a package specification.

14. B. USER_ERRORS

Explanation The USER_ERRORS view is where you can find compilation error messages for all program units that you have attempted to compile, but that are currently INVALID.

15. C. It stops processing the function.

Explanation The RETURN statement, wherever it's encountered during processing, stops processing the function, ignoring whatever statements follow. Most importantly, the RETURN statement includes an expression after the RETURN keyword, and this expression is evaluated and returned through the function itself.

16. C. GRANT EXECUTE ON PURCHASING TO AGREENSPAN;

Explanation When you GRANT EXECUTE on a program unit, all required privileges are automatically granted with it for the purposes of executing that procedure.

17. A. The LINE column of the USER_SOURCE view

Explanation The USER_SOURCE view contains the source code, and the LINE column is the line number for a particular program unit.

18. A. The PL/SQL Interpreter

Explanation Use the PL/SQL Interpreter to type in commands to execute procedures.

19. C. CJONES can execute SCHEDULING.

Explanation CJONES can execute the procedure SCHEDULING, but that doesn't mean CJONES has direct access to the same things that SCHEDULING has direct access to—namely, the CRUISES table.

20. B. USER_OBJECTS

Explanation   Query the USER_OBJECTS view with a WHERE TYPE = 'FUNCTION' AND STATUS = 'INVALID' clause to get the results.

21. C. The PL/SQL Editor

Explanation   The PL/SQL Editor shows compilation errors on the bottom half of the screen, and it automatically places the cursor in the source code at the location of the error.

22. D. DEPTREE

Explanation   The DEPTREE view is the best source of information. DEPTREE uses a CONNECT BY style of SELECT statement on the same information found in the USER_DEPENDENCIES view, which you could also use with some effort. However, DEPTREE is the answer that the OCP exam is looking for in a question like this, unless the question specifies something about an indented hierarchical list, in which case the answer would be IDEPTREE.

23. D. USER_DEPENDENCIES

Explanation   Although you may be able to extract most, and perhaps all, of the information you are looking for from USER_SOURCE, which stores all of the source code, the USER_DEPENDENCIES view is vastly superior. This view breaks out a list of all called objects and unambiguously identifies the owner of each referenced object.

24. B. WNDS

Explanation   The purity level WNDS is Writes No Database State. The others are fictitious.

25. D. It cannot be done.

Explanation   Local procedures and functions are, by definition, only accessible within the PL/SQL block that declares them and cannot be granted to any other calling source.

26. C. You will get an error message.

Explanation   The remote database function recompilation has the effect of flagging your procedure as invalid, but the automatic recompilation that would normally take place when both program units are in the same database does *not* happen automatically when one of the program units is remotely located. The procedure COMPUTE_TAX must be recompiled manually or called a second time in order to successfully execute.

27. C. USER_JOBS

Explanation   The USER_JOBS view is what you can query to identify the current state of batch jobs created with the DBMS_JOB package.

28. C. DHAMILL.FIGURES.EIGHTS;

Explanation   The proper syntax is schema.package.procedure.

29. A, C, D.   A: Subprograms C: Referenced by D: References

Explanation   The Object Navigator shows for each client-side program unit the subprograms the unit contains, any objects that the program unit references, and any other program units that reference this one.

30. C. The developer must trust that the purity levels asserted are actually in force because the compiler isn't checking for them.

Explanation   The TRUST keyword effectively turns off the purity-level compilation check. This is a way that the purity levels can be documented without being enforced, a sort of workaround that is actually required under certain circumstances.

31. C. Overloading

Explanation   Overloading is the process of creating different program units that share the same name, but differ in parameter lists. The purpose is to create the capability for any calls to this program unit to pass in different data types or other different combinations of parameters yet theoretically get the same, or similar, results.

32. B. Declare it in a package body.

Explanation   A private cursor is useful in a package body, where it can be used by one or more packaged procedures and/or functions. However, a private cursor is declared outside of the packaged procedures or packaged functions themselves, yet within the package body, where all private constructs are declared.

33. C. In both the package specification and the package body.

Explanation   You must include the RETURN datatype as part of the function's declared header in the package specification, and you must always repeat the entire declaration as part of the function's code in the package body.

34. C. A package specification in the database

Explanation   Putting the variable declaration in a stored database package specification is the only way to make it available to various program units.

35. D.   It cannot be done.

Explanation   The VALIDATE_PRICE function is a private function and cannot be granted for access from outside of the package.

36. C.   DBMS_SQL

Explanation   The DBMS_SQL package contains procedures and functions that support the capability of PL/SQL program units to issue any dynamically defined SQL statements and, in particular, DDL statements. Note, however, that the new feature of native dynamic SQL is a new alternative to DBMS_SQL that is easier to work with.

37. A.   As two local functions within the same stored database procedure

Explanation   You can create two functions with the same name, but with different parameter lists as local modules within a single PL/SQL block or a single package. However, because namespaces for functions are respected within a single schema, trying to create overloaded functions across schema boundaries is not possible. Stored database functions—that is, functions that are not in a package—cannot be overloaded.

38. D.   This cannot be done.

Explanation   The package specification is the foundation of a package. Without it, there is no package. Therefore, although it's possible to create the package body and store it in the database with a status of INVALID before creating the package specification, once they are both there, there is no statement to remove the specification and leave the body, even in a status of INVALID, in the data dictionary.

39. C.   Declare the cursor in the package specification.

Explanation   Any construct declared in the package specification is inherently public and global. Note that this does not include elements declared within a program unit, which are local to that program unit.

40. A.   VALID

Explanation   Nothing has happened to the procedure AUDIT. The procedure AUDIT in the package is not recognized by the database as the same object as the stored database procedure.

41. A.   ALTER PACKAGE AP_LEDGER COMPILE BODY;

Explanation   The statement in C works, but it recompiles both the specification and the body. The command to compile only the body is A. B and D have bad syntax.

42. C.   A public global constant

Explanation   Public packaged constants, which are global by definition, are declared and defined in the package specification. Public cursors are declared in the package specification, and the SELECT statement could be defined in the package specification as well, except when the SELECT statement is hidden, which requires it to be declared in the package body. Any procedure—public or private— must have its processing section in the package body.

43. D.   The same name of an existing trigger in the same schema

Explanation   Packages are in a different namespace from triggers so they can share the same name within the same schema. However, stored packages, stored (out-of-the-package) procedures, and stored (out-of-the-package) functions are also in the same namespace so these cannot share the same name in the same schema. Any program unit name cannot begin with a number, and the keyword SELECT is reserved and cannot be used as a program unit name.

44. D.   In the package body for all procedures

Explanation   You always put the processing section for any packaged procedure or function in the package specification, regardless of whether the program unit is public or private.

45. B, C.   B: Use the Procedure Builder's debugger to set a breakpoint and step into the package initialization section's execution. C: Insert some DBMS_OUTPUT.PUT_LINE statements in the package initialization section to print the contents of the variables.

Explanation   Both of these are valid steps to take. The original purpose for the DBMS_OUTPUT package was to support these sorts of efforts in order to print out variables for debugging purposes. However, the Procedure Builder debugger feature is a powerful alternative that provides more real-time control during execution.

46. C.   DBMS_JOB

Explanation   The DBMS_JOB package is designed for scheduling batch submissions. There is no DBMS_BATCH package.

47. D.   AFTER

Explanation   By triggering the AFTER event, such as AFTER INSERT OR UPDATE ON tablename, you ensure that the trigger doesn't fire until the DML statement (the INSERT or UPDATE) has been processed. For example, if you trigger the BEFORE, the trigger fires and then the UPDATE statement is processed. If the UPDATE experiences a problem, the UPDATE fails, but the BEFORE trigger has already fired and its results are not rolled back. Finally, this scenario requires a FOR EACH ROW option, not a FOR EACH STATEMENT.

48. B.   As many as you want

Explanation   Although there is a finite number of possible circumstances that fire a trigger, there is no practical limit to the number of triggers you can create for those events. You can create multiple triggers on the same triggering events.

49. B.   The reference to :new is not allowed here.

Explanation   This trigger is a FOR EACH STATEMENT trigger. You can tell because the FOR EACH ROW clause is not included and there is no such thing as a FOR EACH STATEMENT clause. In a STATEMENT-level trigger, you cannot reference :new or :old. On the other hand, references to USER are acceptable and INSERT statements are allowed in the processing section of an AFTER UPDATE statement.

50. B.   The CRUISE_AUDIT trigger is dropped.

Explanation   When a table is dropped, its triggers are also dropped.

51. C.   Use a RAISE statement to raise a user-defined exception and do not handle the exception in the trigger to stop the DELETE.

Explanation   You cannot create an INSTEAD OF trigger on a table; those are only for database views. You should use a RAISE statement to raise a user-defined exception and do not handle it—this forces the exception to propagate out to the DELETE statement itself, stopping it from completing successfully.

52. A, D.   A: CREATE TABLE
D: CREATE VIEW

Explanation   A CREATE trigger fires on any event other than CREATE DATABASE or CREATE CONTROLFILE.

53. C.   Create an ON DATABASE trigger.

Explanation   The ON SCHEMA option has the scope of its own schema owner, whereas the ON DATABASE trigger has the entire database as its scope. There is no ON SCHEMA ALL trigger.

54. B.   INSERTING

Explanation   The conditional predicates are INSERTING, UPDATING, and DELETING.

55. C.   USER_TRIGGERS

Explanation   The entire processing section is included in a single data element within the USER_TRIGGERS view. USER_SOURCE does not include any information about triggers.

56. C.   Disable the trigger.

Explanation   The advantage to disabling triggers is that it leaves the code in the database while rendering the trigger inactive.

57. B, C, D.   B: GRANT
C: RENAME
D: DROP

Explanation   The new DDL trigger capability empowers developers to create triggers on CREATE, ALTER, DROP, GRANT, REVOKE, TRUNCATE, RENAME, and many other DDL statements. However, COMMIT and other transaction control statements themselves do not directly fire triggers.

58. D.   Nothing is wrong.

Explanation   The statement is syntactically fine.

59. A.   Create a separate stored procedure containing the code and call the procedure from the trigger.

Explanation   The concern here is that triggers cannot contain more than 32KB of code. A is the best solution. B is unpredictable because you have no control over the sequencing of trigger firing under a single triggering event. C is a generally good idea, but it does nothing to contribute to the solution. D is not an option under any circumstances.

60. B.   Can optionally specify the time of day that a trigger will fire

Explanation   Okay, so this might be a trick question, but B really is true, although it's not the only thing that WHEN does. The purpose of WHEN is to provide additional logic for further restricting when the trigger will execute. For the WHEN clause to even be considered, the triggering event must have occurred and the trigger must have been fired. The WHEN clause serves as a last chance to further fine-tune the definition of when the trigger will actually be processed and could theoretically include a reference to SYSDATE to determine what time of day the trigger would fire. The WHEN clause is a BOOLEAN statement that allows the trigger to fire when it is true and does not when it is false. WHEN can reference the new and old identifiers.

Index

Symbols

%ROWTYPE variable, 35–36
%TYPE attribute, 34, 77, 394
:new/:old qualifiers, 175–176

A

advanced datatype declaration, 34
ALL_ views, 86
ALL_SOURCE views, 86
ALTER FUNCTION…COMPILE
    command, 107
ALTER PACKAGE…COMPILE
    statements, 137
ALTER PROCEDURE …COMPILE
    command, 94
ALTER PROCEDURE command, 70
ALTER statements
    recompiling packages, 143–145
    triggers, 181
altering
    functions, 107
    procedures, 70–71
ALTER_COMPILE procedure, 257–259
ANALYZE_OBJECT procedure,
    258–259
anonymous blocks, 47, 73

anonymous explicit cursors, 33
anonymous PL/SQL programs, 6
arithmetic expressions
    comparison operators, 18
    NULL values, 17
    processing sections, 15
arithmetic operators, 16
AS reserved word, 66, 138
assignment statements, 21, 111
attributes
    cursors, 32
    implicit cursors, 32
automatic datatype conversion,
    22, 121
avoiding recompilation errors,
    392–393

B

batch jobs, monitoring, 255
BEFORE DELETE triggers, 176
BEFORE INSERT database trigger, 249
BEGIN keyword, 66
BEGIN reserved word, 66
BEGIN statements
    blocks, 40
    implicit cursors, 31
BFILE datatypes, 13

BINARY_INTEGER datatypes, 13
BIND_ARRAY procedure, 272
BIND_VARIABLE procedure, 271–272
BIND_VARIABLE_CHAR
   procedure, 272
BIND_VARIABLE_RAW
   procedure, 272
BIND_VARIABLE_ROWID
   procedure, 272
BLOB datatypes, 13
blocks, 6
   anonymous, 47
   BEGIN statements, 40
   calling functions, 116
   declaration sections, 6, 10
   DECLARE statements, 40
   END statements, 40
   exception handling sections, 7,
      37, 41
   labels, 43
   nested, 41–42
   processing sections, 6, 15
   storing as procedures, 62
BOOLEAN datatypes, 9, 12
BOOLEAN expressions, 17–20
breakpoints, debugging, 331–334,
   337–338
BROKEN procedure, 255
buffer editor, SQL+Plus, 287–288

C

calling
   functions
      from blocks, 116
      from expressions, 110
      from SELECT statements, 112
      from SQL statements, 112
   procedures, headers, 83
   program units, 207
CHANGE procedure, 254

CHAR datatypes, 11
character expressions, NULL
   values, 17
character literals. *See* string literals.
clauses, 172
client-side functions, 113
client-side procedures, Procedure
   Builder, 298
client-side processes, storing
   procedures, 64
client-side program units, 204–208
CLOB datatypes, 13
CLOSE keyword, 30
CLOSE_CURSOR procedure, 268
code
   blocks, defining via procedures, 63
   debugging formatting, 320
COLUMN_VALUE procedure, 271
command line
   executing procedures, 74
   SQL+Plus, 284
comments, 8
common debugging techniques,
   318–319
comparison operators, 19
   arithmetic expressions, 18
   BOOLEAN expressions, 17–18
compilation errors, 318, 323–326
conditional predicates, 177
conditional statements, 22
conditions for triggers, WHEN
   clause, 173
constants
   persistent, 228–229
   PL/SQL, 14
constraining tables, 180
constructs, package specifications, 138
CREATE FUNCTION statements,
   106, 123
CREATE OR REPLACE PROCEDURE
   command, 94

CREATE PROCEDURE command,
66–68, 94
CREATE reserved word, 138
Cursor FOR LOOP statements, 27, 33
CURSOR keyword, 30
cursors, 28
    attributes, 32
    explicit, 30–31
    hiding logic, 234–236
    implicit, 28
    persistent, 232–233
CURSOR_ALREADY_OPEN
    exceptions, 38

D

data dictionary views
    packages, 156–157
    privileges, 364, 367–369
    recording compilation errors, 322
    tracking procedure data, 85
    triggers, 190
database triggers, 49, 170–173, 190,
249, 308
databases, storing procedures, 64
datatypes
    %ROWTYPE declaration, 35–36
    %TYPE declaration, 34
    advanced declarations, 34
    automatic conversion, 22, 121
    BFILE, 13
    BINARY_INTEGER, 13
    BLOB, 13
    BOOLEAN, 9, 12
    CHAR, 11
    CLOB, 13
    DATE, 11
    DEC, 14
    DECIMAL, 14
    DOUBLEPRECISION, 14
    FLOAT, 14

INTEGER, 13
LONG, 12
LONGRAW, 13
MLSLABEL, 13
NATURAL, 13
NCLOB, 13
NUMBER, 11–12
NUMERIC, 14
parameters, 77
PLS_INTEGER, 13
POSITIVE, 13
RAW, 13
REAL, 14
RECORD, 14
ROWID, 13
SMALLINT, 13
TABLE, 14
VARCHAR2, 11
DATE datatypes, 11
DBA_ views, 86
DBA_DEPENDENCIES view, 382
DBA_SYS_PRIVS view, 366
DBMS_DDL package, 257–259, 274
DBMS_JOB package, 251,
254–256, 274
DBMS_OUTPUT package, 247,
250, 274
DBMS_OUTPUT.PUT_LINE
    statement, 267
DBMS_PIPE package, 262–263, 275
DBMS_SQL package, 263,
266–268, 274
DBMS_SQL.COLUMN_VALUE
    function, 266
DBMS_SQL.DEFINE_COLUMN
    procedure, 266
DBMS_SQL.EXECUTE function, 266
DBMS_SQL.EXECUTE statement, 267
DBMS_SQL.FETCH_ROWS
    function, 266
DBMS_SQL.PARSE procedure, 266

DBMS_STANDARD package, 381
DDL triggers, 189
debugging, 340
   code formatting, 320
   common procedures and
      techniques, 318–319
   compilation errors, 318
   Procedure Builder, 330
      breakpoints, 331–334, 337–338
   run-time errors, 318
   SQL+Plus
      compilation errors, 323–326
      execution errors, 329
   tools, error message
      documentation, 321
DECIMAL datatypes, 14
declaration sections, 6, 10, 50
DECLARE keyword, 66
DECLARE statements, 40
declared elements, scope, 42–43
declaring parameters, 76
DECODE function, 16
default purity level, packages, 226
default values, parameters, 77–78, 81
DEFAULT reserved word, 76
definer rights, 358
DEFINE_COLUMN procedure, 269
DEFINE_COLUMN_CHAR
   procedure, 270
DEFINE_COLUMN_RAW
   procedure, 270
DEFINE_COLUMN_ROWID
   procedure, 270
DELETING conditional predicate, 177
dependencies
   multiple database, 388–389
   single database, 386–387
   tracking, 378
DEPTREE view, 382–385, 395
DISABLE statement, 248
disabling triggers, 183

DML (Data Manipulation Language)
   commands, 5
DML triggers, database events, 171
documentation of error messages, 321
dot notation, referencing packaged
   constructs, 151
DOUBLEPRECISION datatypes, 14
dropping
   functions, 108
   packages, 147
   procedures, 72
   triggers, 181
DUP_VAL_ON_INDEX exception, 38

E

elements, declared, 42–43
ELSE clauses, IF statements, 25
ELSIF clauses, IF statements, 25
ENABLE statement, 248
enabling triggers, 183
END IF reserved word, 23
END keyword, 66
END labels, procedures, 69
END LOOP reserved word, 26
END LOOP statements, 26
END statements, blocks, 40
error message documentation, 321
exception handlers, 45
exception handling sections, 7, 37,
   41, 50
EXCEPTION keyword, 41, 66
exception scope, nested blocks, 44–45
exceptions
   system-defined, 38
   user-defined, 39–40
EXECUTE command, 75
EXECUTE function, 270
executing
   commands, SQL+Plus, 286
   procedures, 73–74

execution errors, debugging, 329
EXIT statements, 26
EXIT WHEN keyword, 25
explicit cursors, 28–31
expressions
    calling functions, 110
    functions, 16, 105
    nested parentheses, 16
    processing sections, blocks, 15
    rule of operator precedence, 15

F

FETCH, INTO reserved word, 30
FETCH_ROWS function, 270
FINANCE.REFUND procedure, 254
Find field, Object Navigator, 298
firing triggers, 168, 178
FLOAT datatypes, 14
FOR EACH ROW triggers, 173–175
FOR EACH STATEMENT triggers, 173
formatting of code, debugging, 320
forward declarations, calling local
    subprograms, 209–211
FOUND attribute, cursors, 32
functions, 48, 104, 109, 114, 123
    altering, 107
    as parameter values for
        functions, 111
    assignment statements, 111
    automatic datatype conversion, 121
    calling, 110–112, 116
    client-side, 113
    creating, 106
    DBMS_SQL.COLUMN_VALUE, 266
    DBMS_SQL.EXECUTE, 266
    DBMS_SQL.FETCH_ROWS, 266
    DECODE, 16
    differences from procedures, 105
    dropping, 108
    EXECUTE, 270

expressions, 16
FETCH_ROWS, 270
FUNC_VALIDATE_SHIPS, 174
IF...THEN...END IF statements, 111
IN OUT parameters, 115
invoking, 109
local subprograms, 209
NEXT_ITEM_TYPE, 262
NVL, 17
OPEN_CURSOR, 268–270
overloading, 216
packages, 5
parameters, 105, 115–118
purity levels, 221–223
RECEIVE_MESSAGE, 261
RETURN statements, 107, 119–122
returned values, 113–115
SEND_MESSAGE, 260
storing in Oracle Forms, 113
SUBSTR, 16
FUNC_VALIDATE_SHIPS function, 174

G–H

GET_LINE procedure, 249
global constructs, package bodies,
    141–142
GRANT statements, 362
granting privileges, 362
headers, procedures, 80, 83
hiding cursor logic, 234–236

I

identifiers, 8
IDEPTREE view, 382–385, 395
IF...THEN...END IF statements, 111
IF reserved word, 23
IF statements, 22–25
implicit cursors, 28–29, 32
IN OUT parameters, 76, 79, 94, 115

IN parameters, 76, 93
    default values, 77
    functions, 115
INCREASE_OR_DISPLAY packaged
    procedure, 142
initializing variables, one-time-only
    procedures, 219–220
inner blocks, 46
inner block exception handlers, 45
IN parameters, 78–82
INSERTING conditional predicate, 177
INSTANCE procedure, 254
INSTEAD OF triggers, 185–187
INTEGER datatypes, 13
INTERVAL procedure, 254
INTO reserved word, 28
INVALID status, procedures, 67
INVALID_CURSOR exception, 38
INVALID_NUMBER exception, 38
invoker rights, 358
    packages, 246
    program units, 360–361
invoking
    client-side program units, 206
    functions, 109
    packaged constructs, 151
    procedures, 73–75
    server-side program units, 205
IS reserved word, 66
ISOPEN attribute, cursors, 32
ISUBMIT procedure, 255

J–K

JOB_QUEUE_INTERVAL
    parameter, 252
JOB_QUEUE_PROCESSES
    parameter, 251
keywords
    BEGIN, 66
    CLOSE, 30

    CURSOR, 30
    DECLARE, 66
    END, 66
    EXCEPTION, 41, 66
    EXITWHEN, 25
    OPEN, 30
    TRUST, 225

L

labels
    blocks, 43
    END, 69
libraries, 64, 206–307
literals, 9
local subprograms, calling via forward
    declarations, 209–211
local text editor, SQL+Plus, 289–290
Location Indicator, Object
    Navigator, 298
logical operators, BOOLEAN
    expressions, 20
LOGIN_DENIED exception, 38
LONG datatypes, 12
LONGRAW datatypes, 13
LOOP reserved word, 26
loops, EXIT statements, 25–26

M

MLSLABEL datatypes, 13
modules, 206, 215–216
monitoring
    altered/analyzed object results, 259
    batch jobs, 255
multiline comments, 8
multiple BOOLEAN expressions,
    logical operators, 20
multiple database dependencies,
    388–389

multiple RETURN statements,
   functions, 119
mutating tables, 179

N

named PL/SQL programs, 6
named program units, 47
   database triggers, 49
   functions, 48
   packages, 49
   procedures, 48
names, triggers, 171
namespaces, program units, 217–218
native dynamic SQL, 272–273
NATURAL datatypes, 13
NCLOB datatypes, 13
nested blocks, 41–45, 50
nested parentheses, expressions, 16
nesting statements, loops, 25
NEW_LINE procedure, 249
NEXT_DATE procedure, 254
NEXT_ITEM_TYPE function, 262
nodes, Object Navigator, 294–298
non-DML triggers, 188
NOTFOUND attribute, cursors, 32
NOT_LOGGED_ON exception, 38
NO_DATA_FOUND exception, 38
NULL reserved word, 9
NULL values, 17
NUMBER datatypes, 11–12
Numeric FOR LOOP statements, 27
numeric literals, 9
NUMERIC datatypes, 14
NVL function, 17

O

Object Navigator
   Find field, 298
   Location Indicator, 298

nodes, 294–295, 297–298
   objects, 294
   subnodes, 295
object privileges, program units, 356
objects, Object Navigator, 294
one-time-only procedures, initializing
   variables, 219–220
OPEN keyword, 30
OPEN statements, cursor
   definitions, 32
OPEN_CURSOR function, 268–270
operators
   arithmetic, 16
   comparison, 19
   logical, 20
OR REPLACE option, CREATE
   PROCEDURE command, 68
Oracle Forms, storing functions, 113
OUT parameters, 76–78, 81, 94
outer blocks, 46
overloading
   functions, 216
   modules, 215–216
   program units, 214–215
   subprograms, 215
overview of PL/SQL, 4
overwriting procedures, 68
owner rights, 246, 358

P

package bodies, 139, 158–159
   construct changes, 149
   global constructs, 141–142
   private constructs, 140–141
   public constructs, 141
package constructs, 158
PACKAGE reserved word, 138
package specifications, 137, 158–159
   constructs, 138
   package bodies, 140–142, 149
   purity levels, 225-226

packaged constructs, 155
   packaged program units, 151–152
   referencing, 151
packaged global constructs, 152, 155
packaged procedures,
   INCREASE_OR_DISPLAY, 142
packaged program units,
   151–152, 155
packages, 49, 136
   advantages, 134–135
   data dictionary views, 156–157
   DBMS_DDL, 257–259
   DBMS_JOB, 251, 254–256
   DBMS_OUTPUT, 247, 250
   DBMS_PIPE, 262–263
   DBMS_SQL, 263, 266–268
   default purity level, 226
   dropping, 147
   invoker rights, 246
   owner rights, 246
   prewritten, 5
   PL/SQL, 5
   purity analysis, 381
   recompiling, ALTER statement,
      143–145
   storing procedures, 64
PACK_MESSAGE procedure, 260
PACK_MESSAGE_RAW procedure, 260
PACK_MESSAGE_ROWID
   procedure, 260
parameters, 84, 93
   datatypes, 77
   declaring, 76
   default values, 77–78
   functions, 105, 115–118
   IN OUT, 82
   JOB_QUEUE_INTERVAL, 252
   JOB_QUEUE_PROCESSES, 251
   passing by reference, 83
   procedures, 62–64, 76
   reserved expressions, 77
   SUBMIT procedure, 252

PARSE procedure, 268
passing parameters, 83, 117
persistent constants, 228–229
persistent cursors, 232–233
persistent records, 231–232
persistent states, 228
persistent tables, 231–232
persistent types, 231–232
persistent variables, 228–229
PL/SQL
   blocks, 6
   comments, 8
   constants, 14
   identifiers, 8
   literals, 9
   overview, 4
   packages, 5
   program units, 5
   statements, 8
PL/SQL Editor, 302–304
PL/SQL Interpreter
   debugging breakpoints, 331
   executing program units, 305
PL/SQL packages. *See* packages.
PL/SQL tables, TYPE statements, 212
PLS_INTEGER datatypes, 13
POSITIVE datatypes, 13
Practice Exam #1, 404–424
Practice Exam #2, 436–451
Practice Exam #3, 462–477
PRAGMA RESTRICT_REFERENCES
   statements, 222
PRAGMA statements, advantages, 226
prewritten PL/SQL packages, 5
private constructs, package bodies,
   140–141
privileges
   data dictionary views, 364–369
   granting, 362
   revoking, 362
   roles, 351
   system, 350–351

Procedure Builder, 293
    debugging, 322, 330
        breakpoints, 331–338
    Object Navigator, 294
    PL/SQL Interpreter, executing
        program units, 305
    program units, 298–301, 306
procedures, 48, 62–64, 72, 93
    altering, 70–71
    ALTER_COMPILE, 257
    ANALYZE_OBJECT, 258
    BIND_ARRAY, 272
    BIND_VARIABLE, 271–272
    BIND_VARIABLE_CHAR, 272
    BIND_VARIABLE_RAW, 272
    BIND_VARIABLE_ROWID, 272
    BROKEN, 255
    CHANGE, 254
    CLOSE_CURSOR, 268
    COLUMN_VALUE, 271
    creating, 66
    DBMS_SQL.DEFINE_COLUMN,
        266
    DBMS_SQL.PARSE, 266
    DEFINE_COLUMN, 269
    DEFINE_COLUMN_CHAR, 270
    DEFINE_COLUMN_RAW, 270
    DEFINE_COLUMN_ROWID, 270
    defining code blocks, 63
    differences from functions, 105
    dropping, 72
    END labels, 69
    executing, 73–74
    executing from command line, 74
    FINANCE.REFUND, 254
    GET_LINE, 249
    GET_LINES, 249
    headers, 80, 83
    IN OUT parameters, 82
    IN parameters, 79–80
    INSTANCE, 254

INTERVAL, 254
INVALID status, 67
invoking, 73, 75
ISUBMIT, 255
local subprograms, 209
NEW_LINE, 249
NEXT_DATE, 254
OUT parameters, 81
overwriting, 68
packages, 5
PACK_MESSAGE, 260
PACK_MESSAGE_RAW, 260
PACK_MESSAGE_ROWID, 260
parameters, 62–64, 76, 84
PARSE, 268
PROC_RESET_ERROR_LOG, 66
PUT, 248
PUT_LINE, 248, 266
REMOVE, 253
RUN, 253
stored, 66
storing, 64
SUBMIT, 252
tracking data, 85
UNPACK_MESSAGE, 262
UNPACK_MESSAGE_ROW, 262
UNPACK_MESSAGE_ROWID, 262
USER_EXPORT, 254
VALID status, 67
WHAT, 254
procedures for debugging, 318–319
processing sections, 6, 15, 50
PROC_RESET_ERROR_LOG
    procedure, 66
PROC_UPDATE_CRUISE_STATUS
    procedure, 73
program units, 5, 47, 237
    calling, 207
    client-side, 204, 208
    creating in other schemas, 355
    executing, 305

invoker rights, 360–361
libraries, 206, 307
modules, 206
moving, 306
named, 47
namespaces, 217–218
object privileges, 356
overloading, 214–215
owner rights, 358
PL/SQL, 5
PL/SQL Editor, 302–303
Procedure Builder, 298–301
server-side, 208
storing, 207
system privileges, 353–354
programmer-defined records, TYPE
statememts, 211
PROGRAM_ERROR exception, 38
public constructs
invoking, 151
package bodies, 141
purity analysis, packages, 381
purity levels
functions, 221–223
package specifications, 225–226
PUT procedure, 248
PUT_LINE procedure, 248, 266

Q–R

qualifiers, :old/:new, 175–176
RAISE statements, 39
RAW datatypes, 13
REAL datatypes, 14
RECEIVE_MESSAGE function, 261
recompilation errors, 392–393
recompiling packages, 143–145
RECORD datatypes, 14
records, persistent, 231–232
referencing packaged constructs, 151
REFERENCING clauses, 172

REMOVE procedure, 253
reserved expressions, parameters, 77
reserved words
AS, 66, 138
BEGIN, 66
CREATE, 138
DEFAULT, 76
END LOOP, 26
ENDIF, 23
FETCH, INTO, 30
IF, 23
INTO, 28
IS, 66
LOOP, 26
NULL, 9
PACKAGE, 138
THEN, 23
restrictions, triggers, 179
RETURN statements, 107, 119–123
returned values, functions,
113–115, 120
REVOKE FROM command, 363
revoking privileges, 355, 362
rights, 358
RNPS purity level, functions, 224
roles, 351
ROWCOUNT attribute, cursors, 32
ROWID datatypes, 13
rule of operator precedence, 15, 21
RUN procedure, 253
run-time errors, 318

S

schemas, 350, 355
scope, declared elements, 42–43
SELECT statements
calling functions, 112
implicit cursors, 28–29
explicit cursors, 31
SEND_MESSAGE function, 260

server–side program units, 205, 208
SESSION_PRIVS view, 364
SESSION_ROLES view, 365
SET SERVEROUTPUT ON
    statement, 247
SHOW ERR command, 91–92, 328
SHOW ERRORS command, 91–92
signature mode, 390–391
single database dependencies,
    386–387
single quote characters, 9
single triggers, 171
single-line comments, 8
SMALLINT datatypes, 13
SQL functions, 16
SQL statements, calling functions, 112
SQL+Plus, 284
    buffer editor, 287–288
    command line
        executing procedures, 74
        interface, 284
    debugging, 323
        compilation errors, 323–326
        execution errors, 329
        features, 322
    executing commands, 286
    local text editor, 289–290
SQLCODE function, returning error
    message number, 321
SQLERRM function, returning error
    messages, 321
statements, 8
    assignment, 21
    BEGIN, 40
    conditional, 22
    CREATE...FUNCTION, 106
    Cursor FOR LOOP, 27, 33
    DBMS_OUTPUT.PUT_LINE, 267
    DBMS_SQL.EXECUTE, 267
    DECLARE, 40
    DISABLE, 248
    ENABLE, 248

END, 40
END LOOP, 26
EXIT, 26
IF 22–24
LOOP, 26
nesting via loops, 25
Numeric FOR LOOP, 27
PRAGMA, 226
PRAGMA RESTRICT_REFERENCES,
    222
RAISE, 39
SELECT, implicit cursors, 28–29
SET SERVEROUTPUT ON, 247
UPDATE, 33, 267
WHILE LOOP, 26–27
STORAGE_ERROR exception, 38
stored procedures, 66
stored program units, PL/SQL
    Editor, 304
storing
    procedures, 64
    program units, 207
string literals, 9
SUBMIT procedure, 252
subnodes, Object Navigator, 295
SUBSTR function, 16
system event triggers, 188–189
system privileges, 350–352, 368
    program units, 353–354
    revoking, 355
system-defined exceptions, 38
system-level events, triggers, 169

T

TABLE datatypes, 14
tables
    constraining, 180
    mutating, 179
    persistent, 231–232
    triggers, 184

techniques for debugging, 318–319
text editor, SQL+Plus, 289–290
THEN reserved word, 23
TIMEOUT_ON_RESOURCE
    exception, 38
timestamp mode, 390
TOO_MANY_ROWS exception, 39
tracking dependencies, 378
TRANSACTION_BACKED_OUT
    exception, 39
triggers, 168, 171, 194
    ALTER statements, 181
    attaching to views, 169
    BEFORE DELETE, 176
    bodies, 174
    conditions, WHEN clause, 173
    data dictionary views, 190
    database, 170, 173, 308
    database_events, 171
    DDL, 189
    disabling, 183
    dropping, 181
    enabling, 183
    firing rules, 178
    FOR EACH STATEMENT, 173
    FOR EACH ROW, 173
    INSTEAD OF, 185–187
    names, 171
    restrictions, 179
    single, 171
    system event, 188–189
    system-level events, 169
    tables, 184
    UPDATE, 172
    view, 185
    when-package-loaded, 219
trigger_level clauses, 172
TRUST keyword, 225
TYPE statements, 213
    PL/SQL tables, 212

programmer-defined records, 211
types, persistent, 231–232

U

unhandled exceptions, 45
UNPACK_MESSAGE procedure, 262
UNPACK_MESSAGE_ROW
    procedure, 262
UNPACK_MESSAGE_ROWID
    procedure, 262
UPDATE statements, 33, 175, 267
UPDATE triggers, 172
UPDATING conditional predicate, 177
user-defined exceptions, 39–40
USER_ views, 86
USER_DEPENDENCIES view, 85, 156,
    378–381, 394
USER_ERRORS view, 85, 89–92, 156,
    190, 328
USER_EXPORT procedure, 254
USER_JOBS view, 255–256
USER_OBJECTS view, 85–87, 123,
    156, 190, 259
USER_OBJECT_SIZE view, 85, 88, 156
USER_ROLE_PRIVS view, 365
USER_SOURCE view, 85, 88–89, 156
USER_SYS_PRIVS view, 365
USER_TAB_PRIVS view, 366
USER_TAB_PRIVS_MADE view, 366
USER_TAB_PRIVS_RECD view, 366
USER_TRIGGERS view, 191

V

VALID status, procedures, 67
values, returning for functions,
    113–115, 120
VALUE_ERROR exception, 39
VARCHAR2 datatypes, 11

variables
  %ROWTYPE, 36
  declaration sections, blocks, 10
  initializing, one-time-only
     procedures, 219–220
  parameters, 76
  persistent, 228–229
views, attaching triggers, 169, 185

W–Z

WHAT procedure, 254
WHEN clause, trigger conditions, 173
when-package-loaded triggers, 219
WHILE LOOP statements, 26–27
WNPS purity level, functions, 224
ZERO_DIVIDE exception, 39

INTERNATIONAL CONTACT INFORMATION

AUSTRALIA
McGraw-Hill Book Company Australia Pty. Ltd.
TEL +61-2-9417-9899
FAX +61-2-9417-5687
http://www.mcgraw-hill.com.au
books-it_sydney@mcgraw-hill.com

CANADA
McGraw-Hill Ryerson Ltd.
TEL +905-430-5000
FAX +905-430-5020
http://www.mcgrawhill.ca

GREECE, MIDDLE EAST, NORTHERN AFRICA
McGraw-Hill Hellas
TEL +30-1-656-0990-3-4
FAX +30-1-654-5525

MEXICO (Also serving Latin America)
McGraw-Hill Interamericana Editores S.A. de C.V.
TEL +525-117-1583
FAX +525-117-1589
http://www.mcgraw-hill.com.mx
fernando_castellanos@mcgraw-hill.com

SINGAPORE (Serving Asia)
McGraw-Hill Book Company
TEL +65-863-1580
FAX +65-862-3354
http://www.mcgraw-hill.com.sg
mghasia@mcgraw-hill.com

SOUTH AFRICA
McGraw-Hill South Africa
TEL +27-11-622-7512
FAX +27-11-622-9045
robyn_swanepoel@mcgraw-hill.com

UNITED KINGDOM & EUROPE (Excluding Southern Europe)
McGraw-Hill Education Europe
TEL +44-1-628-502500
FAX +44-1-628-770224
http://www.mcgraw-hill.co.uk
computing_neurope@mcgraw-hill.com

ALL OTHER INQUIRIES Contact:
Osborne/McGraw-Hill
TEL +1-510-549-6600
FAX +1-510-883-7600
http://www.osborne.com
omg_international@mcgraw-hill.com

GET YOUR **FREE SUBSCRIPTION**
TO ORACLE MAGAZINE

Oracle Magazine is essential gear for today's information technology professionals. Stay informed and increase your productivity with every issue of *Oracle Magazine.* Inside each free bimonthly issue you'll get:

- Up-to-date information on Oracle Database, E-Business Suite applications, Web development, and database technology and business trends
- Third-party news and announcements
- Technical articles on Oracle Products and operating environments
- Development and administration tips
- Real-world customer stories

IF THERE ARE OTHER ORACLE USERS AT YOUR LOCATION WHO WOULD LIKE TO RECEIVE THEIR OWN SUBSCRIPTION TO ORACLE MAGAZINE, PLEASE PHOTOCOPY THIS FORM AND PASS IT ALONG.

Three easy ways to subscribe:

① Web
Visit our Web site at www.oracle.com/oraclemagazine. You'll find a subscription form there, plus much more!

② Fax
Complete the questionnaire on the back of this card and fax the questionnaire side only to +1.847.647.9735.

③ Mail
Complete the questionnaire on the back of this card and mail it to P.O. Box 1263, Skokie, IL 60076-8263

Oracle Publishing

FREE SUBSCRIPTION

○ Yes, please send me a FREE subscription to *Oracle Magazine*   ○ NO

To receive a free subscription to *Oracle Magazine*, you must fill out the entire card, sign it, and date it (incomplete cards cannot be processed or acknowledged). You can also fax your application to +1.847.647.9735.
Or subscribe at our Web site at www.oracle.com/oraclemagazine/

○ From time to time, Oracle Publishing allows our partners exclusive access to our e-mail addresses for special promotions and announcements. To be included in this program, please check this box.

○ Oracle Publishing allows sharing of our mailing list with selected third parties. If you prefer your mailing address not to be included in this program, please check here. If at any time you would like to be removed from this mailing list, please contact Customer Service at +1.847.647.9630 or send an e-mail to oracle@halldata.com.

signature (required)   date

X

name   title

company   e-mail address

street/p.o. box

city/state/zip or postal code   telephone

country   fax

YOU MUST ANSWER ALL NINE QUESTIONS BELOW.

① WHAT IS THE PRIMARY BUSINESS ACTIVITY OF YOUR FIRM AT THIS LOCATION? (check one only)

- ☐ 01 Application Service Provider
- ☐ 02 Communications
- ☐ 03 Consulting, Training
- ☐ 04 Data Processing
- ☐ 05 Education
- ☐ 06 Engineering
- ☐ 07 Financial Services
- ☐ 08 Government (federal, local, state, other)
- ☐ 09 Government (military)
- ☐ 10 Health Care
- ☐ 11 Manufacturing (aerospace, defense)
- ☐ 12 Manufacturing (computer hardware)
- ☐ 13 Manufacturing (noncomputer)
- ☐ 14 Research & Development
- ☐ 15 Retailing, Wholesaling, Distribution
- ☐ 16 Software Development
- ☐ 17 Systems Integration, VAR, VAD, OEM
- ☐ 18 Transportation
- ☐ 19 Utilities (electric, gas, sanitation)
- ☐ 98 Other Business and Services

② WHICH OF THE FOLLOWING BEST DESCRIBES YOUR PRIMARY JOB FUNCTION? (check one only)

Corporate Management/Staff
- ☐ 01 Executive Management (President, Chair, CEO, CFO, Owner, Partner, Principal)
- ☐ 02 Finance/Administrative Management (VP/Director/ Manager/Controller, Purchasing, Administration)
- ☐ 03 Sales/Marketing Management (VP/Director/Manager)
- ☐ 04 Computer Systems/Operations Management (CIO/VP/Director/ Manager MIS, Operations)

IS/IT Staff
- ☐ 05 Systems Development/ Programming Management
- ☐ 06 Systems Development/ Programming Staff
- ☐ 07 Consulting
- ☐ 08 DBA/Systems Administrator
- ☐ 09 Education/Training
- ☐ 10 Technical Support Director/Manager
- ☐ 11 Other Technical Management/Staff
- ☐ 98 Other

③ WHAT IS YOUR CURRENT PRIMARY OPERATING PLATFORM? (select all that apply)

- ☐ 01 Digital Equipment UNIX
- ☐ 02 Digital Equipment VAX VMS
- ☐ 03 HP UNIX
- ☐ 04 IBM AIX
- ☐ 05 IBM UNIX
- ☐ 06 Java
- ☐ 07 Linux
- ☐ 08 Macintosh
- ☐ 09 MS-DOS
- ☐ 10 MVS
- ☐ 11 NetWare
- ☐ 12 Network Computing
- ☐ 13 OpenVMS
- ☐ 14 SCO UNIX
- ☐ 15 Sequent DYNIX/ptx
- ☐ 16 Sun Solaris/SunOS
- ☐ 17 SVR4
- ☐ 18 UnixWare
- ☐ 19 Windows
- ☐ 20 Windows NT
- ☐ 21 Other UNIX
- ☐ 98 Other
- 99 ☐ None of the above

④ DO YOU EVALUATE, SPECIFY, RECOMMEND, OR AUTHORIZE THE PURCHASE OF ANY OF THE FOLLOWING? (check all that apply)

- ☐ 01 Hardware
- ☐ 02 Software
- ☐ 03 Application Development Tools
- ☐ 04 Database Products
- ☐ 05 Internet or Intranet Products
- 99 ☐ None of the above

⑤ IN YOUR JOB, DO YOU USE OR PLAN TO PURCHASE ANY OF THE FOLLOWING PRODUCTS? (check all that apply)

Software
- ☐ 01 Business Graphics
- ☐ 02 CAD/CAE/CAM
- ☐ 03 CASE
- ☐ 04 Communications
- ☐ 05 Database Management
- ☐ 06 File Management
- ☐ 07 Finance
- ☐ 08 Java
- ☐ 09 Materials Resource Planning
- ☐ 10 Multimedia Authoring
- ☐ 11 Networking
- ☐ 12 Office Automation
- ☐ 13 Order Entry/Inventory Control
- ☐ 14 Programming
- ☐ 15 Project Management
- ☐ 16 Scientific and Engineering
- ☐ 17 Spreadsheets
- ☐ 18 Systems Management
- ☐ 19 Workflow

Hardware
- ☐ 20 Macintosh
- ☐ 21 Mainframe
- ☐ 22 Massively Parallel Processing
- ☐ 23 Minicomputer
- ☐ 24 PC
- ☐ 25 Network Computer
- ☐ 26 Symmetric Multiprocessing
- ☐ 27 Workstation

Peripherals
- ☐ 28 Bridges/Routers/Hubs/Gateways
- ☐ 29 CD-ROM Drives
- ☐ 30 Disk Drives/Subsystems
- ☐ 31 Modems
- ☐ 32 Tape Drives/Subsystems
- ☐ 33 Video Boards/Multimedia

Services
- ☐ 34 Application Service Provider
- ☐ 35 Consulting
- ☐ 36 Education/Training
- ☐ 37 Maintenance
- ☐ 38 Online Database Services
- ☐ 39 Support
- ☐ 40 Technology-Based Training
- ☐ 98 Other
- 99 ☐ None of the above

⑥ WHAT ORACLE PRODUCTS ARE IN USE AT YOUR SITE? (check all that apply)

Software
- ☐ 01 Oracle9i
- ☐ 02 Oracle9i Lite
- ☐ 03 Oracle8
- ☐ 04 Oracle8i
- ☐ 05 Oracle8i Lite
- ☐ 06 Oracle7
- ☐ 07 Oracle9i Application Server
- ☐ 08 Oracle9i Application Server Wireless
- ☐ 09 Oracle Data Mart Suites
- ☐ 10 Oracle Internet Commerce Server
- ☐ 11 Oracle interMedia
- ☐ 12 Oracle Lite
- ☐ 13 Oracle Payment Server
- ☐ 14 Oracle Video Server
- ☐ 15 Oracle Rdb

Tools
- ☐ 16 Oracle Darwin
- ☐ 17 Oracle Designer
- ☐ 18 Oracle Developer
- ☐ 19 Oracle Discoverer
- ☐ 20 Oracle Express
- ☐ 21 Oracle JDeveloper
- ☐ 22 Oracle Reports
- ☐ 23 Oracle Portal
- ☐ 24 Oracle Warehouse Builder
- ☐ 25 Oracle Workflow

Oracle E-Business Suite
- ☐ 26 Oracle Advanced Planning/Scheduling
- ☐ 27 Oracle Business Intelligence
- ☐ 28 Oracle E-Commerce
- ☐ 29 Oracle Exchange
- ☐ 30 Oracle Financials
- ☐ 31 Oracle Human Resources
- ☐ 32 Oracle Interaction Center
- ☐ 33 Oracle Internet Procurement
- ☐ 34 Oracle Manufacturing
- ☐ 35 Oracle Marketing
- ☐ 36 Oracle Order Management
- ☐ 37 Oracle Professional Services Automation
- ☐ 38 Oracle Projects
- ☐ 39 Oracle Sales
- ☐ 40 Oracle Service
- ☐ 41 Oracle Small Business Suite
- ☐ 42 Oracle Supply Chain Management
- ☐ 43 Oracle Travel Management
- ☐ 44 Oracle Treasury

Oracle Services
- ☐ 45 Oracle.com Online Services
- ☐ 46 Oracle Consulting
- ☐ 47 Oracle Education
- ☐ 48 Oracle Support
- ☐ 98 ther
- 99 ☐ None of the above

⑦ WHAT OTHER DATABASE PRODUCTS ARE IN USE AT YOUR SITE? (check all that apply)

- ☐ 01 Access
- ☐ 02 Baan
- ☐ 03 dbase
- ☐ 04 Gupta
- ☐ 05 IBM DB2
- ☐ 06 Informix
- ☐ 07 Ingres
- ☐ 08 Microsoft Access
- ☐ 09 Microsoft SQL Server
- ☐ 10 PeopleSoft
- ☐ 11 Progress
- ☐ 12 SAP
- ☐ 13 Sybase
- ☐ 14 VSAM
- ☐ 98 Other
- 99 ☐ None of the above

⑧ DURING THE NEXT 12 MONTHS, HOW MUCH DO YOU ANTICIPATE YOUR ORGANIZATION WILL SPEND ON COMPUTER HARDWARE, SOFTWARE, PERIPHERALS, AND SERVICES FOR YOUR LOCATION? (check only one)

- ☐ 01 Less than $10,000
- ☐ 02 $10,000 to $49,999
- ☐ 03 $50,000 to $99,999
- ☐ 04 $100,000 to $499,999
- ☐ 05 $500,000 to $999,999
- ☐ 06 $1,000,000 and over

⑨ WHAT IS YOUR COMPANY'S YEARLY SALES REVENUE? (please choose one)

- ☐ 01 $500, 000, 000 and above
- ☐ 02 $100, 000, 000 to $500, 000, 000
- ☐ 03 $50, 000, 000 to $100, 000, 000
- ☐ 04 $5, 000, 000 to $50, 000, 000
- ☐ 05 $1, 000, 000 to $5, 000, 000

123101

About the BeachFrontQuizzer™ CD-ROM

BeachFrontQuizzer provides interactive certification exams to help you prepare for certification. With the enclosed CD, you can test your knowledge of the topics covered in this book with more than 300 multiple choice questions.

Installation

To install BeachFrontQuizzer:

1. Insert the CD-ROM in your CD-ROM drive.

2. Follow the Setup steps in the displayed Installation Wizard. (When the Setup is finished, you may immediately begin using BeachFrontQuizzer.)

3. To begin using BeachFrontQuizzer, enter the 12-digit license key number of the exam you want to take:

   PL/SQL Program Units   303977796975

Study Sessions

BeachFrontQuizzer tests your knowledge as you learn about new subjects through interactive quiz sessions. Study Session Questions are selected from a single database for each session, dependent on the subcategory selected and the number of times each question has been previously answered correctly. In this way, questions you have answered correctly are not repeated until you have answered all the new questions. Questions that you have missed previously will reappear in later sessions and keep coming back to haunt you until you get the question correct. In addition, you can track your progress by displaying the number of questions you have answered with the Historical Analysis option. You can reset the progress tracking by clicking on the Clear History button. Each time a question is presented the answers are randomized so you will memorize a pattern or letter that goes with the question. You will start to memorize the correct answer that goes with the question concept.

Practice Exams

For advanced users, BeachFrontQuizzer also provides Simulated and Adaptive certification exams. Questions are chosen at random from the database. The Simulated Exam presents a specific number of questions directly related to the real exam. After you finish the exam, BeachFrontQuizzer displays your score and the passing score required for the test. You may display the exam results of this specific exam from this menu. You may review each question and display the correct answer.

NOTE
For further details of the feature functionality of this BeachFrontQuizzer software, consult the online instructions by choosing Contents from the BeachFrontQuizzer Help menu.

Technical Support

If you experience technical difficulties please call (888) 992-3131. Outside the U.S. call (281) 992-3131. Or, you may e-mail bfquiz@swbell.net.